UNDERSTANDING REGULATION

Understanding Regulation
Theory, Strategy, and Practice

....

ROBERT BALDWIN

and

MARTIN CAVE

OXFORD

UNIVERSITY PRESS

OXFORD

UNIVERSITY PRESS

Great Clarendon Street, Oxford OX2 6DP

Oxford University Press is a department of the University of Oxford
It furthers the University's objective of excellence in research scholarship
and education by publishing worldwide in

Oxford New York

Athens Auckland Bangkok Bogotá Buenos Aires Calcutta
Cape Town Chennai Dar es Salaam Delhi Florence Hong Kong Istanbul
Karachi Kuala Lumpur Madrid Melbourne Mexico City Mumbai
Nairobi Paris São Paulo Singapore Taipei Tokyo Toronto Warsaw
with associated companies in Berlin Ibadan

Oxford is a registered trade mark of Oxford University Press
in the UK and in certain other countries

Published in the United States
by Oxford University Press Inc., New York

British Library Cataloguing in Publication Data
Data available

Library of Congress Cataloging in Publication Data
Baldwin, Robert, Dr.
Understanding regulation / Robert Baldwin and Martin Cave.
p. cm.
Includes bibliographical references and index.
1. Industrial policy—Great Britain. 2. Trade regulation—Great
Britain. 3. Industrial policy. 4. Trade regulation. I. Cave,
Martin. II. Title.
HD3616.G73B28   1999   338.941—dc21   98–47348

ISBN 0–19–877437–0
ISBN 0–19–877438–9 (pbk.)

7 9 10 8 6

Typeset in 10/12pt New Century Schoolbook
by Graphicraft Limited, Hong Kong
Printed in Great Britain
on acid-free paper by
Bookcraft Ltd,
Midsomer Norton, Somerset

Acknowledgements

We are grateful to a number of individuals for their help with this book. For research assistance, textual comments, and work on manuscripts, we thank Laura Dachner, Charlotte Hadfield, Nicholas Lambert, and Diana Woodhead.

We also express our appreciation to all of those colleagues at LSE and Brunel who have assisted in a variety of ways—from making suggestions to commenting on drafts—and we thank in particular Julia Black, Damian Chalmers, and Vanessa Finch.

Robert Baldwin would also like to thank his co-teachers on the LSE's M.Sc. in Regulation for broadening his outlook on regulatory issues— Stephen Glaister, Christopher Hood, Bridget Hutter, Judith Rees, Colin Scott, Mark Thatcher, and Ralph Turvey.

Special thanks for her excellent work in turning manuscripts into final copy go to Amanda Tinnams.

Robert Baldwin bears primary responsibility for Chapters 1–14 and 21–3 of the book, Martin Cave for Chapters 15–19, and both authors for Chapter 20.

Contents

Contents

Figures

Tables

Abbreviations

AGM	Annual General Meeting
ALARA	As Low as Reasonably Achievable
ALARP	As Low as Reasonably Practicable
ATLB	Air Transport Licensing Board
BATNEEC	Best Available Technology Not Entailing Excessive Costs
BR	British Rail
BT	British Telecom
C & C	Command and Control
CAA	Civil Aviation Authority
CBA	Cost-Benefit Analysis
CBI	Confederation of British Industry
CCA	Compliance Cost Assessment
CEGB	Central Electricity General Board
CFI	Court of First Instance
CIPFA	Chartered Institute of Public Finance and Accountancy
CMLR	*Common Market Law Review*
CRI	Centre for the Study of Regulated Industries
DAB	Digital Audio Broadcasting
DBRU	Departmental Better Regulation Unit
DG	Director General
DGES	Director General of Electricity Supply
DGFT	Director General of Fair Trading
DGGS	Director General of Gas Supply
DGT	Director General of Telecommunications
DGWS	Director General of Water Services
DGIV	Directorate General IV
DTI	Department of Trade and Industry
ECJ	European Court of Justice
EFILWC	European Foundation for the Improvement of Living and Working Conditions
ELJ	*European Law Journal*
ELR	*European Law Review*
EPA	Environment Protection Agency (US)
EU	European Union
EUI	European University Institute (at Florence)
GCC	Gas Consumers' Council

GYIL	*German Yearbook of International Law*
HSE	Health and Safety Executive
HSWA	Health and Safety at Work Act 1974
ILR	Independent Local Radio
IPPR	Institute for Public Policy Research
IRC	Industrial Reorganisation Corporation
ITA	Independent Television Authority
ITC	Independent Television Commission
JBL	*Journal of Business Law*
LQR	*Law Quarterly Review*
LT	London Transport
MLR	*Modern Law Review*
MMC	Monopolies and Mergers Commission
MS	Member State
MSL	Minimum Service Level
NAO	National Audit Office
NCC	National Consumer Council
NEDC	National Economic Development Council
NLJ	*New Law Journal*
OFFER	Office of Electricity Regulation
OFGAS	Office of Gas Supply
OFLOT	Office of the National Lottery
OFT	Office of Fair Trading
OFTEL	Office of Telecommunications
OFWAT	Office of Water Services
OJLS	*Oxford Journal of Legal Studies*
OMB	Office of Management and Budget
ONP	Open Network Provision
OPRAF	Office of Passenger Railway Franchising
ORR	Office of the Rail Regulator
PCA	Parliamentary Commissioner for Administration (Ombudsman)
PES	Public Electricity Supplier
PL	*Public Law*
PRIA	Preliminary Regulatory Impact Analysis
RA	Radio Authority
RCBA	Risk Cost Benefit Analysis
REC	Regional Electricity Company
RIA	Regulatory Impact Analysis
ROSCO	Rolling Stock Leasing Company
RPI–X	Retail Price Index less efficiency factor X price cap
SFAIRP	So Far As Is Reasonably Practicable
SIB	Securities and Investments Board
SRO	Self-Regulatory Organization

TOR	Tolerability of Risks
TUC	Trades Union Congress
USO	Universal Service Obligation
WTA	Willingness to Accept
WTP	Willingness to Pay
YBEL	*Yearbook of European Law*

Introduction

Our aim in writing this book is to introduce readers to those practical and theoretical issues that we see as central to the study of regulation. We set out to describe the nature of those issues, to indicate how regulatory practitioners and commentators have dealt with them, and to offer arguments on potential responses to regulatory difficulties. The focus is on experience in Britain but points of more general application arise and are dealt with.

Regulation is a topic that has stimulated interest in a host of disciplines—notably law, economics, political science, sociology, history, psychology, geography, management, and social administration. This is a subject, moreover, that calls for a multidisciplinary approach. To give an example: if economists were to devise technically superb schemes of regulation these would come to little if no heed was paid to the warnings of those political scientists and sociologists who point out reasons why, in the real world, those schemes will not produce the ends the economists anticipated. Similarly, in looking at how such schemes can be implemented, lawyers' messages concerning the limitations of different kinds of rules and enforcement processes should be taken on board. Analogous points could be made from the perspectives of other disciplines. This book is written by a lawyer and an economist but will attempt both to draw from a wider range of disciplinary perspectives and to be accessible across disciplines. Highly technical approaches and terminology will be avoided where possible. It is hoped, therefore, that the analysis offered will prove useful to regulatory studies in a wide variety of areas.

What is Regulation?

Regulation is spoken of as if an identifiable and discrete mode of governmental activity[1] yet the term regulation has been defined in a number

---

[1] See R. Baldwin, C. Scott, and C. Hood, *A Reader On Regulation* (Oxford, 1998), ch. 1.

of ways.[2] Selznick's notion of regulation as sustained and focused control exercised by a public agency over activities that are valued by a community has been referred to as expressing a central meaning,[3] but it is perhaps useful to think of the word regulation being used in the following different senses:[4]

As a specific set of commands—where regulation involves the promulgation of a binding set of rules to be applied by a body devoted to this purpose. An example would be the health and safety at work legislation as applied by the Health and Safety Executive.

As deliberate state influence—where regulation has a more broad sense and covers all state actions designed to influence industrial or social behaviour. Thus, command-based regimes would come within this usage but so also would a range of other modes of influence—for instance those based on the use of economic incentives[5] (e.g. taxes or subsidies); contractual powers; deployment of resources; franchises; the supply of information or other techniques.

As all forms of social control or influence—where all mechanisms affecting behaviour—whether these be state-derived or from other sources (e.g. markets)—are deemed regulatory. Within this usage of the term 'regulation' there is no requirement that the regulatory effects of a mechanism are deliberate or designed rather than merely incidental to other objectives.

Regulation is often thought of as an activity that restricts behaviour and prevents the occurrence of certain undesirable activities (a 'red light' concept[6]) but the influence of regulation may also be *enabling* or *facilitative* ('green light') as, for example, where the airwaves are regulated so as to allow broadcasting operations to be conducted in an ordered fashion rather than left to the potential chaos of an uncontrolled market.

Issues on the Regulatory Agenda

There is a tendency in modern Britain to associate regulation with the post-privatization control of the utilities by Directors-General and their

---

[2] See B. Mitnick, *The Political Economy of Regulation* (New York, 1980), ch. 1; A. Ogus, *Regulation: Legal Form and Economic Theory* (Oxford, 1994), ch. 1; G. Majone (ed.), *De-Regulation or Re-Regulation?* (London, 1989).

[3] P. Selznick, 'Focusing Organisational Research on Regulation', in R. Noll (ed.), *Regulatory Policy and the Social Sciences* (Berkeley, Calif., 1985), 363, quoted Ogus, *Regulation*, 1.

[4] See Baldwin, Scott, and Hood, *Regulation*, ch. 1.

[5] On the distinction between command and incentive based regimes see S. Breyer, *Regulation and Its Reform* (Cambridge, Mass., 1982); Ogus, *Regulation*, esp. ch. 11; and R. Baldwin, 'Regulation: After Command and Control', in K. Hawkins (ed.), *The Human Face of Law* (Oxford, 1997).

[6] On 'red light' and 'green light' rules and regulations see C. Harlow and R. Rawlings, *Law and Administration* (2nd edn., London, 1997), chs. 2 and 3; Ogus, *Regulation*, 2.

offices. Media attention focuses almost daily on the activities of such bodies as OFTEL (established by the Telecommunications Act 1984), OFGAS (Gas Act 1986), OFFER (Electricity Act 1989), and OFWAT (Water Act 1991). Regulation has, however, been practised in Britain since at least the Tudor and Stuart periods.[7] In the nineteenth century there was a burgeoning of regulation, with the emergence of specialist regulatory institutions[8] and a host of measures dealing with public health and employment conditions.[9] Developments in the supply of railway, water, gas, and electricity services led to the introduction of controls over prices, safety, and quality of service.[10]

During the twentieth century, public ownership of such utilities as electricity, gas, water, and railways restrained to some extent the development of regulation but a steady growth in regulation nevertheless took place from the 1930s onwards. That decade saw the licensing of goods and passenger carryings by road as well as the advent, in the fishing industry, of marketing boards that fulfilled both operational and regulatory functions.

In the post-war period marketing boards followed in the cotton, crofting, sugar, and iron and steel industries and the first US-style independent regulatory agency was established in Britain in 1954 with the Independent Television Authority. The ITA was innovatory in combining a degree of independence from government with the carrying out of adjudicatory and regulatory, as well as policy-developing, functions. In the United States such independent regulatory bodies had been carrying out key functions of government since the Inter State Commerce Commission was established in 1887 to limit discriminatory pricing by railroads. In the ITA's wake followed a series of regulatory agencies that were created in the 1960s and 1970s to deal with issues in such areas as monopolies, gaming, industrial relations, civil aviation, discrimination, and workplace health and safety.

During the 1980s and 1990s much stress has been placed by governments and commentators on the problems and costs of regulation and the case for deregulating the economy.[11] The privatization drive of the

---

[7] Ogus, *Regulation*, 6–12; 'Regulatory Law: Some Lessons from the Past' (1992) 12 *Legal Studies* 1.

[8] O. MacDonagh, 'The Nineteenth-Century Revolution in Government: A Reappraisal' (1958) 1 *Historical J.* 52.

[9] P. Craig, *Administrative Law* (3rd edn. London, 1994), ch. 2.

[10] See J. Foreman-Peck and R. Millward, *Public and Private Ownership of British Industry 1820–1990* (Oxford, 1994), esp. chs. 1–3, C. Foster, *Privatisation, Public Ownership and the Regulation of Natural Monopoly* (Oxford, 1992), chs. 1 and 2.

[11] See J. Kay, C. Mayer, and D. Thompson (eds.), *Privatisation and Regulation: The UK Experience* (Oxford, 1986); D. Swann, *The Retreat of the State: Deregulation and Privatisation in the UK and US* (Brighton, 1988); K. Button and D. Swann (eds.), *The Age of Regulatory Reform* (Oxford, 1989); also see the White Papers: *Building Business, Not Barriers*, Cmnd. 9794 (London, 1986); *Lifting the Burden*, Cmnd. 9751 (London, 1985);

same period, however, produced a new burst of regulation, carried out by
a host of new regulatory bodies such as OFTEL (1984), OFGAS (1986),
OFFER (1989), OFWAT (1990), and the Office of the Rail Regulator (1993).
In addition, administrative changes have produced a new Environment
Agency in 1996 and from the creation of the National Lottery emerged an
Office of the National Lottery to oversee the providing private operator,
Camelot.

By the mid-1990s some 25 million customers were served by the main
four regulated utilities industries alone, their total annual turnover of
£51 billion represented around 8 per cent of the annual gross domestic
product of the UK and not only the results of regulation but the processes
used to regulate had prompted unprecedented concern. Regulation and
deregulation had moved to positions high on the political agenda. Conservative administrations had sought, since 1985, to deregulate, cut
red tape, and substitute competitive pressures for regulatory action. The
Department of Trade and Industry's Enterprise and Deregulation Unit
had been established in that year in order to review all new legislative
instruments and assess the compliance costs they would impose on
businesses. That body, later called the Deregulation Unit and housed
in the Cabinet Office, had, by 1996 started to subject regulations to a
newly taxing process of 'regulatory appraisal'[12] but the high point of
deregulatory action had come with the passing of the Deregulation and
Contracting Out Act 1994 which *inter alia* had given ministers the power
to use secondary legislative to eliminate burdens and controls. No rigorous
review of the impact of such initiatives was, however, carried out by the
Major government and promises of 'bonfires of red tape' were not fulfilled.

It has, however, been in the field of utilities regulation that the most
urgent political debates have taken place in recent years.[13] Attention has
focused on the issues of efficiency, accountability, and fairness in the system of regulating by means of Directors General and their accompanying offices. A host of books and reports have come from all parts of the
political spectrum to put forward a large number of reform proposals.[14]

Releasing Enterprise, Cm. 512 (London, 1988); Department of Trade and Industry, *Burdens
on Business* (London, 1985); Cabinet Office, *Checking the Cost of Regulation* (London, 1996),
Regulation in the Balance (London, 1996); M. Derthick and P. Quirk, *The Politics of Deregulation* (Washington, 1985); V. Wright, 'Public Administration, Regulation, Deregulation
and Reregulation', in E. Eliassen and J. Kooiman (eds.), *Managing Public Organisations:
Lessons from Contemporary European Experience* (London, 1993).

[12] See *Regulation in the Balance* and Chapter 7 below. Under Labour, the Deregulation
Unit was renamed the Better Regulation Unit in 1997.

[13] For a review of this debate see R. Baldwin, *Regulation in Question* (London, 1995).

[14] See e.g. C. Veljanovski, *The Future of Industry Regulation in the UK* (London, 1993);
Adam Smith Institute, *Who Will Regulate the Regulators?* (London, 1992); P. Hain, *Regulating for the Common Good* (London, 1994); Centre for the Study of Regulated Industries,
Regulating the Utilities: Accountability and Processes (London, 1994); D. Helm, 'Reforming
the Regulatory Frameworks' (Oxford, 1993); National Consumer Council, *Paying the Price*

In this volume we deal with the elements of that debate but we are concerned with more than the reform of utilities regulation. We consider, in the first instance, a number of fundamental questions regarding regulation and we look at sectors beyond the utilities in an attempt to draw parallels and learn lessons.

Part 1 of the book, accordingly, reviews a series of general issues in regulation, namely: why regulate at all (Chapter 2); how the origins of regulation and regulatory changes can be explained (Chapter 3); which strategies can be used to regulate (Chapter 4); and which kinds of body can be used to regulate (Chapter 5). It is then necessary to consider what benchmarks can be used in judging whether regulation is good or not—how evaluations can be made in assessing justifications for regulating or for particular regulatory methods. Chapter 6 looks for such benchmarks and Chapter 7 considers in more detail the role of economic appraisals in assessing regulatory activity.

Chapter 8 looks at how regulation can be enforced on the ground and Chapter 9 examines the problems encountered in choosing types of regulatory standards and in setting acceptable levels of performance.

The particular issues that arise with self-regulatory mechanisms and in regulating risks are explored in Chapters 10 and 11. Chapter 12 discusses the ways in which membership of the European Union affects domestic regulation, the problems posed by attempts to regulate an activity across a number of Member States, and potential responses to such problems. Chapter 13 continues the theme of regulating across borders by reviewing the issues arising when there is competition between different regulators, whether this be across national, industrial, sectoral, or issue-defined borders.

Utilities regulation gives rise to a great deal of current interest and to a number of particular concerns. Chapter 14, accordingly, offers a grounding for that discussion by setting out the basic regulatory structures that have been adopted in the post-privatization utilities sectors.

Part 2 then follows with more detailed discussions of a series of issues and concerns that have arisen in the utilities and other regulatory sectors. Individual chapters look at particular issues or mechanisms such as the control of monopolies (Chapter 15); the balance between regulation and the fostering of competition (Chapter 16); price capping (Chapter 17); measuring efficiency (Chapter 18); quality regulation (Chapter 19), and franchising (Chapter 20). Finally, two chapters

(London, 1993); C. Graham, *Is there a Crisis in Regulatory Accountability?* (London, 1995 and reproduced in Baldwin, Scott, and Hood, *Regulation*); D. Helm, *British Utilities Regulation* (Oxford, 1995); M. E. Beesley (ed.), *Regulatory Utilities: A Time for Change?* (London, 1996), *Regulating Utilities: Broadening the Debate* (London, 1997); DTI Green Paper, *A Fair Deal for Consumers: Modernising the Framework for Utility Regulation*, Cm. 3898 (March, 1998).

deal with issues of special relevance to those assessing the legitimacy of regulatory regimes: accountability (Chapter 21) and procedures and fairness (Chapter 22). Chapter 23 then offers conclusions on approaches to regulatory questions.

FUNDAMENTALS

2

Why Regulate?

Motives for regulating can be distinguished from technical justifications for regulating. Governments may regulate for a number of motives—for example they may be influenced by the economically powerful and may act in the interests of the regulated industry or they may see a particular regulatory stance as a means to re-election. Different commentators may analyse such motives in different ways and a variety of approaches to such analysis will be discussed in Chapter 3. To begin, though, we should consider the technical justifications for regulating that may be given by a government that is assumed to be acting in pursuit of the public interest.[1]

Many of the rationales for regulating can be described as instances of 'market failure'. Regulation in such cases is argued to be justified because the uncontrolled market place will, for some reason, fail to produce behaviour or results in accordance with the public interest.[2] In some sectors or circumstances there may also be 'market absence'—there may be no effective market—because, for example, households cannot buy clean air or peace and quiet in their localities.

1. Monopolies and Natural Monopolies

Monopoly describes the position in which one seller produces for the entire industry or market. Monopoly pricing and output is likely to occur and be sustained where three factors obtain:[3]

[1] For detailed reviews of public interest reasons for regulating see S. Breyer, *Regulation and Its Reform* (Cambridge, Mass., 1982), ch. 1; A. Ogus, *Regulation: Legal Form and Economic Theory* (Oxford, 1994), ch. 3; E. Gellhorn and R. J. Pierce, *Regulated Industries* (St Paul, Minn., 1982), ch. 2; J. Kay and J. Vickers, 'Regulatory Reform: An Appraisal', in G. Majone (ed.), *De-Regulation or Re-Regulation?* (London, 1989); B. Mitnick, *The Political Economy of Regulation* (New York, 1980), ch. 5; C. Sunstein, *After the Rights Revolution* (Cambridge, Mass., 1990), ch. 2; C. Hood, *Explaining Economic Policy Reversals* (Buckingham, 1995).

[2] See also J. Francis, *The Politics of Regulation* (Oxford, 1993), ch. 1.

[3] See Gellhorn and Pierce, *Regulated Industries*, 36–7 and Chapter 15 below. On regulating monopolies generally see C. Foster, *Privatisation, Public Ownership and the Regulation of Natural Monopoly* (Oxford, 1992), ch. 6; Ogus, *Regulation*, 30–3; Breyer, *Regulation and Its Reform*, 15–19; Francis, *Politics of Regulation*, ch. 3; E. Gellhorn and W. Kovacic, *Antitrust Law and Economics* (St Paul, Minn., 1994), chs. 3 and 4.

- a single seller occupies the entire market;
- the product sold is unique in the sense that there is no substitute sufficiently close for consumers to turn to;
- substantial barriers restrict entry by other firms into the industry and exit is difficult.

Where monopoly occurs, the market 'fails' because competition is deficient. From the public interest perspective, the problem with a firm occupying a monopolistic position is that in maximizing profits it will restrict its output and set price above marginal cost. It will do this because if it charges a single price for its product, additional sales will only be achieved by lowering the price on the entire output. The monopolist will forgo sales to the extent that lost revenue from fewer sales will be compensated for by higher revenue derived from increased price on the units still sold. The effects of monopoly, as compared to perfect competition, are reduced output, higher prices, and transfer of income from consumers to producers.

One response to potential monopolies is to use competition (or antitrust) laws so as to create a business environment conducive to competition. Where a 'natural monopoly' exists, however, the use of competition law may be undesirable.[4] A natural monopoly occurs when economies of scale available in the production process are so large that the relevant market can be served at the least cost by a single firm. It is accordingly less costly to society to have production carried out by one firm than by many. Thus, rather than have three railway or electricity companies laying separate networks of rails or cables where one would do, it may be more efficient to give one firm a monopoly subject to regulation of such matters as prices and access to the network. Determining whether a natural monopoly exists requires a comparison of demand for the product with the extent of the economies of scale available in production. If a firm is in a position of natural monopoly then, like any monopoly, it will present problems of reduced output, higher prices, and transfers of wealth from consumers to the firm. Restoration of competition by use of competition law is not, however, an appropriate response since competition may be socially costly and thus regulation of prices, quality, and output as well as access may be called for. The regulator will try to set price near incremental cost (the cost of producing an additional unit) in order to encourage the natural monopolist to expand its output to the level that competitive conditions would have induced.

Not all aspects of a supply process may be naturally monopolistic. As Ogus points out,[5] the economies of scale phenomenon may affect only one part of a given process—for instance the *transmission* of, say,

---

[4] On natural monopolies see M. Waterson, *Regulation of the Firm and Natural Monopoly* (Oxford, 1988), ch. 2; Foster, *Privatisation*, ch. 6.2.

[5] Ogus, *Regulation*, 31.

electricity, rather than its *generation*.[6] The task of many governments and regulators (at least those committed to minimalist regulation) is to identify those parts of a process that are naturally monopolistic so that these can be regulated while other aspects are left to the influence of competitive forces.[7]

2. Windfall Profits

A firm will earn a windfall profit (sometimes called an 'economic rent' or excess profit) where it finds a source of supply significantly cheaper than that available in the market place.[8] It may do so by, say, locating a rich seam of an easily extracted mineral; by coming upon a material efficiency in a production process; or by possessing an asset that suddenly escalates in value—for example a boat in a desert town that has been flooded. Regulation may be called for when it is desired either to transfer profits to taxpayers or to allow consumers or the public to benefit from the windfall.

The rationale for regulating is strongest where the windfall is due to accident rather than planned investments of money, effort, or research. Where such investments have taken place or where society might want to create incentives to search for new efficiencies, products, or areas of demand, there is a case for allowing windfall or 'excess' profits to be retained. Even in the desert town it may be desirable to encourage some individuals to store boats in order to cope with periodic floods.

3. Externalities

The reason for regulating externalities (or 'spillovers') is that the price of a product does not reflect the true cost to society of producing that good and excessive consumption accordingly results.[9] Thus, a manufacturer of car tyres might keep costs to consumers down by dumping pollutants arising from the manufacturing process into a river. The price of the tyres will not represent the true costs that production imposes on society if clean-up costs are left out of account. The resultant process is wasteful because too many resources are attracted into polluting activities (too many tyres are made and sold) and too few resources are devoted by the

---

[6] G. Yarrow, 'Regulation and Competition in the Electricity Supply Industry', in J. Kay, C. Mayer, and D. Thompson, *Privatisation and Regulation* (Oxford, 1986).

[7] See Chapter 16 below, and the White Paper, *Privatising Electricity*, Cm. 322 (London, 1988).

[8] See Breyer, *Regulation and Its Reform*, 21. On the 'windfall tax' see below, pp. 233–5.

[9] See Breyer, *Regulation and Its Reform*, 23–6; Ogus, *Regulation*, 35–8.

manufacturer to pollution avoidance or adopting pollution-free production methods. The rationale for regulation is to eliminate this waste—and to protect society or third parties suffering from externalities—by compelling the internalization of spillover costs—on 'polluter pays' principles.

4. Information Inadequacies

Competitive markets can only function properly if consumers are sufficiently well informed to evaluate competing products.[10] The market may, however, fail to produce adequate information and may fail for a number of reasons: information may cost money to produce (e.g. because researching the effects of a product, such as a drug, may prove expensive). The producer of information, however, may not be compensated by others who use that information (e.g. other manufacturers of the drug). The incentive to produce information may accordingly be low. There may also be incentives to falsify information—where, for example, consumers of the product are ill-positioned to challenge the falsification and seek remedies for damages suffered or where they face high costs in doing so. Areas in which consumers purchase a type of product very infrequently may give rise to this problem. The information produced may, in addition, not be of sufficient assistance to the consumer—for instance because the consumer lacks the expertise required to render technical data useful. Finally, collusion in the market place, or insufficient competition, may reduce the flow of information below the levels consumers might want. Producers, as a group, may thus fail to warn consumers about the general hazards or deficiencies associated with a product. Breyer notes that until the US Government required disclosure, accurate information was unavailable to most buyers in that country concerning the durability of light bulbs, nicotine content of cigarettes, fuel economy for cars, or care requirements for textiles.[11]

Regulation, by making information more extensively accessible, accurate, and affordable, may protect consumers against information inadequacies and the consequences thereof and may encourage the operation of healthy, competitive markets.

5. Continuity and Availability of Service

In some circumstances the market may not provide the socially desired levels of continuity and availability of service. Thus, where demand is

---

[10] See F. Hayek, 'The Use of Knowledge in Society', (1945) 35 *Am. Econ. Rev.* 519; Breyer, *Regulation and Its Reform*, 26–8; Ogus, *Regulation*, 38–41.

[11] Breyer, *Regulation and Its Reform*, 28.

cyclical (for example, as with passenger air transport to a holiday island) waste may occur as firms go through the processes of closing and reopening operations.[12] Regulation may be used to sustain services through troughs—for example by setting minimum prices at levels allowing the covering of fixed costs through lean periods. This would be justified where the extra costs imposed on consumers by pricing rules are less than those caused by the processes of closing and opening services in response to the business cycle. The subsidizing of off-peak by peak travellers will, however, raise issues of equity to be considered alongside questions of social policy. In the case of some products or services—for example water services—it may be considered, as a matter of social policy, that these should be generally available at least to a certain minimum standard. In the unregulated market, however, competition may lead to 'cream-skimming'—the process in which the producer chooses to supply only the most profitable customers—and services may be withdrawn from poorer or more geographically disperse groupings of customers. Regulation may be justified in order to produce socially desirable results even though the cross-subsidizations effected may be criticizable as inefficient and unfair.

6. Anti-competitive Behaviour and Predatory Pricing

Markets may be deficient not merely because competition is lacking; they may produce undesirable effects because firms behave in a manner not conducive to healthy competition. A principal manifestation of such behaviour is predatory pricing. This occurs when a firm prices below costs, in the hope of driving competitors from the market, achieving a degree of domination, and then using its position to recover the costs of predation and increase profits at the expense of consumers. Preconditions for a rational firm to engage in predatory pricing are: that it must be able to outlast its competitors once prices are cut below variable costs and it must be able to maintain prices well above costs for long enough to recover its prior losses. The costs of entry to and exit from the market must, accordingly, allow it this period of comfort before new competition arises. The aim for regulators is to sustain competition and protect consumers from the ill-effects of market domination by outlawing predatory or other forms of anti-competitive behaviour.

7. Public Goods and Moral Hazard

Some commodities, e.g. security and defence services, may bring shared benefits and be generally desired. It may, however, be very costly for those

---

[12] Ogus, *Regulation*, 43–6.

paying for such services to prevent non-payers ('free-riders') from enjoying the benefits of those services. As a result, the market may fail to
encourage the production of such commodities and regulation may be
required—often to overcome the free-rider problem by imposing taxes.

Similarly, where there is an instance of moral hazard—where someone
other than the consumer pays for a service[13]—there may be excessive consumption without regard to the resource costs being imposed on society.
If, for example, medical costs are not met by the patient, but by the state
or an insurer, regulatory constraints may be required if excessive consumption of medical services is to be avoided.

8. Unequal Bargaining Power

One precondition for the efficient or fair allocation of resources in a
market is equal bargaining power. If bargaining power is unequal, regulation may be justified in order to protect certain interests. Thus, if
unemployment is prevalent it cannot be assumed that workers will be
able to negotiate effectively to protect their interests (even leaving aside
informational issues) and regulation may be required to safeguard such
matters as the health and safety of those workers.

9. Scarcity and Rationing

Regulatory rather than market mechanisms may be justified in order to
allocate certain commodities when these are in short supply. In a petrol
shortage, for example, public interest objectives may take precedence over
efficiency so that, instead of using pricing as an allocative instrument,
the petrol is allocated with reference to democratically generated lists of
priorities.

10. Distributional Justice and Social Policy

Allocative efficiency attempts to maximize welfare but is not concerned
with the distribution of that welfare amongst individuals or groups
within society. Regulation may be used to redistribute wealth or to transfer resources to victims of misfortune (e.g. injured parties).[14]

Distrust of individuals' rationality or wisdom may also underpin
another rationale for regulation—paternalism. As a matter of policy

---

[13] See generally G. Calabresi, *The Cost of Accidents: A Legal and Economic Analysis* (New
Haven, 1970).
[14] See Ogus, *Regulation*, 46–51.

not market [handwritten annotation]

society may decide to overrule individuals' preferences on some issues and regulate—for example by demanding that seat belts be worn in motor vehicles. In the strongest form of such paternalism, the decision is taken to regulate even where it is assumed that the citizens involved are possessed of full information concerning products.[15] On a series of other issues, governments may regulate simply in order to further social policies such as the prevention of discrimination based on race, sex, or age.

11. *Rationalization and Coordination*

In many situations it is extremely expensive for individuals to negotiate private contracts so as to organize behaviour or industries in an efficient manner—the transaction costs would be excessive.[16] The firms in an industry may be too small and geographically dispersed to bring themselves together to produce efficiently. (This might happen when small fishing concerns in a sparsely populated area fail to make collective marketing arrangements.) Enterprises may, moreover, have developed different and incompatible modes of production. In these circumstances regulation may be justified as a means of rationalizing production processes (perhaps standardizing equipment in order to create effective networks) and in order to coordinate the market. Centralized regulation holds the advantage over individual private law arrangements where information can be more efficiently communicated through public channels and economies of scale can be achieved by having one public agency responsible for upholding standards.[17]

It is noteworthy that this rationale for regulation is based more on the desire to *enable* effective action to take place than on the need to prohibit undesirable behaviour.

12. *Planning*

Markets may ensure reasonably well that individuals' consumer preferences are met but they are less able to meet the demands of future generations or to satisfy altruistic concerns (e.g. the quality of an environment not personally enjoyed).[18] There is also, as far as altruism is

[15] Ibid. 51–4.

[16] See Ogus, *Regulation*, 41–2; S. Breyer and P. MacAvoy, 'The Federal Power Commission and the Coordination Problem in the Electrical Power Industry' (1973) 46 *S. Cal. LR* 661.

[17] In the transportation sector coordination and regulation by a central agency may be needed in order to organize a route network—see S. Glaister, *Deregulation and Privatisation: British Experience* (World Bank, Washington DC, 1998).

[18] See Ogus, *Regulation*, 54; R. B. Stewart, 'Regulation in a Liberal State: The Role of Non-Commodity Values' (1983) 92 *Yale LJ* 1537; Sunstein, *After the Rights Revolution*, 57–61.

concerned, a potential free-rider problem. Many people may be prepared
to give up some of their assets for altruistic purposes only if they can be
assured that a large number of others will do the same. The problems
and costs of coordination mean that regulation may be required in order
to satisfy such desires.[19]

Conclusions: Choosing to Regulate

There are, as seen above, a number of well-recognized reasons commonly
given for regulating. It should be stressed, however, that in any one sector or industry the case for regulating may well be based not on a single
but on a combination of rationales. As Breyer points out,[20] health and
safety regulation, for example, can be justified with reference to a number of rationales—for example externalities, information defects, unequal
bargaining, and paternalism.

A second point, to be borne in mind in considering whether to regulate, is that the market and all its failings should be compared with
regulation and all its failings. Any analysis of the need to regulate will
be skewed if it is assumed that regulatory techniques will operate perfectly. We will see during this book that all regulatory strategies have
strengths and weaknesses in relation to their implementation as well as
their design. Regulatory and market solutions to problems should be considered in all their varieties and with all likely deficiencies and side-effects
if true comparisons are to be effected.

---

[19] Ogus, *Regulation*, 54.   [20] Breyer, *Regulation and Its Reform*, 34.

TABLE 1. *Rationales for regulating*

Rationale	Main aims of regulation	Example
Monopolies and natural monpolies	Counter ten`dency to raise prices and lower output. Harness benefits of scale economies. Identify areas genuinely monopolistic.	Utilities.
Windfall profits	Transfer benefits of windfalls from firms to consumers or taxpayers.	Firm discovers unusually cheap source of supply.
Externalities	Compel producer or consumer to bear full costs of production rather than pass on to third parties or society.	Pollution of river by factory.
Information inadequacies	Inform consumers to allow market to operate.	Pharmaceuticals. Food and drinks labelling.
Continuity and availability of service	Ensure socially desired (or protect minimal) level of 'essential' service.	Transport service to remote region.
Anti-competitive and behaviour predatory pricing	Prevent anti-competitive behaviour.	Below-cost pricing in transport.
Public goods and moral hazard	Share costs where benefits of activity are shared but free-rider problems exist.	Defence and security services. Health Services.
Unequal bargaining power	Protect vulnerable interests where market fails to do so.	Health and Safety at Work.
Scarcity and rationing	Public interest allocation of scarce commodities.	Petrol shortage.
Distribution justice and social policy	Distribute according to public interest. Prevent undesirable behaviour or results.	Victim protection. Discrimination.
Rationalization and Coordination	Secure efficient production where transaction costs prevent market from obtaining network gains or efficiencies of scale. Standardization.	Disparate production in agriculture and fisheries.
Planning	Protect interests of future generations. Coordinate altruistic intentions.	Environment.

NOT MARKET

3

Explaining Regulation

In explaining how regulation arises, develops, and declines, a number of broad approaches can be adopted.[1] These approaches may set out merely to describe and account for regulatory developments; they may be prescriptive and offer a view on how regulation *should* be organized; or they may serve a combination of these functions. Similarly, accounts of regulation may constitute commentaries on regulatory developments that are delivered with detachment from the sidelines or, together with their proponents, they may participate on the field of play and, intentionally or otherwise, may contribute themselves to regulatory changes.

The part that ideas can play in influencing regulatory developments is itself an issue for debate. Thus, Christopher Hood sees the 'force of ideas' approach as one of four main ways of explaining policy (or regulatory) developments. The essences of the four types of explanation can be set out thus:[2]

1. Where stress is placed on the force of new *ideas* that upset the *status quo* in some way—perhaps through demonstrations of experimental evidence, logical force, or rhetorical power.
2. Where emphasis rests on the pressures of *interests* that act in pursuit of developments that suit their own purposes.
3. Where changes are seen to flow from changes in *habitat* that make old policies obsolete in the face of new conditions—thus economic changes or technological advances may be seen to be driving policy revisions.
4. Where policies are said to *destroy themselves* because of internal problems—as where bureaucratic failings or integral deficiencies of strategy defeat the initial policy and produce changes.

---

[1] For a detailed review of the myriad varieties of regulatory theory see B. Mitnick, *The Political Economy of Regulation* (New York, 1980), ch. 3 and for a briefer account, R. Horwitz, *The Irony of Regulatory Reform: The Deregulation of the American Telecommunications Industry* (Oxford, 1989).

[2] See C. C. Hood, *Explaining Economic Policy Reversals* (Buckingham, 1994), ch. 1 (Hood's analysis refers to 'policy reversals' but is applied here to policy developments generally).

It can be seen that the first three approaches focus on 'external' influences on regimes, the fourth looks to internally generated factors. Of course, accounts of changes in regulation may not fall always neatly into the above categories since, as Hood acknowledges,[3] overlaps and combinations are inevitable (as where, for instance, powerful interests are seen to produce changes by pressing certain ideas against a background of technological advances). In looking at explanations of regulation, however, the above categorization does assist in teasing apart the elements within different approaches and in clarifying the roles played by those approaches in regulatory developments. We may, for instance, consider not only the relative emphases that particular explanations or schools of thought place on the role of ideas, interests, habitats, or internal factors but also the political and practical influence of those explanations or schools and the nature and origins of the forces that drive such explanations.

Most theories of regulatory origin and development can be seen as types of interest theory, though the force that can be exerted by ideas and arguments is recognized in a number of accounts. Among interest theories a broad distinction can be drawn between 'public', 'group', and 'private' versions.

1. Public Interest Theories

Public interest theories centre on the idea that those seeking to institute or develop regulation do so in pursuit of public interest related objectives (rather than group, sector, or individual self-interests). Proponents of regulation thus act as agents for the public interest.[4] Regulation's purpose is to achieve certain publicly desired results in circumstances where, for instance, the market would fail to yield these. (The grounds given for such action are likely to involve reference to one or more of the reasons for regulating outlined in Chapter 2.)[5]

Consistent with such a vision is an emphasis on the trustworthiness and disinterestedness of expert regulators in whose public-spiritedness

---

[3] Ibid. 36.

[4] See e.g. J. M. Landis, *The Administrative Process* (New Haven, 1938); R. E. Cushman, *The Independent Regulatory Commissions* (New York, 1941). For a British public interest account see I. McLean and C. Foster, 'The Political Economy of Regulation: Interests, Ideology, Voters and the UK Regulation of Railways Act 1844' (1992) 70 *Pub. Admin.* 313 at 329: 'Our test of seven hypotheses about the origins of regulation has shown that the best-supported is that both Gladstone and the MPs who voted on his bill were moved by their perceptions of the public interest.'

[5] Public interest visions of regulation may complement 'functionalist' accounts of regulatory origins and developments in so far as functionalism sees regulation as largely driven by the nature of the task at hand (as identified in terms of public needs and interests) rather than by private, individual, or self-interests.

and efficiency the public can have confidence.[6] The public interest approach is still defended by some commentators who argue for the development rather than abandonment of this vision.[7]

A number of problems, theoretical, practical, and political, however, beset the public interest view. A first difficulty is that an agreed conception of the public interest may be hard to identify. Instead, many might contend, regulation generally takes place amidst a clashing of images of the public interest. Public interest theories are said to fail to take into account such clashes.[8]

A further problem stems from doubts concerning the disinterestedness, expertise, and efficiency that the public interest approach attributes to regulators.[9] Thus, it has been argued that regulators may succumb to venality and be corrupted by opportunities for personal profit so that regulation is biased by the pursuit of personal interests.[10] Doubts may also be cast on the competence of regulators, which, it may be alleged, may not be sufficiently high to yield public interest ends—perhaps because rewards and career structures may lack the requisite attractiveness or because training needs and disciplinary emphases are poorly attended to.[11] Finally, capture theorists may suggest that public interest theory understates the degree to which economic and political power influences regulation. Thus, it is argued that regulatory polices and institutions often become (or, in some versions, begin life) subject to the influence of powerful regulated parties, or even politicians or sectors of consumers, so that regulation serves the interests of these parties or sectors rather than those of the wider public.[12]

Even for those capture theorists who are prepared to concede that regulatory regimes are sometimes established in pursuit of public interest objectives, the public interest vision may only be persuasive in relation to the earliest stages of the life-cycle of regulatory affairs.[13]

With regard to results,[14] the public interest perspective is prone to attack on the basis that regulation often seems to fail to deliver public interest

---

[6] See Landis, *Administrative Process*.

[7] See C. Sunstein, *After the Rights Revolution* (Cambridge, Mass., 1990).

[8] See J. G. Francis, *The Politics of Regulation: A Comparative Perspective* (Oxford, 1993), 8. On the public interest as a balancing of different interests; as a compromising approach or a trade-off concept; or as national, social, or particularistic goals see Mitnick, *Political Economy of Regulation*, 92–3.

[9] See G. Stigler, 'The Theory of Economic Regulation' (1971) 2 *Bell J. of Econ.* 3; G. Kolko, *Railroads and Regulation* (Princeton, 1965); Mitnick, *Political Economy of Regulation*, 111–20.

[10] Mitnick, *Political Economy of Regulation*, 94.

[11] See Landis, *Administrative Process*, 66.

[12] See E. S. Redford, *Administration of National Economic Control* (London, 1952), 251–2.

[13] See M. H. Bernstein, *Regulatory Business by Independent Commission* (New York, 1955) (life-cycle theory is discussed below at p. 25).

[14] On which the most telling comment is perhaps that of newly appointed football manager John Bond, who said: 'I promise results, not promises'. Quoted, B. Fantoni, *Private Eye's Colemanballs* (London, 1982).

outcomes. Some observers see this as an indication that appropriate lessons must be learned from failures so that better regulatory regimes can be designed.[15] The message for others is that regulation is doomed to failure and that policies of deregulation should be looked to.

2. Interest Group Theories

Interest group theorists see regulatory developments as the products of relationships between different groups and between such groups and the state. Such theorists generally differ from proponents of public interest accounts in not seeing regulatory behaviour as imbued with public-spiritedness but as a competition for power. Some accounts ('Group Public Interest Approaches')[16] do, however, offer explanations of the public interest that take on board competitions between different versions of that interest. Thus, Bernstein points to the role of regulators in carrying out missions that legislators have negotiated between interest groups, consumers, businesses, and other affected parties—missions that effect compromises but are seen by participants, nevertheless, to be endeavours in pursuit of the public interest.[17] Such visions bridge public interest and group interest approaches.

Versions of interest group theories range from open-ended pluralism to corporatism.[18] Pluralists see competing groups as struggling for power and elections as won by coalitions of groups who use their power to shape regulatory regimes. In contrast, corporatists emphasize the extent to which successful groups are taken into partnership with the state and produce regulatory regimes that exclude non-participating interests.[19] A recent variation on interest group theory is that offered by Leigh Hancher and Michael Moran, who employ the concept of 'regulatory space' within which there is an interplaying of interests concerning regulation.[20]

3. Private Interest Theories

A third broad approach to regulation stresses the extent to which regulatory developments are driven by the pursuit not of public or group but

---

[15] See C. R. Sunstein, 'Paradoxes of the Regulatory State' (1990) 57 *Univ. of Chicago LR* 407.

[16] See Mitnick, *Political Economy of Regulation*, 100.

[17] See M. H. Bernstein, *Regulating Business by Independent Commission* (New York, 1955), 76.

[18] Francis, *Politics of Regulation*; G. Wilson, *Interest Groups* (Oxford, 1990); for a pluralist analysis of government see P. Self, *Political Theories of Modern Government* (London, 1985), 79–107.

[19] See O. Newman, *The Challenge of Corporatism* (London, 1980).

[20] L. Hancher and M. Moran (eds.), *Capitalism, Culture and Regulation* (Oxford, 1989).

of private interests. This general approach thus encompasses theories going under a number of names, notably 'economic', 'Chicago', 'private interest', 'public choice', 'special interest', and 'capture'.

Some economic theories hover between group and private interest approaches. Thus, Kolko argued that US regulation originated in self-interested pressure exerted by business groups who sought such governmental action in order to maximize their profits and stabilize markets.[21] There was no diversion or capture from a public interest mission because regulation was established to serve private business interests in the first place.

The 'Chicago' theory as seen in the writings of George Stigler and Sam Peltzman[22] suggested that where there was a failure of competition, or the existence of monopoly, there would be monopoly profit which the legislature would give the regulator the power to dispose of. The regulated industry thus would have an incentive to influence the regulator so as to benefit from a 'regulatory rent' and there would be a market for regulation. This meant that the regulator would be captured by the industry since industry would have more to lose or gain than the regulator and, more generally, that in political contests, compact, organized interests (say, solicitors) would usually win at the expense of a diffused group (say, users of legal services). The commodity of regulation would go to those who valued it most and producers would thus tend to be better served by regulation than the (more diffused, less organized) masses of consumers. This economic approach assumed that all parties involved in regulation are income maximizers (politicians, for instance, seeking votes to maximize their cash incomes); it assumed that all parties are as well informed as possible and learn from experience; and it also assumed that regulation is costless (hence overall efficiency will not be affected by levels of regulation).[23]

The economic approach, as outlined, is thus consistent with public choice theories that stress the extent to which governmental behaviour can be understood by viewing all actors as rational individual maximizers of their own welfare.[24] Organizations and bureaucracies thus fall to be analysed with reference to the competing preferences of the individuals involved.

[21] G. Kolko, *The Triumph of Conservatism* (New York, 1977).

[22] Stigler loc. cit. n. 9 above; S. Peltzman, 'Towards a More General Theory of Regulation' (1976) 19 *J. Law and Econ.* 211. See also R. Posner, 'Natural Monopoly and Regulation' (1969) 21 *Stanford LR.* 548; id., 'Theories of Economic Regulation' (1974) 5 *Bell. J. of Econ.* 335. W. A. Jordan, 'Producer Protection, Prior Market Structure and the Effects of Government Regulation' (1992) 15 *J. Law and Econ.* 151. G. Becker, 'A Theory of Competition among Pressure Groups for Political Influence' (1983) 98 *Quarterly J. of Economics* 371.

[23] Cf. Peltzman loc. cit. n. 22 above.

[24] Public choice theories thus emphasize the force of *private* interests and preferences in governmental decisions, in stark contrast to public interest accounts; see A. Ogus, *Regulation: Legal Form and Economic Theory* (Oxford, 1994), 58–71.

Emphasis is placed on the propensity of such actors to circumvent official regulatory goals and substitute ends that are self-serving and to act in pursuit of such ends as job retention, aggrandizement, re-election, or the accumulation of personal wealth. The public interest is thus relegated to a small role in the establishment, operation, and development of regulatory regimes. Policies are put into effect so as to enhance wealth or utility positions.[25]

Such approaches have been open to question on a number of fronts.[26] Thus, explaining the nature and origins of preferences in the posited 'markets' for regulation proves difficult. Parties may lack determinate preferences on political or regulatory issues and individuals may behave altruistically in certain important respects. They may, for instance, identify with legislative, group, agency, or bureaucratic objectives and may behave in different ways according to the roles they adopt as, say, consumers of services, career strategists, or professional designers of regulatory policies. Regulators or bureaucrats may, moreover, be prevented from acting in rational, self-serving ways by lack of information, expertise, or commitment. Interest groups' activities may affect regulation in a manner that interferes with the realization of private preferences and regulatory bureaucracies may have lives beyond the sums of their parts. Public choice theories, moreover, ignore or underrate such important motives as ideologies, policy goals, emotional identifications, personality limits, prejudices, and moral stances.[27]

Experience, furthermore, seems to pose as many problems for private interest theories as it does for public interest accounts. Deregulatory developments thus seem difficult to account for in terms of the economic theory. Why, for instance, was there a strong deregulation movement in the 1970s if concentrated business interests were in control of regulatory developments?

On this point, one explanation might be that ideas, rather than pure interests, played a crucial role in moves to deregulate—a contention to be returned to in the next section. Private interest theorists, however, have not given up without a fight. Sam Peltzman himself has sought to rethink the economic approach and assess its power to explain regulatory developments, particularly in the period between the mid-1970s and mid-1980s.[28] He argues that regulation tends to produce incentives for firms to dissipate their wealth (e.g. when faced with controlled prices at

---

[25] See A. Downs, *An Economic Theory of Democracy* (New York, 1957).

[26] See Hood, *Explaining Economic Policy Reversals*, 24 and, generally, P. Dunleavy, *Democracy, Bureaucracy and Public Choice* (London, 1991); P. Self, *Government by the Market?* (Basingstoke, 1993).

[27] Self, *Government by the Market?*, 46.

[28] S. Peltzman, 'The Economic Theory of Regulation after a Decade of Regulation' (1989) *Brookings Papers in Macroeconomics* 1.

a time when costs increase) and that regulatory rents can be eradicated
by regulation itself. A point can thus arrive when a return to the position
prior to regulation becomes more attractive to regulated parties than continued regulation. Peltzman concludes that although the Chicago theory
can tell a coherent story about most of the examples of deregulation (the
latter being explicable in terms of the *disruption* of regulatory rents)
it does, nevertheless, leave some important questions unanswered—for
instance about 'the design of institutions and their adaptability'.[29]

Others have sought to refine the economic approach by considering in
more detail the circumstances in which those seeking the profits extract-
able from monopolistic or protected positions in the market would be
most likely to press for, and obtain, favourable regulation. Thus, Wilson
has built on the Stiglerian vision to argue that regulation is most likely
to be set up to serve the interests of the regulated where a concentrated
group with high stakes is able to secure regulation and favourable wealth
transfers at the expense of a diffused group with low per capita stakes.[30]
In this scenario, the concentrated, high-stake group has incentives to
influence regulation that are unmatched by those of the diffused, low-
stake population. Lobbying for favourable regulation might, however,
be expected to be far less pronounced when both the benefits and costs
of public regulation are either concentrated or diffused. In the former
instance, opponents of regulation might organize as easily as those seeking regulation and, in the case of generally diffused interests, both the
opponents and proponents of regulation find it difficult to organize.
Finally, where the benefits of regulation are diffused and costs are concentrated, opponents of regulation might be expected to be better organized and more forceful than those pressing for regulation.[31]

Such refinements of the economic approach fail, nevertheless, to come
to grips with one of the core problems mentioned by Peltzman—the lack
of any account of the role played by institutional arrangements in the
shaping of regulation. Examining this role is essential, say a number of
commentators, as an antidote to the idea of parties as rational wealth and
vote maximizers. Such institutional positions will be returned to shortly.

The economic approach offers one view of regulatory capture but the
diversion of regulation away from public interest objectives may be
explained quite differently from the perspectives encountered in other
disciplines. Motives can be seen in less simple terms than mere wealth
maximization—to include, for instance, ideological, bureaucratic, or social

[29] S. Peltzman, 'The Economic Theory of Regulation after a Decade of Regulation' (1989)
Brookings Papers Macroeconomics in 40.

[30] J. Q. Wilson, *The Politics of Regulation* (New York, 1980), 357–94. See also M. Olson,
The Logic of Collective Action (Cambridge, Mass., 1965) and Hood, *Explaining Economic
Policy Reversals*, 24–6.

[31] See Hood, *Explaining Economic Policy Reversals*, 25–6.

objectives. Stress, thus, can be placed on the propensity of bureaucrats to seek to maximize agency budgets,[32] or to engage in 'bureau-shaping' so as to create job satisfaction[33] or to maximize the political influence and scope of competencies of the agency.[34]

Contrasts have been drawn between the assumptions of the Chicago school of law and economics—that legislators and regulators seek to maximize their personal wealth—and the position of the 'Virginian' school of political economy which sees legislators and regulators as pursuers of expected votes or ideological ends as well as cash and which gives greater prominence to the interplay of pressure groups.[35] The problem of moving beyond wealth maximization and seeing utility maximization in broader terms is, however, that a loss of predictive power results and it is difficult to attribute relative weights to the various factors (money, votes, ideologies, and other preferences) that are all alleged to be being sought.[36]

Perhaps the best-known capture theory of all does not focus principally on economic interests. Marver H. Bernstein's 'life-cycle' theory makes reference to a variety of forces (internal and external) in accounting for regulatory declines.[37] Writing in 1955, Bernstein described an ageing process in which public interest regulation gave way to capture. Regulation typically begins, on this view, as a policy response to a political call to protect the public from undesirable activity. In the first of four stages of life—termed *gestation*—concerns about a problem result in the creation of a regulatory body. Second there follows *youth* in which the inexperienced regulatory body is outmanœuvred by the regulatees but operates with a crusading zeal. As the first flush of political support for agency objectives dies away, *maturity* follows and devitalization sets in. Regulation becomes more expert and settled but as the agency moves out of the political mainstream it begins to pay increasing attention to the needs of industry. As vitality declines, the agency relies more and more upon precedent when taking decisions and adopts a reactive stance. Finally, *old age*, the fourth stage, arrives to be charactized by debility and decline, resort to ever more judicialized procedures, and the agency giving priority to industrial rather than public interests.

---

[32] See W. A. Niskanen, *Bureaucracy and Representative Government* (Chicago, 1971).

[33] See Dunleavy, *Democracy, Bureaucracy and Public Choice*, 174–209.

[34] See G. Majone, *Regulating Europe* (London, 1996), 65; id., 'Cross-National Sources of Regulatory Policymaking in Europe and the United States' (1991) 11 *J. Publ. Pol.* 76, 94–7.

[35] See C. D. Foster, *Privatisation, Public Ownership and the Regulation of Natural Monopoly* (Oxford, 1992), 386–8; M. A. Crew (ed.), *Deregulation and Diversification of Utilities* (Dordrecht, 1989), 5–20.

[36] Foster, *Privatisation*, 387.

[37] Bernstein, *Regulating Business*. For criticism of the life-cycle theory see e.g. L. L. Jaffe, 'The Independent Agency—A New Scapegoat' (1956) 65 *Yale LJ* 1068; see also P. Quirk, *Industry Influence in Federal Regulatory Agencies* (Princeton, 1981).

4. Force of Ideas Explanations

The deregulatory programmes of the Reagan and Thatcher administrations prompted some commentators to argue that certain changes in
regulation did not stem so much from the pressing of private interests
as from the force of ideas.[38] (In such contexts 'ideas' are taken to refer
to intellectual conceptions 'which express how and why the government
ought to control business'.)[39] Ideas might be distorted by political considerations when being applied but: 'they provide the essential basis
of assumed social realities whereby political leaders explain and justify
their policies to the public, backed by a media which keeps the range of
"realistic" options within narrow limits'.[40]

It has been contended that deregulation, as seen in the United States
in the Reagan era, was driven not by interest group pressures but by
an intellectually guided process of economic rationalism that managed
to benefit dispersed consumer groups at the expense of concentrated producer interests.[41] (Residential consumers, the evidence was said to indicate, benefited from the deregulation.) This argument might itself have
difficulty in explaining why certain ideas take root, how ideas can be separated conceptually from interests, or in accounting for the patchiness
of deregulation,[42] but in so far as it is conceded that ideas possess a force
of their own, the force of ideas approach does usefully qualify economists'
emphasis on the market as the key factor in understanding regulatory
progressions.[43]

[38] Hood, *Explaining Economic Policy Reversals*, 29; see R. A. Harris and S. M. Milkis,
The Politics of Regulatory Change (2nd edn., New York, 1996), esp. ch. 1; on the influence
of public choice ideology see Self, *Government by the Market?*, ch. 3, esp pp. 65–7. On ideas
and policy processes generally see P. A. Hall, 'Policy Paradigms, Social Learning and the
State: The Case of Economic Policy-making in Britain' (1993) 25 *Comparative Politics* 275;
J. Goldstein and R. Keshane (eds.), *Ideas and Foreign Policy: Benefits, Institutions and
Political Change* (Ithaca, NY, 1993).

[39] Harris and Milkis, *Politics of Regulatory Change*, 26.

[40] Self, *Government by the Market?*, p. xii; see also P. G. Hall (ed.), *The Political Power
of Economic Ideas* (Princeton, 1989).

[41] See M. Derthick and P. Quirk, *The Politics of Deregulation* (Washington, 1985) and
Harris and Milkis, *Politics of Regulatory Change*, who argue: 'we must appreciate the history of the underlying ideas and institutions if we are to understand deregulatory outcomes
of the Reagan revolution' (p. 18). Harris and Milkis refer to 'the leadership role played by
intellectual and political elites in establishing a new regulatory regime' (p. 25); on the role
of ideas in European integration and regulation see H. Wallace and W. Wallace (eds.), *Policy-
Making in the European Union* (3rd edn., Oxford, 1996), 22–4.

[42] See Hood, *Explaining Economic Policy Reversals*, 29; J. K. Jacobsen, 'Much Ado about
Ideas' (1995) 47 *World Politics* 283; P. Quirk, 'In Defence of the Politics of Ideas' (1988)
50 *Journal of Politics* 31; also T. E. Keeler, 'Theories of Regulation and the Deregulation
Movement' (1984) *Public Choice* 103; L. W. Weiss and M. W. Klass (eds.), *Regulatory Reform:
What Actually Happened* (Boston, 1986).

[43] For counter-explanations of deregulation see Hood, *Explaining Economic Policy Reversals*, 29–33; Keeler, loc. cit. n. 42 above; Peltzman loc. cit. n. 28 above; Weiss and Klass,
Regulatory Reform.

5. Institutional Theories

A further group of commentators has been highly sceptical of the rational actor model encountered in the economic approach. Institutionalist theorists centre on the notion that institutional structure and arrangements, as well as social processes, significantly shape regulation—that there is more driving regulatory developments than mere aggregations of individuals' preferences.[44] Individual actors are seen by institutionalists as influenced by rules as well as organizational and social settings, rather than as pure rational choice maximizers, and as having preferences that are influenced by institutional procedures, principles, expectations, and norms that are encountered in cultural and historical frameworks.[45] Regulation is thus seen as shaped not so much by notions of the public interest or competitive bargaining between different private interests but by institutional arrangements and rules (legal and other). Forces acting within regulatory bodies are thus emphasized more strongly within institutionalism than in, say, interest theories.

'New institutionalist' approaches come from a variety of disciplinary roots but share a common scepticism about atomistic accounts focusing on the individual.[46] Thus, within the socio-legal literature attention has been paid to principal-agent problems and the difficulties that elected officials encounter when they have to place the implementation of public programmes in the hands of unaccountable officials and agencies.[47] A

[44] See J. March and J. Olsen, 'The New Institutionalism: Organisational Factors in Political Life' (1984) 78 *Am. Pol. Sci. Rev.* 734; J. Meyer and B. Rowan, 'Institutionalised Organisations: Formal Structure as Myth and Ceremony' (1977) *Am. J. Sociol.* 340; W. Scott, 'The Adolescence of Institutional Theory' (1987) 32 *Admin. Sci. Qly.* 493; W. Powell and P. Di Maggio (eds.), *The New Institutionalism in Organizational Analysis* (Chicago, 1991); R. L. Jepperson, 'Institutions, Institutional Effects, and Institutionalism', ibid.; T. A. Koelble, 'The New Institutionalism in Political Science and Sociology' (1995) *Comparative Politics* 231. B. Levy and P. T. Spiller, *Regulations, Institutions and Commitment* (Cambridge, 1996). See also the discussion in J. Black, 'An Economic Analysis of Regulation: One View of the Cathedral' (1997) *OJLS* 699; 'New Institutionalism and Nationalism in Socio-Legal Analysis: Institutional Approaches to Regulatory Decision-Making' (1997) 19 *Law and Policy* 53.

[45] But for a 'transactions cost' approach to institutional choices, which does make 'rational choice' assumptions familiar in economics literature see M. J. Horn, *The Political Economy of Public Administration* (Cambridge, 1995).

[46] See W. Powell and P. Di Maggio, *New Institutionalism*, esp. ch. 1. (On the birth of 'New Institutionalism' see Powell and Di Maggio, p. 11 and March and Olsen loc. cit. n. 44 above.)

[47] See M. D. McCubbins, R. G. Noll, and B. R. Weingast, 'Administrative Procedures as Instruments of Political Control' (1987) 3 *J. Law Econ. Org.* 243; 'Structure Process Politics and Policy: Administrative Arrangements and the Political Control of Agencies' (1989) 75 *Virginia LR* 431 (McNollGast I and II respectively); R. L. Calver, M. D. McCubbins, and B. R. Weingast, 'A Theory of Political Control and Agency Discretion' (1989) 33 *Am. J. Pol. Sci.* 588. For criticism see J. L. Mashaw, 'Explaining Administrative Process: Normative, Positive and Critical Stories of Legal Development' (1990) 6 *J. Law Econ. Org.* 267; T. Moe, 'Political Institutions: The Neglected Side of the Story' (1990) 6 *J. Law Econ. Org.* 213; Levy and Spiller, *Regulations, Institutions and Commitment*. For a European view see M. Bergman and J. Lane, 'Public Policy in a Principal-Agent Framework' (1990) 2 *J. of Theoretical*

notable contribution has been made by McCubbins, Noll, and Weingast (McNollGast) on this front. McNollGast's concern is that administrative agencies and bureaucrats may tend to act in ways contrary to the objectives established in the original legislative compromise and may do so because of coalitional and bureaucratic 'drifts'. Their argument is that bureaucratic deviations from the desires of politicians and legislatures are inherently difficult to control but a solution lies in the use of the 'administrative process'. Elected officials can design procedures to solve the two central problems of political control: 'First, procedures can be used to mitigate the informational disadvantages faced by politicians in dealing with agencies. Second, procedures can be used to enfranchise important constituents in agency decision-making processes.'[48] Thus, to solve the problem of eroding legislative coalitions McNollGast hypothesize that legislators will 'stack the deck' of administrative procedures (i.e. rig these) in favour of the original winning coalition. The effect is to preserve the thrust of the original policy position (or mandate) in the face of declining cohesion in the original political alliances that produced the policy.

Other commentators have sought to add to McNollGast by arguing that problems of bureaucratic and legislative drift can be controlled not merely by using administrative procedures but also by 'stacking' organizational structures and designs. Jonathan Macey,[49] for instance, has contended that the structure and design of agencies can be manipulated 'in ways that reduce the chance that future changes in the political landscape will upset the terms of the original understanding among the relevant political actors'.[50] Regulatory outcomes are, on such a view, said to be influenced by agency structures which affect the kinds of political pressure that various groups are able to exert on the bureaucrats within the agency.

New institutional economists have, for their part, sought to qualify the standard assumptions of microeconomic theory by focusing on the transaction and arguing that individuals may seek to maximize in accordance with certain preference orderings but they do so in the face of cognitive

---

Politics 339. For a review of principal-agent theories in regulation see M. Barrow, 'Public Services and the Theory of Regulation' (1996) 24 *Policy and Politics* 263.

[48] See McNollGast I, 244. On bureaucratic and coalitional drifts see M. J. Horn and K. A. Shepsle, 'Commentary: Structure, Process, Politics and Policy' (1989) *Va. LR* 499.

[49] J. R. Macey, 'Organisational Design and Political Control of Administrative Agencies' (1992) 8 *J. Law Econ. Org.* 93.

[50] Ibid. On the role of institutional structures in explaining regulation in the EU see G. Majone, 'The Rise of the Regulatory State in Europe' (1993) *West European Politics*. In their comparative study of telecommunications regulation, Levy and Spiller (*Regulations, Institutions and Commitment*) emphasize that regulatory performance is affected by the political and social institutions encountered in a country. They urge (controversially) that regulation can only be efficient and satisfactory if adequate state mechanisms are in place to restrain arbitrary administrative action by regulators: see pp. 1, 120.

limits, incomplete information, and difficulties in monitoring and enforcing agreements.[51]

From the political science perspective, a special concern is the nature of collective action and the way that political structures, institutions, and decision-making processes shape political outcomes.[52] A number of writers focus on the mechanics of legislating, the way that this affects substantive results, and the efforts of different political groupings to control each other (e.g. committees of the legislature and regulatory agencies).[53]

In sociology and organization theory, the new institutionalism involves not only a rejection of rational actor models but also an interest in institutions as independent variables; in cognitive and cultural explanations; and in units of analysis that are more than aggregations of individuals' preferences, attributes, or motives. Sociologists have devoted particular attention to the nature and conceptualization of institutions and how certain forms of behaviour and understandings become institutionalized.[54] A sociological approach to capture is thus offered by Grabosky and Braithwaite, who suggest that the closer the regulatory institution is to the regulated firm in terms of experience, outlook, and class (the smaller the 'relational distance') and the greater the frequency of agency to firm contacts, the more likely it is that cooperative arrangements and capture will result.[55] Organizational theorists have tended to focus on the

[51] See Powell and Di Maggio, *New Institutionalism*, 3, and L. Putterman, *The Economic Nature of the Firm* (Cambridge, 1986); O. Williamson, *The Economic Institutions of Capitalism* (New York, 1985); D. C. North, 'Government and the Cost of Exchange in History' (1984) 44 *J. of Econ. History* 255; R. Matthews, 'The Economics of Institutions and the Services of Growth' (1986) 96 *Economic Journal* 903; Horn, *The Political Economy of Public Administration*.

[52] See K. A. Shepsle, 'Institutional Equilibrium and Equilibrium Institutions', in H. Weisburg (ed.), *Political Science: The Science of Politics* (New York, 1986). T. Moe, 'An Assessment of the Positive Theory of Congressional Dominance' (1987) 12 *Legislative Stud. Q.* 475; id., 'Political Institutions: The Neglected Side of the Story' (1990) 6. *J. Law Econ. Org.* 213. For an economic approach to issues of political control see R. L. Calver, M. D. McCubbins, and B. R. Weingast, 'A Theory of Political Control and Agency Discretion' (1989) 33 *Am. J. Pol. Sci.* 588.

[53] See W. H. Riker, 'Implications from the Disequilibrium of Majority Rule for the Study of Institutions' (1980) 74 *Am. Pol. Sci. Rev.* 432; K. A. Shepsle and B. Weingast, 'Structure-Induced Equilibria and Legislature Choice' (1981) 37 *Public Choice* 503; Shepsle and Weingast, 'The Institutional Foundations of Committee Power' (1987) 81 *Am. Pol. Sci. Rev.* 85; B. Weingast and W. Marshall, 'The Industrial Organisation of Congress' (1988) 96 *J. Pol. Econ.* 132; E. Ostrom, 'An Agenda for the Study of Institutions' (1986) 48 *Public Choice* 3; K. A. Shepsle loc. cit. (1986) n. 52 above; T. Moe, 'Interests, Institutions and Positive Theory: The Politics of the NLRB' (1987) 2 *Studies in American Political Development* 236.

[54] See e.g. J. Meyer and B. Rowan, 'Institutionalised Organisation: Formal Structure as Myth and Ceremony' in Powell and Di Maggio, *New Institutionalism*. S. Crawford and E. Ostrom, 'A Grammar of Institutions' (1995) 89 *Am. Pol. Sci. Rev.* 582. R. L. Jepperson, 'Institutions, Institutional Effects and Institutionalism', in Powell and Di Maggio, *New Institutionalism*.

[55] P. Grabosky and J. Braithwaite, *Of Manners Gentle: Enforcement Strategies of Australian Business Regulatory Agencies* (Melbourne, 1986). On relational distance see D. Black, *The Behavior of Law* (New York, 1974), 40–8.

role of organizational structures and processes that are of industry-wide, national, or international scope and the extent to which individual choices are guided by shared organizational experiences, expectations, and understandings.[56]

One strand of regulatory theory that has socio-legal, sociological, cultural, and organizational elements is that represented by Leigh Hancher and Michael Moran,[57] who question portrayals of regulation as contests between public authorities and private interests and argue that regulation involves an intermingling of public and private characteristics that makes it more fruitful to focus on the complex and shifting relationships between and within organizations involved in regulation. Hancher and Moran thus look to understand the way that different institutions come to inhabit a shared 'regulatory space' that is marked out by a range of regulatory issues subject to public decision.

How regulatory regimes compete is a further, and distinct, focal point in explanations of regulation and attention may be paid to relations between domestic institutions as well as regulatory competition across borders.[58] In such analyses questions arise concerning the effect of regulatory competition on such matters as: the rigour of standards; the control (or encouragement) of regulatory capture; and the production of even-handed and effective regulatory regimes across national borders.[59]

Finally, mention should be made of the historical and cultural strands of institutionalism. The former tend to give weight to the influence of past decisions, practices, and procedures in explaining regulatory developments.[60] The latter look to the influence on institutions of informal

---

[56] See Powell and Di Maggio, *New Institutionalism*, 9–10.

[57] See L. Hancher and M. Moran (eds.), *Capitalism, Culture and Regulation* (Oxford, 1989), esp. their chapter 'Organising Regulatory Space'. See also T. Daintith, 'A Regulatory Space Agency' (1989) 9 *OJLS* 534 and C. Shearing, 'A Constitutive Conception of Regulation', in P. Grabosky and J. Braithwaite (eds.), *Business Regulation and Australia's Future* (Canberra, 1993).

[58] See Chapter 13 below; G. Majone, *Regulating Europe* (London, 1996); J. M. Sun and J. Pelkmans, 'Regulatory Competition in the Single Market' (1995) 33 *J. Common Market Studies* 67; C. Scott, 'Competition and Co-ordination in US and EC Telecommunications Regulation', in S. Picciotto, J. McCahery, C. Scott, and B. Bratton (eds.), *International Regulatory Competition and Co-ordination* (Oxford, 1996); S. Woolcock, *Competition among Rules in the Single European Market* (London, 1994); J. P. Trachtman, 'International Regulatory Competition, Externalisation and Jurisdiction' (1993) 34 *Harv. J. of Int. Law* 49; H. Siebert and M. J. Koop, 'Institutional Competition Versus Centralisation: *Quo Vadis* Europe' (1993) 9 *Oxford Rev. of Econ. Policy* 15.

[59] On *comparing* regulation across borders see R. Baldwin and T. Daintith, *Harmonisation and Hazard* (London, 1992) and below, Chapter 11.

[60] See K. Thalem and S. Steinmo, 'Historical Institutionalism in Comparative Politics', in S. Steinmo, K. Thelen, and F. Longstreth (eds.), *Structuring Politics: Historical Institutionalism in Comparative Politics* (Cambridge, 1992); I. McLean and C. Foster, 'The Political Economy of Regulation: Interests, Ideology, Voters and the UK Regulation of Railways Act 1844' (1992) 70 *Pub. Admin.* 313.

rules, procedures, conceptions, myths, ideologies, theories, shared values, beliefs, expectations, and understandings. More particular concerns are cognitive processes, the cultural frameworks of perception, and the relationships between ideas, images or symbols, and practical responses.[61] Influential within cultural approaches to institutions is Mary Douglas's distinction between two basic dimensions of organizations:[62] 'grid' (the degree to which relations are governed by externally imposed rules) and 'group' (the extent to which individuals are incorporated into broader, bounded units). Combining these two dimensions gives four basic ways of life: 'fatalist' (high grid, high group); 'hierarchist' (high grid, low group), 'individualist' (low grid, low group), and 'sectarian' or 'egalitarian' (low grid, high group). Commentators have sought to apply grid-group anlayses in accounting for developments in government and, in using such analyses, have stressed the importance of institutions and groups as well as rule systems in determining social and regulatory developments.[63]

In emphasizing the self-productive aspect of institutions such cultural approaches are consistent with systems theory and the idea that the differentiated functional systems into which society is divided are autopoietic. Each system (law, economy, politics, religion, etc.) is seen to have its own rationality yet to be able to react with its environment so as to self-generate and reproduce.[64] Regulatory developments, accordingly, come to be analysed in terms of the nature, compatibilities, and interactions of autopoietic systems.[65]

---

[61] See Jepperson loc. cit. n. 54 above; J. Meyer, J. Boli, and G. Thomas, 'Ontology and Rationalisation in the Western Cultural Account', in G. Thomas et al. (eds.), *Institutional Structure* (London, 1987); J. Meyer, 'Conceptions of Christendom', in M. Kohn (ed.), *Cross-National Research in Sociology* (London, 1988); id., 'Society without Culture: A Nineteenth Century Legacy', in F. O. Ramirez (ed.), *Rethinking the Nineteenth Century* (New York, 1988), G. M. Thomas, *Revivalism and Cultural Change* (Chicago, 1989); M. Douglas, *How Institutions Think* (London, 1986); M. Thompson, R. Ellis, and A. Wildavsky, *Cultural Theory* (Boulder, Colo., 1990).

[62] M. Douglas, *In the Active Voice* (London, 1982).

[63] See e.g. Thompson, Ellis, and Wildavsky, *Cultural Theory* and A. Wildavsky, 'The Logic of Public Sector Growth', in J. E. Lane (ed.), *State and Market* (London, 1985) (discussed, Hood, *Explaining Economic Policy Reversals*, 98–9).

[64] See G. Teubner (ed.), *Autopoietic Law: A New Approach to Law and Society* (Berlin, 1988); id., *Juridification of Social Spheres* (Berlin, 1987); id., *Law as an Autopoietic System* (Oxford, 1993); N. Luhmann, 'Law as a Social System' (1989) 83 *NWULR* 136; M. King, 'The Truth about Autopoiesis' (1993) 20 *J. of Law and Society* 218; W. H. Clune, 'Implementation as an Autopoietic Interaction of Autopoietic Organisations', in G. Teubner and A. Febbrajo (eds.), *State, Law and Economy as Autopoietic Systems: Regulation and Autonomy in New Perspective* (Milan, 1992); on autopoiesis and self-regulation see J. Black, (1996) 59 *MLR* 24 and for an introduction, King, 'The Truth about Autopoiesis'.

[65] See Black, loc. cit. n. 64 above and G. Teubner, 'After Legal Instrumentalism? Strategic Models of Post-Regulatory Law', in Teubner (ed.), *Dilemmas of Law in the Welfare State* (Berlin, 1985); M. Wilke, 'Societal Regulation through Law', in Teubner and Febbrajo, *State, Law and Economy*.

Conclusions

A review of major approaches to the explanation of regulation may not exhaustively account for the host of potential theories available. It serves, however, to indicate the main tensions and differences of emphasis encountered in the regulatory literature. It would be optimistic, even rash, to suggest that such theories can be synthesized so that reliable predictions can be made about all or most regulatory processes.[66] Different theories exist at differing levels of generality and have varying applications and uses as explanatory tools. For this reason it makes little sense to say whether one explanation or type of explanation carries more conviction than another without reference to a particular issue and context. What can be said is that in seeking to explain particular regulatory developments, an awareness of the variety of available explanations does help the observer to evaluate the insights offered by different theories, to develop a sense of the limitations of and assumptions underpinning those theories, and to identify the kinds of information necessary for applying and testing them.

The study of regulation has developed in many promising ways in recent years.[67] Thus, interdisciplinary approaches have become more widespread and traditional academic boundaries have been crossed between such disciplines as law, political science, and economics.[68] Regulatory theory has come to draw from an ever wider range of sources, from legal theory[69] to political science[70] and anthropology.[71] Regulatory studies have taken on board new issues and concerns—such as attend the topic of risk[72]—and, from a British perspective, a healthy indigenous literature has developed to supplement previously dominant 'borrowings' from across the Atlantic.[73] Themes and approaches do remain to be developed within the body of regulatory studies[74] but regulation is set to grow in importance not merely as a governmental activity and as a subject for party political attention but also as a focus of academic interest.

---

[66] See M. E. Levine and J. L. Forrence, 'Regulatory Capture, Public Interest and the Public Agenda: Towards Synthesis' (1990) *J. Law Econ. Org.* 167.

[67] See the discussion in R. Baldwin, C. Scott, and C. Hood (eds.), *A Reader On Regulation* (Oxford, 1998), ch. 1.

[68] See e.g. D. Helm (ed.), *British Utilities Regulation* (1996).

[69] See e.g. the works of Teubner and Black at n. 64 above.

[70] See e.g. Hood, *Explaining Economic Policy Reversals*; R. A. Harris and S. M. Milkis, *The Politics of Regulatory Change* (2nd edn., New York, 1996).

[71] See e.g. M. Douglas, 'Risk as a Forensic Resource' (1990) 119 *Daedalus* 1.

[72] See below, Chapter 11 and e.g. Royal Society, *Risk: Assessment, Perception, Management* (London, 1992) (containing a useful bibliography of risk studies).

[73] See e.g. A. Ogus, *Regulation: Legal Form and Economic Theory* (Oxford, 1994); M. Armstrong, S. Cowan, and J. Vickers, *Regulatory Reform: Economic Analysis and British Experience* (London, 1994).

[74] For discussion see Baldwin, Scott, and Hood, *Regulation*, ch. 1.

TABLE 2. *Explaining regulation*

Type of Theory	Main Emphasis	Key Problems
Public Interest	Regulator acting in pursuit of public rather than private interests. Regulator disinterested and expert.	Difficult to agree a conception of public interest. Scepticism concerning disinterestedness, and public-spiritedness of regulators. Understates influence of economic power and prevalence of capture in regulation. Concern that public interest outcomes often fail to result. Understates competition for power amongst groups.
Interest Group	Regulation as product of relationships between groups and with the state.	Understates role of private economic power.
Private Interest	Role of private economic interests in driving regulation. Incentives of firms to secure benefits and regulatory rents by capturing regulator.	Assumes that parties in regulation are rational maximizers of own welfare. Difficulty of identifying preferences of parties. Possibility of altruism and public-spiritedness. Informational limitations may limit self-interestedness of actions. Role of groups and institutions may be underemphasized.
Force of Ideas	Role of ideas in steering regulatory developments.	It may be hard to separate the force of ideas from the role of economic interests. Explaining deregulation may be difficult.
Institutional	Influence of organizational rule and social setting on regulation. Actors seen not purely as individuals but as shaped in action, knowledge, and preference by organizational rule and social environments. Principal-agent issues and problems of democratic control of implementation.	How to balance institutional explanations with others in accounting for regulatory changes.

4

Regulatory Strategies

If the state wants to control, say, the pollution of a river it may use a number of strategies. The dumping of noxious substances may be made unlawful or, alternatively, the state may give rewards (e.g. tax deductions) to those existing polluters who reduce the levels of their discharges. Looking to other strategies, manufacturers might be compelled to tell the public how much pollution is caused in making each product or rights might be allocated so as to allow the victims of pollution to recover damages from polluters.

Choosing the right strategy for regulating matters. A regulatory system will be difficult to justify—no matter how well it seems to be performing—if critics can argue that a different strategy would more effectively achieve relevant objectives. How, though, can we map out the array of different regulatory techniques? A starting point is to consider the basic capacities or resources that governments possess and which can be used to influence industrial, economic, or social activity. These have been described as follows:[1]

To command—where legal authority and the command of law is used to pursue policy objectives.

To deploy wealth—where contracts, grants, loans, subsidies, or other incentives are used to influence conduct.

To harness markets—where governments channel competitive forces to particular ends (for example by using franchise auctions to achieve benefits for consumers).

To inform—where information is deployed strategically (e.g. so as to empower consumers).

To act directly—where the state takes physical action itself (e.g. to contain a hazard or nuisance).

To confer protected rights—where rights and liability rules are structured and allocated so as to create desired incentives and constraints (e.g. rights to clean water are created in order to deter polluters).

[1] See C. C. Hood, *The Tools of Government* (London, 1983), 5; T. C. Daintith, 'The Techniques of Government', in J. Jowell and D. Oliver (eds.), *The Changing Constitution* (3rd edn., Oxford, 1994).

A number of basic regulatory strategies are built on the use of the above capacities or resources and can be distinguished from each other as follows.[2]

1. Command and Control

The essence of command and control (C & C) regulation is the exercise of influence by imposing standards backed by criminal sanctions.[3] Thus, the Health and Safety Executive may bring criminal prosecutions against occupiers who breach health and safety regulations. The force of law is used to prohibit certain forms of conduct or to demand some positive actions or to lay down conditions for entry into a sector.

Regulators who operate C & C techniques are sometimes equipped with rule-making powers (as is often the case in the USA). In the UK, however, it is common for regulatory standards to be set by government departments through primary or secondary legislation and then enforced by regulatory bureaucracies. C & C thus involves the setting of standards within a rule, it often entails some kind of licensing process to screen entry to an activity, and may set out to control not merely the quality of a service or the manner of production but also the allocation of resources, products, or commodities and the prices charged to consumers[4] or the profits made by enterprises.

The strengths of C & C regulation (as compared to techniques based, say, on the use of economic incentives such as taxes or subsidies) are that the force of law can be used to impose fixed standards with immediacy and to prohibit activity not conforming to such standards. In political terms, the regulator or government is seen to be acting forcefully and to be taking a clear stand: by designating some forms of behaviour as unacceptable; by excluding dangerous parties from relevant areas; by protecting the public; and establishing penalties for those engaging in offensive conduct. Some forms of behaviour can thus be outlawed completely and the ill-qualified can be stopped from practising activities likely to produce harms. The public, as a result, can be assured that the might of the law is being used both practically and symbolically in their aid.

C & C regulation is not, however, problem-free and, during the 1980s in particular, a number of North American socio-legal scholars and

---

[2] On regulatory strategies in general use see S. Breyer, *Regulation and Its Reform* (Cambridge, Mass., 1982), esp. ch. 8; A. Ogus, *Regulation: Legal Form and Economic Theory* (Oxford, 1994), esp. Parts III and IV; N. Gunningham and P. Grabosky, *Smart Regulation* (Oxford, 1998), ch. 2.

[3] On command and control and alternatives see R. Baldwin, 'Regulation: After Command and Control', in K. Hawkins (ed.), *The Human Face of Law* (Oxford, 1997).

[4] For more detailed discussion of price control mechanisms see Chapter 17 below.

economists alleged a series of weaknesses.[5] Such concerns were echoed by many politicians on both sides of the Atlantic—particularly those predisposed to doubt the value of governmental rather than market-based modes of influence.

Capture

A first worry was that in C & C regulation the relationships between the regulators and the regulated might tend to become too close and lead to capture—the pursuit of the regulated enterprises' interests rather than those of the public at large.[6] A number of versions of capture theory have been put forward.[7] 'Life-cycle' accounts suggest that agencies progress through various stages until, lonely, frightened, and old, they become the protectors of the regulated industry, rather than of the public interest;[8] 'interest group' explanations stress the extent to which regulators can be influenced by the claims and political influence of different groups; and 'private interest' or economic analyses see regulation as a commodity liable to fall under (or to be established under) the sway of the economically powerful.[9]

The proximity of regulator to regulatee relationships that is associated with C & C techniques might be thought to be particularly conducive to capture in so far as agencies, when drawing up and enforcing rules, must rely to some extent on the cooperation of the regulated firms. Thus, the argument runs, regulators require a good deal of information in order to carry out their functions—say to fix appropriate standards on issues such as acceptable pollution levels or price increases. The primary, and best, source of such information will often be industry. The regulator, accordingly, requires some assistance from the regulated firms in order to make C & C regulation work. This gives the regulated firms a degree of leverage over regulatory procedures and objectives, a leverage that, over time, produces capture.

In response to allegations that C & C regulation is particularly prone to capture it should be noted that many versions of capture theories would

[5] See e.g. Breyer, *Regulation and Its Reform*; R. B. Stewart, 'Regulation and the Crisis of Legalism in the United States', in T. Daintith (ed.), *Law as an Instrument of Economic Policy* (Berlin, 1998); id., 'The Discontents of Legalism: Interest Group Relations in Administrative Regulation' (1985) *Wisconsin LR* 685; E. Bardach and R. Kagan, *Going by the Book: The Problem of Regulatory Unreasonableness* (Philadelphia, 1982) Gunningham and Grabosky, *Smart Regulation*, 44–7.

[6] See C. Hood, *Explaining Economic Policy Reversals* (Buckingham, 1994), 21.

[7] For a review of these see B. Mitnick, *The Political Economy of Regulation* (New York, 1980); also see P. J. Quirk, *Industry Influence in Federal Regulatory Agencies* (Princeton, 1981); G. Wilson, 'Social Regulation and Explanations of Regulatory Failure' (1984) 32 *Pol. Stud.* 203.

[8] See M. H. Bernstein, *Regulating Business by Independent Commission* (New York, 1955) and discussion above at p. 25.

[9] See R. Posner, 'Theories of Economic Regulation' (1974) 5 *Bell J. of Econ.* 335; G. Stigler, 'The Theory of Economic Regulation' (1971) 2 *Bell J. of Econ.* 3.

attribute capture to factors that operate in a manner unaffected by the particular regulatory technique employed. They might point, for instance, to broad political, institutional, or economic considerations.

Legalism

A second major concern with C & C regulation has been its alleged propensity to produce unnecessarily complex and inflexible rules, and indeed, a proliferation of rules that leads to over-regulation, legalism, delay intrusion on managerial freedoms, and the strangling of competition and enterprise.[10] Eugene Bardach and Robert Kagan have expressed concern at the extent to which US regulators have tended to over-regulate with over-inclusive rules (rules that apply to an unnecessarily wide array of instances or actions) and have given a number of reasons why such problems tend to occur. Firstly, rule-makers find it very difficult to design precisely targeted rules (the informational demands are severe) and the tendency is to avoid such design and drafting difficulties by writing over-inclusive rules. Secondly, for political reasons, regulators tend to respond to particular problems or tragedies with general, or 'across-the board', rules and solutions. This gives the appearance of 'doing something about that sort of thing'. Third, pressures to reduce discretions in favour of the 'rule of law' (so as to make regulatory actions rule-governed) may come from politicians, those regulated, or consumers, and these pressures may induce the excessive production of rules. Fourth, regulators often wish to respond to a mischief before public concern dies down—while the memory of the disaster is still fresh. Working to the resultant short time scales tends to produce rules that are broad-brush rather than precisely targeted. Finally, there is what is dubbed the 'regulatory ratchet'[11] whereby regulatory rules tend to grow rather then recede because revisions of regulations are infrequent; work on new rules tends to drive out attention to old ones; and failure to carry out pruning leads the thickets of rules to grow ever more dense.[12]

In the context of British telecommunications OFTEL has argued that detailed, prescriptive rules can be a barrier to entry, can inhibit competition, and can discriminate between incumbent licensed operators and new entrants. OFTEL has urged a movement away from control by means of detailed rules contained in the licences of those given privileged access, towards 'open state' regulation that is based on general authorizations and which gives a stronger role to general competition and

---

[10] See Stewart, loc. cit. (1988) n. 5 above; Bardach and Kagan, *Going by the Book*; G. Teubner, *Juridification of Social Spheres* (Berlin, 1987).

[11] Bardach and Kagan, *Going by the Book*, ch. 7.

[12] On responses to these problems see R. Baldwin, *Rules and Government* (Oxford, 1995), 183–5 and below, Chapter 19.

consumer protection laws, backed up by detailed guidance only where necessary.[13]

Standard Setting

Setting appropriate standards has been argued to pose major difficulties for regulators because the informational demands are so severe.[14] Thus, anti-competitive effects must be addressed; the appropriate *type* of standard must be selected—be this an output standard specifying a level of performance or an input standard calling for a particular design or specification of operation or machinery—and the level of exposure to judicial review may be high[15]. Setting the appropriate level of performance is, moreover, technically difficult and liable to be contentious. To give a simple instance, employing the example of pollution again, even if it is assumed that the regulator knows the beneficial values of particular levels of cleanliness in a river, and is clear on social objectives, setting the optimal levels of allowable pollution (the levels that minimize the sum of abatement and damage costs) would require data on the differing abatement costs of all of the various polluters on the riverbank. The efficient level of pollution will, indeed, be specific to each enterprise yet the regulator has usually to produce a generalized rule.

Enforcement

A final major difficulty said to be particularly associated with C & C regimes is that of enforcement. The complex rules attending such regimes have to be brought to bear on the ground by bodies of officials or inspectors but enforcement is expensive, the techniques used give rise to contention, and the effects of enforcement are said to be uncertain.[16] On the latter point, for instance, the rules used in C & C systems may be too narrow or too broad in scope. They may, accordingly, fail to cover conduct that should be controlled or else may constrain activity that should be unrestricted. In addition, there may be problems of 'creative compliance' —the practice of avoiding the intention of the law without breaking the terms of the law.[17]

---

[13] See OFTEL, *Second Submission to the Culture, Media and Sport Select Committee: Beyond the Telephone, the Television and the PC—Regulation of the Electronic Communications Industry* (London, Mar. 1998).

[14] See Chapter 9 below for a general discussion of standard setting, also Breyer, *Regulation and Its Reform*, 109–19, Ogus, *Regulation*, ch. 8.

[15] See Ogus, *Regulation*, ch. 8.

[16] For further discussion of enforcement see Chapter 8 below and Baldwin, *Rules and Government*, ch. 6.

[17] See below, pp. 102–3.

Regulators employing C & C techniques thus face substantial difficulties of rule use. Not only must the rules employed be capable of enforcement and be accessible to regulated firms or individuals, but the appropriate types and levels of standards must be fixed, problems of scope (or inclusiveness) must be overcome, and issues of creative compliance dealt with. Such problems, moreover, must often be faced in political environments that are unlikely to produce the resources necessary for effective enforcement and are hostile to rules that impose compliance costs on industry or interfere with managers. In the light of such difficulties, some commentators advocate a move away from command-based strategies towards alternative 'constitutive', 'less restrictive', or 'incentive-based' styles of control.[18] The strategies now to be described may be seen as the main alternatives to C & C style of regulation.

2. Self-Regulation and Enforced Self-Regulation[19]

Self-regulation can be seen as a substitute for C & C though it might also be portrayed as self-administered C & C.[20] Simple self-regulation usually involves an organization or association (e.g. a trade association) developing a system of rules that it monitors and enforces against its own members or, in some cases, a larger community.[21] Such regimes are commonly instituted in professions or trades so as to hold government regulation and legislative controls at bay (examples may be found in the British advertising, press, and insurance industries).

Self-regulation can be classified as 'enforced' when it is subject to a form of governmental structuring or oversight. A regime may thus be mandated under legislation, as was the case in the UK financial services sector with the network of self-regulatory organizations (SROs) established under

[18] See Stewart, loc. cit. (1988) n. 5 above; Breyer, *Regulation and Its Reform*. On incentive-based regulation see Ogus, *Regulation*, ch. 11. For a European view of the limits of command law see G. Teubner, *After Legal Instrumentalism? Strategic Models of Post-Regulatory Law*, EUI Working Paper No. 100 (Florence, 1984).

[19] For a more detailed discussion of self-regulation see Chapter 10 below.

[20] See I. Ayres and J. Braithwaite, *Responsive Regulation: Transcending the Regulation Debate* (Oxford, 1992), ch. 4; J. Braithwaite, 'Enforced Self-Regulation: A New Strategy for Corporate Crime Control' (1982) 80 *Mich. LR* 1466; J. Black, 'Constitutionalising Self-Regulation' (1996) 59 *MLR* 24. On varieties of self-regulation see A. I. Ogus, 'Rethinking Self-Regulation' (1995) 15 *OJLS* 97.

[21] See Baldwin, Scott, and Hood, *Regulation*, ch. 1, who cite the Advertising Standards Authority as an example of self-regulation with a jurisdiction extending beyond members. On self-regulation generally see A. Page, 'Self-Regulation: The Constitutional Dimension' (1986) 49 *MLR* 141; id., 'Financial Services: The Self-Regulatory Alternative', in R. Baldwin and C. McCrudden, *Regulation and Public Law* (London, 1987); R. Baggott and L. Harrison, 'The Politics of Self-Regulation', in G. Richardson and H. Genn (eds.), *Administrative Law and Government Action* (Oxford, 1995).

the Financial Services Act 1986.[22] Statutes may subject self-regulation to scrutiny and approval by a government department or agency—as is the case with the trade association codes of practice approved by the Director General of Fair Trading under the Fair Trading Act 1973.[23]

Self-regulatory methods have proved popular with a number of governments and commentators.[24] Thus, Ayres and Braithwaite have suggested that systems of enforced self-regulation, under which organizations make their own rules but have to submit them to public agencies for approval, bring a number of advantages as compared to traditional C & C regimes. The strengths of enforced self-regulation have thus been said to be:

- The high level of commitment of firms and associations to 'their own' rules.
- Well-informed rule-making.
- Low costs to government.
- A close fit between regulation and the standards firms accept as realistically attainable.
- Greater effectiveness in detecting violations and in securing convictions where prosecution is necessary.
- The greater comprehensiveness of rules.
- The potential of self-regulatory rules for rapid adjustment to changing circumstances.
- More effective complaints procedures.

Ogus has argued that self-regulatory regimes based on consensual bargaining or involving competition between self-regulatory structures have the potential to meet traditional criticisms of self-regulation if such regimes incorporate some measure of external constraint. Those criticisms, however, possess some force and the following main concerns should be noted:

- The costs to the public purse of approving self-regulatory rules may be considerable.
- The rules written by self-regulators may prove self-serving and may not be immune from the problems afflicting rules in C & C regimes (e.g. difficulties attending legalism, standard-setting, and enforcement).
- The procedures employed to produce rules may be subject to the objection that they lack openness, transparency, accountability, and acceptability to the public and to consumers of services.

---

[22] See A. Page and R. Ferguson, *Investor Protection* (London, 1992); C. Mayer, 'The Regulation of Financial Services: Lessons from the UK for 1992', in M. Bishop, J. Kay, and C. Mayer (eds.), *The Regulatory Challenge* (Oxford, 1995).

[23] See Baldwin, Scott, and Hood, *Regulation*, ch. 1 and I. Ramsay, 'The Office of Fair Trading', in Baldwin and McCrudden, *Regulation and Public Law*.

[24] For arguments in favour of self-regulation see Ayres and Braithwaite, *Responsive Regulation*, and Ogus loc. cit. n. 20 above, p. 15.

- Compliance units within firms may not always retain their independence and the public may not trust self-regulatory bodies to apply the rules in the public or consumer interest.
- Where self-regulatory regimes contain powers to make and enforce rules and to sanction transgressors, difficult doctrinal questions may arise as to their broader subjection to the principles of administrative law.[25]
- The public may demand that the government take responsibility for a sector or an issue.

British experience with enforced self-regulation is limited but elements of the approach are encountered. The Health and Safety Executive, for instance, has experimented with self-regulation under supervision and employs self-assessment procedures. Fair trading legislation has relied, particularly in the 1970s, upon trade association codes of practice while financial services regulation has involved a degree of monitored self-regulation.

Enforced self-regulation can, finally, be seen as an important element in techniques where combinations of different regulatory strategies are employed. Ayres and Braithwaite have suggested thinking in terms of a pyramid strategy.[26] Within this approach self-regulation is favoured as the initial response to a mischief and where desired results are not achieved, enforced self-regulation involving greater state monitoring is seen as appropriate. Only when these strategies fail, it is said, should regulation with discretionary punishment, and finally with mandatory punishment, be resorted to.[27]

The feasibility of progressing through different regulatory strategies within such a scheme is a central challenge to be faced by proponents of the pyramidic approach.

3. Incentive-Based Regimes

Regulating by means of economic incentives might be thought to offer an escape from highly restrictive, rule-bound, C & C regimes.[28] According to the incentives approach, the potential mischief causer, say a polluter, can be induced to behave in accordance with the public interest

---

[25] See Black, loc. cit n. 20 above and Chapter 10 below.

[26] Ayres and Braithwaite, *Responsive Regulation*.

[27] See J. T. Scholtz, 'Cooperative Regulatory Enforcement and the Politics of Administrative Effectiveness' (1991) 85 *Am. Pol. Sci. Rev.* 118.

[28] See Ogus, *Regulation*, ch. 11; T. C. Daintith, 'The Techniques of Government'; R. Breyer and R. B. Stewart, 'The Discontents of Legalism: Interest Group Relations in Administrative Regulation' (1985) *Wisconsin LR* 685. On the limitations of incentive-based regimes see J. Braithwaite, 'The Limits of Economism in Controlling Harmful Corporate Conduct' (1982) 16 *Law and Society Review* 481.

by the state or a regulator imposing negative or positive taxes or deploying grants and subsidies from the public purse. Thus, not only can taxes be used to penalize polluters but rewards can be given for reductions in pollution or financial assistance can be given to those who build pollution-reducing mechanisms into their production or operational processes. An example of such an incentive strategy at the broadest level was the proposal by the Chancellor of the Exchequer, Gordon Brown, to cut the vehicle excise duty for the cleanest and smallest cars by £50 in his March 1998 budget.[29]

The posited advantages of such schemes are numerous. They are, for instance, said to involve relatively low levels of regulatory discretion (as compared to C & C systems) because financial punishments or rewards operate in a mechanical manner once the regime is established. These low levels of discretion and structured modes of application reduce the dangers of regulatory capture in so far as regulators are not involved in constant negotiations, close relations, and information exchanges with regulatees as in the usual C & C scheme.

They are also said to leave managers free to manage. It is up to the regulated firm, not the bureaucrat or regulator, to balance the costs of polluting against those of abatement in a particular context and to devise means of reducing the mischief most efficiently. Managers are, accordingly, able to be more flexible concerning their modes of production than most C & C regimes allow.

Incentive-based regimes are, additionally, claimed to involve relatively light burdens of information collection and costs yet to produce results by creating economic pressures. They, moreover, are said by proponents to encourage individual regulated firms to reduce harmful conduct as much as possible (to give an 'incentive to zero') not merely down to the level that is demanded by the standard stipulated in a C & C regime—a standard liable, in any event, to be fairly lax because C & C regulators tend, for political reasons, to have to set a general standard soft enough to be met by poorer performers in the industry without causing financial crises or unacceptable unemployment.

The advantages of incentive regimes can, however, be exaggerated and a number of cautionary points should be borne in mind.[30] Such systems

---

[29] Mr Brown proposed also to increase the tax on low sulphur diesel by a penny less than ordinary diesel fuel. He was, however, criticized by environmental groups for postponing action on earlier proposals for taxing water pollution and quarrying (see *Financial Times*, 18 Mar. 1998). A differential tax on leaded and unleaded petrol was introduced in Britain in 1987. On regulation by taxation see A. Ogus, 'Corrective Taxation as a Regulatory Instrument', in C. McCrudden (ed.), *Regulation and Deregulation* (Oxford, 1999); also at (1998) 61 MLR. 767; S. Rose-Ackerman, 'Efficient Changes: A Critique' (1973) 6 *Can. J. Econ.* 572; W. J. Baumol, 'On Taxation and the Control of Externatilies' (1972) 62 *Am. Econ. Rev.* 307; P. Burrows, 'Pricing versus Regulation for Environmental Pollution', in A. J. Culyer (ed.), *Economic Policies and Social Goals* (London, 1974).

[30] For evaluation see Ogus, *Regulation*, 250–6 and Breyer, *Regulation and Its Reform*, 278–80.

often have to be put into effect by means of highly complex systems of rules (the field of taxation, for instance, is not one renowned for simplicity).[31] Many of the problems associated with C & C regulation might thus be replicated in putting such systems into effect on the ground. Inspection and enforcement mechanisms might, moreover, have to be employed to prevent regulatees evading their liabilities (e.g. to taxes). The system might, thus, come to resemble C & C regulation and the distinction between incentives and penalty mechanisms might be less than first appeared.[32]

Proponents of incentive systems tend to assume that those regulated operate on the whole in an economically rational manner. In practice, however, many problems (e.g. hazards in the workplace) are the product of irrational, accidental, or negligent behaviour.[33] Incentive mechanisms may, accordingly, influence responsible parties more effectively than irresponsible, careless, or ill-informed individuals or firms—yet it is the latter group who are most in need of regulation. Regulatory lag may also prove a significant problem with incentive regimes because they operate indirectly. Thus, within a firm the effects of tax incentives may have to be transmitted from finance directors through operations managers to floor staff and this, even if successful, may take some time—the fish in the river may long be dead. Incentives may thus prove to be poor regulatory tools where periodic crises occur in the sectors involved or where such sectors are subject to rapid economic change.

A core difficulty with incentive regimes may be predicting the effect on the ground of a given incentive. To continue the river pollution example, it will be very difficult to predict how much a certain tax bite will clean up the river. The effect on each firm sited on the river will differ and will depend, *inter alia*, on the profit derived within each production process from each unit of pollution. Fixing incentive levels may thus make informational demands at least as severe as those encountered within C & C regimes.

The mechanical application of incentives may also bring disadvantages. Within C & C systems, enforcement can be used flexibly in an effort to achieve desired results and to limit the imposition of restrictions on particular firms or individuals where unduly onerous effects would result. In so far as incentive regimes operate mechanically, such tailoring to individual circumstances will not be possible. If a flexible and discretionary approach is adopted in relation to incentives (and there is no reason why

---

[31] See R. S. Markovits, 'Antitrust: Alternatives to Delegalisation', in G. Teubner (ed.), *Juridification of Social Spheres* (Berlin, 1987).

[32] See Bardach and Kagan, *Going by the Book*, chs. 8, 9, and 10; J. Braithwaite, 'The Limits of Economism in Controlling Harmful Corporate Conduct' (1982) 16 *Law and Society Review* 481.

[33] See Braithwaite, loc. cit. n. 28 above.

this cannot be the case) another supposed difference from, and advantage over, C & C regulation falls away.

Presentationally and politically, a move from C & C towards incentive regimes may prove popular with firms regulated (especially where subsidies are offered) but public concern may arise on the grounds that socially harmful activity is not being stigmatized or condemned and that a licence is being given for undesirable behaviour.[34] Subsidies may be objected to as making payments from the public purse to those engaged in offensive conduct and negative incentives or taxes may be criticized not only for their failure to designate certain acts as unacceptable but also for taking away from industry the very resources that might have been committed to measures aimed at avoiding the undesirable consequences of their actions (e.g. to filtration systems). As far as democratic accountability and access to the regulatory process are concerned, similar consultative and other procedures to those used in command and control regulation may be used. If it is hard to predict the effects of given incentives on the ground, however, it may be difficult to produce the results that such democratic inputs favour and this can be seen as a distancing of accountability and access.

4. Market-Harnessing Controls

Competition Laws

A direct method of regulating by channelling market forces is to influence competition within an area. Competition laws can thus be used instead of, or in conjunction with, regulation in order to sustain such levels of competition as will ensure that the market provides adequate services to consumers and the public.[35]

Such laws can also be used to control market behaviour so as to prevent anti-competitive or unfair practices such as 'predatory pricing' by dominant operators (setting prices for one's products below cost in order to drive competitors from the market)[36] or effecting cross-subsidies from monopolistic to competitive sectors.

The telecommunications industry provides an example of competition law being used instead of classical C & C regulation. Thus, in contrast to

---

[34] See Ogus, *Regulation*, 225; also W. Beckerman, *Small is Stupid: Blowing the Whistle on the Greens* (London, 1995).

[35] On competition law generally see R. Whish, *Competition Law* (3rd edn. London, 1993). For an example of a regulatory agency coming to grips with competition issues see OFTEL, *Effective Competition: Framework for Action* (London, 1995) and for advocacy of a move from C & C or prescriptive rules towards reliance on competition and consumer protection laws see OFTEL, *Second Submission*. On regulation versus competition see below, Chapter 16.

[36] See J. Vickers, 'The Economics of Predatory Prices' (1985) 6 *Fiscal Studies* 24.

the UK's use of a sectoral agency (OFTEL) with sector-specific rules (the Telecommunications Act 1984), the New Zealand Government, on privatizing in the late 1980s, relied on general competition laws, applied in the courts, as a mechanism for influencing the telecommunications industry.

The broad advantages of reliance on competition laws are that they can be applied across the board to different sectors, the need for industry-specific regulation is avoided, and barriers to entry may be lower than in regimes incorporating large numbers of highly prescriptive rules. Consistent principles can also be developed across sectors and there are economies of scale in applying rules broadly.

Competition laws produce lower levels of intrusion into firms' internal decisions than are involved in C & C regimes and flexibility in the industry tends to be greater under competition law regimes than in cases where behaviour is structured by an overseeing agency. Finally, enforcement involves relatively light burdens on the public purse because it depends on private actions in courts rather than action by publicly-funded regulatory agencies. Experience in New Zealand telecommunications suggests, however, that a number of drawbacks can be encountered when heavy reliance is placed on competition laws.[37] The broad principles established in competition laws may, for instance, not provide solutions to operational, technical, or commercial problems. Such issues are left to the parties to resolve in the courts and more effective solutions might, under certain conditions, be produced by a specialist overseeing agency. An agency, moreover, might develop and apply a greater level of expertise than the parties or the courts in dealing with such issues as the economics of interconnections. Guidelines established by a regulatory agency can reduce uncertainties and transaction costs for operators more efficiently than competition laws or the courts.

The courts system may, furthermore, be slow to develop guidelines on central industrial issues. Thus, following difficulties concerning the application of general competition rules to a dispute over interconnection by a new entrant (issues fought from New Zealand to the Privy Council in 1994[38]) the New Zealand Government considered whether a new mix of institutions and rules would be appropriate.[39] One difficulty encountered in relying on judicially developed principles on such issues as interconnection is that rulings only emerge as cases happen to arise. Principles, accordingly, may develop sporadically, slowly, and may leave key issues untouched. Developing such principles, moreover, may involve asking

---

[37] For reviews of New Zealand experience see: New Zealand Commerce Commission, *Telecommunications Industry Inquiry Report* (Wellington, June 1992); C. Blanchard, 'Telecommunications Regulation in New Zealand: How Effective is "light-handed" regulation?' (1994) 18 *Telecommunications Policy* 154–64.

[38] See *Clear Communication* v. *New Zealand Telecommunications Corp.* [1994] 6 TCLR 138 (1995) 1 NZLR 385 (PC).

[39] See Baldwin, Scott, and Hood, *Regulation*, ch. 1.

the courts to stand in the shoes of business people and to make business decisions.[40] Evidential problems may also compound such reliance on the courts, thus, competition law may have a limited role in dealing with entry barriers where it is difficult to show these have been established on purpose by a dominant undertaking.

To point to some of the problems to be anticipated in using competition laws is not, of course, to say that such laws cannot play a very useful role in combination with other mechanisms of influence, such as C & C regulation in the classical style. Competition laws can thus substitute for excessively prescriptive C & C regulation on some issues and the latter can be used to impose structures and final solutions for industries in circumstances where competition law would be slow to provide answers on these fronts.

Franchising

Franchising is a system control that can be employed in naturally monopolistic sectors to replace competition *in* the market with competition *for* the market. It has been employed notably in the British independent television, radio, and rail industries. The underlying idea is that if applicants for franchises make competitive bids for an exclusive (or at least protected) right to serve a market for a given period and under conditions, they will bid on assumptions of efficient operation and, as a result, consumers will benefit—they will be served by operators who are not under immediate competitive pressure but who will behave in many ways as if they are. A fuller discussion of franchising is offered in Chapter 20.

Regulation by Contract

Government departments or agencies can use the state's wealth and spending power to achieve desired objectives by specifying these in the contracts it agrees with enterprises. It can be stipulated, for example, that parties contracting to supply goods or services shall pay their own employees a minimum wage.[41] The regulatory aspects of the contract may be incidental to the main purpose, which may be commercial, but the effect is to impose a regulatory standard across all firms contracting with the government. There is no need for a command base. A form of

[40] See Commerce Commission, op. cit. n. 37 above, p. 83, quoted G. Bitondo, 'Detailed Regulation v. Competition Policy in Telecommunications: The Case of Interconnection Agreements in the UK and New Zealand' (1996), on file, LSE Regulation Library.

[41] See T. C. Daintith, 'Regulation by Contract: The New Prerogative' (1979) *Current Legal Problems* 41. On governing through contracts see I. Harden, *The Contracting State* (Buckingham, 1992) and N. Lewis and J. Goh, *The Private World of Government* (Sheffield, 1998).

contracting out—Compulsory Competitive Tendering (CCT)—of local authority services has been used by government as a means of reducing service costs and it brings with it local authority regulation of those who provide services under contractual terms. In some sectors, similarly, dependence on public funding has been used as a basis for encouraging both the development of self-regulation and the imposition of 'consensual forms of regulation'.[42]

Tradeable Permits

A further technique that seeks to harness markets is the use of tradeable permits to engage in an activity that has been deemed to require control (e.g. discharging pollutants into a water course). Like franchising, the strategy can be used to control both entry into the market and subsequent behaviour within the market. Examples of the use and advocacy of tradeable permits are to be found. Thus, since 1991 the US Environment Protection Agency (EPA) has sought to control sulphur dioxide emissions by allocating tradeable emission permits to coal-burning electric power plants and in October 1996 the European Commission was reported[43] to be considering recommending that airport take-off and landing slots should be open to trading by airlines rather than allocated by national slot coordinators.

In typical regimes the public agency issues a given number of permits and each of these allows a specified course of behaviour (e.g. a polluting discharge of a fixed amount). Following the initial allocation, permits may be traded and this allows, say, a generating company to switch to cleaner fuels and sell its excess allowances to other firms. The initial distribution of permits may be carried out by auction or according to public interest criteria. The incentives within such systems are provided by the market in permits.

Advantages claimed for the strategy are, first, that permits can be allocated to those who will generate most wealth per unit of pollution. This is because those willing to pay most for the permits will be those who derive the most profit from polluting—in this sense it can be argued (at least on a set of not uncontentious assumptions), that the pollution is being put to the use that society values most. Second, the incentive to reduce harmful behaviour can, as in taxation regimes, operate down to zero since the process of abatement will release permits for resale until the point where no harm is being done at all. Third, managers, again, are less restricted than in C & C regulation because they are free to decide

---

[42] See Baldwin, Scott, and Hood, *Regulation*, ch. 1; M. Cave, R. Dodsworth, and D. Thompson, 'Regulatory Reform in Higher Education in the UK: Incentives for Efficiency and Product Quality', in Bishop, Kay, and Mayer, *Regulatory Challenge*.

[43] See *Financial Times*, 4 Oct. 1996, p. 1.

whether and how to reduce harmful conduct in order to release permits. Fourth, regulatory discretions (and dangers of capture) are kept low because markets rather than bureaucrats are imposing restraints, and, finally, regulatory costs are low since, once established, the market in permits runs on its own accord.

The problems to be anticipated in relation to schemes with marketable permits are, however, numerous.[44] Enforcement still has to be carried out to prevent non-permit holders from creating harms and to stop permit holders from exceeding the terms of their permits. Inspectorates accordingly require funding. Regulatory lag may also be a problem. If, for example, permits are used to control river pollution, it may be difficult to adjust pollution levels rapidly so as to cope with sudden drops in the river's capacity to absorb pollution (as might occur in a heatwave or drought). The difficulty is that permits are already issued, they are in the market place and bearing a given value. (A response to the difficulty might be to give permits a floating value, one adjustable by the regulator. This would give flexibility but might prejudice the operation of the market and would impose severe informational demands on the regulator.)

Permits, moreover, do not provide the resources needed to compensate the victims of harmful conduct and, politically, permits may create difficulties with electorates since they may be seen as 'licences to pollute'. The system, in addition, demands that there be a healthy market in permits—which calls for such factors as a large number of potential buyers possessed of adequate information. If the market is deficient (perhaps because of uncertainties or lack of information) the value of permits may be low and the incentives to desist from harmful conduct may be weak. (This, it has been suggested, is why there has been a problem in the US Environment Protection Agency's scheme of control for carbon dioxide.[45]) A further problem is that markets in permits may allow hoarding and the creation of barriers to enter into certain markets. This will be more likely where conditions favour collusion between certain large firms. The effects may be generally anti-competitive and may be unfair to less well-resourced firms. As for the areas where markets in permits can be used, some harms or pollutants may have to be prohibited absolutely and, accordingly, the tradeable permit system will be inappropriate. Finally, it should be cautioned that democratic accountability and influence may be low once the system is up and running since the market (and its degree of genuine competitiveness) will govern the price to be placed on pollution. Where markets are imperfect it is also likely that information flowing into the public domain is below optimal levels.

[44] See Ogus, *Regulation*, ch. 7; Breyer, *Regulation and Its Reform*, ch. 8.

[45] See R. Lapper and L. Morse, 'Market Makers in CO_2 Permits', *Financial Times*, 1 Mar. 1995, and B. Van Dyke, 'Emissions Trading to Reduce Acid Deposition' (1992) 100 *Yale LJ* 2707.

5. *Disclosure Regulation*

Structuring the disclosure of information provides a mode of regulation that is not heavily interventionist. It does not regulate the production process, the level of output allowed, prices charged or the allocation of products. Disclosure rules usually prohibit the supply of false or misleading information and may also require mandatory disclosure—perhaps obliging suppliers to provide information to consumers on price, composition, quantity, or quality (familiar demands in the food and drinks sectors).[46] Disclosure regulation may also involve the supply of information to the public directly by a scrutinizing regulator or governmental official. Thus in October 1997 the Agriculture Minister, Jack Cunningham, first put into action a policy of 'naming and shaming' food manufacturers who failed to comply with regulations on safety, product quality, and authenticity. Following a departmental survey, the Minister named sixteen pork and bacon brands as guilty of failing to declare the added water content of their products. These included suppliers of Tesco and J. Sainsbury.[47]

Disclosure regulation allows consumers of products and services (or even voters more generally) to make decisions on the acceptability of the processes employed in producing those products or services. To rely on consumer or voter preferences in this manner does, however, restrict the potential of disclosure as a regulatory instrument.

The main problems to be anticipated are, first, that users of the information disclosed, be they consumers or other citizens, may make mistakes; they may fail to use the information properly; fail to understand the implications of the data given; misassess risks; neglect to collect the full range of relevant information; lack the resources to research issues fully; and so may come to harm. Second, information users may not respond in anticipated ways to the flow of information. Consumers, when purchasing products, may choose according to price rather than other considerations. They may, for instance, buy cheap products without responding to information suggesting that dangers are involved in consumption or that production of the goods involves a host of socially undesirable consequences (e.g. discharges of polluting effluents).

Third, the costs of producing the information may be excessive, as may the costs of processing it. Thus, if information disclosure rules were employed instead of C & C regulation in relation to food safety, a visit to the supermarket would involve a very lengthy process of scrutinizing

---

[46] In the food sector there is a pressure group devoted to disclosure—the Food Labelling Agenda (FLAG).
[47] See *Financial Times*, 29 Oct. 1997: ' "Naming and Shaming" over pork product labels'.

labels. It might, in many circumstances, be far more efficient for consumers to rely on the expertise and protection of public regulators and inspectorates rather than depend on their own individual assessments of risks.

Fourth, the risks associated with some products or activities may be so great that policy-makers may feel that it is inappropriate merely to inform affected parties about these matters and C & C methods may be deemed necessary.[48] Fifth, where information regulation is employed there is always a danger that the information will be inaccurate and unjustifiable claims made. Policing of the quality of information will, accordingly, be necessary. This increases the costs of information-based regulatory regimes. Finally, standards may have to be applied to various items of information so that affected parties may make appropriate use of any data given. In the absence of such standards information may be offered in a manner that does not assist, for example, consumers. Thus 'may cause cancer' is a phrase that discloses little concerning the size of any risk of cancer generated by using the product.

Given the above limitations of disclosure regulation, the case for the strategy is liable to be strongest where: the hazard involved is not potentially catastrophic or the difference between high- and low-quality products or processes is not likely to give rise to grave consequences; the relevant information can be processed at a reasonable cost; risks can be assessed accurately by affected parties; consumers of the products at issue, or other affected parties, can be relied upon to give proper consideration to the information given; and the accuracy and utility of information can be monitored and ensured through enforcement at acceptable cost.

6. *Direct Action*

Governments can use their resources to achieve desired results by taking direct action. Rather than set and enforce standards on, say, dust extraction levels in factories, central governments or local authorities can build properly ventilated premises and lease these to private manufacturers. Public ownership of infrastructure can, moreover, be combined with the franchising out of operations (leasing for fixed periods subject to conditions on use and renewal would produce similar results). Long-term investments can, by such methods, be rendered amenable to planning by government and the replacement of unsatisfactory operators can be facilitated. Thus, in the period to 1991, the public regulator in the independent television sector, the Independent Broadcasting Authority,

---

[48] See I. Ramsey, *Consumer Protection* (London, 1989).

owned and operated the transmission infrastructure and franchised out programme making, and in London the bus transport network is publicly owned but routes are put out to competitive tendering or franchising.[49]

An advantage of direct action is that public money can be used to ensure protection in circumstance where firms, particularly small ones, might not invest in the required measures. A degree of subsidization may, by such means, be effected and public resources used to assist firms to reduce harms rather than to fund C & C enforcement regimes or to apply penalties that take money away from the enterprises that are asked to spend on avoiding undesired consequences.

Such subsidization may give rise to distributional issues—concerning access to subsidized premises, for instance—but there is no reason why the prices of leases cannot be set so as to avoid criticism. A more difficult problem, may, however, be that the public funding of a certain aspect of a production process may encourage firms to build operations around the funded element. As a result, innovation may not be driven by the market and the enterprise's responsiveness to markets and potential new technologies or processes may be blunted. Thus if the well-ventilated manufacturing premises are publicly owned and there are no other controls on dust levels in the air, there is little incentive for the private sector to devise new, more efficient ways to control dust.

7. Rights and Liabilities

In the case of the factory that pollutes the river, the state might decide not to tax pollution or impose standards in a C & C regime, but to allocate rights (for example to the enjoyment of clean water) so as to encourage socially desirable behaviour.[50] Thus, the argument goes, the prospective polluter will be deterred from such activity by his or her potential liability to pay damages when sued by the holder of the right to clean water (say, the angling club or the riparian owner downstream). The deterrent effect will be the quantum of expected damages multiplied by the probability of those damages being inflicted. In economic terms the efficient level of deterrence is that which will ensure that the factory owner will spend money on avoiding pollution up to the point where the cost of avoidance exceeds the value of the damage caused by the pollution. (Beyond

---

[49] See S. Glaister, D. Kennedy, and T. Travers, *London Bus Tendering* (London, 1995) and S. Glaister, *Deregulation and Privatisation: British Experience* (World Bank, Washington DC, 1998).

[50] See generally Breyer, *Regulation and Its Reform*, 174–7; G. Calabresi and A. Melamed, 'Property Rules, Liability Rules and Inalienability: One View of the Cathedral' (1972) *Harv. LR* 1089.

that point it is efficient to let the pollution occur and compensate the 'victims' rather than spend on abatement.)

If society desires this efficient level of deterrence, difficulties are encountered because the precise deterrent effects of liability rules are difficult to predict. Rights and mirroring liabilities may fail to deter efficiently for a number of reasons. Many undesirable events, for example, are the results of accidents, random events, and irrational behaviour. Deterrence, for this reason, does not operate in a mechanical and frictionless manner.[51]

Enforcement costs for individuals may prove discouraging and lead many parties not to proceed to enforce their rights. Coordinating between victims may not always prove feasible or it may involve high transaction costs. Evidential difficulties may reduce to a low level the probability of proving that the harm involved was caused by the actions of the defendant polluter. (If there is only a 50 per cent chance of proving causation this halves deterrence. Uncertainties in the legal rules creating rights and liabilities will have a similar effect.) Many victims in the pool of victims may lack the resolve to proceed against the harm-causer and, to the extent that claims are not pursued, deterrent effects will be sub-optimal.

In reflection of such factors, the harm causer will be likely to be able to settle out of court for negotiated sums that are lower than those that would create efficient levels of deterrence. Courts, of course, might attempt to correct for levels of deterrence that are too low—for example by granting damages that do not merely compensate for harms done but also include a punitive element that makes up for the under-deterrence liable to arise for the reasons cited. The courts will, however, face considerable informational hurdles if taking this course. The judiciary would find it extremely difficult to amass all relevant information about the array of potential actions for damages likely to follow, say, a pollution incident. If such actions are brought separately and serially, the court will not know at a given time in the process how many claims are to be aggregated in calculating total deterrence nor will it be able to assess the gravity of claims to be brought at a future date.

A final problem is that insurance may limit the deterrent effect of liability rules and may generally make deterrence very difficult to assess. Under certain conditions, insurance may spread risks very widely and undermine deterrence. On the other hand, very high or even excessive levels of deterrence (and for firms financial difficulties) may be caused if

---

[51] See D. Harris et al., *Compensation and Support for Illness and Injury* (Oxford, 1984), 328 and on the deficiencies of liability rules in providing compensation see ch. 12.

insurance is subject to restrictions, withdrawals, and crises so that effective cover at affordable prices is not available. Thus, in the tort sector, what has been described as a crisis was experienced in the mid-1980s in the United States and Canada[52] and it has been the unpredictability of the liability insurance market that has urged a number of North American commentators to look to regulatory devices as alternatives to the tort system.[53]

8. Public Compensation/Social Insurance Schemes

Economic incentives to avoid undesirable behaviour can be created not merely by systems of taxation and subsidy but also by schemes of compensation or insurance that link premiums paid to performance records. One field in which a good deal of research into insurance-based incentives has been conducted is that of the working environment.[54] A review conducted in 1994[55] pointed to a number of insurance-based schemes dealing with workplace safety and health around the world. National schemes were encountered in several EU countries, the USA, Canada, Japan, and New Zealand, with strategies under development in Denmark, Poland, and elsewhere. These were all no-fault liability schemes and essentially compensatory, though some also provided means of funding improvements in conditions—as in the French, Swedish, and Albertan systems.

In the typical scheme, workers surrender their rights to sue employers for damages relating to health and safety failings, and, in return, are entitled to statutory compensation, often amounting to full payment of lost earnings plus costs. The employer's premiums depend on their organization's past claims experience.[56]

[52] See V. Finch, 'Personal Accountability and Corporate Control: The Role of Directors and Officers Insurance' (1994) 57 *MLR* 880, 915.

[53] See e.g. G. Priest, 'The Current Insurance Crisis in Modern Tort Law' (1987) 96 *Yale LJ* 521; R. B. Stewart, 'Crisis in Tort Law? The Institutional Perspective' (1987) 54 *Univ. of Chicago LR* 184; M. Trebilcock, 'The Social Insurance—Deterrence Dilemma of Modern North American Tort Law: A Canadian Perspective on the Liability Insurance Crisis?' (1987) 24 *San Diego LR* 929.

[54] See the work of the European Foundation for the Improvement of Living and Working Conditions (EFILWC), a European Community institution, reported in: *Catalogue of Economic Incentive Systems for the Improvement of the Working Environment* (Dublin, 1994) and S. Bailey (ed.), *Economic Incentives to Improve the Working Environment* (Dublin, 1994).

[55] EFILWC, *Catalogue*.

[56] See S. Bailey, 'Economic Incentives for Employers to Improve the Management of Workplace Risk'—paper to W. G. Hart Legal Workshop, 4 July 1995.

A central issue attending such schemes is whether state-administered or private insurance mechanisms should be employed. In relation to private provision, doubts exist concerning the extent to which private insurance companies can be relied upon to provide incentives to improve working conditions. The primary concern of private insurers is not to reduce hazards but to generate profits for shareholders. Such insurers might not be prepared to spend money to isolate poor-risk, dangerous employers beyond profit-maximizing levels. It is true that competition in the insurance market will to some extent drive insurance companies to spend money on discriminating between risks but there are limits to competitive pressures and, in any event, there is a tension between the basic function of insurance (to spread risks) and risk discrimination (isolating poor risks). This tension also imposes limits on the willingness of private insurers to identify poor risks and apply localized economic incentives.

In such conditions, the tendency will be to confine risk discrimination to those sectors in which statistical guidance on the quantum of risks is readily available and affordable. Thus, in motor insurance, with a wealth of accidents, and, as a result, useful data available at reasonable cost, discrimination might be high whereas in relation to workplace safety—where accidents are infrequent but often serious—weak statistics might be expected to lead to low levels of risk discrimination and the linking of cover and premiums to very broadly defined categories of risk.

For such reasons, the European Foundation for the Improvement of Living and Working Conditions (EFILWC) has proposed a publicly administered scheme linking premiums not to statistics on accident records—which were said 'not to make any sense' for firms with under 100 employees[57]—but to factors that could be measured properly such as the conditions of the working environment, the state of the factory's machinery, and so on. Such schemes, said the EFILWC, would encourage the accurate reporting of accidents, whereas reliance on past accident records might be expected to encourage firms to massage their statistical returns—for example, by placing pressure on employees not to report accidents (e.g. by offering bonuses to accident-free teams of workers, and creating peer pressures not to report). Insurance-based schemes might also be combined with the use of incentives to improve conditions by allowing premium reductions to companies taking harm-reducing measures (e.g. moving to the use of low-emission materials or low-noise machines).

---

[57] EFILWC, *Catalogue*, 19.

The further advantages pointed to by proponents of insurance-based schemes[58] are that they make employers conscious of the costs of their actions. Employers considering increasing pressures on workers to take risks so as to escalate production levels will be aware that the potential extra profits derived from improved production will have to be weighed against the potential increases in insurance premiums that will follow an inspection by the insurance fund. Prevention will thus be given a higher priority by firms than would be the case under C & C regulation because harms will impinge more directly on their profits. Insurance-based schemes are said to offer incentives and financial motivations to *all* employers in contrast with C & C strategies which are so expensive to enforce that they are patchily and poorly applied .on the ground.

A further strength claimed for incentive schemes is that they can achieve incentives to go better than fixed standards—indeed, incentives to zero can be instituted. This contrasts with C & C systems which offer incentives to comply with designated standards but not to perform to higher standards. Employers, it is also said, will respond to the emergence of new hazards under incentive schemes without the need for new legislation.

To balance such sanguinity, however, some caveats do have to be entered. Compensation for workers may produce some undesirable incentives. Thus, if compensation is seen as generous or an easy option, this may encourage some individuals to accept injuries, dangers, or disabilities in return for cash. To work properly, moreover, such a scheme would have to involve the periodic inspection and rating of all employers and their premises. The resource implications are huge. Thus, inspection as envisaged would not be possible in the UK using the present staffing and resources of the Health and Safety Executive, whose current scheme of inspection involves, in the case of medium-sized firms, several years between visits. It might, indeed, be argued that the important difference between the proposed insurance scheme and the existing C & C system lies in the assumptions that are made concerning resources; that with a commensurate increase in resources, C & C could achieve as much.

The differences between an insurance-based scheme and C & C regulation may, thus, be liable to overstatement. In the former, inspectors would check compliance with rules designed to limit risks and would penalize non-compliance by imposing an adjusted premium. In C & C regimes, fines or administrative orders take the place of premiums as sanctioning devices. The insurance-based scheme, it could be contended, is merely a C & C regime with a variation in the sanction. Fines, after all, might be described as disincentives.

---

[58] Ibid. 24–5.

Conclusions: Choosing Regulatory Methods

In deciding whether to regulate or to leave matters to the market it is wise, as noted in the last chapter, to be realistic about the levels of performance that can be expected of regulatory regimes. To compare a friction-free vision of regulation with the imperfect operation of the market is to bias any analysis in favour of regulation. Similarly, in comparing different regulatory strategies, an effort must be made to take into account all the respective difficulties that will be encountered in their implementation. Thus, to compare C & C, with all its enforcement difficulties, to a series of 'less-restrictive' devices that are assumed to be enforceable in a problem-free manner is not to offer a balanced perspective.[59]

Enforcement, as has been noted, is not a difficulty confined to C & C regimes.[60] Nor, moreover, should the *positive* aspects of enforcement be ignored when reviewing C & C regulation. Enforcement procedures can be seen as the lifeblood of many regulatory systems. In Britain, for instance, enforcement practices tend to be more flexible, more administrative, and less prosecutorial than those encountered in the USA, where the most committed critics of C & C are to be found. C & C operates on the ground in a less restrictive and legalistic fashion on this side of the Atlantic and it is the enforcement practices adopted that ameliorate many of the difficulties encountered in C & C regimes.[61] The objections to C & C, it could be said, often relate to a style of applying C & C regulation—one that is not the norm, say, in Britain.

The difference between C & C and other regimes may, indeed, be one prone to exaggeration since, as noted, many or most schemes require implementation through rules—be these command or incentive based. Proponents of C & C have to cope with difficulties of fixing the appropriate level of precision and inclusiveness in rules, of using rule formulations that cope with potential creative compliers, and of incorporating the right kinds of standards.[62] 'Alternative' regulatory methods often need rules, however, on matters such as: *when* incentives will apply; the *conditions* under which franchises will be held or marketable permits transferred; the *kind of information* to be disclosed; the *use* of publicly provided premises; the *extent and form* of liabilities; or the *nature* of premium variations in a social insurance system. Just as enforcement

---

[59] For an argument viewing C & C as a 'last resort' see Breyer, *Regulation and Its Reform*, ch. 9.

[60] See Ogus, *Regulation*, 250–6; Breyer, *Regulation and Its Reform*, 278–80; R. Smith, 'The Feasibility of an Injury Tax Approach to Occupational Safety' (1974) 38 *Law and Cont. Prob.* 730; P. Burrows, *The Economic Theory of Pollution Control* (Oxford, 1979), 33–5.

[61] See D. Vogel, *National Styles of Regulation: Environmental Policy in Great Britain and the United States* (Ithaca, NY, 1986).

[62] See Chapter 9 below and generally Baldwin, *Rules and Government*.

difficulties cannot be assumed away when moving to alternative or 'less restrictive' regulatory methods, neither, it should be repeated, can those problems that attend rule-making processes.[63]

It should also be cautioned that an historical association between certain regulatory methods and certain styles of implementation—for example between C & C and the use of highly restrictive rules—should not be taken as a demonstration of inevitable or exclusive linkage. In North America in the 1980s an enthusiasm for alternative methods of regulation was to a degree fuelled by concerns that C & C methods had led to a 'crisis of legalisation'.[64] Other possible causes of over-proliferation and complexity in rules can, however, be pointed to. Relevant factors may have been: the particular demands made of regulators by North American judges when seeking to control the rationality, fairness, and accessibility of rules and rule-making processes; the existence of certain conditions leading to litigiousness; the operation of certain statutory rule-making procedures; or the political contexts within which particular regulatory institutions operated.[65] Given the potential relevance of such factors, it is difficult to conclude with confidence that a move from C & C to alternative strategies constitutes even a start in combating excessive legalization. There may be a temptation when considering 'alternative' regulatory methods, to isolate their least attractive features and designate these as C & C intrusions—that, however, is, again, to rig the debate.

Finally, it should be remembered that, in most regulatory contexts combinations of regulatory methods tend to be employed. Thus, potential polluters may face some C & C regulations but also may be subject to licensing or franchising conditions or sets of incentives operating though taxation and subsidy rules. They may have to supply information of various kinds, they are likely to be enmeshed in a network of liability rules, and may be able to avail themselves of publicly provided assets or services. In relation to a given regulatory issue it is, accordingly, necessary to look for the particular mixture of regulatory strategies that will best meet desired objectives—procedural and substantive.[66]

At this point, it is necessary to identify the objectives of regulatory regimes—to establish benchmarks for the evaluation of regulatory systems. Without these it is difficult to say what is good or bad regulation. The search for benchmarks will be discussed in Chapter 6 after we have considered the kinds of bodies that are involved in regulating.

[63] See E. Markovits, 'Antitrust: Alternatives to Delegalisation', in Teubner, *Juridification of Social Spheres*.

[64] See R. B. Stewart, 'Regulation and the Crises of Legalisation in the United States', in Daintith, *Law as an Instrument of Economic Policy*, 108–9.

[65] See e.g. Bardach and Kagan, *Going by the Book*, and R. A. Kagan, 'Should Europe Worry about Adversarial Legalism?' (1997) 17 *OJLS* 165.

[66] See Gunningham and Grabosky, *Smart Regulation*, 14–19; ch. 6.

TABLE 3. *Regulatory strategies: posited strengths and weaknesses*

Strategy	Example	Strengths	Weaknesses
1. *Command & Control*	Health and Safety at Work	Force of law. Fixed standards set minimum acceptable levels of behaviour. Screens entry. Prohibits unacceptable behaviour immediately. Seen as highly protective of public. Use of penalties indicates forceful stance by authorities.	Intervenes in management. Prone to capture. Complex rules tend to multiply. Inflexible. Informational requirements severe. Expensive to administer. Setting standards is difficult and costly. Anti-competitive effects. Incentive is to meet the standard, not go better. Enforcement costly. Compliance costs high. Inhibits desirable behaviour.
2. *Self-Regulation*	Insurance Industry	High commitment to own rules. Well-informed rule-making. Low cost to government. Coincidence of regulatory standards and the standards that industry sees as reasonable. Enforcement efficiency. Comprehensive rules.	High cost of approving rules. Rules may be self-serving. Legalism not necessarily avoided. Rulemaking procedures may be closed to public or consumers. Enforcement may be weak or may favour the industry.

TABLE 3. (*cont'd*)

Strategy	Example	Strengths	Weaknesses
		Flexibility. Effective complaints. Can combine with external oversight.	Public may not trust self-enforcers. Legal oversight may be problematic. Public may want governmental responsibility.
3. *Incentives*	Differential tax on leaded and unleaded petrol	Low regulator discretion. Low-cost application. Low intervention in management. Incentive to reduce harm to zero, not just to standard. Economic pressure to behave acceptably.	Rules are required. Poor response to problems arising from irrational or careless behaviour. Predicting outcome from given incentive difficult. Mechanical, so inflexible. Regulatory lag. Politically contentious as rewards wrongdoer and fails to prohibit offence.
4. *Market-Harnessing Controls* (a) *Competition Laws*	Airline Industry	Responses to market driven by firms not bureaucrats. Can be applied across industries. Economies of scale in use of general rules. Low level of intervention. Flexibility for firms.	No expert agency to solve technical or commercial problems in the industry. Uncertainties and transaction costs. Courts slow to generate guidance. Principles develop sporadically.

TABLE 3. (*cont'd*)

Strategy	Example	Strengths	Weaknesses
(*b*) *Franchising*	Rail, Television, Radio	Enforcement is low cost to public.	Evidential difficulties.
		Low level of restriction.	Need to specify service.
		Respects managerial freedoms.	Tension of specification and responsiveness/ innovation.
		Allows competition for market as substitute for competition in the market.	Uncertainties impose costs on consumers.
		Managers rather than bureaucrats respond to market preferences.	Requires competition for franchise but may be few bidders.
			Need to enforce terms of franchise.
(*c*) *Contracting*	Local Authority refuse services	Combines control with service provision.	Potential confusion of regulatory and service roles.
		Sanctioning by economic incentive or non-renewal.	Poor transparency and accountability.
		Easier to operate than licensing system.	Judicial control weak.
(*d*) *Tradeable Permits*	Sulphur dioxide emissions (USA)	Pollution by greatest wealth producer.	Enforcement may require inspectorate.
		Incentive to reduce harm to zero.	Regulatory lag, lack of rapid response in crisis.
		Managerial freedom considerable.	No compensation for victims.
		Regulatory discretion low.	Requires healthy market for permits.
		Regulatory costs low.	Barriers to entry may be created.
			Some harms need to be prohibited absolutely.

TABLE 3. (*cont'd*)

Strategy	Example	Strengths	Weaknesses
5. *Disclosure*	Mandatory disclosure in food/drink sector	Low intervention. Allows consumer to decide issues. Lower danger of capture. Useful in low-risk sectors.	Information users may make mistakes. Economic incentives (e.g. price) may prevail over information (on e.g. risk). Cost of producing information may be high. Risks may be so severe as to call for prohibition. Policing of information quality and fraud may be required. Information may be in form undermining its utility.
6. *Direct Action*	State-supplied work premises	Can separate infrastructure provision from operation. Assures acceptable level of provision. Useful where small firms in poor position to behave responsibly. Allows state to plan long-term investments.	Fairness of subsidies may be contentious. Funding costly. Public sector involvement contentious. Innovations may not be market driven.
7. *Rights and Liabilities Laws*	Rules of tort law; right to e.g. light or clean water	Self-help. Low intervention. Low cost to State.	May not prevent undesired events that result from accidents and irrational behaviour.

TABLE 3. (*cont'd*)

Strategy	Example	Strengths	Weaknesses
			Individuals may not enforce due to costs.
			Evidential difficulties and legal uncertainties reduce enforcement.
			Victims may lack resolve and information to proceed so deterrence sub-optimal.
			Difficult for courts to deter efficiently.
			Insurance may temper deterrent effects.
8. *Public Compensation / Social Insurance*	Workplace safety schemes (USA, Canada, Japan, New Zealand)	Insurers provide economic incentives.	Incidence levels may be too low to allow risk discrimination.
		Low intervention in management.	Tension of loss-spreading and incentive to behave responsibly.
		Low danger of capture.	
		Encourages accurate reporting of incidents.	Inspection and scrutiny of performance expensive.
		Makes employers aware of costs of activities.	May operate in very similar manner to command and control mechanism.
		Good coverage, applied to all employers.	
		No need to legislate for each individual harm.	

5

Who Regulates? Institutions and Structures

Regulation can be carried out by a variety of bodies and the nature of the regulating institutions can affect not merely the style of regulation and the strategies employed but also the success with which regulatory ends are achieved.[1]

If 'regulation' takes on board the first two meanings discussed in Chapter 1 (as a specific set of commands or as deliberate state influence) the main categories of regulator can be given as follows:

- self-regulators;
- local authorities;
- Parliament;
- courts and tribunals;
- central government departments;
- regulatory agencies;
- Directors General.

In Britain, examples of each kind of regulator can be pointed to and in relation to each one a number of particular concerns tends to be associated.

1. Self-Regulators

Self-regulation typically involves an organization regulating the standards of behaviour of its membership. The controls at issue may be entirely voluntary and quite informal or subject to degrees of governmental supervision and legislative structuring.[2] Self-regulatory systems have

---

[1] On British regulatory institutions and their development see A. Ogus, 'Regulatory Law: Some Lessons from the Past' (1992) 12 *Legal Studies* 1; T. Prosser, *Law and the Regulators* (Oxford, 1997), ch. 2; C. Foster, *Privatisation, Public Ownership and the Regulation of Natural Monopoly* (Oxford, 1992), chs. 1–4; R. Baldwin and C. McCrudden, *Regulation and Public Law* (London, 1987), ch. 2. On institutional explanations of regulatory developments see above pp. 27–31.

[2] See Chapter 10 for a further discussion of self-regulation and for a classification of regulatory systems, see R. Baggot, 'Regulatory Reform in Britain: The Changing Face of Self-Regulation' (1989) 67 *Pub. Admin.* 435.

operated in Britain since at least medieval times when supervision of such matters as work conditions, wages, production levels, and product quality was carried out by craft guilds—bodies commonly acting under powers granted in royal charters of incorporation.[3] At the present day, self-regulatory bodies operate in a host of professions and in sectors such as advertising, press, and sports.

Self-regulatory bodies are capable of acting governmentally while possessing the institutional, and often legal, structures and interests of private bodies.[4] They generally regulate entry to an association, formulate their own rules, and enforce discipline. A familiar kind of self-regulation is, accordingly, exemplified by the Law Society, which controls the solicitors' profession.[5]

Other self-regulators, however, may be subject to complex schemes of governmental oversight. Thus, the Financial Services Act 1986 established a three-tier regime involving, at its head, ministerial and legislative supervision.[6] The former Securities and Investments Board (SIB) occupied the middle tier with a Chair and governing members appointed (and removable) by the Secretary of State and the Governor of the Bank of England acting jointly.[7] SIB promulgated rules, statements of principles, and Codes of Practice concerning the conduct of investment business. It also recognized and oversaw the operations of Self-Regulatory Organizations (SROs) which regulated investment business on a day-to-day basis subject to the requirements of the 1986 Act and SIB's own rules. (The SROs are companies limited by guarantee but, unlike SIB, their power is contractual, not derived from statute.) SIB had to report annually to the Secretary of State who, in turn, reported to Parliament but SROs simply had to adhere to Companies Acts requirements for annual reports.

As institutions, self-regulatory bodies may be favoured by policy-makers over central departments or statutory agencies for a number of reasons other than their utility in keeping central government small or the desire to avoid confrontations with powerful groupings. Stress may be placed on their expertise and familiarity with an area, on the speed with which they can be established, on their willingness and ability to

---

[3] See Ogus, loc. cit. n. 1 above.

[4] See J. Black, 'Constitutionalising Self-Regulation' (1996) 59 *MLR* 24. On enforced self-regulation see I. Ayres and J. B. Braithwaite, *Responsive Regulation* (Oxford, 1992), ch. 4.

[5] See generally R. Baldwin, *Regulating Legal Services* (Lord Chancellor's Department, London, 1998).

[6] See A. Page, 'Financial Services: The Self-Regulatory Alternative', in Baldwin and McCrudden, *Regulation and Public Law*.

[7] In 1997 the Government published plans to replace SIB with a new Financial Services Authority (FSA) which would take over, *inter alia*, former SIB functions, and self-regulatory organizations such as the Investment Management Regulatory Organization and the Personal Investment Authority. The FSA has already taken over the responsibilities of the SIB and will take over the duties of the self-regulatory organizations in 1999/2000 in accordance with new financial services legislation.

produce rules quickly, and (factors cited in the financial services sector[8]) their amenability to innovation, capacity to produce an internationally competitive industry, effectiveness and speed as enforcers, and independence from government.

When, however, private bodies carry out governmental functions this does give rise to concerns on some fronts. A core question is how such bodies should be held to account and 'constitutionalized' within a system of government.[9] Issues arise concerning the governmental machinery needed to oversee self-regulators; the role of the courts in reviewing such bodies; how the processes and organizational structures of self-regulation can be designed to ensure that interests beyond those of association members can be taken on board;[10] and how grievances against association members can be handled acceptably by an organization that has been appointed by the membership.

2. *Local Authorities*

For centuries a host of issues has been regulated in Britain at the local level. In the Tudor period, for instance, local justices controlled such matters as rural wages, the prices that could be charged for certain products, and the supply of corn in times of shortage.[11] At the start of the nineteenth century local regulatory functions were carried out not merely by justices of the peace but by a variety of bodies such as municipal corporations, parishes, the police, and a range of special purpose bodies.[12] The forces of industrialization and urbanization, however, gave rise to a developed structure of local government and local authorities assumed regulatory responsibilities on a range of topics which, by the 1930s, included development control, planning, environmental health, public spaces, and consumer protection. In a number of other areas, direct action was taken and services were provided under such headings as policing, fire, social work, refuse disposal, education, and housing.

---

[8] See M. Moran, *The Politics of the Financial Services Revolution* (London, 1991), 68–79, A. Page, loc. cit. n. 6 above, pp. 304–5 and White Paper, *Financial Services in the United Kingdom: A New Framework for Investor Protection*, Cmnd. 9432 (London, 1985); L. C. B. Gower, *Review of Investor Protection: A Discussion Document* (London, 1982).

[9] See Black, loc. cit. n. 4 above; C. Graham, 'Self-Regulation', in G. Richardson and H. Genn, *Administrative Law and Government Action* (Oxford, 1994) and also G. Borrie, 'The Regulation of Public and Private Power' [1989] *Public Law* 552; Lord Woolf, 'Public Law—Private Law: Why the Divide?' [1986] *Public Law* 220; *R v. Panel on Takeovers and Mergers ex p. Datafin plc and another* [1987] 1 All ER 564.

[10] See R. Mayntz, 'The Conditions of Effective Public Policy: A New Challenge for Policy Analysis' (1983) 11 *Policy and Politics* 123.

[11] See Ogus, loc. cit. n. 1 above, p. 7; Foster, *Privatisation*, 61–5.

[12] See M. Loughlin, *Local Government in the Modern State* (London, 1986), ch. 1.

Local authority regulation provides for democratic control by those with detailed knowledge of an area, control that is liable to be more responsive to particular regional concerns than a regime run by a central government department or agency. A move towards centralized regulation might, however, be argued for in certain circumstances: where there is a need to coordinate controls or impose uniform standards across a number of localities; where the pooling of expertise in a central body is necessary to realize the benefits of certain technologies; where a close linkage with central government policies is required; where conflicts of interest or capture by dominant interests may give rise to difficulty at the local level; or where economies of scale can be derived from a centralized approach.[13]

3. Parliament

In the eighteenth and nineteenth centuries, Parliament imposed direct control over a number of industries by passing bills (mostly private) to lay down in considerable detail the limits of allowable conduct (the railway industry of the last century is an outstanding example of parliamentary regulation[14]). The statutes involved were tailored to particular circumstances, so that every new railway line, waterworks, gas works, or electricity generating plant had its own bill discussed in Parliament by a specially appointed committee. The Acts produced were thus the equivalent of the licences, combined with statutes, that are found in modern utilities regulation.[15]

Experience in the railway industry in the last century pointed to a number of weaknesses in parliamentary regulation.[16] Individual consideration of bills by separate committees did not produce coherence or consistency of regulation. No system of general rules and principles emerged—at least until Gladstone's Regulation of the Railways Act of 1844. Enforcement of the Acts was through the courts and judges frequently departed from the intentions of the parent committees.[17] Members of Parliament sitting on committees resented advice from officials and tended to ignore that advice. This produced low levels of expertise and encouraged inconsistency. Parliament, moreover, failed to set up an expert body to advise the committees on railway regulation and so did not counter the expertise of the railway companies.

---

[13] See Chapter 13 below and for a classic discussion of regulatory competition at local authority level see C. Tiebout, 'A Pure Theory of Local Expenditures' (1956) 64 *J. Pol. Econ.* 416—discussed below, Chapter 12.

[14] See Foster, *Privatisation*, ch. 1.

[15] For an outline of the structure of modern utilities regulation see Chapter 9 below.

[16] For details see Foster, *Privatisation*, 20–36.

[17] See A. T. Hadley, *Railroad Transportation: Its History and Its Laws* (London, 1890), 135–7.

The system was also prone to capture. The railway lobby was so strong in Parliament and in the committees that bills were not dealt with on their merits (Foster reports, also, that in 1845 at least 157 MPs were railway stockholders[18]). Finally, Parliament proved not to be an institution capable of monitoring the operation of the Acts in an adequate manner. Maximum rates were fixed but were not revised or subjected to oversight. As a result, the companies routinely made excessive profits by exploiting dominant or monopolistic positions and by taking advantage of technological advances that lowered costs. Even after the passing of the Railways Act 1844 and the institution of rate of return regulation on a twenty-one-year cycle, the companies found ways to bypass such controls by diluting stock values and over-investing.

4. Courts and Tribunals

Regulation by judicial bodies has a long and continuing history, particularly in the transport sector. Following the failure of parliamentary regulation of the railways, a judicial tribunal, the Railway Commission, was set up by statute in 1873 to make rulings on rates and preferences. By 1888 the Commission had been strengthened (and renamed the Railway and Canal Commission). It had the authority of a high court, was presided over by a judge with two lay assessors, and cases were argued before it by barristers under legal procedures and rules of evidence. The subsequent history was one of procedural evasions by railway companies, of high costs and ineffectual action on rates. The Commission was replaced by a slightly less judicial body, the Railway Rates Tribunal, in 1921. This was renamed the Transport Tribunal in 1947 but its procedures remained highly legalistic with legal representation and lengthy trial-type hearings.

It was in the aviation industry, however, that the limitations of judicial regulators were most starkly exposed.[19] By 1960 judicialized regulatory regimes had been operating in the railways industry for almost a century and in the road goods and passenger transport industries for three decades. In that year, the Civil Aviation (Licensing) Act established the Air Transport Licensing Board (ATLB). This body saw itself as a judicial tribunal and controlled route entry and domestic prices for air services. It relied on public trial-type hearings both to allocate licences and to develop policy through establishing a 'case law'. In three major respects, however, the judicial method failed. First, it failed to coordinate policies with the government of the day. ATLB decisions were not linked

---

[18] Foster, *Privatisation*, 21.

[19] See R. Baldwin, *Regulating the Airlines* (Oxford, 1985) and 'Civil Aviation Regulation from Tribunal to Regulatory Agency', in Baldwin and McCrudden, *Regulation and Public Law*.

to ministerial strategies for obtaining the traffic rights that operators needed in order to fly international routes and around a third of all appeals from ATLB decisions to ministers were allowed. As a result, the Board could not sustain a competition policy. The ATLB became a step-ping stone en route to the real decision-maker, the Minister. Second, the ATLB failed to develop, by means of its decisions, a set of durable standards or policies and was increasingly accused of arbitrariness and capriciousness. Third, the Board failed (because of lack of resources and an attachment to judicial methods) to develop the expertise in aviation policy-making that would have allowed it to stand up to the aviation specialists in the Board of Trade. As a result, it reacted to events rather than planned for the industry.

To summarize, Britain has experience of judicialized regulatory bod-ies but trial-type procedures as operated by courts and tribunals have generally not lent themselves well to decision- or policy-making in the complex, shifting, and politically sensitive world of economic regulation.[20] In some instances, specialist, expert, regulatory agencies have developed as a response to the perceived inadequacies of such judicial bodies.[21]

5. Central Government Departments

The exercise of state power through ministerial departments only became the norm in the middle of the last century.[22] The rise of the depart-ment reflected Parliament's growing dissatisfaction with the system of government by independent boards. Thus, when the Poor Law Commis-sion was replaced by a ministry in 1847 this marked Parliament's desire to control government action by allocating functions to persons answer-able in the House. From that time onwards, departments have carried out a wide range of operational and regulatory functions. Examples of modern departmental regulation include safety on North Sea oil rigs,[23] merchant shipping, and company direction.

Accountability to Parliament may be a strength of the ministerial depart-ment but a number of factors can be cited as reasons why ministerial schemes of control have tended to give way to agencies in twentieth-century regulation.

[20] On trial-type procedures and decisions on multi-centred ('polycentric') issues see L. Fuller, *The Morality of Law* (New Haven, 1964), 83; J. Jowell, *Law and Bureaucracy* (Dunellan, 1975), 151–5, 213–14. For a discussion of the more successful use of trial-type procedures by the Civil Aviation Authority see Baldwin, *Regulating the Airlines*.

[21] See Baldwin, *Regulating the Airlines*.

[22] See e.g. P. Craig, *Administrative Law* (3rd edn., London, 1994), ch. 2.

[23] For discussion of this industry and the choice of departmental, rather than agency regulation (by e.g. the Health and Safety Executive) see W. G. Carson, *The Other Price of Britain's Oil* (Oxford, 1982).

One reason for moving towards agencies may be the perceived need to take issues 'out of party politics' either in order to give continuity of policy development and longer-term planning in a sector or so as to achieve fairness in adjudication—so that, for instance, choices between different applicants for licences will be seen to be made in a manner free from suspicions of political bias.[24] Agencies, furthermore, may be less prone than ministers to interfere in day-to-day commercial affairs and decisions that are viewed as properly managerial. The scale of central government may also be kept within manageable proportions by avoiding ministerial regimes. (Electorates may indeed be given the impression that government is being reduced.[25])

It may also be doubted whether government departments will bring the same levels of expertise and efficiency to bear on a topic as would bodies specifically devoted to the task and able to create both career structures and employment conditions tailored to the sector.[26] Finally, where a new regime of regulation is to be introduced as a response to public pressure (perhaps following a disaster or other burst of concern), the use of departmental controls will not give as dramatic an impression of government action as the establishment of a new regulatory agency.

6. Regulatory Agencies

Regulatory agencies are bodies that act on behalf of central government but are not central Departments of State. One of their strengths, as institutions, is an ability to combine governmental functions. They often decide disputes between parties, promulgate rules, and enforce those rules.[27] Their regulatory work is usually directed at a particular sector (as with the Civil Aviation Authority) or at a specific problem (as with the Health and Safety Executive). Such agencies have multiplied in numbers through the last half-century. Perhaps the first regulatory agency established in Britain along the lines of the great US regulatory commissions (that began with the Interstate Commerce Commission in 1887) was the Independent Television Authority, set up in 1954 with independent status to license television programme-makers in the public interest. A host of agencies followed in the 1960s and 1970s including the Industrial Reorganization Corporation (IRC) of 1966, the Race Relations Board (1965),

---

[24] See F. M. G. Willson, 'Ministries and Boards: Some Aspects of Administrative Development since 1832' (1955) *Pub. Admin.* 43 and (on freedom from political influence in decision-making) Baldwin, *Regulating the Airlines*, ch. 7.

[25] See C. C. Hood, 'Keeping the Centre Small' (1978) 26 *Pol. Stud.* 30.

[26] See e.g. the Fulton Committee on the Civil Service, Cmnd. 3638 (London, 1968).

[27] See generally Baldwin and McCrudden, *Regulation and Public Law*. (In the case of a number of agencies, regulatory rules are made by Parliament or ministers and then enforced by agencies.)

Monopolies Commission (1965), and the Civil Aviation Authority (1972). The trend continued through the 1980s and into the 1990s with bodies such as the Environment Agency (1996).

Public ownership in the utilities sectors delayed the advent of regulatory agencies to some extent in Britain but a number of factors (often related to concerns about the limitations of courts, tribunals, and central departments) militated in favour of regulation by specialist independent agency. There was a growing perception by policy-makers and legislators during this century that certain industries and activities required a special and continuing form of control—that in relation to, say, discrimination or broadcasting, reliance could not be placed solely on sporadic forays by individuals in the ordinary courts.[28] It was, moreover, thought that such fields demanded the development of broad policies and strategies and that these could not properly be developed by thinly staffed courts operating on a case-by-case basis. It was, in addition, felt necessary to mix functions such as adjudication, policy-making, and enforcement which could not be combined in a tribunal or court and could not be carried out by a government department, at least where adjudication was involved, because departments would be seen to be lacking independence, or worse, politically biased. Further factors were the growth of new technologies and greater appreciations of complex social problems which were thought to call for *expert* decision-makers and agencies able both to attract staff of high calibre and to train them as career professionals in particular sectors of regulation.

The regulatory agency thus came to occupy a prominent place on the governmental stage. Typically, a parent statute would empower the Secretary of State to establish the agency as a legal corporation and to appoint the Chair and members of the governing board. The agency would act independently of the ministerial department, with its own staff, but the minister would have overall powers of key appointment and direction.[29]

To summarize, agencies as regulatory institutions hold the advantage over ministerial departments in so far as they offer a greater degree of continuity of policy, they combine a wider range of functions successfully, they may adjudicate free from political taint, and can develop high levels of special expertise. As compared to courts, agencies offer a better-resourced capacity to develop plans and policies for their sector and can combine adjudication with a host of other functions such as direct enforcement.

Major concerns with agencies flow, however, from the combining of functions. A constant danger is of falling between stools so that agency adjudications are seen as tainted by policy-making concerns; planning is

[28] See Baldwin and McCrudden, *Regulation and Public Law*, 22.
[29] Powers of direction were generally phrased in narrow terms and can be viewed as distinct from powers to give policy guidance of a more wide-ranging kind—see *Laker Airways Ltd* v. *Department of Trade* [1977] QB 643 and Baldwin, *Regulating the Airlines*, 113.

made difficult by reliance on trials and public hearings; and political oversight undermines both adjudicative neutrality and the ability of the agency to devise plans and policies.[30]

7. Directors General

The privatizations of the British Utilities that were commenced in the 1980s were effected with statutes that gave regulatory powers, not to boards or commissions, but to single individuals—Directors General.[31] We are, now familiar with the work of the Directors General who were appointed in such fields as Telecommunications (1984), Gas Supply (1986), Water Services (1989), and Electricity Supply (1989).

Each of these individuals is assisted by an office (OFTEL, OFGAS, OFWAT, and OFFER). Bodies of this kind might be viewed as regulatory agencies but for the fact that the Directors General are the single independent regulators for their industries. The basic structure of British utilities regulatory regimes is set out in more detail in Chapter 14 but at this stage we focus on the position of the Director General. He or she is appointed by the Secretary of State and must exercise his or her powers in accordance with general statutory duties. Directors Generals' decisions may be reviewed in the courts or appealed to the Monopolies and Mergers Commission and accountability to the Government comes primarily through annual reporting and treasury financial controls. Parliamentary oversight includes auditing and value for money examination by the Comptroller and Auditor General, scrutiny by the Public Accounts Committee, Select Committees, and the Parliamentary Commissioner for Administration. Directors General are also required by statute to consult publicly on major actions such as proposals to change providers' licence conditions or to make enforcement orders.

The rationale for attaching regulatory powers to an individual has been described thus: 'Observation of the operation of regulatory systems overseas, especially in the United States, led the Government to seek to develop a quicker and less bureaucratic system of regulation. This was centred on the idea of a single, independent regulator for each industry, operating without undue bureaucracy and supported by a small staff.'[32] It was considered, further, that personal responsibility for regulation would reassure the public who could identify regulation with an individual protector of their interests rather than some vague commission of faceless persons.

[30] See Baldwin, *Regulating the Airlines*, ch. 10.

[31] For a review of the work of Directors General see National Audit Office, Report by the Comptroller and Auditor General, *The Work of the Directors General of Telecommunications, Gas Supply, Water Services and Electricity Supply*, HC 645 Session 1995–6 (24 July 1996) (hereafter NAO Report).

[32] NAO Report, para. 2.3.

In the 1990s, however, proposals for replacing Directors General with Commissions have been made with some frequency, a Director General of Telecommunications has himself advocated such a change, and the Government is instituting reforms to reduce the dangers that attend individual regulation.[33] Such reforms are discussed in Chapter 22 below.

Conclusions

Different kinds of regulatory institution have varying strengths and weaknesses. It could be said in broad terms, for instance, that self-regulators tend to be strong on specialist knowledge but weak on accountability to the public; local authorities strong on local democratic accountability, weak on coordination; Parliament strong on democratic authority, weak on sustained scrutiny; courts and tribunals strong on fairness, weak on planning; central departments strong on coordination with government, weak on neutrality; agencies strong on expertise and combining functions, weak on accountability; Directors General strong on specialization and identification of responsibility, weak on spreading discretionary powers.

The set of qualities that is desirable of a regulator in a given regulatory context may vary according to the kinds of issues and problems that may arise and their frequency. The pattern of issues and problems encountered is likely to call for specific regulatory capacities. Thus, where choosing between different applicants for franchises or licences, and being seen to do so fairly, is a central requirement, this might point in the direction of a court or agency. If, on the other hand, the key capacity is the ability to develop policies in a way that is accountable and closely linked to governmental strategies for the economy, this might militate in favour of regulation by a ministerial department.

As for choosing the benchmarks by which to judge the performance of regulators, and their suitability to given tasks, it is time to be more explicit. The next chapter, accordingly, turns to matters of evaluation.

[33] See Director-General of Telecommunications, *Submission to Review of Utility Regulation* (London, 1997) and also C. Veljanovski, *The Future of Industry Regulation in the UK* (London, 1993), 60–2; John Baker (National Power), 'Re-think of the Regulator's Role', *Observer*, 6 Apr. 1994; Sir Iain Vallance (British Telecom), 'Time is up for this regime of regulators', *Evening Standard*, 10 Mar. 1995; *Financial Times*, Leader 10 Mar. 1995; H. McRae, 'The Regulators Must Go by the Board', *Independent*, 23 Feb. 1995; Tony Blair spoke in favour of regulatory panels on 16 May 1995 (Institute for Public Research Conference; 'Regulating in the Public Interest', London). The DTI Green Paper, *A Fair Deal for Consumers: Modernising the Framework for Utility Regulation*, Cm. 3898 (Mar. 1998) suggests (pp. 44–5) that individualized regulation brings dangers of unpredictability, unaccountability, and discontinuity and the DTI White Paper, *A Fair Deal for Consumers: A Response to Consultation* (London, July 1998) proposes three-person boards for the telecommunications and energy sectors.

TABLE 4. *Who regulates?*

Institution	Example	Strengths	Weaknesses
Self-Regulators	Legal Profession	Expertise of staff. Support of industry or profession. Ability to produce rules seen as reasonable by membership.	Seen as self-interested and serving members not public interests. Accountability low. Judicial scrutiny limited. Closed procedures. Questionable independence of complaints mechanisms. Need for governmental oversight.
Local Authorities	Environmental Health	Democratically established. Local knowledge.	Inconsistencies and coordination between regions may be poor. Central government may interfere or exert real control. Expertise may be lower than where knowledge is pooled centrally. Conflicts of interest with other functions (e.g. of service provision).
Parliament	Railways of nineteenth century	Democratic authority high. Accountability strong.	Consistency between committees, lack of general principles.

TABLE 4. (*cont'd*)

Institution	Example	Strengths	Weaknesses
			Enforcement, monitoring may be weak. Limited expertise.
Courts and Tribunals	Transport Sector	Procedures seen as fair and open.	Conflicts with government policies may undermine regulation. Case law may produce policy only sporadically. Limited expertise and ability to plan or develop guidelines.
Central Government Departments	North Sea Oil Extraction	Coordination with government policies high. Accountability of minister to Parliament.	Some issues need to be taken out of politics. Seen as politically biased. Short-term horizons of ministers limit planning. Tendency to interfere on day-to-day basis. Smacks of large government. Expertise limited. Appears less dynamic than creation of new regulatory agency.
Agencies	Civil Aviation Authority	Independence from government. Special expertise applied by career regulators.	Combining functions may lead to reduced performance of those functions.

TABLE 4. (*cont'd*)

Institution	Example	Strengths	Weaknesses
		Continuity of policy-makers and ability to plan for industry.	Accountability limited.
			May suffer from ministerial interference and conflicts of agency/ departmental policies.
		Can combine policy-making, adjudication and enforcement.	
Directors General	Utilities	Focus of responsibility on individual.	Narrow experience of individual, compared to board.
		Decisiveness.	Pressure on individual great.
			Cult of personality.
			Fears of capriciousness, and 'rule of man'.
			Lack of continuity of policy on change of Director General.
			Limited accountability.

6

What is 'Good' Regulation?

To decide whether a system of regulation is good, acceptable, or in need of reform it is necessary to be clear about the benchmarks that are relevant in such an evaluation.[1]

A temptation for some economists may be to assert that regulation is good if it is efficient in the sense that it maximizes wealth.[2] It can be objected, however, that wealth maximization provides no ethical basis for action, that it cannot justify any particular distribution of rights within society, and that, as a result, it cannot be used to measure regulatory decisions affecting rights.[3]

This is because there is circularity in the assertion that one should distribute rights (e.g. to pollute or to be free from pollution) in a manner that maximizes wealth. For every particular, given, distribution of wealth there is a specific allocation of further rights that will maximize wealth —thus, how best to allocate the new supply of petrol would be governed by who owns the machinery that burns petrol.[4] Deciding distributional

---

[1] See generally, R. Baldwin and C. McCrudden, *Regulation and Public Law* (London, 1987), ch. 3; R. Baldwin, *Rules and Government* (Oxford, 1995), ch. 3; J. O. Freedman, *Crisis and Legitimacy* (Cambridge, 1978).

[2] See R. A. Posner, 'Utilitarianism, Economics and Legal Theory' (1979) 8 *J. Legal Stud.* 103; id., 'Wealth Maximisation Revisited' (1985) 2 *Notre Dame J. of Law, Ethics and Pub. Policy* 85.

[3] See R. Dworkin, 'Is Wealth a Value?' [1980] 9 *J. Legal Stud.* 191; id., 'Why Efficiency' (1980) 8 *Hofstra LR* 563; id., *A Matter of Principle* (Cambridge, Mass., 1986), ch. 13; S. Kelman, 'Cost-Benefit Analysis: An Ethical Critique' (1981) 5 (1) *Regulation* 33; A. Kronman, 'Wealth Maximisation as a Normative Principle' (1980) 9 *J. Legal Stud.* 227; C. G. Veljanovski, 'Wealth Maximisation, Law and Ethics: On the Limits of Economic Efficiency' (1981) 1 *Int. Rev. Law and Econ.* 5; E. J. Weinrib, 'Utilitarianism, Economics and Legal Theory' (1980) 30 *U. Toronto LJ* 307; C. Fried, 'Difficulties in the Economic Analysis of Rights', in G. Dworkin, G. Bermont, and P. Brown (eds.), *Markets and Morals* (Washington, 1977). For a review of the literature see N. Duxbury, *Patterns of American Jurisprudence* (Oxford, 1995), 400–6.

[4] This statement assumes that there are transaction costs. If there are no transaction costs and parties can bargain in a friction-free manner then, as the Coase Theorem tells us, *any* distribution of rights will maximize wealth and the owners of petrol burning machines will end up using the petrol even if it is not allocated to them in the first instance. This implies, again, that wealth maximization offers no help at all in deciding how to allocate rights. See R. Coase, 'The Problem of Social Cost' (1960) 3 *J. Law and Econ.* 1; Veljanovski loc. cit. n. 3 above and L. A. Bebchuck, 'The Pursuit of a Bigger Pie: Can everyone Expect a Bigger Slice?' (1980) 8 *Hofstra LR* 671.

issues on the basis of wealth maximization, accordingly, assumes a given distribution from the start. Similarly, it is circular to state that rights should be allocated to those who value them most—valuation itself depends on assumptions about the allocation of rights (one can only value if one has something to value with or else the valuation takes place in the realms of fantasy). Questions of justice, it follows, cannot be answered by economists' appeals to efficiency and distributional questions such as whether it is right to allow an extra unit of pollution (thus shifting the balance of rights from, say, river user A to polluting factory owner B) have to be made on the basis of grounds other than efficiency.

This is not to say that efficiency may not be a factor to be taken into account in making regulatory judgements.[5] We may, in deciding how to allocate rights between, say, polluters and potential victims, want to take on board the wealth implications of particular distributional choices. What we should be wary of is using efficiency as a single measuring rod or justification for regulatory decisions. This will involve either circularity, as noted, or the assumption that the present distribution of wealth, together with a bias in favour of those with wealth, is acceptable.[6]

A further moral objection to wealth maximization relates to its implication that it is right to allow B to interfere with A's rights (e.g. by polluting their river or exposing them to a hazardous substance) if B generates enough wealth to compensate A for the harm done. Human beings, the objection runs, have certain basic rights that it would be morally objectionable to put up for sale. Certain risks, it might similarly be said, should not be imposed on individuals' lives no matter what the price, compensation, or wealth gain on offer.[7]

A more plausible approach to regulatory evaluation can be arrived at by looking at those arguments that have general currency when regulatory arrangements and performance are discussed in the public domain. Certain arguments have force in debating whether this or that regulatory action or regime is worthy of support (is 'legitimate'). These arguments involve reference to one or more of five key tests:

- Is the action or regime supported by legislative authority?
- Is there an appropriate scheme of accountability?
- Are procedures fair, accessible, and open?
- Is the regulator acting with sufficient expertise?
- Is the action or regime efficient?

[5] On economists' contributions see R. Cooter and T. Ulen, *Law and Economics* (Glenview, Ill., 1988), ch. 1 and see Chapter 7, below, on the cost-benefit testing of regulation.

[6] Those possessing wealth will gain in efficiency-based decisions because they value rights more highly and are better placed than poorer persons to generate further wealth from the rights at issue: see C. E. Baker, 'The Ideology of the Economic Analysis of Law' (1975) 5 *Philosophy and Public Affairs* 3; G. Minda, 'Towards a More "Just" Economics of Justice—A Review Essay' (1989) 10 *Cardozo LR* 1855.

[7] For governmental acknowledgment of this point see HM Treasury, *The Setting of Safety Standards* (London, 1996), 9.

The five tests, or criteria, should be explained before their role in assessing regulation is discussed further.

1. The Legislative Mandate

This criterion suggests that regulatory action deserves support when it is authorized by Parliament, the fountain of democratic authority. If the people, through Parliament, have instructed certain regulators to achieve result X, and those regulators can point to their having produced result X, then they are in a position to claim public support. They have fulfilled their mandate.

It might be very proper to judge regulators according to their success in fulfilling their mandates. Unfortunately, however, it is seldom easy to state in precise terms what this should involve. Most regulatory statutes give regulators broad discretions and implementing the mandate thus involves interpretation.[8] A statute, for example, may order a regulator to protect the interests of consumers but it may be silent on the balance to be drawn between industrial and domestic or large and small consumers' interests.

Such statutes, moreover, often set out objectives that exist at mutual tension. Achieving certain objectives may necessarily involve trading off performance in relation to other stated objectives. Regulatory statutes, in addition, often give regulators scope for exercising judgement and devising solutions. (They do this because legislators generally have limited information and expertise in specialist areas and, though knowing that there is a problem, tend not to know how to solve it.) It is, in such cases, impossible to point to clear objectives. Legislators, furthermore, may deliberately avoid setting down precise objectives because they want regulators to have the freedom to cope with problems as they arise in the future. For all of these reasons, regulators are seldom, if ever, involved in the mechanical transmission of statutory objectives into results on the ground[9] and the mandate benchmark, though of relevance, will rarely provide an easy answer to questions of legitimation.

2. Accountability or Control

Regulators with imprecise mandates may, nevertheless, claim that they deserve the support of the public because they are properly accountable

---

[8] See K. C. Davis, *Discretionary Justice* (Chicago, 1969), 39 and on British utilities see T. Prosser, *Law and the Regulators* (Oxford, 1997), 15–31. Lowi suggested that many US regulatory statutes were devoid of any meaningful guidelines—see T. J. Lowi, *The End of Liberalism* (1969 and 2nd edn., New York, 1979).

[9] On the 'transmission-belt' model of implementation and its inadequacies see R. B. Stewart, 'The Reformation of American Administrative Law' (1975) 88 *Harv. LR* 1667.

to, and controlled by, democratic institutions. Thus, a regulatory agency might claim that it is accountable for its interpretation of its mandate to a representative body and that this oversight renders its exercise of powers acceptable.[10]

A difficulty with this criterion is that controversy will often attend the selection of the individuals and bodies that provide accountability. If Parliament itself or another elected institution is not the body holding the regulator to account then the arrangement may be criticized as unrepresentative. Where control is exercised by certain institutions (e.g. courts) the competence of those institutions in specialist areas may also be called into question. Issues also arise as to the appropriate degree of accountability, the resources that should properly be devoted to accountability, and the acceptability of any trade-off between accountability and the effective pursuit of regulatory objectives.[11]

3. Due Process

The basis of the due process claim is that public support is merited because the regulator uses procedures that are fair, accessible, and open. Thus, attention is paid to equality, fairness, and consistency of treatment but also to the levels of participation that regulatory decisions and policy processes allow to the public, to consumers, and to other affected parties. The underlying rationale of such a claim is that proper democratic influence over regulation is ensured by due process being observed and that this influence has a legitimating effect.[12]

The criterion is, again, however, limited in so far as further guiding principles are required in order to explain, for example, who should be able to participate and in what manner. Trade-offs once more have to be made against the effective implementation of the mandate. Thus, more participation may lead to less effective decision-making and eventually to stagnation in the regulatory system. To expand participatory rights beyond a certain point may not, moreover, be consistent with the development and exercise of expertise and judgement.

Disputes may also arise concerning the appropriate *mode* of participation. Lawyers, for instance, may see certain (perhaps formal or trial-type) methods of participation as appropriate in circumstances that those from other disciplines (e.g. political science or economics) might see as calling for quite different arrangements.

[10] See G. E. Frug, 'The Ideology of Bureaucracy in American Law' (1984) 97 *Harv. LR* 1277, 1355–61, 1334–9.

[11] On accountability generally see Chapter 21 below and C. Graham, *Is There a Crisis in Regulatory Accountability?* (London, 1996).

[12] See Stewart, loc. cit. n. 9 above.

4. Expertise

Certain regulatory functions may require the exercise of expert judgement. This is liable to be the case where the decision-maker has to consider a number of competing options or values and come to a balanced judgement on incomplete and shifting information. In these circumstances, the regulator may claim support on the basis of his or her expertise, and the nature of the task at hand, rather then offering to give reasons, or justifications. 'Trust to my expertise' is the essence of such a claim.[13] Experts thus assert that they will come to the most appropriate decision and achieve the best results most rapidly when freed from duties of explanation.

One problem with this test is that it may be difficult for the public to assess whether the decisions arrived at have been appropriate or effective. (It may be difficult to tell what would have happened had alternative decisions been made.) Claims of expertise may also be questionable where the expert fails to explain why *this* issue demands expert judgement (a communications failure that the expert may say flows from the lack of expertise of the lay public). A natural distrust by lay persons of those who lay claim to expertise also serves to undermine demands of support from specialists. This may be the case particularly where experts refuse to give full reasons for their actions, deny access to decision-making processes, or pursue narrow and arcane modes of analysis. Conflicts of opinion between experts again affect their credibility. Nor can it be assumed that experts are neutral—decisions involving judgements will inevitably have a political aspect as competing interests are affected by regulation and as tensions are resolved in a particular manner.

Within the 'risk society', it can be argued, the case for trusting to experts grows ever weaker. Commentators such as Beck and Giddens[14] argue that in risk society traditional securities can no longer be relied on, that increasingly society is preoccupied with the future and 'manufactured risks'—those that are produced by mankind, not nature, that stem from technological advances so as to create new risk environments for which history provides us with very little previous experience and whose uncertainties cannot be 'solved' by further scientific advances. Experience, accordingly, tells us more and more often that we cannot rely on experts to guide us in our choices but must insist on a new political dialogue built on the death of deference to those claiming special expertise.

---

[13] For a defence of expertise see J. M. Landis, *The Administrative Process* (New Haven, 1938); for discussion see J. Mashaw, *Bureaucratic Justice* (New Haven, 1983), 26–9.

[14] For concise reviews of issues see U. Beck, 'The Politics of Risk Society' and A. Giddens, 'Risk Society: The Context of British Politics', both in J. Franklin (ed.), *The Politics of Risk Society* (Cambridge, 1998). See also U. Beck, *Risk Society* (London, 1992); id., *The Reinvention of Politics* (Cambridge, 1997); A. Giddens, *Beyond Left and Right* (Cambridge, 1994).

5. Efficiency

A regulator may claim support on the basis of acting efficiently and, in doing so, may make two kinds of claim. The first of these urges support on the basis that the legislative mandate is being implemented at the least possible level of inputs or costs and there is productive efficiency.[15] This, of course, is a claim afflicted by all the problems discussed above in relation to the mandate—notably those arising from the imprecision of that mandate. It is particularly difficult to measure efficiency when the mandate fails to set down consistent or coherent objectives[16] or where a regulator's functions intermesh with those of other agencies and departments.[17] It is difficult, moreover, to assert that a particular method of regulating achieves 'better' results than alternative methods when the latter have not been put to the test in the relevant arena.

A second version of the efficiency claim urges support on the basis that the regulation at issue leads to results that are efficient—as judged by criteria set down with a degree of independence from the mandate. Reference might thus be made to the regulatory regime's allocative efficiency (whether it is impossible to redistribute goods to make at least one consumer better off without making another consumer worse off) and its dynamic efficiency (whether there is encouragement of desirable process and product innovation and whether the system produces flexible responses to changes in demand).[18]

Leaving aside the problem of showing that alternative systems would not offer superior performance, such claims present difficulties because, as noted, efficiency is not a value independent of distributional considerations and efficiency in itself provides no answers on distributional issues or in defining the regulatory mandate. The pursuit of efficiency may, indeed, conflict with legislative statements on distributional matters and, accordingly, the appropriateness of efficiency claims may be especially questionable in those spheres of regulation where distributive concerns are central.[19]

The extent of a conflict between efficiency and social or distributional objectives may itself be a matter of dispute. Thus, Prosser[20] has contested

[15] One can distinguish effectiveness as addressing the issue of whether desired results are actually achieved (irrespective of costs).
[16] See C. G. Veljanovski, 'Cable Television: Agency Franchising and Economics', in Baldwin and McCrudden, *Regulation and Public Law*.
[17] See P. P. Craig, 'The Monopolies and Mergers Commission: Competition and Administrative Rationality', ibid.
[18] See Cooter and Ulen, *Law and Economics*, 17–18; R. Baldwin and M. Cave, *Franchising as a Tool of Government* (London, 1996), section 4.1.
[19] See R. Baldwin and C. C. Veljanovski, 'Regulation by Cost Benefit Analysis' (1984) 62 *Pub. Admin.* 51.
[20] See Prosser, *Law and the Regulators*, 15–24.

Foster's[21] view that the performance of British utilities regulators should be judged according to the benchmark of efficiency. The objection is that the main utilities statutes do not make maximizing economic efficiency an overriding regulatory goal and that a series of social obligations and non-economic ends (such as are implied in the concept of universal service) are legislative objectives of at least equal importance—that regulatory goals are 'mixed and include irretrievably varied rationales, economic and social'.[22]

6. The Role of the Five Criteria

The above five claims, it can be seen, are all fraught with difficulties but collectively they constitute a set of benchmarks for assessing regulatory regimes. These are the rationales that are employed and have currency in real-life debates on regulation and its reform.[23] Arguments in support of (or arguments criticizing) regulators that do not fall under these five headings will be deemed irrelevant by most members of the public. Thus, if I argue that the Director General of OFGAS should be supported in her work because she is kind to animals or gives to charity, this will be seen as missing the point. If I say that she deserves support since she is achieving her statutory objectives; acting in a fully accountable, open, and fair manner; bringing expertise to bear and making good use of her resources, these are likely to be seen as relevant points.

Judging the extent to which regulation is legitimate is not to offer a sociological assessment of the actual support that a regulator enjoys (this might have been achieved by good public relations or even misrepresentation); it is, rather, to offer an assessment of the legitimacy that a regulator *deserves*.[24] What matters is the collective justificatory power of the arguments that can be made under the five headings. Strong claims across the board point to regulation that deserves support, generally weak claims indicate a low capacity to justify.

How, though, can trade-offs between claims be dealt with? How, can it be said whether a weakening of rights of participation in return for improvements in satisfying the statutory mandate is a good or a bad thing?[25]

[21] C. Foster, *Privatisation, Public Ownership and the Regulation of Natural Monopoly* (Oxford, 1992), ch. 9.

[22] Prosser, *Law and the Regulators*, 24. See also Chapter 7 below the on the application of cost-benefit testing to regulation.

[23] See Baldwin, *Rules and Government*, 47.

[24] See R. Barker, *Political Legitimacy and the State* (Oxford, 1990), 20–7; D. Beetham, *The Legitimation of Power* (London, 1991), 13.

[25] See Baldwin, *Rules and Government*, ch. 3, for a more extended discussion and for comment on such an approach see T. Prosser's book review of *Rules and Government* at (1996) 59 *MLR* 762–5.

The answer is that, at the end of the day, the weight that individuals place on each legitimating argument will reflect their personal political philosophies and, in the absence of all persons agreeing on the nature of an ideal world, we will differ on matters of weighting. What we do seem to agree on, however, is the benchmarks themselves. Any perusal of debates on regulation will reveal their exclusive usage.[26]

This means that, short of those discussing regulation simply exposing their political differences, much can still be said in making assessments of regulatory performance. It can be asked, notably, whether performance on one of the five fronts can be improved significantly without material loss on another. (This kind of discussion is the meat and drink of most regulatory debates.)

Where trade-offs between different kinds of claim are involved, resolution will demand reference to a political philosophy or position. Designers or reformers of regulation should bear in mind, however, that performance under some headings (e.g. the legislative mandate) may be linked, under certain conditions, to performance under other headings (e.g. fairness and openness of processes). Thus, if a regulatory regime is perceived by the public or industry to be unfair, the regulator may enjoy low levels of cooperation and this may impede performance in satisfying the mandate. This means that a reformer may not have the option of effecting an extreme trade-off between fairness or openness and more efficiency in achieving mandated ends—public reaction will stand in the way of achieving this efficiency. The implication is that, whatever the philosophy of the regulatory designer or reformer, that individual or institution should be wary of endorsing regulatory designs that score conspicuously badly on any of the five tests—performance as judged on the other criteria may be affected detrimentally.

How, then, can legitimacy be improved in the real world? The answer is by taking steps to improve ratings according to the five tests. To give

---

[26] For examples see Baldwin, *Rules and Government*, 47. To take more recent instances: in June 1997 Margaret Beckett, President of the Board of Trade, announced the Government's Review of Utility Regulation and stated that its objective was to secure value, quality, and choice to consumers (a reading of the mandate for the utilities), guided by principles of fairness, transparency, consistency, and predictability (aspects of fairness) together with accountability and the provision of incentives to managers to innovate and improve efficiency (these objectives are set out in the terms of reference of the review at Annex A of the DTI Green Paper *A Fair Deal for Consumers*, Cm. 3898 (Mar. 1998). See also paragraph 7.2 of the Green Paper on key elements of an 'effective and legitimate' regime (clear legal framework; effective structuring and resourcing; transparency; accountability; open procedures for challenging decisions; predictability and consistency; timeliness; and cost acceptability). In January 1998 the Better Regulation Task Force (an independent advisory body appointed by the Public Service Minister and assisted by the Better Regulation Unit of the Office of Public Service) published a 'Critics' Guide' to good regulation. It highlighted five key principles of good regulation: transparency; accountability; targeting (the aims of the mandate rather than unintended side-effects); consistency (again, an aspect of fairness); and proportionality (an aspect of efficiently achieving mandated objectives).

some brief examples, under the mandate, measures could be taken to improve the clarity of the mandate and achieve agreement on its terms. A regulatory body could, thus, publish its vision of the mandate and hold discussions on this. Alternatively, regulators and ministers could, at periodic intervals, jointly produce statements of aims in explanation of the mandate and these could be put to Parliament for approval.[27] Regulators' claims to be properly accountable might be improved by such steps as the creation of a specialist parliamentary select committee (a House of Commons Select Committee on Regulated Industries) or by strengthened (perhaps publicly funded) standing consumer bodies for specific industries or products. Due process claims could be improved by reforms to increase information flows and participation in regulatory decision- and policy-making and there might, for instance, be a role for statutory or court-mandated requirements that regulatory rules be disclosed whenever they are in operation. Expertise claims might be reinforced by legislative or administrative actions to designate those issues that are matters of judgement for the regulator and by improving levels of training and resources where these are inadequate. Efficiency claims might be strengthened by taking steps to clarify the mandate and by improving flows of information to the public. Whether cost-benefit testing of regulation has a role on this front is discussed in the following chapter.

To summarize: regulatory regimes and actions can be assessed by making judgements about the merits of legitimating claims under the five headings set out. To assess in this manner is not to evaluate the moral correctness or legality of the regulatory action or regime but to make a judgement as to its worthiness of public support. In making that judgement, personal visions have to be tempered by considering the responses of other parties. Assessing regulation thus involves areas of agreement (on benchmarks) but also of divergence (on the weighting of different desiderata). Debates on the merits of particular regulatory approaches and of potential reforms can, nevertheless, make fruitful use of the five benchmarks and these criteria will be referred to throughout the course of this book.

[27] For discussion of ministerial policy guidance systems see R. Baldwin, *Regulating the Airlines* (Oxford, 1985), ch. 9 and below, Chapter 21.

TABLE 5. *Benchmarks for regulation*

Claim to Legitimacy	Essence of Claim	Problems
Legislative Mandate	Authorization from elected legislature.	Parliament's intention may be vague.
		Stated objectives for regulation may exist in tension or conflict.
		Parliament may have delegated the power to flesh-out objectives.
		Large discretions may be given to regulators.
Accountability or Control	Regulator is properly accountable and controlled and so is democratically responsive.	Is the body holding to account properly representative?
		Is the trade-off of accountability and efficiency acceptable?
Due Process	Support is merited because procedures are sufficiently fair, accessible, and open, to expose to democratic influence.	Who should be allowed to participate?
		What is the acceptable trade-off between openness or accessibility and efficiency?
		Is the *mode* of participation appropriate?
Expertise	'Trust to my expertise' because a judgement has to be made on the basis of a number of factors and variables and specialized knowledge skills and experience have to be applied.	Public is poorly positioned to evaluate expertise.
		Difficult for expert to explain reasoning or judgement to lay persons.
		General distrust of experts and arcane language.
		Public desire for openness and accountability.
		Conflicts between experts undermine public confidence.
		Public may see experts as self-interested or captured.
		Public sceptical of neutrality of regulatory decisions where certain parties gain advantages.
Efficiency	Legislative mandate is being implemented efficiently.	See problems of legislative mandate claims.
	Efficient results are produced.	Conflicts with legislative mandate may arise.
		Distributional questions may be begged or left out of account.
		Measuring efficiency is difficult.

7

The Cost-Benefit Testing
of Regulation

This chapter considers the role of cost-benefit testing and other forms of economic appraisal as means of evaluating and influencing regulatory activity.[1] It asks whether there is a case for applying economic appraisals to regulation in spite of arguments that regulatory regimes should satisfy values other than efficiency.

1. From Cost-Benefit Analysis to Compliance Cost Assessment to Regulatory Appraisal

British cost-benefit testing in the regulatory arena has been strongly influenced by experience in the United States of America. In 1981 President Ronald Reagan issued Executive Order 12291 and required all executive agencies in the United States to submit all major regulations to cost-benefit analysis (CBA) and only to put forward for presidential approval those regulations predicted to produce a surplus of benefits. The burden of proof rested on the agencies putting forward the regulation—they had to be able to demonstrate cost effectiveness.

The stated objectives of Order 12291 were to reduce the burden of regulation, to increase agency accountability, to provide for more effective presidential oversight of the regulatory process, and to ensure better-reasoned

---

[1] See generally, T. O. McGarity, *Reinventing Rationality: The Role of Regulatory Analysis in the Federal Bureaucracy* (Cambridge, 1991); R. Baldwin, *Rules and Government* (Oxford, 1995), ch. 7; G. Bryner, *Bureaucratic Discretion* (New York, 1987) and on economic appraisal of regulation in Britain see G. R. Baldwin and C. G. Veljanovski, 'Regulation by Cost-Benefit Analysis' (1984) 62 *Pub. Admin.* 51; J. Froud, R. Boden, A. Ogus, and P. Stubbs, 'Toeing the Line: Compliance Cost Assessment in Britain' (1994) 24 *Policy and Politics* 4; J. Froud and A. Ogus, ' "Rational" Social Regulation and Compliance Cost Assessment' (1996) 74 *Pub. Admin.* 221; A. Ogus, 'Risk Management and Rational Social Regulation', in R. Baldwin (ed.), *Law and Uncertainty* (London, 1996); A. Ogus, *Regulation: Legal Form and Economic Theory* (Oxford, 1994), 153–65; R. H. Pildes and C. R. Sunstein, 'Reinventing the Regulatory State' (1995) 62 *Univ. of Chicago LR* 1.

justifications for regulating. Agencies had to prepare a Preliminary Regulatory Impact (PRIA) for final major rules and then a Regulatory Impact Analysis (RIA). The RIA would not only set out the costs and benefits of proposed regulation but had to outline alternative approaches that might achieve the given regulatory goals at lower cost. Since not all benefits (or costs) could be quantified in monetary terms, non-quantifiable benefits had to be described.

Scrutiny of appraisals was carried out by a central unit in the Office of Management and Budget (OMB) which was given the responsibility for determining the adequacy of the RIA. The OMB scrutinized with zeal from the inception of the system and commentators have concluded that, although OMB review has produced withdrawal or rejection of proposed regulations in a fairly small percentage of cases, the impact of CBA scrutiny has been very significant in US regulation.[2] In the USA the broad system continues to this day under the Clinton administration.[3]

In Britain the origins of economic appraisal are to be found in the mid-1980s in the work of the Enterprise Unit of the Cabinet Office and in concerns, particularly within the Conservative Government, to reduce regulatory burdens on business.[4]

After various moves between departments, the current British appraisal system is now run centrally by the Cabinet Office Better Regulation Unit, with Departmental Better Regulation Units (DBRUs) given responsibility for ensuring that officials in their Departments prepare appraisals for all proposals likely to affect business. All UK and EC regulatory proposals affecting business, charities, and voluntary organizations are now required to submit to Regulatory Appraisal incorporating a Compliance Cost Assessment (CCA).

The CCA calculates the costs to businesses of complying with a proposed regulatory option, and it is intended to inform Ministers of such costs before decisions to regulate are approved so that 'unnecessary' burdens on business can be avoided.[5] It will, amongst other things:

---

[2] See e.g. McGarity, *Reinventing Rationality*, 22.

[3] In 1993 President Clinton issued Executive Order 12866, which maintained the basic process instituted by President Reagan and the importance of CBA in decision-making but introduced some modifications such as new disclosure requirements; see Pildes and Sunstein loc. cit. n. 1 above.

[4] See e.g. DTI, *Burdens on Business* (London, 1985); White Papers: *Lifting the Burden*, Cmnd. 9571 (London, 1985); *Building Business, Not Barriers*, Cmnd. 9794 (London, 1986); *Releasing Enterprise*, Cm. 512 (London, 1988); DTI, *Counting the Cost to Business* (London, 1990); DTI, *Checking the Cost to Business* (London, 1992); DTI, *Cutting Red Tape for Business* (London, 1991); DTI, *Cutting Red Tape* (London, 1994); DTI, *Thinking about Regulation* (London, 1994); HM Treasury, *Economic Appraisal in Central Government* (London, 1991); Deregulation Unit, Cabinet Office, *Checking the Cost of Regulation: A Guide to Compliance Costs Assessment* (London, 1996); *Regulation in the Balance: A Guide to Regulatory Appraisal Incorporating Risk Assessment* (London, 1996) (see now revised edition of 1998).

[5] Deregulation Unit, *Checking the Cost of Regulation*, 1.

- outline the intended effect of a proposed measure;
- summarize compliance costs for a typical business and for all businesses affected;
- give key information about effects on international competitiveness;
- summarize business sectors likely to be affected and estimate numbers involved;
- estimate total recurring and non-recurring costs of compliance for a typical business;
- outline the results of a 'small business litmus test' (based on comments by two or three typical small businesses on the impact of the regulation);
- detail how compliance costs will be monitored;
- summarize alternative approaches and reasons why lower cost alternatives were rejected.

The risk assessment that, from 1996 onwards, accompanies a CCA in a Regulatory Appraisal identifies the potential benefits associated with various options and, where possible, places a value on these benefits so that they may be compared with the costs imposed on consumers, business, and the Government. It is the risk assessment that moves the CCA system, as formerly employed in the UK, significantly away from mere calculation of costs and in the direction of CBA on the United States model. The approach of the new Labour Government of 1997 is to move further towards a cost-benefit balancing approach by combining risk assessments with Appraisals and calling on regulators to show that quantified benefits outweigh costs.

The risk assessment system of 1996 sought to do the following:[6] identify the problem and the harm involved; estimate the risk associated with the harm (this involves assessing the probability or frequency of the harm arising as well as its likely magnitude); identify regulatory options; estimate the impact of the options on the risk; place a monetary value on expected benefits of each option; compare the costs with the benefits—by taking the costs to business as calculated in the CCA and adding costs to consumers and to Government; and identify any important issues of equity or other political considerations.

2. Appraising Economic Appraisals

Advocates of economic appraisal mechanisms make a number of claims that can be seen as addressing the five benchmarks for regulation discussed in the last chapter.

---

[6] See Deregulation Unit, Cabinet Office, *Regulation in the Balance*.

The legislative mandate—appraisals are said to improve the pursuit of mandated policy goals by measuring regulatory alternatives against such goals.

Accountability—appraisals subject rule-makers to an objective eye; they reveal costs borne by society; they expose policy judgements; and avoid the pursuit of hidden agendas within bureaucracies.

Due process—appraisals keep rule-making procedures open and encourage access to those who argue for alternative options; they avoid moving towards premature solutions and guide towards rational decision-making.

Expertise—appraisals encourage experts to clarify their justifications for regulating in a particular way; they highlight the need to review goals; and draw attention to gaps in information and to research needs.

Efficiency—appraisals conduce to more effective regulation by insisting on strategies that minimize costs for given benefits; they encourage the systematic use of information on the advantages and disadvantages of policies; and they identify 'correct' decisions on an efficiency basis.

When, however, we consider how appraisals are affected by the variety of legal, political, and practical constraints that impinges on regulatory or governmental actions, the above claims may, in many respects, seem overstated.

Thus, with regard to claims under the legislative mandate heading, a problem arises if efficiency tests are sought to be satisfied in the face of statutory objectives that are not stated in efficiency terms. The tension between statutory objectives and a CBA will be greatest where the statute is strongly redistributive or promotes ends other than efficiency.[7] Economic appraisers' actions might thus be liable to judicial review if attempts are made to overrule mandates in favour of efficiency-related ends unsanctioned by the legislation.[8]

As for accountability and due process, a problem with CBA testing may be that the process of analysis may mask policy-making and come between regulatory rule-makers and those being consulted. It may, accordingly, reduce accountability and participatory access. This may occur if the analysis stresses quantifiable factors to the detriment of 'softer' components or if policy issues are buried in a mass of economic technicalities and arcane language.[9] Nor can it be assumed that economic appraisal is a neutral, value-free exercise. Analysts conducting such appraisals may operate with certain prejudices, for instance biases

---

[7] See C. R. Sunstein, 'Cost Benefit Analysis and the Separation of Powers' (1981) 23 *Arizona LR* 1267.

[8] See e.g. the test in *Wednesbury* [1948] 1KB 223. The European Court of Justice has also ruled that economic factors may not be superimposed on a directive—see C-44/95 *R* v. *Secretary of State for the Environment ex p. Royal Society for the Protection of Birds*, ECJ, FC, 11 July 1996 (reported *Financial Times*, 8 Oct. 1996).

[9] See P. Self, *Administrative Theories and Politics* (2nd edn. London, 1978), 212.

against regulation or favouring the satisfaction of private preferences, rather than values associated with procedural rights or collective or public goals—and CBAs may be prone to manipulation by prejudiced parties.[10]

Accountability may also become fragmented by the process of appraisal. Thus, such oversight in the US has been said to obscure responsibilities and reduce democratic accountability so that it becomes unclear who bears final responsibility for regulatory decisions—the agency, the OMB, federal judges, or elected individuals.[11]

Further concerns under the due process heading are that participatory rights may be devalued in so far as economic analysis may, in practice, offer certain groupings unfairly preferential access to the policy-making and regulatory processes and that it may allow well-organized private groups and regulated industries to dictate national policy. The OMB has been criticized on this front[12] and in Britain the DTI made it clear during the Conservative years of the 1980s and 1990s that its appraisal procedures were designed specifically to offer privileged business access to regulatory rule-making processes.[13]

As for the exercise of regulatory expertise, economic analysis may operate, again, in a prejudicial manner. OMB review in the USA has been said to work not so much as a means of imposing objective, rational scrutiny on regulators but as a means of exerting control over the substantive policies of regulators—as a way to give preference to undisclosed goals.[14] This may devalue regulatory expertise (not to say accountability and the satisfaction of the mandate) in so far as regulators may be slow to develop balanced regulatory rules if they anticipate reorientation of those rules through the analysis process. Regulatory authority, moreover, may be shifted from specialist agencies to less expert regulatory review staff who not only lack in-depth knowledge in relevant areas but do not have the time or resources to conduct properly expert assessments.

Finally, in relation to efficiency claims, it might be contended that CBA testing militates in favour of policies that maximize net social benefits but CBAs do not hold out the prospect of clear-cut answers to regulatory problems and a number of technical difficulties afflict the appraisals process. Sceptics might also urge that the process tends to produce not better regulation but burdens and delays for regulators—that it does not

---

[10] See P. Self, *Econocrats and the Policy Process: The Politics and Philosophy of Cost Benefit Analysis* (Basingstoke, 1975).

[11] See S. Breyer, *Regulation and Its Reform* (Cambridge, Mass., 1982).

[12] Ibid. 285–6; E. D. Olson, 'The Quiet Shift of Power: OMB Supervision of Environmental Protection Agency Rulemaking under Executive Order 12291 (1984) 4 *Va. J. Nat. Resources* 31; noted Pildes and Sunstein, loc. cit. n. 1 above, p. 5.

[13] See the White Paper, *Building Business, Not Barriers*; Chapter 21 n. 3, below.

[14] See Bryner, *Bureaucratic Discretion*, 285–6; Pildes and Sunstein loc. cit. n. 1 above, p. 4.

lead towards the right kind or level of regulation but to the reduction of regulation even where it is beneficial.[15]

Distributional Issues

CBA testing may apply efficiency yardsticks but distributional concerns may be the primary rationales for regulatory programmes. On these questions CBAs will offer little help. They tend to assume, for instance, that the present distribution of wealth is acceptable; that this does not skew the analysis; and that regulation or deregulation has an insignificant distributional effect. In reality, though, the way that people attribute value is a product, at least in part, of their wealth and to ignore this biases CBAs in favour of those with economic power.[16] If, moreover, the existence of a regulatory regime implies that the given distribution of wealth is undesirable (for example because polluters are externalizing some of the costs of production and are accordingly enjoying too much wealth) it may be a mistake to presuppose, for the sake of a CBA test, that the present distribution is satisfactory. The legislature's choice of regulation for either explicit or implicit redistributive purposes may be inconsistent with the use of CBA as a benchmark for regulatory rules.

Data Constraints and Measurement

Technical difficulties beset most economic appraisals. Assessing the impact of a piece of regulation may, for instance, be difficult because adaptive responses are involved.[17] (Regulations requiring the wearing of hard hats on construction sites may reduce skull fractures but workers wearing hats may behave generally more dangerously because they feel protected. As a result, leg and arm injuries may increase.) Quantification of such displacement effects may be very difficult to build into a CBA.

The costs and benefits associated with a regulation will also depend on how it is enforced and the pattern of compliance that results. Again, predicting enforcement and compliance behaviour gives rise to serious quantification difficulties. The effects on industry may involve 'hidden' costs such as reductions in productivity, a dulling of incentives, expenditure

[15] See R. V. Percival, 'Checks without Balance: Executive Office Oversight of the Environment Protection Agency' (1991) *54 Law and Cont. Prob.* 127. In March 1998 the US Senate considered the Regulatory Improvement Bill—proposed legislation to increase the complexity of the economic analyses to be conducted by would-be rule-makers. Opponents of the Bill characterized it as an attempt to paralyse efforts to protect the public interest—see *Financial Times*, 10 Mar. 1998.

[16] See H. Otway, 'Public Wisdom, Expert Fallibility: Towards a Contextual Theory of Risk', in S. Krimsky and D. Golding (eds.), *Social Theories of Risk* (Westport, Conn., 1992).

[17] See S. Peltzman, 'The Effects of Automobile Regulation' (1975) 83 *J. Pol. Econ.* 677; W. K. Viscusi, 'The Impact of Occupational Safety and Health Regulation' (1979) 10 *Bell J. of Econ.* 117.

on responding to regulation, and distortions on investment and production
—these factors further aggravate quantification problems. Regulatory analysts will often lack the time, resources, and data to explore such factors
in detail.[18] Any information available 'off the shelf' is liable to come from
industry and be subject to bias. The interests of, and costs borne by, large
numbers of unorganized or ill-represented individuals may in such a
process be inadequately considered and the public interest insufficiently
attended to in the CBA.

Benefit measurement is likely to be at least as difficult as quantifying costs because there is liable to be an absence of relevant data (on
e.g. the value of cleaner rivers) and economists may differ by several
orders of magnitude when valuing such benefits as human life or good
health.[19] Many intangibles will defy pricing and CBA testing procedures usually recognize this by requiring non-quantifiable benefits to
be described. The danger of the CBA process is, however, that 'hard'
figures take precedence over 'soft' factors that are less susceptible to
quantification in numerical terms. Regulation tends to occur where
markets have, for various reasons, failed, and, accordingly, there tends
to be an absence of good market-based data in exactly those circumstances
where there is a case for regulating. This suggests that CBAs will be at
their least persuasive or reliable where the need for rational and effective regulation is greatest.[20]

CBAs may also beg questions about the valuation of different risks.
Thus, Pildes and Sunstein argue that experts and lay persons may
value, say, the avoidance of certain hazards, quite differently. Lay
persons may, for instance, value reductions in the risks of certain modes
of death more highly than others because some deaths are particularly
dreaded.[21] CBAs based on expert valuations may accordingly fail to take
on board competing approaches to evaluation. CBAs may, moreover, deal
with aggregations of costs and benefits whereas the public may be concerned to know how distributions of costs and benefits will be produced
—to know who wins and who loses from a regulatory action.

Implementation Problems

If appraisal mechanisms are to be applied to regulators then a bureaucratic mechanism will be required in order to carry these out. One

[18] See McGarity, *Reinventing Rationality*, 126–32.
[19] US studies have used valuations of life ranging from $300,000 to $3.5m.—see
McGarity, ibid. 275; C. Noble, *Liberalism at Work* (Philadelphia, 1986), 112–15.
[20] See Baldwin and Veljanovski, loc. cit. n. 1 above, p. 56.
[21] Pildes and Sunstein, loc. cit. n. 1 above, pp. 50–2; see more generally Chapter 11 below;
S. Hill, *Democratic Values and Technological Choices* (Stanford, Calif., 1992), 55–89;
P. Slovic, 'Perception of Risk', in S. Krimsky and D. Golding (eds.), *Social Theories of Risk*
(Westport, Conn., 1992).

immediate danger is of duplication and adding to the cost and weight of governmental bureaucracy. (In the USA the average cost of an analysis was put at $100,000 over a decade and a half ago.[22]) If extra resources are not allocated to regulators, a straight diversion of money from regulation to analysis is effected. This leads to the criticism that analysis is best seen as a way of slowing down regulatory activity rather than as a means of improving regulation.[23] A balanced view is perhaps that economic scrutiny can be expected to deter the making of extravagantly inefficient rules but can also be expected to increase the resource requirements for making a desirable regulatory rule.

The constraints that attend the implementation of appraisals may also cast further doubts on the notion that CBAs encourage the consideration by policy-makers of a wide variety of regulatory options. Included amongst those constraints are: limitations on information; the costs of analysis; the need to select and analyse facts with a policy end in sight; the need to meet political or policy-making deadlines; the attachment of policy-makers to certain types of solution or modes of analysis; and the limited ability of top policy-makers to consider widely ranging options.[24] In real life, economic appraisers may be tied to appraising options that have already been identified by policy-makers.

Delay is a particular problem occasioned by CBA testing. Some regulatory actions may have to be taken rapidly to respond to crises and satisfactory CBAs, accordingly, may not be feasible in the timescales presented. Other deadlines, as noted, may restrict the level of analysis that can be achieved.

The most serious impediment to the effective use of CBA within regulation has been said to be the bureaucratic resistance encountered.[25] This may be due to a variety of causes. Regulatory officials may, for instance, distrust economic analysis and its techniques; they may be wedded to established responses to problems; or they may think that economic analyses impede the compromises and bargains that have to be struck in regulatory and political life. (British Civil Service traditions, in particular, may encourage a rejection of CBA styles of policy discussion.) Regulators, moreover, may have their own interests and policy objectives which they do not see in pure efficiency-seeking terms. These may

[22] US General Accounting Office, *Improved Quality, Adequate Resources and Consistent Oversight Needed if Regulatory Analysis is to Help Control Costs of Regulations* (Washington DC, 1982).

[23] See Bryner, *Bureaucratic Discretion*, 83–4; A. B. Morrison, 'OMB Interference with Agency Rule-making: The Wrong Way to Write a Regulation' (1986) 99 *Harv. LR* 1059: C. De Muth and D. Ginsberg, 'White House Review of Agency Rule-making' (1986) 99 *Harv. LR* 1075.

[24] McGarity, *Reinventing Rationality*, 160.

[25] See D. Braybrooke and C. E. Lindblom, *A Strategy of Decision* (New York, 1963) on the limitations of a comprehensive approach to planning.

be the results of, for example, statutory requirements, organizational traditions, personal and bureaucratic objectives, or managerial interests. Forces within the regulatory and governmental processes may, accordingly, thwart the CBA testing process.

Conclusions

Economic appraisals techniques present significant problems under all five of our test headings. This is not, however, to argue that such appraisals have no place in evaluation regulation. There is a role for the appraisal of costs and benefits in regulation but it is a constrained one because of imperfections in appraisal systems and the need to satisfy non-efficiency values such as are involved under the mandate, accountability, due process, and expertise headings. To make regulation, and questions as to its extent, *turn* on CBA testing would be to give efficiency too central a place in regulatory affairs. What can be done is to use economic appraisals not to impede regulation (as an end in itself), or in order to give business a preferential say in regulatory policy-making, but as a supplement to the policy-making process. This might be achieved by adopting the following approach.[26]

Appraisals should focus on questions set by policy-makers, not by the appraisers themselves, and should look to the costs and benefits of 'live' proposals for rules. They should briefly note alternative methods of achieving set objectives but should not purport to offer a comprehensive review of options with a 'correct' solution. They should avoid spurious elaboration and levels of technicality that impede policy discussions, and values that the appraisal cannot take into account should be explicitly identified and addressed.

Assumptions on imponderables should be spelled out as should those on enforcement and adaptive responses, and particular groups or individuals should not be given preferential access to appraisal processes.

Appraisals, and the information upon which they are based, should be openly disclosed as a part of the rule-making process. Such documents should be available to the public and to the scrutinizing agents and committees of Parliament. The limitations of appraisals, in general, and of the particular appraisal, should be openly disclosed. Participatory mechanisms should be incorporated into the appraisals process in order to allow citizens to express their judgements about different risks in different contexts;[27] and, finally, the courts should continue to ensure that appraisals do not loom so large in the rule-making process as to constitute

---

[26] See Baldwin, *Rules and Government*, 215.
[27] A proposal of Pildes and Sunstein loc. cit. n. 1 above, p. 75.

a resort to irrelevant considerations, or indeed do not themselves take into account irrelevant considerations.

Such a way of dealing with economic appraisals pays heed to those commentators who argue that economic approaches to risk-benefit analysis should be guided by democratic processes and ethical principles, should allow participation by affected parties, and should be exposed to alternative assessment techniques.[28]

Finally, it bears stressing that the most fundamental objection to a purely economic approach—one tailoring regulation to economically efficient ends—is an ethical one. To aim for efficient solutions is, as indicated in the last chapter, no morally justifiable answer to questions regarding the distribution of rights and issues of justice since wealth maximization provides no convincing normative basis for action.[29]

---

[28] See Chapter 11 below on risk-benefit analysis and K. S. Shrader-Frechette, *Risk and Rationality* (Berkeley, Calif., 1991). Note Pildes and Sunstein's criticism of the proposal in S. Breyer, *Breaking the Vicious Circle* (Cambridge, Mass., 1993), 59–63, that an expert elite should advise on the rationalization of regulatory priorities. They urge that this places too much emphasis on the technical as opposed to the democratic side of regulation—Pildes and Sunstein loc. cit. n. 1 above, 86–7.

[29] For criticism of cost-benefit analysis as efficiency based see D. Kennedy, 'Cost-Benefit Analysis of Entitlement Problems: A Critique' (1981) 3 *Stanford LR* 387; R. S. Markovits, 'Duncan's Do Nots: Cost-Benefit Analysis and the Determination of Legal Entitlements' (1984) 36 *Stanford LR* 1169; M. S. Baram, 'Cost-Benefit Analysis: An Inadequate Basis for Health, Safety and Environmental Regulatory Decisionmaking' (1980) 8 *Ecology LQ*; M. Sagoff, 'At the Shrine of our Lady of Fatima or Why Political Questions are not all Economic' (1981) 23 *Arizona LR* 1283; C. R. Sunstein, 'Cost-Benefit Analysis and the Separation of Powers' (1981) 23 *Arizona LR* 1267.

Enforcing Regulation

Regulation is generally used to influence behaviour in the real world and regulatory processes can be thought of as comprising three stages: the enactment of enabling legislation; the creation of regulatory administrations and rules; and the bringing to bear of those rules on persons or institutions sought to be influenced or controlled.[1] This third, enforcement, stage is as vital to the success of regulation as the first two. Astute enforcement can remedy design defects in regulatory mechanisms and ill-enforcement can undermine the most sophisticated designs of regulation. Thus, skilled field enforcers can use their discretions to apply rules selectively so as to solve problems or to temper excessively restrictive bodies of legislation.[2] On the other hand, failures to identify and deal with breaches of rules may reduce regulatory statutes to mere paper exercises.[3]

This chapter looks at five central issues relating to enforcement:

- styles of enforcement;
- rules and enforcement;
- when to intervene;
- how much to enforce;
- controlling corporations.

1. Styles of Enforcement

Regulatory officials seek to gain compliance with the law not merely by resort to formal enforcement and prosecution but by using a host

---

[1] See generally, B. M. Hutter, *Compliance: Regulation and Environment* (Oxford, 1997), ch. 1; id., *The Reasonable Arm of the Law?* (Oxford, 1988); K. Hawkins, *Environment and Enforcement* (Oxford, 1984). On private enforcement see J. Braithwaite, 'Enforced Self-Regulation' (1982) 80 *Mich. LR* 1461; I. Ayres and J. Braithwaite, *Responsive Regulation* (Oxford, 1992), ch. 4; C. D. Shearing and P. D. Stenning (eds.), *Private Policing* (Beverly Hills, Calif., 1986); W. Landes and R. Posner, 'The Private Enforcement of Law' (1975) 4 *J. Legal Stud*. 1.

[2] See P. Fenn and C. Veljanovski, 'A Positive Economic Theory of Regulatory Enforcement' (1988) 98 *Economic Journal* 1055, 1069.

[3] For a general review of why regulation may fail see P. N. Grabosky, 'Counterproductive Regulation' (1995) 23 *Int. J. of Sociology of Law* 347.

of informal techniques including education, advice, persuasion, and negotiation.[4]

Reiss has thus drawn an important distinction between 'compliance'[5] approaches to enforcement, which emphasize the use of measures falling short of prosecution in order to seek compliance with laws, and 'deterrence'[6] approaches which are penal and use prosecutions in order to deter future infractions.

Compliance approaches can be seen as holding conformity to the law as a more central objective than deterrence approaches, which may also involve a stronger retributive dimension.[7] Within the compliance strategy Hutter has distinguished two sub-strategies that she terms the *persuasive* and the *insistent* approaches.

Both aim to secure compliance but the persuasive approach is more accommodating. Officials educate, coax, and cajole offenders into complying with the law, they explain rationales for laws and possible means of compliance, and do so in a patient, open-ended way.[8] The insistent strategy is less flexible and there are defined limits to the tolerance of officials who will increase pressures when compliance is not forthcoming within a limit period. Cultural differences may also be seen as producing differences in enforcement styles. It has been said that the American system of enforcement tends to be more adversarial, litigious, and deterrence-based than the more compliance-oriented British approach[9] but caution should be exercised in viewing national approaches as homogeneous—variations of styles may be encountered even within single agencies (on which, more below).[10]

On the relative effectiveness and desirability of compliance and deterrence approaches to enforcement, there are a number of conflicting

---

[4] See Hawkins, *Environment and Enforcement*; Hutter, *Compliance*; G. Richardson, A. Ogus, and P. Burrows, *Policing Pollution* (Oxford, 1988); W. G. Carson, 'Some Sociological Aspects of Strict Liability and the Enforcement of Factory Legislation' (1970) 33 *MLR* 396; R. Cranston, *Regulating Business* (London, 1979); A. Reiss, 'Selecting Strategies of Social Control over Organisational Life', in K. Hawkins and J. Thomas (eds.), *Enforcing Regulation* (Boston, 1984).

[5] See Reiss loc. cit. n. 4 above. Richardson et al., *Policing Pollution*, use the term 'accommodative' for this style.

[6] Hawkins uses the term 'sanctioning' for this approach.

[7] See Hutter, *Compliance*, 15.

[8] This strategy is said to approximate to Braithwaite, Walker, and Grabosky's notion of the Diagnostic Inspectorate in their article 'An Enforcement Taxonomy of Regulatory Agencies' (1987) 9 *Law and Policy* 321.

[9] See e.g. D. Vogel, *National Styles of Regulation* (Ithaca, NY, 1988) and for a USA/ Sweden comparison see S. Kelman, *Regulating America, Regulating Sweden* (Cambridge, Mass., 1981).

[10] On variations within the Health and Safety Executive's inspectorates see R. Baldwin, *Rules and Government* (Oxford, 1995), 143 and C. D. Drake and F. B. Wright, *Law of Health and Safety* (London, 1983), 24.

arguments.[11] Proponents of deterrence tend to argue that compliance approaches are indicative of capture, lack of enforcement resources, and of regulator and regulatee having sufficient identification with each other (through shared experience, contacts, staff exchanges, or familiarity) as to make routine prosecution unthinkable.[12] Deterrence approaches and strict enforcement, in contrast, are said often to prove highly effective in changing corporate cultures so as to produce improved standards of behaviour, and management systems that reduce the risks of infringement.[13] Deterrence approaches treat infractions seriously by stamping errant conduct as unacceptable—they accordingly reinforce and give effect to social sentiments of disapproval and this enhances social pressures to comply. Such approaches, it is urged moreover, can induce political shifts so that firmer approaches to regulation can be taken.[14] Tough approaches to enforcement make it rational for firms to give a high priority to compliance.

In defence of compliance approaches it may be argued that they involve an efficient, cost-conscious use of resources and can be justified as economically rational rather than indicative of capture.[15] Prosecutions are so costly in time and money that selective use of less formal mechanisms may produce higher levels of compliance for a given level of state expenditure than is possible with routine prosecution.[16] Legalistic enforcement, it can also be said, can often prove inflexible; it may fail to identify the best ways to improve performance; it may cause resentment, hostility, and lack of cooperation in those regulated and this, in turn, may reduce the effectiveness of enforcement as well as increase overall costs.[17]

A further criticism of strict enforcement is that it may produce undesired side-effects (e.g. driving certain firms out of business and causing unemployment) and these consequences may alienate the public—again reducing regulatory effectiveness. Compliance strategies, on the other hand, can provide responses to risks (as opposed to harms actually inflicted) and can do so more effectively than deterrence approaches. They can thus

---

[11] For a head-to-head confrontation see the exchange between F. Pearce and S. Tombs, 'Ideology, Hegemony and Empiricism' (1990) 30 *BJ Crim*. 424 and K. Hawkins, 'Compliance Strategy, Prosecution Policy and Aunt Sally' (1990) 30 *BJ Crim*. 144 and 'Enforcing Regulation: More of the Same from Pearce and Tombs' (1991) 31 *BJ Crim*. 427. See also Ayres and Braithwaite, *Responsive Regulation*, 20–35.

[12] See R. Brown, 'Theory and Practice of Regulatory Enforcement: Occupational Health and Safety Regulation in British Columbia' (1994) 16 (1) *Law and Policy* 63.

[13] See E. Bardach and R. Kagan, *Going by the Book* (Philadelphia, 1982), 93–5.

[14] See Pearce and Tombs loc. cit. n. 11 above, p. 434.

[15] See Fenn and Veljanovski, loc. cit. n. 2 above; C. G. Veljanovski, 'Regulatory Enforcement: An Economic Study of the British Factory Inspectorate' (1983) 5 *Law & Policy Quarterly* 75; Hawkins, *Environment and Enforcement*, 198–202.

[16] See Baldwin, *Rules and Government*, ch. 6.

[17] See P. Kagan and J. Scholz, 'The Criminology of the Corporation and Regulatory Enforcement Strategies', in Hawkins and Thomas, *Enforcing Regulation*.

prevent more harms from occurring.[18] They are consistent with making exceptions where there is a case for them—rather than imposing uniform requirements where this makes no sense.[19]

Instead of drawing a stark contrast between compliance and deterrence approaches to enforcement it is possible, however, to see enforcement as involving a progression through different compliance-seeking strategies and sanctions. Ian Ayres and John Braithwaite comment: 'To reject punitive regulation is naive; to be totally committed to it is to lead a charge of the light brigade. The trick of successful regulation is to establish a synergy between punishment and persuasion.'[20]

These two authors introduce the concept of enforcement pyramids. One of these pyramids involves a hierarchy of sanctions, the second, a hierarchy of regulatory strategies. In this model of 'responsive regulation' those regulated are subjected to increasingly interventionist regulatory responses as they continue to infringe and to less interventionist actions as they come to comply. At the base of the enforcement pyramids are the least intrusive interventions and at the pinnacle the most intrusive. The first response regulatory action is that at the base of the pyramid and, accordingly, most regulation tends to take place in the realm of persuasion and self-regulation. Applying this model, Hutter has portrayed the two pyramids encountered in the three British inspectorates she studied in the way shown in Figure 1.[21]

To portray enforcement in the above manner is not, however, to deny that different bodies of enforcers possess their own particular styles.[22] Accounting for variations in regulatory styles, either in general or in particular instances, is, indeed, a discrete line of enquiry itself. Thus, Kagan[23] explains variations in regulatory enforcement styles with reference to four factors: legal design; social and economic environment; political environment; and internal leadership. Hawkins has suggested that prosecutions are most likely to be pursued when infringements are flagrant, repeated, or extreme in their culpability or consequences[24] and

[18] See e.g. R. Brown and M. Rankin, 'Persuasion, Penalties and Prosecution', in M. L. Friedland (ed.), *Securing Compliance* (Toronto, 1990).

[19] See Bardach and Kagan, *Going by the Book*, 58.

[20] Ayres and Braithwaite, *Responsive Regulation*, 25, see also J. Braithwaite, *To Punish or Persuade* (Albany, NY, 1985).

[21] Hutter, *Compliance*, 227, 229. The three inspectorates studied were the Factory Inspectorate, Industrial Air Pollution Inspectorate, and Railway Inspectorate. The sanctions pyramid set out by Ayres and Braithwaite (*Responsive Regulation*, 35) escalates through the layers: persuasion; warning letter; civil penalty; criminal penalty; licence suspension; licence revocation. The pyramid of enforcement strategies (ibid. 39) escalates: self-regulation; enforced self-regulation; command regulation with discretionary punishment; command regulation with non-discretionary punishment.

[22] See Hutter, *Compliance*, 231; Baldwin, *Rules and Government*, 143–4.

[23] R. Kagan, 'Regulatory Enforcement', in D. H. Rosenbloom and R. D. Schwartz (eds.), *Handbook of Regulation and Administrative Law* (New York, 1994); Hutter, *Compliance*, ch. 9.

[24] See Hawkins, *Environment and Enforcement* and Hutter, *Reasonable Arm of the Law?*

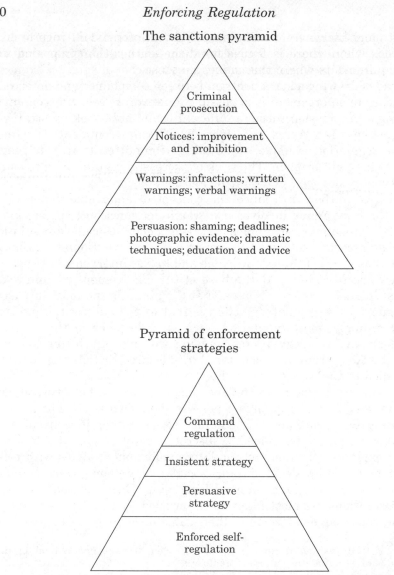

The sanctions pyramid

Criminal
prosecution

Notices: improvement
and prohibition

Warnings: infractions; written
warnings; verbal warnings

Persuasion: shaming; deadlines;
photographic evidence; dramatic
techniques; education and advice

Pyramid of enforcement
strategies

Command
regulation

Insistent strategy

Persuasive
strategy

Enforced self-
regulation

FIG. 1. *The sanctions pyramid and the pyramid of enforcement strategies*

Hutter[25] has pointed to the following conditions as conducive to informal
and accommodative styles: a high degree of social consensus on the value
of compliance; a generally high level of compliance and low incidence of
serious breaches; an ability to bluff in negotiations on compliance (where

---

[25] Hutter, *Reasonable Arm of the Law?*, 149–53; see also N. Shover et al., *Constructing a Regulatory Bureaucracy* (Albany, NY, 1982); Kelman, *Regulating America*, 111.

there is a high incidence of well-disposed but ill-informed infringers); high resource levels; low costs of inspection; the absence of strong media or political calls for hard-line prosecution; a high level of integration of enforcing officials into the relevant community; and close personal or social relationships between enforcers and potential compliers.

2. Rules and Enforcement

Enforcement may be affected by the kinds of regulatory rules involved and not all kinds of rule can be enforced with the same degree of success.[26] Rules may fail for a number of reasons, for example, because they are too vague or too long and complex to understand readily or to enforce; or because they prohibit desirable behaviour or they do not cover certain undesirable conduct. Different regulatory contexts, furthermore, may demand rules with different qualities or dimensions.

Rules may vary according, *inter alia*, to: degree of specificity or precision; extent, coverage, or inclusiveness; accessibility and intelligibility, legal status and force; and the prescriptions or sanctions they incorporate.[27] Rules, moreover, have to be employed by enforcers in conjunction with different compliance-seeking strategies—be these prosecutions, administrative sanctions, or processes of persuasion, negotiation, advice, education, or promotion.

Different enforcement strategies may thus call for different kinds of rule. If prosecutions are the main mode of enforcement this may call for precise rules so that guilt or innocence can be established easily (as a result, these rules may be long and complex). If broad promotion of good practice is to be used (e.g. in leaflets or guidance) then less precise but more accessible rules may be more effective.

As to the selection of enforcement strategies (and, accordingly, accompanying rule types) this, it has been argued, requires an analysis of the kinds of regulatee being dealt with.[28] If the regulatee is well intentioned (i.e. wishes to comply) and is ill-informed (about legal requirements or how to meet these), prosecution may be a lower priority than educating and promoting—since information rather than a big stick is required. Accessible rules will, accordingly, be useful. The well-intentioned, well-informed regulatee will be able to cope with more detailed rules. The

---

[26] See generally, Baldwin, *Rules and Government*; id., 'Why Rules Don't Work' (1990) 53 *MLR* 321; J. Black, *Rules and Regulators* (Oxford, 1997); id., 'Using Rules Effectively', in C. McCrudden (ed.), *Regulation and Deregulation* (Oxford, 1999); C. Hood, *Administrative Analysis: An Introduction to Rules, Enforcement and Organisations* (Brighton, 1986); C. S. Diver, 'The Optimal Precision of Administrative Rules' (1983) 93 *Yale LJ* 65.

[27] For other approaches to the dimensions of rules see Black, *Rules and Regulators*, 21 and Diver loc. cit. n. 26 above.

[28] See Baldwin, *Rules and Government*, ch. 6; Ayres and Braithwaite, *Responsive Regulation*, ch. 2.

ill-intentioned, ill-informed category may demand a higher level of prosecution and, accordingly, precise rules will be in order. Finally, the ill-intentioned, well-informed regulatee will demand strategies, rules, and sanctions that can cope with deliberate rule avoidance and mixtures of general and specific rules may be appropriate.[29]

Effective enforcement thus calls for judgements to be made concerning blends of enforcement strategies and the rule types that will best produce compliance. This suggests that informers and rule-makers should ask the following questions:[30]

- What is the undesirable behaviour, or mischief at issue?
- Who is responsible for the mischief?
- Which enforcement strategies will best lead the mischief creators to comply?
- Which types of rules best complement those strategies?

Such an approach presupposes that types of regulatee can be identified in the various sectors regulated. This will allow strategies and rules to be designed accordingly. If this is not possible or sectors have numbers of different kinds of regulatee, it may be necessary for agencies to equip their enforcers with an array of rules and strategies to cope with all eventualities. This is very costly in rule-making resources. It can similarly be cautioned that pyramidic approaches to enforcement involve progressing through various strategies in a serial fashion and this may also make large demands on rule-making resources since those different strategies should ideally be matched with different types of rule. When types of regulatee can be identified, a specific and a targeted, rather than a pyramidic, enforcement strategy may constitute a more effective use of resources.[31]

Creative Compliance

Even if compliance with rules is achieved by enforcers this is not the end of the story. Enforcement may fail for two main further reasons. The first of these is what has been termed 'creative compliance'.[32] This

[29] See the discussion of creative compliance below.

[30] See Baldwin, *Rules and Government*, ch. 6, 'Why Rules Don't Work' loc. cit. n. 26 above, and 'Governing with Rules', in G. Richardson and H. Genn (eds.), *Administrative Law and Government Action* (Oxford, 1994) for a discussion of these questions and reasons why rule-makers may fail to adopt such an approach to rule-making. (They tend to assume enforcement is unproblematic and do not seek information on enforcement; they tend to underestimate the political problems involved in making rules; and they are subject to disruptive political pressures from within and beyond the organization.)

[31] See Baldwin, *Rules and Government*, 158 n. 25 and Ayres and Braithwaite, *Responsive Regulation*, ch. 2.

[32] See D. McBarnet and C. Whelan, 'The Elusive Spirit of the Law: Formalism and the Struggle for Legal Control' (1991) 54 *MLR* 848; id., 'Challenging the Regulators: Strategies for Resisting Control', in McCrudden (ed.), *Regulation and Deregulation*; D. McBarnet, 'Law, Policy and Legal Avoidance' (1988) *J. L. Soc.* 113.

is the process whereby those regulated avoid having to break the rules and do so by circumventing the scope of a rule while still breaching the spirit of the rule. Let us suppose that, in order to protect small shops, a government legislates to prohibit shops with over 10,000 square metres of floor space from opening on Sunday afternoons. A retail firm might creatively comply with such a rule by dividing its 12,000 square metre operation into two linked operations of 6,000 square metres. It complies with the law but avoids the thrust of the legislation.

In some fields (e.g. taxation) whole industries are devoted to creative compliance and the challenge for regulatory rule-makers and enforcers is to devise ways to keep the problem under control. This may be difficult for a number of reasons. As McBarnet and Whelan note, regulated industries may apply political pressure to regulators and demand detailed rules so that the rule of law and principles of certainty are served but such types of rules may in reality be the very formulations that are most easily side-stepped by creative compliers. One response, as noted, is to reinforce detailed rules with open-textured and general rules that are more difficult to circumvent.[33]

Inclusiveness

A second reason why enforcement that successfully produces compliance may still fail is that ill-formulated rules may prove over- or under-inclusive.[34] They may discourage desirable behaviour or fail to prevent undesirable behaviour. Bardach and Kagan[35] suggest that regulators tend to over-regulate with over-inclusive rules for a number of reasons. Amongst these are, first, the costs of gaining the information necessary for targeting rules perfectly. These costs can be very high and rule-makers tend to solve the problem by writing over-inclusive rules and relying on selective enforcement. (This conveniently shifts costs from rule-makers to enforcers.) Second, rule-makers tend to opt for broad-brush solutions to problems. Third, pressure to avoid regulatory discretions and produce equal treatment under law tends to trade off efficiency for more rules. Finally, working on a problem while the political iron is hot tends to be necessary for rule-makers and the resultant tight deadlines rule out the precise targeting of rules.

Under-inclusiveness, on the other hand, may also result from informational problems. Thus, a rule may fail to come to grips with certain

---

[33] See, for example, the general duties for employers set out in sections 2–9 of the Health and Safety at Work Act 1984 which may catch employers who creatively comply around more precisely formulated regulations on workplace health and safety.
[34] See Black, *Rules and Regulators*, 7–10.
[35] Bardach and Kagan, *Going by the Book*, 66–77.

hazards because the regulator has not been able to develop the information necessary to identify the cause of the hazard.

Rules, moreover, that deal with problems of inclusiveness, or coverage, may give rise to other problems. Colin Diver explains this well by supposing the need for a rule to stop airline pilots from flying when the social cost of allowing them to continue flying exceeds the social benefits of not having to replace them.[36] He suggests three formulations for such a rule.

Model I   No person may pilot a commercial aircraft after their sixtieth birthday.

Model II   No person may pilot a commercial aircraft if they pose an unreasonable risk of an accident.

Model III   No person may pilot a commercial aircraft if they fall within one of the following categories. (There follow tables giving combinations of values for numerous variables including years, levels of experience, age, height, weight, blood pressure, heart-rate, eyesight, and a host of other medical factors affecting pilot performance.)

Model I is the most transparent and accessible rule. It is easily understood and easy to enforce but gives rise to problems of inclusivity. Some pilots aged over 60 may present lower risks to passengers than some (unhealthy) pilots aged under 60. Model II offers a response to inclusivity (it states the rule's purpose) but, though accessible on its face, is vague, lacks clarity, and, for this reason, is difficult to enforce because it needs to be fleshed out and made precise. Model III scores well on inclusivity and it precisely identifies hazard-causing factors (provided that it is constantly revised and supported by research on health risks). It is likely, however, to be very lengthy, technically complex, and difficult to apply without expert training or the hiring of specialized consultants. It will also be extremely expensive for rule-makers to write and gain necessary agreement on an exhaustive list of hazard-creating medical conditions. Model III is also likely to give rise to greater problems of creative compliance than Models I and II.[37]

Problems of over- and under-inclusiveness can also be approached by considering when it is better, in the face of uncertainty, to err on the side of over- or under-inclusiveness in regulating. Shrader-Frechette examines this issue in asking whether it is better to err by prohibiting the use of a technology that is falsely seen as dangerous but is really acceptable

---

[36] See Diver loc. cit. n. 26 above.

[37] Thus a pilot suffering from a medical condition on the prohibited list might take a drug to remove that condition but the drug might create another dangerous—but unlisted—condition.

and safe (a 'Type I' error) or by allowing the use of a technology that is falsely seen as safe but which is really unsafe (a 'Type II' error).[38]

Type I errors are sometimes referred to as 'producer risks'[39] and Type II as 'consumer risks'. In practice, Shrader-Frechette contends, risk assessors tend to err on the side of avoiding Type I errors for a number of reasons: because pure science researchers prefer to suppose that no connection exists than to posit an effect (e.g. that a substance causes cancer);[40] because producers are seen as enjoying something analogous to a 'presumption of innocence' that places the burden on those asserting a harmful effect; and because many risk assessments are conducted by persons closely associated with, and sympathetic to, the product or technology at issue.[41]

Shrader-Frechette's argument, however, is that it is better, when uncertain, to err on the side of avoiding Type II errors—better to protect consumers rather than defend the producer's rights to sell products— because the burden of proof regarding risk acceptability should be placed on the person wishing to reduce producer rather than consumer risks.[42] She puts forward a number of reasons for this suggested approach:

- It is more important to protect from harm than to enhance welfare.
- Producers reap most of the benefits of a new technology, they should accordingly bear most of the risks and costs.
- Consumers merit greater protection than industry since they have less information and fewer resources with which to deal with hazards.

[38] See K. S. Shrader-Frechette, *Risk and Rationality* (Berkeley, Calif., 1991). Such issues arise in making decisions on whether to regulate an area at all as well as when deciding whether to draft an anticipated rule to cover a particular activity.

[39] Ibid. 132.

[40] See C. F. Cranor, *Regulating Toxic Substances* (New York, 1993), ch. 4. It has been argued elsewhere that less rigorous standards of proof are typically required to prevent the possibility of a Type II error than a Type I error—see G. Brennan, 'Civil Disaster Management: An Economist's View' (1991) 64 *Canberra Bulletin of Pub. Admin.* 30–3. Stephen Tindale argues that the precautionary principle ('giving the environment the benefit of any reasonable doubt') has been seen in operation in some areas (e.g. new medicines or substances liable to enter the human food chain such as drinking water or meat containing growth hormones) but the Panglossian principle (optimism in the face of worrying evidence and the placing of the burden on those seeking to demonstrate that a risk arises) has also been encountered, notably in the environmental area (e.g. global warming, dog faeces, leukemia clusters around Sellafield, pesticides, and lead pollution). The prevalence of the Panglossian approach, Tindale says, leads to the undermining of respect for politics and those in authority—see S. Tindale, 'Procrastination and the Global Gamble', in Franklin (ed.), *Politics of Risk Society* and also A. Jordan and T. O' Riordan, 'The Precautionary Principle in UK Environmental Law and Policy', in T. Gray (ed.), *UK Environmental Policy in the 1990s* (Basingstoke, 1995).

[41] Beck argues that in 'risk society' in general, technological advances create new risks far more rapidly than conventional democratic mechanisms can devise responses—this would imply a tendency to under-regulate and to regulate in an under-inclusive manner (see U. Beck, 'The Politics of Risk Society', in Franklin (ed.), *Politics of Risk Society*).

[42] Beck also argues that the burden of proof should rest on risk creators to prove safety— ibid. 21.

- Lay persons should be accorded legal rights to bodily security—to minimize industry risk on efficiency grounds offends notions of such security and would be morally offensive.
- Producers may not always be able to compensate persons harmed by their products; it is better, accordingly, to err on the side of eliminating harms at source.
- If there is uncertainty about the level of harms it is difficult to justify imposing a risk on consumers.
- On democratic grounds there ought to be no imposition of risks without the informed consent of those who are to bear the risks.
- If consumers have not given informed consent, industry ought to bear the burden of proving that imposing a consumer risk is justified.
- Minimizing consumer risk is less likely to threaten social and political stability than minimizing producer risk.

Contrary to the above approach it can be contended that even if one accepts the value of consumer protection, there are a number of reasons why one might on occasions want to favour producer rather than consumer protection and accordingly err on the under-inclusive side when imposing restrictions on industry. First, if one accepts that rule-makers tend to write over-inclusive rules for a number of reasons (as discussed above) there may be a case for countering this tendency by consciously erring towards under-inclusiveness in particular cases of uncertainty.[43] Second, one might put a value on economic liberty as a good in itself or favour under-inclusiveness where compliance costs are liable to be extremely high and the benefits of a rule are low (a regulation might be proposed in such circumstances for reasons of social justice rather than on efficiency grounds). Third, if the rule at issue exerts control at the stage of preventing a dangerous action occurring (e.g. by licensing an activity) rather than at the stage where the dangerous action has occurred or the harm has been caused,[44] there may be a case for erring on the side of under-inclusion if the costs of prevention are liable to be very high and if any problems of under-inclusiveness can be countered by controls at the act or harm stage.

To summarize, rule-making does affect both the way that enforcement is carried out and the effectiveness of enforcement activity. It can be seen also that rule-making involves complex trade-offs between, amongst other things, attempts to solve problems of inclusivity; efforts to contain creative compliers; and endeavours to produce rules that can be enforced effectively in the field.[45]

---

[43] See Brennan, loc. cit. n. 40 above, p. 33.

[44] On stages of intervention see the following section of this chapter.

[45] On trading-off problems of inclusiveness against other factors such as costs of enforcement see Diver loc. cit. n. 26 above, 74–8 and Baldwin, *Rules and Government*, 180–5.

3. *When to Intervene*

Regulators can intervene in economic or social activity not merely by different methods but at different stages in the processes that lead to harms. Thus, action can be taken to *prevent* a dangerous act or situation arising (e.g. hotels can be inspected and licensed before opening to guests in order to ensure that fire hazards do not arise); action can be taken in response to the *act* of creating a dangerous situation (e.g. operating a hotel without fire doors or sprinklers); or action can be prompted by the realization of a *harm* (e.g. injuring a hotel guest in a hotel fire). Similarly, the kinds of standards incorporated in regulatory rules may be directed towards different stages of the processes leading to harms. Thus, applying *specification* (or *design*) standards (e.g. demanding a certain type of machine be used for a procedure) has the effect of controlling the circumstances leading to dangerous acts (which will not occur if a safe design of machine is used). Applying *performance* (or *output*) standards looks to the seriousness of the dangerous acts that are involved in a procedure and *target* standards focus on the harms that result (e.g. the amount of pollution damage to the river).[46]

Shavell has distinguished three stages of intervention, in which actions are respectively preventive, act-based, and harm-based, and has considered the circumstances that favour particular stages of regulatory intervention.[47]

Preventive Actions

One circumstance in which preventive action is called for is where the costs of rectifying a dangerous state of affairs may be high. It may thus be better to prevent a dangerous design of steel foundry from being built than to try and change matters post-construction. Another reason for acting preventively is that a potentially catastrophic danger may otherwise arise. For both of these reasons, nuclear reactor designs are approved and licensed before the reactor is built. To allow a reactor to be constructed and then to demand changes to improve safety would be hugely expensive and to intervene only when a reactor was being run dangerously would be to run an unacceptably high risk of a catastrophe occurring. Conversely, where the potential harm is relatively small, there may be a stronger case for intervening at the harm stage since failures to deter through punishing harm-causers will not prove catastrophic.

A further reason for preventive action is that in some circumstances, preventive steps can be successfully employed without the use of a heavy

---

[46] For further discussion of standard setting see below, Chapter 9.
[47] See S. Shavell, 'The Optimal Structure of Law Enforcement' (1993) *J. Law and Econ.* 255.

regulatory hand. Thus, a television advertisement on public safety (for example on dipping car headlights properly when night driving) may prevent a large number of dangerous acts and serious harms from arising but it neither interferes greatly with drivers nor involves strong sanctions or expensive enforcement activity. By comparison, intervening at the act stage—by stopping drivers and bringing legal proceedings for failing to use lights properly—involves a good deal of driver inconvenience and state enforcement expense. It may also fail to prevent a large number of harms from ensuing. Waiting until the harms occur (the injuries and deaths) will demand expensive prosecutions and severe sanctions and such actions may (for reasons discussed below) also fail efficiently to prevent future harms from occurring.

The potential of preventive strategies is often restricted by informational difficulties. It may not be easy to predict when certain dangerous situations or harms may occur. To prevent dangerous driving manœuvres would thus be difficult and costly. Even if all drivers had an inspector sitting in their vehicle it would be difficult for the inspector to anticipate when a dangerous turn or stop was about to happen.[48] It may accordingly be more efficient to exert control at the act or harm stage by imposing sanctions for the act of dangerous driving or for causing an accident. It may, similarly, be difficult for regulators to anticipate all potential sources of harm (e.g. of damaging levels of noise in industrial processes). Preventing dangerous activity in such circumstances may, accordingly, make very severe informational demands and prove very expensive. In terms of administrative costs it will often be cheapest of all for the state to wait until the stage when harms have been caused since only a small proportion of dangerous acts will result in actual harms and so a smaller enforcement case load will be involved.

Act-based Interventions

Intervening at the act stage may be more useful than at the preventive stage when prevention would be expensive to accomplish. Thus it might be costly and intrusive to demand prior approval for all operations on a construction site. Resources are more effectively deployed in inspecting such sites and sanctioning dangerous actions—for example using insecure scaffolding.

Act-stage intervention may be preferable to harm-stage control where it is difficult to hold firms or individuals to account for causing harms. This may well be the case where a harm may arise from a number of concurrent sources. Thus, if it is known that ingesting certain particles

---

[48] See Shavell loc. cit. n. 47 above, p. 272. The licensing and testing of drivers does, however, constitute prevention at the most general level.

may cause cancer but it is also known that the disease can be caused by a number of other common hazards (e.g. smoking), it may be preferable to regulate, say, the act of causing workers to ingest the particles than to look at the harm and attempt to establish that a particular cancer has been caused by the particles rather than some other agent.

Where the dangerous act can be identified far more easily than the resultant harm, there is, again, a case for act-based intervention. The harms caused by some acts may be cumulatively very serious but highly diffused (e.g. in the pollution field) and it will be more effective to enforce at the act level then to deal with huge numbers of individually small claims.

Intervening at the act stage may also be preferable to harm-based sanctioning where the latter will under-deter the causing of further harms. Act-based sanctions can be smaller and more frequently applied than harm-based ones because no injury has yet occurred and the instances of infraction are greater in number (since not all dangerous acts lead to harms). In order to obtain the same levels of deterrence from harm-based sanctions the fines involved may have to be extremely high given that a hazard creator may estimate the chance of actually producing a harm as extremely small and of being fined as even smaller. If the firms causing harms are unlikely to be able to pay such fines they will be under-deterred. In some sectors there will be a correlation between poor resourcing and the causing of harms and, accordingly, there will tend to be particular problems of under-deterrence through harm-based intervention. Where potential harms may vastly exceed the resources of the causers of harm (e.g. where ill-resourced firms may injure or kill large numbers of persons) there is liable to be under-deterrence and unacceptably low incentives to take appropriate care.

Harm-based Interventions

Enforcement costs may sometimes militate in favour of intervening at the stage of harm rather than of dangerous act. It may be cheaper for the state to punish the causers of the relatively small number of instances of harm than to pursue the much larger number of persons who perform dangerous acts that are liable to cause harms in some instances. It follows from what has been said above that a policy of severely sanctioning harms will only deter adequately if detection is sufficiently effective and if potential offenders are likely to be able to pay the large fines involved (or serve the prison terms).

It cannot, however, be assumed that in all cases it is easier to apply sanctions to harms than to acts. If a construction firm erects cheap but unsafe scaffolding and makes it difficult for a regulator to detect harms —for example by rewarding injury-free teams of workers with bonuses and thereby generating peer group pressures on workers not to report injuries—it may be easier for a regulator to sanction the (highly visible) act of using dangerous scaffolding than to punish the firm for occasioning harm to the worker.

4. How Much to Enforce

It is not sensible for regulators to aim for perfect compliance or the complete elimination of a hazard. This is because enforcement costs tend to rise alongside increases in levels of compliance and a point will arrive where the costs of further enforcement are not justified by the gains. Breyer refers to this as the problem of the last 10 per cent[49] and quotes Sheldon Meyers: 'it frequently is relatively cheap to reduce risks from 0 to 99 per cent, more expensive to go from 90 per cent to 99 per cent and more expensive to go from 99 per cent to 99.9 per cent'.[50]

In economic terms the socially optimal level of enforcement occurs at the point where the extra costs of enforcement exceed the resulting additional benefits to society.[51] Included within the costs of enforcement are the following:

- the costs of agency monitoring;
- the expenses of processing and prosecuting cases;
- the defence costs (of innocent and guilty parties);
- the costs of misapplications of law, convicting the innocent, and deterring desirable behaviour.

The gains from enforcement lie principally in reductions of harmful behaviour—be this from preventing the particular offender from causing harm or from deterring others. A further gain, however, flows from reductions in private enforcement costs. Thus, when public enforcement agencies forestall a harm, this saves private individuals or firms from having to spend money on protecting their entitlements.

In calculating the deterrent effects of enforcement activity the economic approach assumes *inter alia* that potential offenders are actors who seek to maximize their own welfare in an informed, rational manner. For each potential offender deterrence flows from the expected punishment, which is the probability of punishment times the magnitude of the punishment (e.g. the quantum of the fine).

---

[49] S. Breyer, *Breaking the Vicious Circle* (Cambridge, Mass., 1993), 10–13.

[50] S. Meyers, 'Applications of *De Minimis*', in C. Whipple (ed.), *De Minimis Risk* (1987), 102.

[51] See generally, G. Becker, 'Crime and Punishment: An Economic Approach' (1968) 76 *J. Pol. Econ.* 161; I. Ehrlich, 'The Economic Approach to Crime—a Preliminary Assessment', in S. Messinger and E. Bittner, *Criminology Yearbook* (London, 1979); Ogus, *Regulation*, 90–4; Shavell loc. cit. n. 47 above; G. J. Stigler, 'The Optimum Enforcement of Laws' (1970) 78 *J. Pol. Econ.* 526; T. Gibbons, 'The Utility of Economic Analysis of Crime' (1982) 2 *Int. Rev. Law and Econ.* 173.

From the regulator's point of view, a key calculation is how much the group of potential offenders will be deterred by the regulator's current or prospective approach to enforcement.[52] Factors to be taken on board include not merely the level of fines or other sanctions liable to be applied and the probability of inflicting these on offenders, but also the private benefit likely to be derived from offending and the social cost of the offence. The overall wealth of the offender has also to be considered. If an offending firm cannot pay a large fine (because, say, this would drive the enterprise into insolvency and cause unemployment) a combination of small fines and high probability of application would be more appropriate than using large penalties infrequently. Similarly, if severe sanctions are unlikely to be applied for reasons of social justice (the courts may consider the offence minor) a high probability of application will have to be used especially if the gains from offending are high.

Where, on the other hand, enforcement resources are limited and the probability of bringing sanctions to bear is, as a result, low, it may be rational for the regulator to press the appropriate authorities for penalties great enough to compensate for this improbability.[53] In response to arguments that fairness imposes limitations on the quantum of a punishment for a given offence, the regulator may reply that what matters in real life is the *expected* punishment—that if governments want low-resource regulation they have to be prepared to impose high penalties.

To balance such talk of economic rationality it should, first, be noted that policy and equitable considerations may often govern enforcement decisions. Thus, as a matter of policy, society may want to deter certain activities very strongly and not rely on an efficiency-based balancing of expected gains and penalties. Secondly, the assumptions of economically rational man may be questioned. In the real world most harms are not the result of rational calculations concerning costs and benefits—they are the products *inter alia* of human failings, poor information and training, tiredness, short cuts, and accidents.[54] In so far as the model of rational man fails accurately to describe those persons or firms that are regulated the regulator may feel (and be) justified in placing less emphasis on deterrence and more on active inspection and intervention in the regulated activity.

[52] On the imperfections of the expected cost approach to deterrence see T. Makkai and J. Braithwaite, 'The Limits of the Economic Analysis of Regulation: An Empirical Case and a Case for Empiricism' (1993) 15 (4) *Law and Policy* 271.

[53] In September 1997 the Chief Executive of the Environment Agency made a strong public attack on the current level of fines for environmental offences. During the same month, Michael Meacher, the Environment Minister, announced that the Government was drawing up plans for large increases in fines for persistent corporate polluters; *Financial Times*, 17 Sept. 1997.

[54] Makkai and Braithwaite, loc. cit. n. 52 above.

5. Controlling Corporations

Enforcement officials face a series of difficulties in seeking to control errant firms. Key issues concern the sanctions that can be used to influence such firms; the extent of corporate criminal fault; and the difficulties of proving liability.[55]

Sanctions

Regulators can resort to administrative or criminal sanctions in dealing with corporations. Administrative measures operate without recourse to the courts and can be provided for either in statutes or in contracts (e.g. within the terms of franchises). Examples of statutory administrative sanctions include improvement and prohibition notices which respectively require remedial actions to be taken within a fixed period or which order the discontinuance of a hazardous activity (e.g. the stopping of a dangerous production line).[56] Contractually based measures may include licence revocations, curtailments, or suspensions.

Fines. Criminal sanctions normally involve fines since imprisoning firms is not feasible—though directors may be found criminally liable as individuals, for example, where their personal gross negligence has resulted in a death.[57] To impose fines on firms that, say, pollute waterways or impose health risks on employees, can, however, give rise to difficulties. The firm may engage in activities liable to cause harms that have a value that exceeds any fine they are able to pay. Any potential fine will accordingly under-deter.[58] Firms, moreover, may treat fines as a normal business expense and may be able to pass the cost of fines through to

---

[55] On criminalizing corporations see generally: C. Wells, *Corporations and Criminal Responsibility* (Oxford, 1993); L. H. Leigh, *The Criminal Liability of Corporations in English Law* (London, 1969); id., 'The Criminal Liability of Corporations and other Groups: A Comparative View' (1982) 80 *Mich. LR*; J. C. Coffee, 'No Soul to Damn, No body to Kick' (1981) 79 *Mich. LR* 386; C. Clarkson, 'Kicking Corporate Bodies and Damning their Souls' (1996) 59 *MLR* 557; B. Fisse and J. Braithwaite, 'The Allocation of Responsibility for Corporate Crime' (1988) 11 *Sydney LR* 468; C. Stone, 'The Place of Enterprise Liability in the Control of Corporate Conduct' (1980) 90 *Yale LJ* 1; R. A. Kagan and J. T. Scholz, 'The Criminology of the Corporation and Regulatory Enforcement Strategies', in Hawkins and Thomas, *Enforcing Regulation*; T. Kaye, 'Corporate Manslaughter: Who Pays the Ferryman?', in D. Feldman and F. Meisel (eds.), *Corporate Commercial Law: Modern Developments* (London, 1996).

[56] See Health and Safety at Work etc. Act 1984 ss. 21, 22.

[57] Following the Lyme Bay canoeing tragedy in which four teenagers were drowned, both the Managing Director of the company that owned the responsible outdoor activity centre and the company itself were found guilty of manslaughter; see Kite and Others, *The Independent*, 9 December 1994.

[58] See Coffee loc. cit. n. 55 above, pp. 389–93.

consumers or even employees.[59] Large fines may prejudice the firm's survival and insolvency may punish innocent parties such as employees or customers.

Fines remove ready cash from the company which might have been spent on measures to limit the harms at issue (e.g. on new filtration systems to reduce pollution). Fines that do come to bear on the corporation may, however, not deter or influence the actual decision-maker within the management structure,[60] and fines do not ensure that the problem at issue will be remedied or that the causes of failure within the corporation will be identified.

Alternative ways of sanctioning corporations have been suggested in an attempt to improve on the deficiencies or fines. Proposals include the following.

Equity Fines.[61] Under an equity fine system the convicted corporation is required to issue a given number of shares to the state's victim compensation fund. The shares would have a value equivalent to the cash fine necessary to deter the illegal activity. This strategy has the supposed advantages that it reduces the negative effect of corporate penalties on workers and consumers since the costs of deterrence are concentrated on the shareholders (whose shares lose value as a result of the mandated issue). These shareholders will accordingly have an incentive to discipline managers. The threat of insolvency and harm to employees and the community is removed. High penalties can be imposed because the market valuation of the typical corporation vastly exceeds the cash resources available to it (cash that would be the target of any fines imposed). Cash is not removed from the corporation and so spending on harm avoidance is not prejudiced. Managers' interests are aligned with those of the corporation in so far as stock options will lose value on a mandated issue. Mandated issues will produce managerial fears of takeovers and this will provide an incentive to good behaviour on the part of managers and, finally, shareholders will demand internal controls to reduce dangers of stock dilution through mandated issues. These controls will help avoid regulatory infringements.

Equity fines are thus superior to fines in a number of respects but they may not prove popular with governments that are opposed to state equity holdings and they share, with fines, the weakness that their deterrent value depends on the probability of apprehension and punishment.

---

[59] In response it can be argued that consumers should pay a price for goods that reflects the costs of production (which should include any social costs imposed e.g. by pollution); see B. Fisse, 'Sentencing Options against Corporations' (1990) *Criminal Law Forum* 211; C. Stone, 'Controlling Corporate Misconduct' (1977) *Public Interest* 55; Coffee loc. cit. n. 55 above.

[60] See Fisse and Braithwaite loc. cit. n. 55 above.

[61] See Coffee loc. cit. n. 55 above, pp. 413–15.

They, furthermore, make little contribution to the reform of the corporation's internal procedures and do not ensure that guilty managerial parties will be disciplined.[62]

Punitive Injunctions.[63] Courts could use punitive injunctions to require corporations to remedy their internal controls and to introduce (perhaps at punitive expense) preventive equipment or procedures.

Corporate Probation[64] *and Enforced Accountability.*[65] Judges might monitor the activities of a convicted organization and insist on reporting, record-keeping, and auditing mechanisms designed to remedy identified failings and to hold individuals to account. Corporations can be ordered to undertake enquiries, apply discipline, and report on steps taken and senior managers can be threatened with personal criminal liability if they fail to take such steps to the satisfaction of the court. As with punitive injunctions, particular errant managers or sections of management could be identified and their deficiencies addressed by this method.

Community Service and Compensation Orders. Courts might compel corporations to provide certain services for the community or to compensate individuals or groups in an attempt both to make good harms done and to signify the need for corporate rehabilitation.

Adverse Publicity. Orders can instruct corporations to place notices in the media informing the public of their failings and of remedial measures taken.

All such devices have their strengths, weaknesses, and areas of most useful application. It is perhaps appropriate, therefore, for regulators and courts to approach corporate failure with the full array of such sanctions within their contemplation and to apply them bearing in mind not merely the need to punish and rehabilitate corporations but also the interests of the public in compensation, where appropriate, and in more effective compliance.

The Extent of Corporate Fault and Proving Liability

For many years attributing criminal fault to corporations in Britain has been rendered difficult because the criminal law has developed with an eye to individual fault and it has been necessary to show that an individual managerial representative of the company has been blameworthy. The criminal law has sought to find an individual in the company who has carried out the prohibited act (*actus reus*) with the guilty mind (*mens rea*) that the relevant offence requires. This identification of an

---

[62] See Wells, *Corporations*, 35.

[63] See Fisse and Braithwaite loc. cit. n. 55 above, p. 500.

[64] See Coffee loc. cit. n. 55 above, pp. 448–57; Stone loc. cit. n. 59 above; Wells, *Corporations*, 36–7.

[65] See Fisse and Braithwaite loc. cit. n. 55 above.

individual who is sufficiently important in the corporation structure to represent the corporation's directing mind and will has been the under-pinning doctrine of the criminal law.[66] Its deficiencies were exposed following the P & O case of 1990[67] which arose from the deaths of 187 people in the capsize of the *Herald of Free Enterprise* after it set sail with open doors at Zeebrugge in 1987. Acquittals were directed in the case of the P & O company and its five most senior employees since it could not be proved that the risks of open-door sailings were obvious to any of the senior managers and accordingly no *mens rea* could be attributed to the company.[68]

Recently, however, a less restrictive view of corporate criminal liability has been taken in the courts. The Privy Council, in the *Meridian* case,[69] has rejected exclusive reliance on the identification test and indicated that acts and knowledge can be attributed to a company by courts considering whose acts, knowledge, or state of mind was *for the purpose* of a particular law to count as belonging to the company. Thus, instead of applying a simple identification test, the judges would, in such an approach, consider the language of a rule, its content and policy, and construe corporate liability accordingly. The functions actually performed by individuals in the company become relevant rather than their status in the company hierarchy—a mode of reasoning liable to lead to corporate responsibility for the acts of those at lower levels than would be the case under exclusive reliance on the identification principle.

The restrictiveness of the *Tesco* identification doctrine has also been circumvented by a different route—that of vicarious liability.[70] Thus in *National Rivers Authority* v. *Alfred McAlpine Homes East* [1994] CLR 760, two employees were responsible for allowing wet cement to pollute a controlled water, but, at trial, their employing company was acquitted of the statutory pollution offence under the identification doctrine of *Tesco* v. *Nattrass*. On appeal, however, the Divisional Court applied the doctrine of vicarious liability. The court looked at the purpose of the pollution legislation, bore in mind that the offence was one of strict liability (that is it did not require proof of a guilty mind, only that the

---

[66] See *Tesco Supermarkets Ltd* v. *Nattrass* [1972] AC 153; *HL Bolton (Engineering) Co. Ltd* v. *T. J. Graham and Sons Ltd* [1957] 1 QB 159. See generally N. Lacey and C. Wells, *Reconstructing Criminal Law* (2nd edn., Clandon, 1990), 512–23.

[67] *R* v. *Alcindor and Others* (Central Criminal Court, 19 Oct. 1990), *R* v. *P & O European Ferries (Dover) Ltd* (1980) 83 GAPP. R. 72.

[68] Clarkson loc. cit. n. 55 above, p. 561. Inquiries found companies to be seriously at fault, but no successful prosecutions for manslaughter were brought, following the 1987 King's Cross fire (in which 31 died); the 1988 Clapham rail crash (in which 35 died), and the 1988 Piper Alpha oil platform disaster (in which 167 died).

[69] *Meridian Global Funds Management Asia Ltd* v. *The Securities Commission* [1995] 3 WLR 413; also R. Grantham, 'Corporate Knowledge: Identification or Attribution?' (1996) 59 *MLR* 732.

[70] See Clarkson loc. cit. n. 55 above, pp. 563–6.

accused caused the prohibited action), and held that the nature of the offence demanded that vicarious liability be imposed on the company for the acts of employees (whether they represented the directing mind and will of the company or not). This approach has been followed in the Court of Appeal[71] and in cases where proof of negligence has been required[72] though the House of Lords has cautioned that (at least under the Merchant Shipping Act 1988) a company could not be held liable for each and every wrongful act committed by any employee.[73]

The problems left unsolved by the *Meridian* approach are, first, that it is not wholly clear when the action of a person who does not represent the directing mind and will of the company will be attributed to the company.[74] Second, it is still necessary to find some person within the company who perpetrated the criminal acts yet, in real life, regulatory failings may (as in the P & O case) stem from general managerial slackness and failures to allocate responsibilities rather than from the identifiable actions of particular individuals.

The Law Commission has suggested that there should be a new offence of 'corporate killing' in which criminal responsibility might be attributed to corporations where there is management failure that causes a death and the failure constitutes conduct falling far below what could reasonably be expected of the corporation in the circumstances.[75] Other commentators[76] have suggested that corporate liability might flow either, as now, through an individual's wrongdoing (by vicarious liability or identification) or through aggregation—where it would be asked whether, given the information held by a number of responsible officers, the company had the guilty mind required by the offence;[77] or through 'holistic liability' whereby liability might flow from an examination of the company's structure.

Regulatory enforcement officials, as can be seen, face not inconsiderable legal difficulties in attempting to hold corporations to account by means of the criminal law. (Whether holding to account through contractually based rules presents analogous difficulties will depend in

[71] See *R* v. *British Steel Plc* [1995] 586.

[72] *Tesco Stores Ltd* v. *Brent LBC* [1993] 2 All ER 718; *Re: Supply of Ready Mixed Concrete* (No. 2.) [1995] 1 All 135.

[73] *Seabound Offshore Ltd* v. *Secretary of State for Transport* [1994] 2 All ER 99.

[74] See Clarkson loc. cit. n. 55 above, p. 566.

[75] In relation to manslaughter—see Law. Com. No. 237, *Legislating the Criminal Code: Involuntary Manslaughter* (1996) paras 8.1–8.77 and Draft Involuntary Manslaughter Bill s. 4 (1). In October 1997 Home Secretary Jack Straw argued in favour of a 'corporate killing' offence at the Labour Party Conference. See also TUC, *Paying the Price for Deaths at Work* (London, 1994).

[76] Wells, *Corporations*, 144–5.

[77] The Law Commission (para. 7.33) did not favour the adoption of the aggregation principle. On treating companies on the same lines as individuals see Clarkson loc. cit. n. 55 above.

large part on the drafting of the particular contract.) A number of legal issues, as indicated, are yet to be resolved and so uncertainties remain. A final question is also left hanging: why, in any event, punish corporations criminally?[78]

A first reason is that community disapproval calls, in some instances, for the stamp of criminalization to be imposed. A second is that use of the criminal law provides a set of useful incentives that are of value even when there is no great need to stigmatize conduct as particularly heinous. A third is that corporations, just like individuals, can make decisions and have the capacity to change their policies and procedures and accordingly do meet the conditions of blameworthiness and responsibility.[79] They can, moreover, be deterred by threats of punishment. Finally, the corporation may be better placed than the state to put right its internal failings and so it may be sensible to use the criminal law to give the firm an incentive to do this. The corporation, moreover, is more likely (for informational and evidential reasons) to apply sanctions to an errant manager than is the state and the ensuing higher 'expected punishment cost' that flows from internal controls means that higher levels of deterrence may be attained by punishing the corporation, and leaving it to take further action, than are secured by focusing the criminal law directly on the errant employee.

Conclusions

Enforcement can influence regulatory success or failure not merely by affecting the achievement of the right objectives. It can also impinge on the quality of regulatory processes. There is, however, as much art as science in enforcement since trade-offs have to be made on a number of fronts—between, for example, punishing infringers and maximizing compliance levels or between preventing creative compliance and producing rules that are easily enforced. In making these trade-offs issues of accountability, due process, and expertise arise. It may, for example, be necessary to use high levels of discretion in a regime of flexible and targeted enforcement if the 'right' results are to be produced, but questions of accountability and fairness are involved and it is proper that trade-offs with legitimate efficiency gains should be argued out by regulators. Not only does enforcement demand that highly complex trade-offs and balances be carried out, it demands that these be justified. The need for regulatory legitimacy, it should be emphasized, runs through the entire regulatory process.

[78] See Leigh, *Criminal Liability*; Coffee loc. cit. n. 55 above, part II.
[79] Fisse and Braithwaite loc. cit. n. 55 above.

Setting Standards

Regulatory rules often link a regulatory response (e.g. a fine, tax, or administrative order) to a standard of performance. Use of standards is not exclusive to command and control regimes and standard-setting issues may arise as commonly when incentives rather than sanctions underpin regulation.[1] Regulators are faced with two core questions when standards are incorporated into rules. Which types of standards should be used? What level of performance should be demanded? This chapter examines how those questions can be answered and reviews the general problems of standard setting.[2]

1. Which Types of Standards?

Standards vary across a number of dimensions. As was seen in the last chapter, a key issue in enforcement is the timing or stage of process at which the regulator wishes to intervene. A standard may look to behaviour at the *prevention* stage, it can focus on the *act* that gives rise to a harmful result, or it can look to the *harmful result* itself. Thus a rule might apply a standard to the safety policies that a firm is called upon to develop in order to *prevent* injuries; an alternative (or additional) rule might attach a sanction to dangerous *acts* and apply a standard to the use of equipment (e.g. scaffolding) that is dangerous if employed improperly; and a further rule might apply a standard to define the *harmful result* of an activity and to impose sanctions accordingly.

Standards can thus be divided into three categories in correspondence with these three stages of intervention.

---

[1] On standard setting generally see A. Ogus, *Regulation: Legal Form and Economic Theory* (Oxford, 1994), chs. 8, 9; S. Breyer, *Regulation and Its Reform* (Cambridge, Mass., 1982), ch. 5; G. Richardson et al. *Policing Pollution* (Oxford, 1983), 35–8. For a detailed study of standard setting in the health and safety sector see HM Treasury, *The Setting of Safety Standards* (London, 1996).

[2] This chapter does not deal with the scope (or inclusiveness) of standards or rules, on which see Section 2 of Chapter 8, above.

Specification (or Design) Standards

Specification standards focus on prevention by controlling the processes that give rise to dangerous situations—by demanding, for example, that industrial activities conform to specification on plant construction, equipment to be used, or modes of operation. Such standards can be relatively inexpensive to enforce (since monitoring compliance with a given specification is a fairly simple operation) and a further advantage is that compliance costs may be readily calculated. (If use of a particular design of machinery is required then this can be costed quite easily.) Such standards are, however, highly intrusive in so far as the regulator is strongly involved in structuring, say, the manufacturing process. The technique may also inhibit innovation and the development of new, perhaps safer and more efficient, designs of equipment or operation. The regulated firm is called upon to install the specified design and has no incentive to innovate—indeed it is the regulator who has to lead the way technically. This may be desirable in certain sectors where the regulator possesses expertise and information unavailable to private producers but in other sectors it may be preferable to allow private designers and researchers to generate technological advances, not least for reasons of international competitiveness.

A further problem with specification standards is the difficulty of predicting the total harm that will result from the anticipated use of the specified equipment or method. Suppose a process is specified on the basis that it will produce each hour only a given level of pollution in a river. This will not guarantee the survival of life in the river unless the number of hours of use is stipulated and enforced. If the river's capacity to absorb pollution varies (according to flow and temperature levels) it will be particularly difficult to achieve desired ends by using specification standards.

Performance (or Output) Standards

Performance standards demand a given level of delivery at the act stage but do not specify how that delivery is to be arrived at. In the pollution field an emission standard comes within this category and may govern the concentration of a pollutant that may be discharged from a given point. The focus is on the level of risks that a process creates rather than the actual harms done.

Such standards are less technologically restrictive than specification standards—they offer, and give, firms an incentive to design processes with superior performance levels—but it is still difficult to relate different levels of performance to regulatory goals, for example, to calculate the cumulative consequences of discharges for the watercourse.[3] Enforcement costs are also liable to be higher with performance than with specification standards since it will be more difficult to check ongoing levels of pollution throughout the day and night than to see if the specified filtration system is in use.

Target Standards

Target standards seek to overcome the problems of linking standards to regulatory goals by stating those goals directly. These standards prescribe no particular type of process or level of risk creation but call for the avoidance of certain harmful consequences (e.g. removing the water's capacity to support fish life). The advantage of such standards is that firms are left free to decide how best (and most cheaply) to achieve the set targets. It is the firms, moreover, rather than the state regulators that have to bear the costs of calculating how to achieve stipulated targets. Where, however, the harms at issue are caused by firms who are insufficiently resourced or coordinated to calculate the best means of achieving targets, it may be socially efficient to collect information centrally in the regulatory agency and to employ specification (or design) standards.

2. What Level of Performance should be Demanded?

If the regulators of an activity were to call for the total eradication of risks, this would generally mean that the activity could not be carried out. Reducing harms or risks of harm becomes more and more expensive as reductions advance and so the question arises: How can regulators, in controlling harms or risks, fix standards at the right levels?

One response is to seek to set optimal levels on efficiency grounds by a process in which the costs of harm avoidance are balanced against the benefits. There are, however, objections to making regulatory decisions turn purely on considerations of efficiency—these were discussed in Chapters 6 and 7. Society might, for instance, want to place an absolute ban on the use of some items of dangerous equipment (e.g. unguarded saws[4]) and might want to do so to protect certain rights rather than to reflect a balancing of costs and benefits. This is not to say, however, that

---

[3] 'Ambient' standards do, however, look to the maximum pollution concentration permitted in the environment at a given place and 'receptor' standards look to the perceptible harm that a discharger causes to the environment. These can be seen as bridges between performance and target standards. On specification and performance standards see J. Braithwaite, 'The Limits of Economism in Controlling Harmful Corporate Conduct' (1982) 16 *Law and Soc. Rev.* 481 and Richardson et al., *Policing Pollution*, 37–40.

[4] See the Factories Act 1961 section 14, which requires every dangerous part of any machinery to be securely fenced—it is not permissible to argue that this is impractical or expensive.

decisions primarily concerned with the distribution of rights should pay no heed to the costs and benefits involved. Judgements as to the optimal level of harm abatement demanded by a regulatory standard may quite properly be informed by economists' approaches even if they are not driven by these.[5]

Standards, and the way these are stated, may, in practice, be influenced *inter alia* by lay, historical, political, commercial, and other factors.[6] Thus, if safety standards are taken as an example, it is possible to distinguish between four different approaches.[7]

Traditional Formulations

These may demand that potentially dangerous activities be made wholly safe or *as safe as possible* or they may adopt a *rule of thumb*. The latter approach demands that dangers should not be allowed to increase, even if the balance of costs and benefits changes. Examples would be stipulations that the annual number of fatal commercial air crashes or cumulative atmospheric pollution levels should not be allowed to increase above current figures.

Working Limits and Targets

Working limits are used to define, in flexible terms, the maximum levels of risks, emissions, or harms allowed within good practice. Targets are aspirational and give policies presentational focus—thus published targets for road accident deaths might be used to set goals for promoting safety.

Cost-Benefit Trade-Offs

Some standards may explicitly allow the costs of avoiding dangers to be weighed (in varying degrees) against the benefits of greater safety. In the health and safety field a series of formulations allow the balancing and these are covered by acronyms such as ALARP, ALARA, SFAIRP, and BATNEEC.[8]

Tolerability Approaches

If it is accepted that standards ought to look to individuals' rights and distributional questions but should also take on board considerations of

---

[5] See HM Treasury, *Setting of Safety Standards*.

[6] For other influences see the different explanations of regulatory developments that are reviewed in Chapter 3.

[7] See HM Treasury, *Setting of Safety Standards*, 6–9 on which this section builds.

[8] Standing for: As Low as Reasonably Practicable; As Low As Reasonably Achievable; So Far As Is Reasonably Practicable; and Best Available Technology Not Entailing Excessive Costs. On cost-benefit analysis and regulation see Chapter 7, above.

costs and benefits, a combined approach can be adopted. An example is
the Tolerability of Risks (TOR) framework developed by the Health and
Safety Executive (HSE) in the 1980s. This framework applies a cost-benefit
approach to standards but imposes absolute maximum levels of risk, set
on the basis of equity. It is accepted that risks of harm beyond certain
levels shall not be imposed even in exchange for very high gains. It is
also accepted, however, that below such levels, a cost-benefit approach
can be explicitly employed.

Efficient Standard Setting: The Problems

An efficiency-based strategy would aim to set standards so as to achieve
optimal loss abatement—that is to fix levels at which total benefits would
exceed total costs by the greatest amount.[9] Even leaving aside distributional and perceptual issues,[10] a series of problems faces those who seek
to apply such a strategy.[11] Thus, suppose an agency responsible for a
single district sets out to fix a standard for the maximum number of
potentially harmful dust particles per cubic metre of air that it will allow
in its factories. The following difficulties are likely to be encountered.
The first concerns information. It is generally difficult and expensive for
agencies to acquire unbiased data for use in standard setting.[12] Those
industries that are subject to regulation will possess most of the relevant
raw data but they will tend to distort this information when passing it
to the controlling agency (e.g. exaggerating anticipated compliance costs)
and firms may use the possession of information as a lever with which
to exert influence over the agency. Independent data may be very expensive to generate in-house and resort to experts in the field may produce
findings that are tainted by the industry's influence over the experts they
frequently employ as consultants. Pressure groups and other branches
of government may be in no better a position to generate data than the
regulator.

A second problem is that assessing the costs of imposing a standard
is an enormously complex matter even assuming away the general
informational problems just noted. An initial calculation concerns the
expenses of rule-making, administration, monitoring compliance-seeking,

---

[9] See Ogus, *Regulation*, 153–4 and T. Makkai and J. Braithwaite, 'The Limits of the
Economic Analysis of Regulation: An Empirical Case and a Case for Empiricism' (1993)
15 *Law and Policy* 271. ('The trouble is that the optimum level of stringency in a regulatory standard identified by an economic analysis is always false' (p. 272).)

[10] On the problems that different perceptions of dangers and risks present for 'rational'
regulators see Chapter 11 below.

[11] On the difficulties of applying cost-benefit approaches to regulation generally see Chapter 7 above.

[12] See Breyer, *Regulation*, 109–12.

and enforcement. A further, more difficult matter relates to compliance costs—the expenses of bringing equipment up to standard and any losses that may be incurred, for example, through diminutions in the efficiency of the manufacturing process (e.g. a slowing down of the production line due to the operation of safety guards). If each factory in a district is operating different dust-emitting and controlling processes, calculations will have to relate to each and every set of premises. The side-effects of regulation also have to be anticipated. Thus, increasing the rigour of a standard may change enforcement strategies or policies and also make enforcement more difficult (changing even the equipment demanded for measuring compliance). Patterns of compliance, furthermore, may not be constant but may be dynamic. Factory owners may, for example, give up on complying with standards if they see them as unreasonable or draconian[13] and the relationship between degrees of regulatory rigour and levels of compliance may be indirect and uncertain.[14]

Other unintended effects of fixing standards at particular levels may have to be assessed and these can include: displacement from one mode of production to another that is less regulated and (perversely) more harm-causing;[15] creative compliance and the avoidance of regulatory purposes by shifts in production methods;[16] and the over-deterrence of desirable activity by frightening manufacturers into withdrawals from the field.[17] Increased rigour in standards may also create barriers to entry that prevent competition from developing in a sector—it may, additionally, distort existing competition within the sector. Putting figures on such indirect costs may be extremely difficult because the effects at issue are often diffused and difficult to track and data is not readily available.

A third difficulty that standard-setters are likely to encounter is that of calculating benefits. Cost and benefit calculations are affected by a number of common difficulties (e.g. assumptions concerning displacement and enforcement effects) but benefit assessments may be particularly fraught because regulatory benefits tend to be more diffused (temporally and spatially) and less easily located than costs.[18] (One factory may bear the costs but a host of workers and passers-by may benefit from harm reductions.) Causal connections between benefits and the imposition of a standard may be difficult to establish, never mind quantify, and figures cannot be placed on non-market benefits especially if these stand to be enjoyed over an extended period of time.[19]

---

[13] See Makkai and Braithwaite loc. cit. n. 9 above. [14] Ibid.

[15] See P. Grabosky, 'Counterproductive Regulation' (1995) 23 *Int. J. of Sociology of Law* 347.

[16] See above pp. 102–3.

[17] On over- and under-inclusiveness see Chapter 8 above, pp. 103–6.

[18] Ogus, *Regulation*, 156. [19] Ibid. 156–9.

Conclusions

Standard-setting cannot be reduced to a mechanical process in which the regulator calculates an optimal strategy and level of rigour in an uncontentious manner. As a consequence, standard-setting procedures tend, in the real world, to involve lengthy rounds of negotiation and revision, compromise and accommodation.[20] These procedures may be influenced by the internal politics of the regulatory institution as much as the external political environment within which regulation takes place.[21] It is because standard-setting is a non-mechanical matter, involving politically contentious judgements, that its legitimacy cannot be established readily by appeals to the expertise of the regulator. It is not surprising, accordingly, that the fairness and transparency of standard-setting processes as well as the accountability of the standard-setters, are factors that tend to loom large when such legitimation is under discussion.

[20] On the 'Problem of Process' and rule-making see R. Baldwin, *Rules and Government* (Oxford, 1995), 167–9.

[21] Ibid. 169–74.

10

Self-Regulation

Self-regulation can be seen as taking place when a group of firms or individuals exerts control over its own membership and their behaviour.[1] In Britain it is encountered in a number of professions and sports and in sectors such as financial services, advertising, insurance, and the press. A host of arrangements can be seen as self-regulatory and variations in the characteristics of self-regulatory regimes can be identified.[2] A first variable is the governmental nature of self-regulation. An association may self-regulate in a purely private sense—in pursuit of the private ends of its membership—or it may act governmentally in so far as public policy tasks are delegated to private actors or institutions.[3] Both forms

---

[1] On self-regulation in general see J. Black, 'Constitutionalising Self-Regulation' (1996) 59 *MLR* 24; A. Ogus, 'Rethinking Self-Regulation' (1995) 15 *OJLS* 97; National Consumer Council, *Self-Regulation* (London, 1986); A. Page, 'Self-Regulation: The Constitutional Dimension' (1986) 49 *MLR* 141; id., 'Self-Regulation and Codes of Practice' (1980) *JBL* 30; id., 'Financial Services: The Self-Regulatory Alternative', in R. Baldwin and C. McCrudden, *Regulation and Public Law* (London, 1987); R. Baggott and L. Harrison, 'The Politics of Self-Regulation' (1986) 14 *Policy and Politics* 143; Bardach and Kagan, *Going by the Book*, ch. 8; I. Ayres and J. Braithwaite, *Responsive Regulation* (Oxford, 1992), ch. 4; R. Baggott, 'Regulatory Reform in Britain: The Changing Face of Self-Regulation (1989) 67 *Pub. Admin.* 435; C. Graham, 'Self-Regulation', in G. Richardson and H. Genn (eds.), *Administrative Law and Government Action* (Oxford, 1994).

[2] See Ogus, loc. cit. n. 1 above, pp. 99–100. Legislation is now in process to end self-regulation in financial services.

[3] See Graham, loc. cit. n. 1 above; Baggott loc. cit. n. 1 above; and for studies of self-regulation in particular sectors see S. Dawson et al., *Safety at Work: The Limits of Self-Regulation* (Cambridge, 1988); R. Baldwin, 'Health and Safety at Work: Consensus and Self-Regulation', in Baldwin and McCrudden, *Regulation and Public Law*; R. Ferguson, 'Self-Regulation at Lloyds' (1983) 46 *MLR* 56; M. Moran and B. Wood, *States, Regulation and the Medical Profession* (Buckingham, 1993); V. Finch, 'Corporate Governance and Cadbury: Self-Regulation and Alternatives' (1994) *JBL* 51; R. Cranston, *Consumers and the Law* (2nd edn. London, 1984), ch. 2; I. Ramsay, *Consumer Protection* (London, 1989); A. G. Jordan, *Engineers and Professional Self-Regulation* (Oxford, 1992); Sir D. Calcutt, *Review of Press Self-Regulation*, Cm. 2135 (London, 1992–3); J. J. Boddewyn, *Global Perspectives on Advertising Self-Regulation* (Westport, Conn., 1992); M. Moran, *The Politics of the Financial Services Revolution* (London, 1991); R. Ferguson and A. Page, 'The Development of Investor Protection in Britain' (1984) 12 *Int. J. of Sociology of Law* 287; L. C. B. Gower, *Review of Investor Protection*, Cmnd. 9125 (London, 1984); J. Black, *Rules and Regulators* (Oxford, 1997); Office of Fair Trading (OFT), *Voluntary Codes of Practice* (London, 1996); OFT, *Raising Standards of Consumer Care: Progressing Beyond Codes of Practice* (London, 1998). For a study of 'Responsible Care' in the Australian Chemical Industry see N. Gunningham and P. Grabosky, *Smart Regulation* (Oxford, 1998), ch. 4.

of activity may, indeed, be combined. The process of self-regulation may, moreover, be constrained governmentally in a number of ways—for instance by statutory rules; oversight by a governmental agency; systems in which ministers approve or draft rules; procedures for the public enforcement of self-regulatory rules; or mechanisms of participation or accountability. Self-regulation may appear to lack any state involvement but in reality it may constitute a response to threats by government that if nothing is done state action will follow.[4]

A second variable concerns the extent of the role played by self-regulators. A full role may involve the promulgation of rules, the enforcement of these on the ground, and the monitoring of the whole regulatory process. Self-regulation, however, may be restricted to one of these functions —where, for instance, rules are drafted by a self-regulatory organization but are enforced and monitored by a public agency. Self-regulation may merely operate as an element within a regulatory regime—a point to be returned to below.

The degree of binding legal force that attaches to self-regulatory rules is a third variable to be noted. Self-regulation may operate in an informal, non-binding, voluntary manner or it may involve rules of full legal force that are enforceable in the courts. Finally, self-regulatory regimes may vary in their coverage of an industrial sector—they may apply to all those who participate in an activity (perhaps because screening or licensing of entry is applied) or they may cover only those who join an association voluntarily.

1. Why Self-Regulation?

The case for self-regulation, or incorporating elements of self-regulation into governmental regulation, rests principally on considerations of expertise and efficiency. Worries about self-regulation tend to centre on concerns relating to mandates, accountability, and the fairness of procedures.

Expertise

A familiar claim in favour of self-regulation is that self-regulatory bodies can usually command higher levels of relevant expertise and technical knowledge than is possible with independent regulation—

---

[4] See Black loc. cit. n. 1 above, p. 27. The fear that such threats may induce was recently noted by Roger Cowe in the *Guardian*'s City Column: 'Accountants have not been seized out of the blue with a desire for regulation. They are terrified of having it done for them by a Government that has already stripped them of the power to regulate on investment advice' (21 Feb. 1998). (In February 1998 the six professional bodies administering the accountants' self-regulatory regime proposed the creation of an independent Review Board to oversee self-regulation (see *Financial Times*, 24 Feb. 1998).)

that, for instance, financial services practitioners know much more about their sector than a civil servant or bureaucrat ever could. It can be counter-claimed that such expertise and knowledge can be 'bought in' by bodies independent of the profession or membership, but proponents of self-regulation may respond that it is the ongoing proximity of links with the profession or membership that keeps expertise honed and information up to date—that such ongoing links are unlikely to be sustained where regulators are fully independent of the regulated group.

An aspect of expertise also relates to regulatory effectiveness.[5] It can be argued that self-regulators have a special knowledge of what regulated parties will see as reasonable in terms of regulatory obligations. This level of understanding, it may be claimed, allows self-regulators to make demands that are acceptable to affected firms or individuals and this produces higher levels of voluntary compliance than is likely to be the case with externally imposed regimes of control. Misjudging levels of acceptability, the proponents of self-regulation argue, leads to low levels of voluntary compliance, high enforcement costs for taxpayers, and inefficient controls.

Efficiency

One set of arguments used by advocates of self-regulation emphasizes the potential of self-regulation to produce controls efficiently. Thus it is contended that self-regulators, with their easy access to those under control, experience low costs in acquiring the information that is neces-sary to formulate and set standards. They, furthermore, have low mon-itoring and enforcement costs and they are able to adapt their regimes to changes in industrial conditions in a flexible and smooth manner because they act relatively informally and tend to enjoy the trust of the regulated group.

The informality of voluntary self-regulatory systems can also be said to provide remedies where more formal systems would not. Thus, on 5 February 1998, Lord Wakeham, Chairman of the Press Complaints Com-mission (PCC), expressed fears in the House of Lords that if the Human Rights Bill were to graft a 'statutory superstructure' onto the voluntary press complaints system of self-regulation, negative consequences might flow. He argued that voluntary self-regulation allowed disputes to be resolved swiftly because of the commitment of newspaper editors and the amicable, informal way that the PCC conducted its work. It also, he said, allowed ordinary people to take up complaints against the press without having to find large sums of money. A move to place the scheme

---

[5] On self-regulation and implementation see W. Streek and P. C. Schmitter (eds.), *Private Interest Government: Beyond Market and State* (London, 1985), 22–5.

on a statutory footing, he feared, would place the courts in control and would change the dispute resolution process into one characterized by legal defensiveness and lack of cooperation. Resolving differences and servicing apologies would be far more difficult within a legalistic system than in a cooperative regime and the legal expenses involved would make remedies unavailable to ordinary citizens.[6]

As far as costs to the public purse are concerned, a further point in favour of self-regulation is that it tends to be paid for by those engaging in the regulated activity—this contrasts with the costs of external, or independent, regimes which are usually borne by the taxpayer.

Not all arguments under the efficiency heading do, however, favour self-regulation. Where self-regulation operates as a voluntary mechanism not all of those who participate in a sector may subscribe to self-regulation. Much here depends on the incentives to participate that are provided by a self-regulatory system. These may include qualifications, certificates, or marks of quality (e.g. doctor, architect, British Standards); access to trading space (e.g. on exchanges); or avoidance of exclusions or boycotts of non-members (e.g. trade associations or cartels). Such incentives may often prove powerful but where they are not fully effective, it is common for organizations to seek explicit recognition from the state and controls to make membership compulsory.[7] Self-regulation comes then to operate within a state-maintained framework. Where membership is not exhaustive, the public may prove to be ill-protected by a regime that controls the most responsible members of a trade or industry but leaves unregulated those individuals or firms who are the least inclined to serve the public interest.[8] In some sectors, indeed, the role of self-regulation has been severely limited because of difficulty in controlling mavericks to the extent necessary to assuage public concerns.[9]

---

[6] See *The Times*, 6 Feb. 1998, p. 46. See also J. Black, *Rules and Regulators* (Oxford, 1997), 30–7 on 'interpretive communities' and the effect of shared interpretations in obviating the need for detailed specifications through rules.

[7] See T. Daintith, 'Regulation' in International Association of Legal Science, *International Encyclopaedia of Comparative Law* (Tübingen, 1997), vol. xvii, ch. 10, p. 20.

[8] See Cranston, *Consumers and the Law*, 39. On the 'consensual paradox' and the tendency to regulate those who are least in need of regulating see Baldwin, 'Health and Safety at Work', in Baldwin and McCrudden, *Regulation and Public Law*, 151–3. The NCC (*Self-Regulation*, 6) has argued that those who have not agreed to follow the self-regulatory scheme tend to be the main source of consumer problems (noted, Graham loc. cit. n. 1 above, p. 195). The Director General of Fair Trading's report *Timeshare* (London, 1990) argued that limited membership of the controlling Timeshare Developers' Association meant that self-regulation was not working and that legislation was necessary in the timeshare sector. See also OFT, *Raising Standards of Consumer Care*, on the problem of the non-applicability of codes to non-members and the case for moving towards standards rather than codes.

[9] Graham, loc. cit. n. 1 above, p. 196, cites the estate agencies sector as one in which voluntary self-regulation was encouraged by the Office of Fair Trading with little success and legislative measures were subsequently taken.

Mandates

The essence of a mandate claim is that the regulation at issue serves legitimate ends—as identified with reference commonly to a set of legislative objectives. Apart from the usual problems of determining the content of the mandate, the special difficulty with some self-regulatory regimes is that the relevant objectives may be drawn up by bodies with no democratic legitimacy—for instance by the members of a private association. It is then hard to justify actions that affect parties outside the association or to argue that the public interest is being served.

Such difficulties are less severe in self-regulatory regimes that are directed towards objectives that are set down in statutes or where individuals or groups with some democratic legitimacy have a role in drawing up objectives—for example where a Secretary of State, a local authority, or other elected body fixes aims. Even in such cases, however, those sceptical of self-regulation may assert that special problems of capture arise—that such legitimate objectives or rules will tend to be subverted to private purposes where their pursuit and application is given over to a private body that is accountable to its private members and is in effective control of relevant information.[10] It can be said that this will be the case particularly where the self-regulator's functions include updating and formulating policies, interpreting rules, and adjudicating on applications of those rules. As far as enforcement is concerned, it has been alleged that self-regulatory bodies have an especially poor record in protecting the public interest through enforcing standards against errant members.[11] In numerous studies reference has also been made to the tendency of self-regulatory bodies to act anti-competitively on access requirements and prices so that members' interests rather than those of the public are served.[12]

Accountability

Critics of self-regulatory systems may see their existence as making manifest the capture of power by groups who are not accountable through

---

[10] See Ogus loc. cit. n. 1 above, pp. 98–9.

[11] See Cranston, *Consumers and the Law*, 41, 60–2; R. Abel, *The Legal Profession in England and Wales* (Oxford, 1988), 250–8; Ogus loc. cit. n. 1 above, p. 99. The OFT has noted that the large majority of trade associations have neither the powers nor the will to exercise effective control over those who breach codes of practice—see OFT, *Raising Standards of Consumer Care*, 16–17: 'trade associations, set up for the benefit of members, frequently are neither comfortable nor effective in the role of sectoral regulator'.

[12] See e.g. S. Domberger and A. Sherr, 'The Impact of Competition on Pricing and Quality of Legal Services' (1989) 9 *Int. Rev. Law and Econ.* 41; A Shaked and J. Sutton, 'The Self-Regulating Profession' (1981) 47 *Rev. Econ. Stud.* 217.

normal democratic channels.[13] It would be a mistake, however, to think that all such systems are wholly unaccountable and free from controls other than those applied by members. As already indicated, self-regulators may be subject to non-member controls in a host of ways, notably to constraints deriving from the following:

- statutory prescriptions and objectives;
- rules that are drafted by or approved by other bodies or ministers;
- ministerial guidelines or criteria for consideration by the self-regulator;
- parliamentary oversight of the delegated legislation that guides the self-regulator;
- departmental purse strings and the influence that these provide;
- agency oversight;
- informal influences from government that are exerted in the shadow of threatened state regulation;[14]
- judicial review;[15]
- complaints and grievance-handling mechanisms (e.g. ombudsmen);[16]
- reporting and publication requirements laid down by government or Parliament.

Lack of accountability is thus not a necessary feature of self-regulation. The public are not liable to trust self-regulators, however, or see them as legitimate if they are seen to be able to circumvent external controls, or to be more strongly accountable to their members than to the public or those affected by their activities.

The key problem in identifying the proper level and form of accountability lies in deciding whether the self-regulation at issue is a matter of private control (a matter for resolution between members) or whether it is governmental (in so far as it affects the public interest) and merits democratic (or judicial) accountability accordingly. For their part, the courts have struggled to produce a clear line on the liability of self-regulatory bodies to judicial review.[17] The judiciary have, for technical and pragmatic

---

[13] See Ogus loc. cit. n. 1 above, pp. 98–9; N. Lewis, 'Corporatism and Accountability: The Democratic Dilemma', in C. Crouch and R. Dove (eds.), *Corporatism and Accountability* (Oxford, 1990); I. Harden and N. Lewis, *The Noble Lie* (London, 1986). Graham, loc. cit. n. 1 above, p. 203, makes the point that self-regulators operate outside the scope of the departmental select committees of the House of Commons and there is no equivalent to scrutiny by the National Audit Office, though the Office of Fair Trading does exercise some review in the financial services sector and areas where it has approved codes of practice.

[14] Page, loc. cit. n. 1 above, p. 149, cites the example of the Takeovers Panel. In 1968 the Government and Governor of the Bank of England threatened direct governmental regulation of takeovers unless the City Code was made more effective.

[15] On which see Black loc. cit. n. 1 above and Page loc. cit. n. 1 above.

[16] See e.g. A. Mowbray, 'Newspaper Ombudsmen: The British Experience' (1991) *Media Law and Practice* 91.

[17] See Black loc. cit. n. 1 above, who cites as examples of 'current confusion', *R* v. *Lloyds ex p. Briggs* [1993] Lloyds LR 176 (Lloyds Council not liable to review) and *R* v. *Insurance Ombudsman ex p. Aegon Life Assurance Ltd*, *The Times* 7 Jan. 1994 (Insurance Ombudsman Bureau not subject to review).

reasons, proved reluctant to review the sporting associations[18] but, in cases from *Datafin*[19] onwards,[20] have decided that bodies whose source of power derives neither from statute nor the prerogative, may, nevertheless, be reviewed where they exercise public law functions, their power has a public element, or there is a 'governmental interest' in the decision-making power in question. Identifying when power is 'public' or governmental for the purposes of review has not, however, been made easy by the judges, who have applied a number of tests and stated, for instance, that where private power extends over substantial areas of economic activity, or affects the public interest and the livelihood of many individuals, this will not necessarily be subject to the rules of public law.[21]

How can the courts move towards a more coherent approach? Black has suggested that the courts, at least, should not look to the 'public' or other nature of the self-regulatory body when considering what systems of accountability are appropriate but should look to the nature of the particular action or decision at issue; that a multifaceted approach to 'public' be taken (one recognizing the public nature of actions mediating different systems[22] within society rather than simply state-to-individual relations); and that self-regulators be required to adopt processes that empower affected parties rather than give expression to existing power relationships and parties of influence.[23] The value of such an approach lies in seeing each self-regulatory action or decision in its particular governmental context and in tailoring attendant calls for accountability accordingly. It recognizes that one body can have a number of different personae or functions—acting governmentally or in a regulatory manner on some issues but also being a corporate body, entering into contracts as a commercial enterprise or behaving as an employer in other contexts. It also urges that, as well as providing scrutiny through judicial review, the courts should seek to set the decisions or functions at issue in an institutional and procedural context that allows affected parties to participate appropriately. Such a flexible, or particularized, approach to accountability does, however, make it difficult to make general statements about acceptable arrangements.

---

[18] See e.g. *Law* v. *National Greyhound Racing Club* [1983] 3 All ER 300; *R* v. *Disciplinary Committee of the Jockey Club ex p. Aga Khan* [1993] 2 All ER 853; *R* v. *Jockey Club ex p. RAM Racecourses* [1993] 2 All ER 225; *R* v. *Football Association ex p. Football League* [1993] 2 All ER 833.

[19] *R* v. *Panel on Take-overs and Mergers ex p. Datafin Plc and another* [1987] 1 All ER 564.

[20] See, for example, *R* v. *Chief Rabbi ex p. Wachmann* [1993] 2 All ER 249.

[21] See Hoffman LJ in *R* v. *Disciplinary Committee of the Jockey Club ex p. Aga Khan* [1993] 2 All ER 853 at 875. Monopoly power does not ensure control at public law—see e.g. *R* v. *Chief Rabbi ex p. Wachmann* [1993] 2 All ER 249; for criticism see D. Pannick, 'Who is Subject to Judicial Review and in Respect of What?' [1992] *PL* 1.

[22] That is, different 'functional systems' such as the political, economic, and legal systems.

[23] See Black loc. cit. n. 1 above, pp. 54–6.

Fairness of Procedures

As already indicated, schemes of self-regulation are liable to criticisms of unfairness in so far as non-members may be affected by regulatory decisions to which they have poor or no access. Past experience suggests that self-regulators have a sporadic, unstructured, and patchy record of consulting those with interests in the workings of their systems.[24] Third parties may also be excluded from the negotiations that establish self-regulatory regimes and their objectives, in the first place.[25]

The courts might act to demand proper access for affected parties on the lines noted above in discussing accountability but, as yet, self-regulators are free from general legal duties to consult non-members before taking decisions or devising policies. Nor are they subject to general duties to give reasons for the actions or decisions that they have taken.

The National Consumer Council (NCC)[26] has argued that self-regulatory regimes must be able to command public confidence and has advocated that self-regulatory schemes should operate from within statutory frameworks and that each one should, *inter alia*, include the following basic features:

- strong external involvement in the design and operation of the scheme;
- as far as practicable, a separation of the operation and control of the scheme from the institutions of the industry;
- full representation of consumers and other outsiders on the governing body of the scheme;
- clear statements of principles and standards governing the scheme —normally published in a code;
- clear, accessible, and well-publicized complaints procedures to deal with code breaches;
- adequate sanctions for non-observance of codes;
- the maintenance and updating of the scheme;
- annual reporting.

To summarize on the case for self-regulation, the acceptability or otherwise of a self-regulatory regime falls to be judged, at the end of the day, by the five criteria discussed above and for each rule or regime the relevant trade-offs have to be assessed. A key consideration may be whether the expertise and efficiency gains to be achieved by self-regulation do out-balance any weaknesses in mandate definition, accountability, and

---

[24] See Graham loc. cit. n. 1 above, p. 198.
[25] See I. Ramsay, 'The Office of Fair Trading: Policing the Consumer Market Place', in Baldwin and McCrudden, *Regulation and Public Law*, 191.
[26] NCC, *Self-Regulation*, esp. p. 15. See Graham loc. cit. n. 1 above and the reservations of Lord Wakeham concerning the placing of regimes on a statutory basis—discussed above.

fairness that will remain after appropriate steps have been taken to ward off criticisms on these fronts.

It was noted above that self-regulation may play a part as an element within a scheme of regulation. A mechanism allowing for self-assessment may, for example, be incorporated within a regulatory compliance system, or a role may be given to regulated firms (or organizations thereof) in drafting the rules that government officials will enforce. It may be that such a combination of self-regulation and regulation will offer a level of performance and acceptability that is unobtainable by resorting to either strategy singly.

In order to throw more light on the potential of such 'partial' self-regulatory mechanisms and to move towards identifying the kinds of context in which use of such mechanisms will lead to superior results than externally imposed regulation, we now consider a well-known approach to self-regulation.

2. A Particular Strategy: Enforced Self-Regulation

Ayres and Braithwaite[27] distinguish enforced self-regulation from 'co-regulation'. Co-regulation they take to refer to industry-association self-regulation with some oversight and/or ratification by government.[28] Enforced self-regulation, in contrast, involves negotiations between the state and individual firms so as to establish regulations that are particular to each firm.[29] In some contexts (by no means all, say Ayres and Braithwaite), it will be 'more efficacious' for the regulated firms to take on some or all of the legislative, executive, and judicial regulatory functions—that is, to devise their own regulatory rules, or monitor compliance, or punish and correct episodes of non-compliance. Two key elements underpin their concept of enforced self-regulation: (1) public enforcement of privately written rules and (2) publicly mandated and

---

[27] I. Ayres and J. Braithwaite, *Responsive Regulation* (Oxford, 1992), ch. 4.

[28] See P. Grabosky and J. Braithwaite, *Of Manners Gentle: Enforcement Strategies of Australian Business Regulatory Agencies* (Melbourne, 1986).

[29] Examples of enforced self-regulatory regimes are suggested by Ayres and Braithwaite (*Responsive Regulation*, 116–17), notably the rules of civil aviation safety that are prepared by air carriers and enforced by the Federal Aviation Administration and the mine safety rules that are privately drafted but ratified by the Department of Labour and criminally enforced. Between co-regulation and enforced self-regulation lies 'negotiated rule-making' on US lines. The Negotiated Rule Making Act 1990 sets out, in detail, procedures for negotiating rule-making in the USA. This envisages, *inter alia*, that where there are a limited number of identifiable interests who will be significantly affected by a rule, where these interests can be adequately represented on a rule-making committee, and where a consensus on a proposed rule is reasonably likely, an agency may appoint a committee and proceed with a negotiated rule-making process. Agencies such as the Environmental Protection Agency, the Occupational Safety and Health Administration, and the Federal Aviation Administration have used such procedures.

publicly monitored private enforcement of those rules.[30] Thus, the primary function of government inspectors would be to audit the efficiency and toughness of self-enforcement mechanisms, but old-style direct government monitoring would still be necessary for firms too small to mount their own compliance-seeking operations. Violations of privately written and publicly ratified rules would, moreover, be punishable by law.

The attractions of enforced self-regulation are said to be numerous. The state cannot afford to enforce adequately and, as a result, inspection coverage tends to be 'abysmal'. Self-regulation can expand coverage dramatically, ease pressure on the public purse, and lead to businesses bearing the costs of their own regulation. Self-regulation can increase the quality, frequency, and rigour of inspections for rule infringements. It will also tend to involve more highly trained inspectors than governmental regulation.[31]

Corporate compliance staff, moreover, are likely to have better knowledge of 'where the bodies are buried' than external inspectors and corporate compliance staff may possess more extensive powers with which to detect infringements than are available to public officials. Under enforced self-regulation each company writes a set of rules tailored to the specific context of the firm and these rules would be scrutinized by a regulatory agency. This brings the further advantage, in, say, the environmental field, of better protections for the public because more stringent rules can be demanded of firms with lower compliance costs. Non-uniform standards can thus produce better results than uniform rules which unduly restrict some firms yet are too lax in the case of others.

Firm-specific rules, it is also claimed, can be more precise than industry-wide rules which tend to be highly complex or else vague because they attempt to deal with a problem in all its possible contexts.[32] The introduction of new rules is also easier with firm-specific rules since it is not necessary to await industry-wide agreement. Enforced self-regulation, in addition, encourages firms to design custom-made regulatory systems and firms designing their own specific rules will control more aspects of their activities than would be the case with external regulators who would lack the necessary time and resources. Such firms would, moreover, be more committed to rules that they have devised than to externally imposed rules and this would encourage compliance.

---

[30] Julia Black argues that enforced self-regulation as conceived by Ayres and Braithwaite is not self-regulation proper since self-regulation best describes the situation in which 'a collective group imposes regulation on its components'—see J. Black, 'An Economic Analysis of Regulation: One View of the Cathedral' (1997) 16 *OJLS* 699 at 706.

[31] On self-monitoring and constitutional issues see W. Howarth, 'Self-Monitoring, Self-Policing, Self-incrimination and Pollution Law' (1997) 60 *MLR* 200.

[32] On the complexity of across-the-board rules see R. Baldwin, *Rules and Government* (Oxford, 1995), 162.

Offenders, in turn, would be more effectively disciplined than under governmental regulation because firms can be rewarded for strong systems of discipline. This contrasts with the incentive to conceal infringements under government regulation. Finally, burdens of proof may be lower under enforced self-regulation and more violations will be dealt with by disciplinary steps than would be the case with prosecutions. The more precise and less complex rules that are associated with enforced self-regulation may, again, encourage effective enforcement.

Systems of enforced self-regulation are not, however, problem free and, as is clear from the work of Ayres and Braithwaite and others,[33] a series of difficulties can be anticipated. Ill-intentioned, ill-informed, or inefficient firms may fail to devise appropriate rules. Experience with self-assessment procedures in the British health and safety sector suggests that such firms are very likely to do nothing and await the response of the government regulator.[34] This point applies to the monitoring and enforcement as well as to the drafting of rules. Rule-making and rule-approval costs, moreover, would be large since the government regulator would have to scrutinize a large number of particular rules (often devised with low levels of commitment and competence) instead of devising a single set of general rules.[35] Where firms regulated are small in size and numerous it may be more efficient to rely on government officials to enforce rules than to rely on firms to mobilize independent inspectoral expertise. Similarly, there may be advantages in centralized regulation where the accumulation of expertise in a government body is likely to lead to more rigorous innovation than would be the case with firm-specific controls. Firm-specific drafting of rules may, also, lead to higher levels of industry capture, and worse protections for consumers and the public, than would be the case with government regulation. Firms would expend large sums on devising rules to suit their interests and to circumvent the spirit of government requirements. The state would have to spend similarly large sums to avoid such diversion from public interest objectives. (Whether this is the case or not may depend *inter alia* on the distribution of interests, resources, costs, and benefits in a sector.) Ensuring adequate access to rule-making processes for consumers and

---

[33] Ayres and Braithwaite, *Responsive Regulation*, 120–8; Baldwin, *Rules and Government*, ch. 6; J. Black, 'Talking about Regulation' [1998] *PL* 77.

[34] Baldwin, *Rules and Government*, 162–4.

[35] Black, loc. cit. (1998) pp. 98–100, notes the contention of Ayres and Braithwaite, *Responsive Regulation*, 121, that approval costs can be reduced by routinizing the approvals process. She objects, however, that failing to deal with rules individually undermines the whole enforced self-regulation enterprise. The Office of Fair Trading (OFT, *Raising Standards of Consumer Care*, 13) has, moreover, recently cited the heavy resource demands involved in negotiating, monitoring, and revising voluntary codes of practice and has suggested moving towards introducing core standards to replace codes.

affected interests would also prove extremely difficult if firm-specific drafting was adopted.

Inconsistencies of standards might result from the rule approvals process
—because, for instance, concessions might be made to economically weak
firms (to protect employment) or, in contrast, made to economically
powerful firms in reflection of their political influence or organizational
muscle. In such scenarios middle-range firms would be prejudiced. Some
firms, indeed, might be severely damaged by the costs that enforced self-
regulation would impose on them. In some areas the expenses of drafting rules might be bearable, in others they might put the survival of weaker
firms at risk.

A principal objection to allowing firms to write their own rules might
be that this 'replaces absolute standards with a moral relativism'.[36]
Finally it could be cautioned that managers may not be committed to
regulate in a manner consistent with the public interest where this diverges
from their own and the firm's private interests, and that, even in the case
of well-intentioned firms, the frictions inherent in the rule approvals
process may frequently remove the commitment to the rules that is a
supposed advantage of enforced self-regulation.

The above points suggest that enforced self-regulation offers no simple solution to the traditional problems of regulatory rule-making and
enforcement. They also indicate, however, that different industrial,
social, and economic conditions may call for different blends of regulation and self-regulation, indeed for different models of regulation and
self-regulation, to be used in harness. The kinds of consideration discussed in looking at enforcement in Chapter 8 will, moreover, assist
in attempting to identify the most desirable of such blends. Attention
should thus be paid to the mischiefs to be regulated, the nature of those
who create such mischiefs, the enforcement strategies necessary to combat errant behaviour, and the types of rule that best complement those
strategies.

Conclusions

As with many other regulatory distinctions, the contrast between regulation and self-regulation can be portrayed in ways that are too stark.[37]
Nearly all regulatory mechanisms incorporate some elements of self-
regulation—whether this involves an input into the drafting of rules
or a firm's monitoring its own compliance. Nearly all self-regulatory
mechanisms of governmental significance are subject to some degree of

---

[36] Ayres and Braithwaite, *Responsive Regulation*, 123.

[37] See D. Swann, 'The Regulatory Scene', in K. Button and D. Swann, *The Age of Regulatory
Reform* (Oxford, 1989), 4.

external state influence—even if this is merely the 'shadow' of potential governmental regulation. The trick, as was shown in discussing enforced self-regulation, is to make use of that mix of regulation and self-regulation that best serves legitimate governmental purposes and so merits the strongest claims to support. Analysis of particular regulatory tasks and contexts is essential in bringing about that deployment as is an awareness of the potential of different varieties of regulation and self-regulation.

Regulating Risks

Regulation can be seen to be centrally concerned with the control of risks—be these of illnesses caused by exposure to carcinogens or of inadequate utility services, or of losses caused by incompetent financial advice. To see regulation in terms of risk control adds, moreover, to our understanding of regulatory decisions, methods, and priorities. It does so by exposing a number of difficulties attending the management of uncertainties and the construction of regulatory questions and answers.

This chapter looks, in three parts, at the problems of defining and assessing risks, at the regulatory challenges posed by risks, and at certain proposed solutions to risk regulation.

1. Defining and Assessing Risks

At a common sense level it might be asserted that regulatory efforts should be devoted, as a first priority, to the reduction of the most severe risks that we face in society. A glance at the literature on risks reveals, however, that identifying and assessing risks is no simple matter.[1]

A general definition of risk sees it as the probability that a particular adverse event will occur during a stated period of time, or result from a particular challenge.[2] Important distinctions have, however, been drawn between different types of risk. Thus, probabilistic and unpredictable risks have been differentiated.[3] In the case of the former, assessments of probability can be based on available statistics concerning past incidents. With unpredictable risks, evidence of a causal connection between events may be weak and unquantifiable. Some events may be 'one-off', non-repeating

[1] For introductions to the risk literature see Royal Society, *Risk: Analysis, Perception, Management* (London, 1992); S. Krimsky and D. Golding, *Social Theories of Risk* (Westport, Conn., 1992). On assessments in practice see Interdepartmental Liaison Group on Risk Assessment (ILGRA), *The Use of Risk Assessment in Government Departments* (London, 1996).

[2] See Royal Society, *Risk*, 2; B. Fischhoff, S. Watson, and C. Hope, 'Defining Risk', in T. S. Gluckman and M. Gough (eds.), *Readings in Risk* (Washington, 1993); O. Renn, 'Concepts of Risk: A Classification', in Krimsky and Golding, *Social Theories*.

[3] See e.g. P. Sprent, *Taking Risks* (London, 1988), ch. 2.

risks where probabilities cannot be estimated and subjective assessments must be made. A related distinction lies between 'objective' and 'subjective' risks. The former are seen as scientifically assessable by experts and probabilistic, the latter as non-expert perceptions by the lay public.[4]

A further division can be drawn between *voluntarily undertaken* risks (e.g. from taking oral contraceptives or diet drinks) and *societally imposed* risks (e.g. from nuclear power stations) where citizens have little choice as to exposure. Again, *discrete* risks can be separated from *pervasive* risks, where the former are highly identifiable threats and events of a precise, bounded nature (e.g. earthquakes) and the latter are the risks borne as part of the 'normal' functioning of society—as, for example, presented by polluted air, water, and soil.[5]

A core concern of risk studies has been to explain how risks are, or should be, perceived, assessed, quantified, and responded to.[6] Here a number of broad and varying approaches can be identified.

Technical perspectives, as seen in actuarial approaches, look to the relative frequencies of events amenable to 'objective' observation (e.g. numbers of deaths) and assess probabilities by extrapolating from statistics on past events. Similarly, in epidemiological studies, populations exposed to a risk are compared to control populations and attempts are made to quantify relationships between risks and harms. Engineering approaches attempt to assess the probabilities of failures in complex systems even where there is insufficient data on the given system as a whole. Fault-tree or event-tree analyses are used and the failure probabilities for each component in the tree are evaluated before all such probabilities are sought to be synthesized.

Technical approaches, in general, seek to anticipate harms, average events over time and space, and use relative frequencies to specify probabilities. They are associated with the view that decisions on risks can be made on the basis of objective evidence that can be treated mathematically to produce a numerical result. This perspective has been used not merely to assess the quantum of risks but also their social acceptability. This latter application has, however, been much criticized by social scientists[7] on the grounds that what persons perceive as undesirable

---

[4] For a critique of this distinction see e.g. B. Wynne, 'Institutional Mythologies and Dual Societies in the Management of Risk', in C. Kunnreuther and E. U. Lay (eds.), *The Risk Analysis Controversy* (1983). On the way that regulatory bodies assess risks in the USA see C. F. Cranor, *Regulating Toxic Substances* (New York, 1993), esp. ch. 4.

[5] See M. Waterstone (ed.), *Risk and Society: The Interaction of Science, Technology and Public Policy* (Dordrecht, 1991).

[6] See generally Royal Society, *Risk* and B. Fischhoff, P. Slovic, S. Lichtenstein, S. Reid, and B. Combs, 'How Safe is Safe Enough?' (1978) 9 *Policy Sciences* 127.

[7] See e.g. M. Douglas, *Risk: Acceptability According to the Social Sciences* (London, 1985); O. Renn, loc. cit. n. 2 above; A. Mazur, 'Bias in Risk-Benefit Analysis' (1985) 7 *Technology in Society* 25; U. Beck, *Risk Society* (London, 1992); L. Clarke, *Acceptable Risk* (Berkeley, Calif., 1989).

depends on their values and preferences and that technical strategies tend to undervalue objectives such as equity, fairness, public participation, and resilience.[8] Objectors have also contended that judgements are involved in selecting, defining, and structuring the 'risk problem' and that these influence subsequent conclusions.[9] Such criticisms have eroded not only the idea of objectivity in risk assessment but also the presumed difference between expert and lay public views of risk—the critics of technical approaches hold that both technical and lay assessments of risks involve human interpretation, judgement, and subjectivity.[10] This, we will see below, has implications for those seeking to legitimate different regulatory approaches to risk.

The *economic perspective* on risk transforms undesired effects into subjective utilities so that comparisons between different risks and benefits can be made using the currency of personal satisfaction. This provides a means of integrating risk analyses into decision processes in which various costs and benefits are assessed in pursuit of the allocation of resources in a way that maximizes their utility for society.

Central difficulties for the economic approach[11] are how individuals' subjective utilities can be aggregated; how costs imposed on parties beyond the immediate transaction can be taken on board; how future risks are accounted for; how monetary units can be placed on risks of health losses or deaths; and how utilitarian, wealth-maximization or contractarian ethics can be justified. The economic approach thus begs serious distributional questions and makes contestable assumptions both about the rationality of market decisions and concerning the freedom of choice and quality of information encountered in the market place. It is said to involve a range of judgements and modelling assumptions and be highly prone to manipulation.[12] It, moreover, involves a bias towards the wealthy since all methods of placing a monetary value on life (e.g. making reference to willingness to pay, insurance calculations, or court awards) are in some way based on the wealth of the victim and impliedly encourage saving the lives of the wealthy and imposing risks on the poor.[13]

---

[8] J. F. Short, 'The Social Fabric at Risk: Towards the Social Transformation of Risk Analysis' (1984) 49 *Am. Soc. Rev.* 711. For official acceptance that risk regulation 'cannot be reduced to a set of rules based on universal formulae for quantifying and valuing costs and benefits' but involves ethical and perceptual problems see HM Treasury, *The Setting of Safety Standards* (London, 1996).

[9] See C. J. H. Vlek and P. J. M. Stollen, 'Rational and Personal Aspects of Risk' (1980) 45 *Acta Psychologica* 273. Cranor, *Regulating Toxic Substances*, 10.

[10] Royal Society, *Risk*, 97; B. Fischhoff, *Risk: A Guide to Controversy* (Washington DC, 1989).

[11] See e.g. P. Slovic, B. Fischhoff, and S. Lichtenstein, 'Rating the Risks' (1979) *Environment* 4; M. S. Baram, 'Cost-Benefit Analysis: An Inadequate Basis for Health, Safety and Environmental Regulatory Decisionmaking' (1980) 8 *Ecology LQ* 463.

[12] See P. Self, *Econocrats and the Policy Process: The Politics and Philosophy of Cost-Benefit Analysis* (Basingstoke, 1975).

[13] See H. Otway, 'Public Wisdom, Expert Fallibility: Towards a Contextual Theory of Risk', in Krimsky and Golding, *Social Theories*.

The *psychological approach* to the definition and measurement of risk focuses upon individual cognition and such questions as how probabilities are perceived; how preferences relating to risks can be accounted for and how contexts shape individuals' risk estimations and evaluations. Thus, several factors have been said to impinge on perceptions of seriousness of risks.[14] These include:

- catastrophic potential;
- degree of personal control over the size or probability of the risk;
- familiarity with the risk;
- degree of perceived equity in sharing risks and benefits;
- visibility of the benefits of risk taking;
- potential to impose blame on risk creators;
- delay in the manifestation of harm;
- voluntariness with which the risk is undertaken.

Risk, within such an approach, is seen as a multidimensional concept that cannot be reduced to a mere product of probability and consequences. Such a focus on the individual is, however, said to underplay the extent to which perceptions are affected by group, social, institutional, and cultural factors.[15]

Sociologists have addressed this under-emphasis by attending to social relations and institutions as influences on risk perception and by examining the ways that moral positions and valuations affect responses to risk. They have tended to stress the limitations of technical approaches and to argue that expert knowledge is not value free but conditioned by social contexts; that public attitudes to risk are affected by a wide range of variables and that public tolerance of risk is a political issue in which the degree of public involvement in risk management processes may play an important role.[16]

At a more general level, Ulrich Beck and other sociologists have talked of the 'risk society' in which we now live. This begins 'where nature ends' in the sense that risks are no longer imposed from outside and suffered as a matter of fate but are 'manufactured'—they are the products of mankind's decisions, options, science, politics, industries, markets, and capital.[17] In this risk society we increasingly struggle to negotiate

---

[14] See Royal Society, *Risk*, ch. 5; Renn, loc. cit. n. 2 above; P. Slovic, B. Fischhoff, and S. Lichtenstein, 'Perceived Risks, Psychological Factors and Social Implications' (1981) 376 *Proceedings of the Royal Society of London* 17; L. Gould et al., *Perceptions of Technological Risks and Benefits* (New York, 1988).

[15] See Royal Society, *Risk*, 11, 108; A. Plough and S. Krimsky, 'The Emergence of Risk Communication Studies: Social and Political Context' (1987) 12 *Science, Technology and Human Values* 4.

[16] See S. Krimsky and D. Golding in Krimsky and Golding, *Social Theories*, 356; A. Giddens, *Beyond Left and Right* (Cambridge, 1994).

[17] See U. Beck, *Risk Society* (London, 1992); Giddens, *Beyond Left and Right*; U. Beck, 'The Politics of Risk Society' and A. Giddens, 'Risk Society: The Context of British Politics', both in J. Franklin (ed.), *The Politics of Risk Society* (Cambridge, 1998).

the future, science can no longer be looked to for answers, and conventional political mechanisms do little to assure us. The challenge is said to be to develop political processes that will come to grips with these new risk-related issues.[18]

Cultural theorists, in turn, have contended that attitudes to risk vary according to cultural biases—attitudes and beliefs shared by a group—and that risk is a plastic concept allowing the development of no single measure by which different cultural biases towards risk can be compared.[19]

Such cultural approaches to risk have been linked with psychological and sociological treatments in the work of 'social amplification theorists' who suggest that signals concerning risks are filtered through social amplification stations (e.g. groups of scientists; the media; pressure groups and politicians) and that this filtering intensifies or minimizes certain aspects of risks.[20] Other social scientists have focused on risk communication and have attended to the ways that messages about risks are conveyed; the politics of such message passing and the institutional and cultural contexts under which risk messages are formulated and conveyed.[21]

To summarize, a host of different approaches to the definition and measurement of risks can be taken. These very differences raise issues about regulatory responses to risks and the ways in which risk regulation regimes can be justified or legitimated. Thus, high confidence in technical approaches to risk might lead to an emphasis on leaving risk regulation to experts and in establishing regulatory priorities with reference to technical evaluations. In contrast, a strong belief that risks are socially constructed might be taken to suggest that regulatory priorities and policies cannot be left to the 'objective' evaluations of experts but have to emerge from democratically legitimate processes of debate and consultation.

2. Risks: The Regulatory Challenges

A first challenge for regulators is to identify those risks that need to be reduced as matters of first priority and to do so in a manner meeting public approval. As seen above, a material problem may arise from the

[18] See Giddens, *Beyond Left and Right*.

[19] See Douglas, *Risk*; M. Douglas, *Risk and Blame* (London, 1992); M. Douglas and A. Wildavsky, *Risk and Culture* (Berkeley, Calif., 1982); M. Schwarz and M. Thompson, *Divided We Stand: Redefining Politics, Technology and Social Choice* (Hemel Hempstead, 1990). On the limitations of cultural theory see S. Rayner, 'Culture Theory and Risk Analysis', in Krimsky and Golding, *Social Theories*.

[20] See e.g. R. E. Kasperson et al., 'The Social Amplification of Risk: A Conceptual Framework' (1988) 8 *Risk Analysis* 177; R. E. Kasperson et al., 'The Social Amplification of Risk: Progress in Developing an Integrative Framework', in Krimsky and Golding, *Social Theories*.

[21] See Royal Society, *Risk*, ch. 5.5; H. J. Otway and B. Wynne, 'Risk Communication: Paradigm and Paradox' (1989) 9 *Risk Analysis* 141; S. Krimsky and A. Plough, *Environmental Hazards: Communicating Risks as a Social Process* (Dover, Mass., 1988).

tension between 'technical', 'rational', or 'expert' approaches and the perceptions of the public. The priorities that the public might establish will tend to appear irrational to experts since citizens' perceptions of risk will be distorted by the range of factors noted above (e.g. the degree of personal control, familiarity, etc.) and will not correspond to figures based on products of probability and magnitude of harm. Not only will members of the public respond 'irrationally' to risks but democratic processes may have limited potential to cope with information about risks.[22] Questions thus arise concerning the role of the public in decision-making on risks; on whether (and how) people should be informed of the risks they face; and the means by which decisions regarding risks can be legitimated in the eyes of the public. One strand of the risk literature explores models of decision-making that aim to reduce conflicts about risk assessment and focuses on the potential of adversarial processes, administrative rules, and judicial review to legitimize risk regulation.[23] More general concerns are the extent and quality of information relating to risks; the reasons why there may be informational inadequacies when decisions on risks are taken; and the costs of risk-related information.[24] One view sees differences in public and expert perceptions of risk as a key element in the 'vicious circle' of factors that diminishes public trust in regulatory institutions, inhibits more rational regulation, and contributes to random selection of regulatory priorities as well as inconsistencies of regulatory approach.[25]

A second regulatory challenge is to manage and regulate risks in an effective and acceptable manner.[26] The stage at which intervention should take place is a central issue. Risk management may involve the adoption of strategies to minimize the *production* of risks or it may be concerned with mitigating the adverse *effects* of hazards through implementing such measures as warning procedures, safety mechanisms, and contingency plans.

Thus, a distinction is to be drawn between instruments that are active (which seek to modify the source of the risk—for example by dynamiting the avalanche slope) and those which are passive and lessen undesirable effects (e.g. by evacuating populations within the potential avalanche path). This question of whether risk managers and regulators should anticipate

[22] S. G. Hadden, *A Citizen's Right to Know: Risk Communication and Public Policy* (Boulder, Colo., 1989); D. J. Fiorino, 'Citizen Participation and Environmental Risk: A Survey of Institutional Mechanisms' (1990) 15 *Science Technology and Human Values* 226; J. Handman and E. C. Penning-Rowsell (eds.), *Hazards and the Communication of Risks* (Aldershot, 1990).

[23] See S. Jasanoff, 'The Misrule of Law at OSHA', in D. Nelkin (ed.), *The Language of Risk* (Beverly Hills, Calif., 1985).

[24] See K. R. MacCrimmon and D. A. Wehrung, *Taking Risks* (New York, 1982), 15–17.

[25] See S. Breyer, *Breaking the Vicious Circle: Toward Effective Risk Regulation* (Cambridge, Mass., 1993) (discussed further below).

[26] See C. Hood and D. Jones, *Accident and Design* (London, 1997).

and prevent or should promote resilience and the capacity to withstand harms is a recurring issue in the risk management literature.[27]

Another important concern is the design of institutions and techniques for managing risk. Involved here is the fundamental question of when risks should be seen as matters of public concern rather than left for private handling.[28] Issues considered in the literature include the role of insurance mechanisms in shaping responses to risks and how insurance interacts with legal and regulatory structures relevant to risk taking. Particular interests are the effects of insurance on the incentives created by liability rules and the problems of moral hazard and adverse selection within the insurance mechanism.

Choosing the appropriate regulatory technique is a further challenge that is also the subject of an extensive literature[29] involving attention to institutions, modes of enforcement,[30] and the optimal way to target regulation on risks. On the last point, a key question is whether risk managers, if they are to err, should choose, where possible, to do so by rejecting true hypotheses about causes of harm and under-regulating risks rather than by accepting false hypotheses and regulating when there is no true justification for this.[31]

Further questions of technique arise. A first is whether risk management or regulation should be 'blame-oriented'—with precise allocation of liability and resultant incentives to take care—or whether a greater focus should be placed on collective or corporate design rather than individual blame.[32] A second issue is whether risk managers should rely on qualitative risk evaluations as opposed to more quantitative assessments. Those sceptical of quantitative methods stress their susceptibility to problems of value assumptions, qualitative data, administrative difficulties, equity, public acceptability, the lack of a single risk decision framework, and effectiveness.[33]

---

[27] See e.g. B. A. Turner, *Man-Made Disasters* (London, 1978); H. D. Foster, *Disaster Planning* (New York, 1979); A. Wildavsky, *Trial without Error: Anticipation Versus Resilience as Strategies for Risk Reduction* (Sydney, 1985); id., *Searching for Safety* (New Brunswick, NJ, 1988).

[28] See M. T. Katzman, 'Pollution Liability Insurance and Catastrophic Environmental Risk' (1988) *Journal of Risk and Insurance* 75.

[29] On regulatory strategies see Chapter 3 above; A. Ogus, *Regulation: Legal Form and Economic Theory* (Oxford, 1994) and C. Hood, *The Tools of Government* (Basingstoke, 1983).

[30] On regulatory enforcement see Chapter 8 above.

[31] That is by making 'Type II' rather than 'Type I' errors—see Chapter 8 above, pp. 104–6; G. Brennan, 'Civil Disaster Management: An Economist's View' (1991) 64 *Canberra Bull. of Pub. Admin.* 30.

[32] Compare R. A. Posner, *Economic Analysis of Law* (3rd edn., Boston, 1986), 147–51 and B. Fisse and J. Braithwaite, 'Accountability and the Control of Corporate Crime', in M. Findlay and R. Hogg (eds.), *Understanding Crime and Criminal Justice* (Sydney, 1988); E. Bardach and R. Kagan, *Going by the Book* (Philadelphia, 1982).

[33] See J. Adams and M. Thompson, *Risk Review* (London, 1991) and A. Gorz, *Critique of Economic Reason* (London, 1989).

A third question is whether a basis of knowledge can be generated that is adequate to found effective institutional designs for risk management. On the one hand, it is asserted that principles of good institutional design can be set down[34] but, on the other, sceptics point to current limitations in knowledge about the handling of risks in organizations. A fourth issue concerns the extent to which reductions in risks have to be traded off against other basic goals or alternative risk reductions. Some commentators, however, contest the view that trade-offs always have to be made and point to instances where actions designed to reduce risks have positive rather than negative effects on such matters as productivity and efficiency.[35]

The final issue to be noted returns to the theme of democratic acceptability and concerns the degree of participation in risk management decisions that is appropriate. One approach stresses the need for broad access to risk management processes and thereby accountability.[36] It is, further, argued that where scientific evidence about risks is inconclusive there is a specially strong case for incorporating an 'extended peer community' of experts into risk management decisions.[37] The alternative view, however, doubts the benefits of broad participation, stresses the dangers of giving weight to 'unfounded public fears', and argues for rational decisions by small groups of well-informed experts.[38]

In summary, seeing regulation in terms of risks highlights a series of challenges that face regulators. Positions taken in relation to the issues discussed above will often link to the issue of confidence in forecasting and quantifying risks in an agreed manner. High confidence on these fronts will tend to favour anticipatory actions and the specification of outputs; low confidence will tend to favour emphasis on resilience, the specification of processes, and qualitative debates concerning uncertainties.

3. 'Solutions' to Risk Regulation

Risk regulators, it is clear from the above, face difficult problems in seeking legitimation, not least because of divergences in expert and lay perceptions of risk. What, then, can be done to improve the force of legitimating arguments? This section reviews two kinds of response. The first is based principally on an expertise rationale and the second on the accountability and due process rationales.

---

[34] See T. Horlick-Jones, *Acts of God?* (London, 1990).
[35] See E. Tait and L. Levidov, 'Proactive and Reactive Approaches to Risk Regulation' (1992) *Futures* 219.
[36] See S. Beder, 'The Fallible Engineer' (1991) *New Scientist* 38.
[37] Royal Society, *Risk*, 164.
[38] See R. S. Yalow, 'Radioactivity in the Service of Humanity' (1985) 60 *Thought* 517; Breyer, *Breaking the Vicious Circle*.

Stephen Breyer exemplifies the first approach in his book *Breaking the Vicious Circle: Towards Effective Risk Regulation*.[39] For Breyer, the regulation of small but significant health risks is plagued by three serious problems: *tunnel vision*—where there is over-regulation to the point that it brings about more harm than good; *random agenda selection* —where regulatory priorities are driven by issues coming to the public's attention rather than by rational appraisals of risks; and *inconsistency*— where agencies use different methods to calculate the effects of regulation and the values that regulators implicitly attach to the saving of a statistical life vary widely from one programme or agency to another.

The causes of these problems are said, again, to be threefold and constitute a 'vicious circle' that diminishes trust in regulatory institutions and increasingly inhibits more rational regulation. The causes are: *public perceptions*—in which the public's evaluation of risk problems 'differs radically from any consensus of experts in the field' and does not reflect a 'rational' set of priorities;[40] *congressional action and reaction*— a tendency to respond to risks with detailed statutory directions that later experience shows to be inappropriate; and *uncertainties in the technical regulatory process*—the limitations of knowledge, data, and predictive power that afflict regulatory processes.

Breyer's solution involves institutional changes that reflect the view that a 'depoliticised regulatory process might produce better results'.[41] His suggestion has two parts: first, that a new career path be established to provide a group of civil servants with experience in working with health and environmental agencies, Congress, and the Office of Management and Budget; second, that a small centralized administrative group be formed from such civil servants, one with a mission of producing a coherent risk programme and a set of rational priorities covering risk regulatory programmes.[42] The group would have jurisdiction over different agencies and would have a degree of political insulation to allow it to withstand various political pressures. It would have prestige, authority, and expertise and would rationalize right across government. Its authority would flow from its outputs 'insofar as a systematic solution produces technically better results, the decision will become somewhat more legitimate'.[43]

The difficulty with Breyer's proposal is that it involves heavy emphasis on legitimation through expertise at the expense of legitimation through emphasis on democratic policy-making, accountability, and due process in the form of participation. Breyer suggests that the group's proposals, plans, and findings would be openly available for comment and criticism but at root what is proposed is a level of insulation from

---

[39] (Cambridge, Mass., 1993).   [40] Ibid. 33.
[41] Ibid. 56.   [42] Ibid.   [43] Ibid. 63.

politics such as will allow the 'rational' decisions of experts to establish priorities for risk regulation rather than public perceptions and desires. This presupposes to a considerable degree that risk prioritizing can be dealt with technically as a mere product of probability and extent of harm. As already noted, however, a number of commentators might be expected to object strongly that experts are no more 'rational' than lay persons, that in 'risk society' scientists and experts create as many uncertainties as they dispel,[44] and that risk priorities are perceptual, distributional, and political matters that must be negotiated through exchanges of views rather than laid down from on high by experts making hidden value judgements.[45] It can, furthermore, be objected that striving for greater rationality in the form of increased scientific accuracy concerning risks may, beyond a certain stage, involve costs, delays, legal challenges, and the creation of new uncertainties that are socially undesirable—that this may produce a tendency both to under-regulate and to introduce mistakes into regulatory processes. The value of more detailed risk analysis can, thus, be said to depend on normative judgements about the chosen uses to be made of such information.[46]

A contrasting approach to that of Breyer is offered by Shrader-Frechette, who points to certain strengths of risk cost benefit analyses (RCBA)—notably their systematic nature, clarity concerning social costs, and superiority to arbitrary, intuitive, and expert modes of decision-making.[47] Shrader-Frechette, nevertheless, seeks to remedy some of the weaknesses of RCBA by application of 'scientific produralism'. This process seeks to improve RCBA by three devices. The first of these is *ethical weighting*. This involves imposing a negative weight to the imposition of certain particularly undesirable risks and it is envisaged that the public or its representatives could be involved in deciding which weighting scheme best represents its values. The central idea is that ethical considerations rather than the RCBA itself should govern priorities.[48] The

---

[44] See J. Durant, 'Once the Men in White Coats Held the Promise of a Better Future', in Franklin, *Politics of Risk Society*: 'science is no longer simply regarded as a source of solutions, it is increasingly seen as part of the problem.'

[45] See e.g. Giddens, *Beyond Left and Right* and Beck, *Risk Society*. For a review of Breyer's thesis see V. B. Flatt, 'Should the Circle be Unbroken?' (1994) 24 (4) *Environmental Law* 1707. Flatt contends, *inter alia*: 'many of the "problems" with inconsistent risk values are not problems at all but actual policy choices that reflect societal values other than the explicit reduction of risk to human life' (p. 1713); 'some of our regulatory choices are not value judgements about *what* we should pay for regulation but rather *who* should pay' (p. 1718).

[46] See Cranor, *Regulating Toxic Substances*, 120 and 130 who argues that the 'science-intensive' approach to regulation is slow because of its concern to develop 'perfect' regulations.

[47] See K. S. Schrader-Frechette, *Risk and Rationality* (Berkeley, Calif., 1991).

[48] See also the Tolerability of Risk (TOR) approach noted in Chapter 9 above, and discussed in HM Treasury, *Setting Safety Standards*, 8–9, which allows risk cost benefit only within equitably established boundaries. Cranor suggests in *Regulating Toxic Substances* that, in relation to such problems as those posed by carcinogens, scientific knowledge and

second device is the use of *alternative risk analyses and evaluations*. Several risk analyses can be commissioned or allowed in relation to a single risk issue and this, it is suggested, will reveal information and assumptions more clearly than is possible with a single analysis. It will also allow citizens, as opposed to experts, to have a greater role in determining risk choices—it will lead policy-makers to rely on procedural and democratic, rather than merely scientific, methods of evaluating and managing risks.[49] Finally, *weighted expert opinions* can be used to give emphasis in policy-making processes to the forecasts of experts whose risk estimates have been 'vindicated by past predictive success'—a process that comes to grips with the absence of any uncontroversially objective way to calculate risks in so far as it offers a checking system.

'Scientific proceduralism' thus rejects any assumption that risks can be estimated in a value-free way. It asserts the need to democratize RCBA and it stresses the value of open, pluralistic approaches in revealing realities. The technique, as set out by Shrader-Frechette, leaves open a number of unresolved issues—whether, for instance, weighting procedures oversimplify ethical considerations; whether democratic participation is better served by separating this from the RCBA than by weighting; how weighting processes can be combined with RCBA; whether policy-making in the real world allows the use of alternative and multiple RCBAs (and whether this will lead to confusion); and the extent to which expertise in one area of risk analysis can be transported to other areas. What is noteworthy for our purposes, however, is the proposed route to legitimation and the urging that risk analyses must be conducted within frameworks of greater participation and accountability—this contrasts quite starkly with Breyer's emphasis on expertise.

Conclusions

To focus on the uncertainties involved in regulating a sector or topic is to set out to deal with a particular set of difficulties. Issues arise relating to the perception of risk; the definition and classification of risks; and the construction of 'risk problems'. Particular concerns in the control of

data for risk estimates is inadequate and that this presents a choice: to desist from regulating or to make decisions on the basis of available evidence and non-scientific policy considerations. Allowing the science-intensive perspective to dominate would thus lead to under-protection of the public, increased regulatory costs, and decreased policy accountability. The way forward, he states, is via the use of explicitly made policy guidelines and the *combination* of policy and scientific judgements. 'Once it is recognised that risk assessment (and regulation) is in part a function of policy considerations, public input, especially in a democratic form of government, becomes a relevant consideration to shape the process' (p. 134).

[49] Shrader-Frechette, *Risk and Rationality*, 187.

risks relate to divergences in lay and expert approaches; to the use of information in regulating uncertainties; and the susceptibility of risk control regimes to democratic and participatory mechanisms. As was seen in discussing the proposals of Breyer and Shrader-Frechette, very different approaches to 'rational' risk regulation can be taken and the role of rationality in risk control is itself contentious.

Seeing regulation in terms of risks, and an awareness of the literature on risk control that is encountered in many disciplines, does add new dimensions to our understanding of regulation. It prompts new questions about perceptions of regulatory priorities, the construction and development of regulatory agendas, and the legitimation of both regulation and regulatory reviews.

Regulation in the European Context

Few domestic regulatory regimes in the European Union are unaffected by governmental actions taken at the European level. In many sectors the domestic regime is strongly influenced by European rules and in some areas it has been acknowledged that the main source of regulatory law has moved from the Member State to Europe.[1] At the level of European Union government, a 'regulatory state' has been said to have arisen as the European institutions have become regulators themselves.[2]

This chapter considers the challenges both of regulating at the European level and of regulating within Europe. It starts by reviewing the general problems of European level regulation, proceeds to examine the strategies for regulating that have been developed by European institutions, and then examines the relationship between European and Member State levels of regulation.

1. The Problems of European Regulation

If reference is made to the regulatory benchmarks discussed in Chapter 6, it can be seen that European-level regulation presents difficulties at least as severe as those faced by Member State regulators.

---

[1] By 1990 the head of the UK Health and Safety Commission had conceded that the European Community had to be regarded as the 'principal engine' of health and safety law. See Health and Safety Commission, *Plan of Work for 1990/1 and Beyond* (HMSO, London, 1989), p. viii. On the development of Community Law in the health and safety sector see R. Baldwin and T. Daintith, *Harmonisation and Hazard* (London, 1992) and R. Nielsen and E. Szyszczak, *The Social Dimension of the European Community* (2nd edn., Copenhagen, 1993); D. Rowland, 'Enforcement of Health and Safety at Work, with Special Reference to the UK', in C. Harding and B. Swart (eds.), *Enforcing European Community Rules* (Aldershot, 1996). On developments in the utilities see S. Sayer, 'The Impact of the European Union on UK Utility Regulation', in M. E. Beesley (ed.), *Regulating Utilities: A Time for Change?* (London, 1996); L. Hancher, 'Utilities Policy and the European Union', in P. Vass (ed.), *CRI Regulatory Review 1996* (London, 1996); J. Pelkmans, 'Utilities Policy and the European Union', in P. Vass (ed.), *CRI Regulatory Review 1997* (London, 1997). On the decline in national regulatory competence in the environment policy, social policy, product safety, and fundamental rights fields see S. Weatherill, 'Implementation as a Constitutional Issue', in T. Daintith (ed.), *Implementing EC Law in the United Kingdom* (Chichester, 1995).

[2] See G. Majone, 'The Rise of the Regulatory State in Europe' (1993) 17 *West European Politics* 77; id., *Regulating Europe* (London, 1996).

Mandates

A British regulator usually has problems in claiming legitimacy through implementing a mandate because the content of the mandate is almost always open to interpretation. Few difficulties are encountered, however, in asserting that Parliament is a democratically legitimate body. In Europe the legitimacy of the Parliament is by no means beyond dispute and if European regulation is justified by reference to, say, a Directive, there are further problems concerning the basis of legislative authority as well as the content of the mandate.[3] First, the linkage between the Directive and the authorizing treaty term may be extremely loose or contentious[4] and may be the responsibility of the unelected Community institutions, with the elected organ, the European Parliament, playing a limited role.[5] Second, the extent to which the UK Parliament has sanctioned a particular provision may be highly questionable and strongly disputed. The mandate may derive from the Community policy-making process rather than any domestic Parliament. Third, reference may be made in some European rules to standards made by private bodies and the lines of democratic authority in such cases may be particularly weak.[6]

Finally, a mode of legislation such as the Directive incorporates a large measure of discretion as to implementation through Member State law

---

[3] See e.g. J. Weiler, 'After Maastricht: Community Legitimacy in Post-1992 Europe', in W. Adams (ed.), *Singular Europe: Economy and Polity of the European Union after 1992* (Ann Arbor, 1992). It should also be borne in mind that traditional attitudes to mandates and their precision may vary across Europe with populations attuned to continental codes and drafting styles being more sympathetic to open-ended mandates than, say, those familiar with English common law approaches. On European legislation generally, see P. Craig and C. Harlow (eds.), *Lawmaking in the European Union* (Dordrecht, 1998).

[4] On disputes as to the Treaty basis of a Directive see the 'Titanium Dioxide' case: Case 300/89 *Commission* v. *Council* [1991] ECR 1-2867 and Case 155/91 *Commission* v. *Council* [1993] ECR 1-939. On stretching the use of an Article see J. Weiler, 'The Transformation of Europe' (1991) 100 *Yale LJ* 2403 (extracted in P. Craig and G. de Burca, *EC Law* (London, 1995), 105–11).

[5] See R. Baldwin, *Rules and Government* (Oxford, 1995), 272–3. On the 'democratic deficit' within the EU generally see S. Williams, 'Sovereignty and Accountability in the European Community' (1990) 61 *Pol. Q.* 299; C. Harlow, 'A Community of Interests' (1992) 55 *MLR* 331; L. Hancher, '1992 and Accountability Gaps' (1990) 53 *MLR* 669; K. Featherstone, 'Jean Monnet and the "Democratic Deficit" in the European Union' (1994) 32 *J. Common Market Studies* 149; S. Andersen and K. Eliassen, *The European Union: How Democratic is It?* (London, 1996); D. Curtin, 'The Constitutional Structure of the European Union' (1993) 30 *CMLR* 17; B. Boyce, 'The Democratic Deficit of the European Community' (1993) 46 *Parliamentary Affairs* 458; P. Raworth, 'A Timid Step Forwards: Maastricht and the Democratisation of the European Community' (1994) 19 *ELR* 16; J. Weiler et al., 'European Democracy and Its Critique' (1995) 4 *West European Politics* 24; *Report of the Reflection Group* SN 520/95 (Dec. 1995). On 'fusion' theory and democratic legitimation at the supranational level see W. Wessels, 'An Ever Closer Fusion? A Dynamic Macropolitical View on Integration Processes' (1997) 35 *J. Common Market Studies* 267.

[6] On private standard setting in the EU and on delegations of power see K. Lenaerts, 'Regulating the Regulatory Process: "Delegation of Powers" in the E. C.' (1993) 18 *ELR* 23; R. Lauwaars, 'The "Model Directive" on Technical Harmonisation', in R Bieber, R. Dehousse, J. Pinder, and J. Weiler, *1992: One European Market* (Baden-Baden, 1988).

rather than offers a precise mandate—it is only binding 'as to the result to be achieved' and leaves to the Member State 'the choice of form and methods'.[7]

Accountability

It might be argued that the European Parliament holds regulators to account in the EU but, again, it can be countered that there is a 'democratic deficit' within the EU and a gap between powers conferred to the Community and the controls of the elected Parliament.[8] As for accountability through the openness of the participatory process generally, the criticism made in relation to domestic regulation—that this is attuned to the large-scale, well-resourced enterprise rather than the small or medium-sized firm—applies all the more on the Community stage.[9] Nor can it be said with conviction that Member State Parliaments make up for the weakness of the European Parliament by offering strong scrutiny of European legislation—national parliaments have little or no input into Commission proposals on regulatory rules (they cannot, for instance, amend Community legislation) whereas governmental input through bureaucratic structures is considerable.[10] In this sense, any shift from domestic to European-level regulation involves a movement away from parliamentary towards governmental and bureaucratic control.[11] There are, furthermore, problems with governmental input into European policy-making in so far as unanimity in the Council is no longer required in certain areas (e.g. on market completing issues) and so the citizens of a Member State may be regulated by a provision that their representing minister has been outvoted on.

Legal control is exercised in the EU by the European Court of Justice (ECJ), which can review the legality of Regulations, Directives, and Decisions which are binding and it can decide whether legal effects are

---

[7] See Art. 189 EC.

[8] See references on 'democratic deficit' at n. 5 and on the European Parliament's role in European legislation see D. Chalmers, *European Union Law Vol. 1* (Aldershot, 1998), 182–90 and Baldwin, *Rules and Government*, 273–83.

[9] But cf. Harlow loc. cit. n. 5 above on access to policy-making processes in the EU.

[10] See generally E. Smith (ed.), *National Parliaments as Cornerstones of European Integration* (London, 1996); P. Norton (ed.), *National Parliaments and the European Union* (London, 1996); K. Neunreither, 'The Democratic Deficit of the European Union: Towards Closer Cooperation between the European Parliament and the National Parliaments' (1994) 29 *Government and Opposition* 299; P. Birkinshaw and D. Ashiagbor, 'National Participation in Community Affairs: Democracy, the UK Parliament and the EU' (1995) 33 *CMLR* 499. National parliamentary participation in the EC legislative procedure was addressed at Amsterdam in a protocol: *Protocol to the TEC on the Role of National Parliaments in the European Union*. The protocol requires, *inter alia*, that Commission legislative proposals be made in sufficient time to allow domestic parliamentary scrutiny.

[11] On the need for early parliamentary input into the community legislative process see Hansard Society, *Making the Law* (London, 1992), paras. 539–46.

to be given to 'soft law' measures.[12] Judicial review is, however, a limited mechanism of accountability. The ECJ's resources are finite; review tends to be sporadic and depends on there being a party with the knowledge and financing to bring an action; the ECJ looks to the legality, not merits or substance, of regulatory rules or actions and the breadth of the discretions given to the community institutions limits their vulnerability to judicial review.

Due Process and Fairness

It is perhaps in claiming that European level regulation is transparent, accessible, and fair that the most severe difficulties are encountered. The essence of this claim is that parties affected by a regulatory rule have been dealt with openly and fairly—in a Community of fifteen Member States, fairness is of special importance. The lack of openness in Community law-making has been criticized from a number of directions[13] and in 1992 the high-level Sutherland Report stressed the need for the Commission to introduce better procedures for making citizens aware of proposed legislation at an early stage; for disclosing background information; for debating issues of subsidiarity; for ensuring transparency in legislative processes; and for achieving wide and effective consultation on commission proposals.[14] Nor do key developments in EU

[12] On 'soft law' in the EU see Baldwin, *Rules and Government*, ch. 8; K. C. Wellens and G. M. Borchardt, 'Soft Laws in European Community Law' (1989) 14 *ELR* 267; F. Beveridge and S. Nott, 'A Hard Look at Soft Law', in Craig and Harlow, *Lawmaking*. A criticism of soft law is its propensity to avoid judicial review—see Della Cananea, 'Soft Law and State Aids', in I. Harden et al., *State Aids* (1993).

[13] See Chalmers, *European Union Law Vol. 1*, 190; and F. Snyder, 'The Effectiveness of European Community Law' (1993) 56 *MLR* 19; Hansard Society, *Making the Law*, para. 570–1; P. P. Craig, 'Democracy and Rule-making within the EC: An Empirical and Normative Assessment' (1997) 3 *European Law Journal* 105; J. Lodge, 'Transparency and Democratic Legitimacy' (1994) 32 *J. Common Market Studies* 343; J. C. Piris, 'After Maastricht, are the Community Institutions More Efficacious, More Democratic, More Transparent?' (1994) 19 *ELR* 949.

[14] See P. Sutherland et al., *The Internal Market after 1992: Meeting the Challenge*, Report to the EEC Commission by the High Level Group on the Operation of the Internal Market (Brussels, 1992) (The Sutherland Report), 11–12, 28–30. The *Report of the Reflection Group* produced for the 1996 inter-Governmental Conference stressed five goals under the heading of transparency: access to information; the provision of information to experts and society in general prior to legislative proposals being made; the provision of information to national parliaments with time to comment at the start of the legislative process; the opening up of the workings of the Community institutions; and the rendering of Union law more accessible—see Craig loc. cit. n. 13 above, p. 119 and *Report of the Council of the Functioning of the Treaty on European Union* (Luxembourg, 1995), paras. 13–15. Access has been given to the public on documents held by the Commission and Council—see *Code of Conduct concerning Public Access to Council and Commission Documents* OJ 1993 340/41— adopted by the Council and Commissions officially in Decisions 93/371/EC, OJ 1993 L 340/43, and 94/90/EC, OJ 1994 L 46/58 respectively. The Amsterdam summit of 1997 moved towards a general principle of open government for EU citizens—see Chalmers, *European Union Law Vol. 1*, 200.

policy-making techniques inevitably increase transparency. The increase in legislative tempo that followed the Single European Act of 1986 was a step not liable to strengthen claims to openness and, again, the privatization of standards-making that supports the New Approach to technical harmonization (discussed below) is open to the criticism that it favours business interests rather than consumer organizations, who tend to lack the resources required to participate effectively in the standard-setting process.[15] It has been proposed that European regulatory processes might be formalized along the lines set out in the US Administrative Procedure Act 1946 and that new rights to public hearings should be introduced,[16] but such steps are yet to be taken.

This is not to say, however, that European administrative law does not play a significant role in controlling the openness of laws and regulations. Article 190 demands that Regulations, Directives, and Decisions adopted jointly by the European Parliament and the Council or by the Council or Commission 'shall state the reasons on which they are based'.[17] This requirement applies not only to legislative norms but also to individualized administrative decisions and is broader in scope than the rules encountered in many Member States. A reason-giving requirement potentially makes the decision-making process more transparent by allowing affected parties to know the reasoning behind a measure or decision; it thus facilitates participation and it encourages decision-makers to be clear about the rationales for their actions. A reason-giving requirement also facilitates the exercise of review by the European Court of Justice (ECJ), allowing it to scrutinize the purposes for which powers are used and the proportionality of actions taken.

The force of the reason-giving requirement in European law depends on the approach to judicial review taken by the ECJ. It has been argued that a number of background factors, familiar to US observers, point in the direction of an increasingly rigorous approach to review.[18] These

---

[15] See Lodge loc. cit. n. 13 above; A. McGee and S. Weatherill, 'The Evolution of the Single Market: Harmonisation or Liberalisation?' (1990) 53 *MLR* 578. On lobbying see S. Mazey and J. Richardson, 'The Commission and the Lobby', in G. Edwards and D. Spence, *The European Commission* (2nd edn., London, 1997); W. Streek and P. Schmitter, 'From National Corporalism to Transnational Pluralism: Organised Interests in the Single Market' (1991) 19 *Politics and Society* 133; C. Harlow, 'A Community of Interests: Making the Most of European Law' (1992) 55 *MLR* 331; S. Mazey and J. Richardson (eds.), *Lobbying in the European Community* (Oxford, 1993); R. Pedler and P. Van Schendeden (eds.), *Lobbying in the European Union* (Aldershot, 1994).

[16] See R. Dehousse et al., *Europe after 1992*, EUI Working Paper 92/31 (Florence, 1992). For arguments against full-scale legislative codification of EC administrative procedures, but in favour of codification of 'general principles of good administration' see C. Harlow, 'Codification of EC Administrative Procedures? Fitting the Foot to the Shoe or the Shoe to the Foot' (1996) 2 *ELJ* 3.

[17] See Craig and de Burca, *EC Law*, 107–12; 496–505; M. Shapiro, 'The Giving Reasons Requirement' (1992) *U. Chic. Legal Forum* 179; id., 'Codification of Administrative Law: The US and the Union' (1996) 2 *European Law Journal* 26.

[18] See Shapiro loc. cit. n. 17 above (1996).

factors include the growing desire for transparency and participation that accompanies a movement of regulatory authority from Member State capitals to Brussels; growing suspicions within the EU concerning Brussels regulators; increasing fears of technology and technocracy; and the removal of those business and governmental elites that formerly negotiated regulatory compromises at national level to the periphery of European policy-making—a removal that leads them to exert pressure for greater access to, and transparency of, European regulatory and legislative processes.

For its part, the ECJ has indicated that the extent of the Article 190 reason-giving requirement depends on the nature of the measure in question,[19] but the court has proved reluctant to require the Commission to enter into a dialogue with affected parties and to discuss with them all issues of fact and law involved in administrative proceedings.[20] Where any particular procedural requirements are deemed to be essential by the ECJ (a matter of construction for the ECJ) the court will also act under Article 173 and exercise review. The following procedural requirements have been held to be essential for such purposes: the requirement to give a hearing;[21] the duty to provide reasons;[22] and the duty to consult.[23] It remains to be seen whether the ECJ will follow the route to activism seen in the USA but a movement in that direction will take the court nearer to centre stage on issues of procedural fairness.

Turning from the role of administrative law to the institutional structure of the Community, an area of particular concern to those interested in regulation is the comitology of Europe and its effect on transparency.[24] The Community has come to rely on committees so much that an estimated 400 to 1,000 committees are encountered within the EC's institutional structure.[25] Such resort to committees began in the 1960s in the agricultural policy area with the 'management committee procedure' whereby a committee made up of national representatives would be consulted by the Commission prior to decisions. In 1968 the 'regulatory committee procedure' came on the scene to institutionalize cooperation

---

[19] Case 5/67 *Beus* [1968] ECR 83, 95; see also Case 24/62 *Germany* v. *Commission* [1963] ECR 63.

[20] Cases 240–2, 261–2; 268–9/82 *Stiching Sigarellenindustrie* v. *Commission* [1985] ECR 3831; see Shapiro loc. cit. n. 17 above (1992).

[21] Case 17/74 *Transocean Marine Paint* v. *Commission* [1974] ECR 1063.

[22] Case 24/62 *Germany* v. *Commission* [1963] ECR 63.

[23] Case 138/79 *Roquette Freres SA* v. *Council* [1980] ECR 3333.

[24] See generally E. Vos, 'The Rise of Committees' (1997) 3 *ELJ* 210; K. St C. Bradley, 'The European Parliament and Comitology: On the Road to Nowhere' (1997) 3 *ELJ* 230; C. Joerges and J. Neyer, 'From Intergovernmental Bargaining to Deliberation Political Process: The Constitutionalisation of Comitology' (1997) 3 *ELJ* 273; R. H. Pedler and G. F. Schaefer (eds.), *Shaping European Law and Policy: The Role of Committees and Comitology in the Political Process* (EIPA, Maastricht, 1996); W. Sauter and E. Vos, 'Harmonisation Under Community Law: the Comitology Issue', in Craig and Harlow, *Lawmaking*.

[25] See Vos loc. cit. n. 24 above, p. 213.

between the Member States and the Commission[26] and in the following years 'advisory committees' were created by the Council in a number of areas to issue opinions on designated topics. This plethora of committees carries out the functions of policy-making and implementation, consultation of interests, and the supply of needed expertise and information to the preparatory and implementation phases of the decision-making process.

The main problems posed by the comitology are, first, that it may change the institutional balance within the Community—the fear is that including powerful committees within decision-making detracts from the Commission's independent right of decision, and, in turn, from the European Parliament's right of supervision.[27] A second worry is that the rise of committees prejudices the overall legitimacy of Community decision-making since the obscure processes of committee-driven policy preparation and implementation undermine the transparency of Community decision-making, blur national and Community competencies, and thwart the processes of democratic oversight.[28]

Following considerable dispute between the EC institutions, the Council in 1987 rationalized the committee procedures to apply on the delegation of powers to the Commission.[29] Committees have been given legal approval by the European Court of Justice and committees, it should be pointed out, may have a role in reducing the mistrust that Member States may have of each other and also in producing cooperative approaches to problems.

Concerns still remain, however, concerning the lack of transparency of EC committees, the effect of committees on European Parliament scrutiny of commission activity, the paucity of information concerning their membership and activities,[30] the lack of generalized rules on procedures and composition,[31] and the extent to which there should be more wide-ranging consultation of interests than is offered through the comitology.

On the question of substantive as opposed to procedural fairness, the difficulty for European regulators lies in demonstrating that European laws and regulations are applied with equal rigour on the ground so that, say, producers of goods in different Member States compete on a level

[26] Where the Commission wishes to adopt measures not in accordance with such a committee's opinion it must submit the proposed measure to the Council, which will act by qualified majority.

[27] See Vos loc. cit. n. 24 above, p. 214.

[28] See e.g. P. Kapteyn and P. VerLoren van Themaat (2nd edn. by L. Gormley), *Introduction to the Law of the European Communities* (Deventer, 1989), 244.

[29] The Comitology Decision—Decision 87/373/EEC—limits the number of committee structures and lays down procedures to be observed by the Commission. The advisory, management, and regulatory categories of committee were adopted.

[30] See e.g. Bradley loc. cit. n. 24 above p. 252.

[31] On developing general procedures in the Community see C. Harlow loc. cit. n. 16 above (1996).

playing field. In the case of a regulatory regime that is driven by a Directive, fairness demands that Member States not only transpose the Directive into domestic law in an equivalent manner but that they enforce it with similar efficiency and resolve—matters to be returned to below in looking at efficiency and effectiveness.

Expertise

Claims to expertise tend always to be treated with suspicion (see Chapter 6) but a special difficulty for European regulators lies in making a case that collecting the views of Member State experts during rule-making produces a *cumulative* expertise. It may, on the contrary, be the case that Member State regulators compete and seek to have their own approach to a problem adopted on the larger stage. The result may be the amassing of contradictory advice and the emergence of a patchwork of regulatory measures and approaches.[32] Resolving such tensions may not always be possible and attempted resolutions may not produce a highly expert judgement—as opposed to something typifiable as a political compromise. Consultative processes are, moreover, liable to produce numbers of 'expert' judgements that differ from those of Commission staff. The Commission itself may also lack the resources to deal fully and openly with all the 'expert' inputs it receives from Member States and interested parties.

One response to such problems is to delegate European-level functions to expert regulatory agencies. Such a strategy brings with it a further set of legitimation problems and these will be discussed in Section 2 below when regulatory strategies are reviewed.

Efficiency and Effectiveness

Claims that Euro-regulation produces results effectively and efficiently are again more difficult to make than equivalent domestic claims. This is not least because European regulation, in the main, only pursues results indirectly[33] with the Council or the Commission enacting Community policies and laws and the authorities of Member States implementing these.[34] Effectiveness and efficiency accordingly have to be measured

[32] On clashes of diverse policy traditions in European regulation see A. Heritier, 'The Accommodation of Diversity in European Policy-Making and its Outcomes: Regulatory Policy as Patchwork' (1996) 3 *J. of European Public Policy* 149.

[33] Direct community enforcement is largely confined to the areas of external trade and competition—see B. Swart, 'From Rome to Maastricht and Beyond', in C. Harding and B. Swart, *Enforcing European Community Rules* (1996). See, however, the discussion of enforcement agencies in Section 2 of this chapter.

[34] See Snyder, loc. cit. n. 13 above, and on implementing Euro-regulation see T. C. Daintith (ed.), *Implementing EC Law in the United Kingdom* (Chichester, 1995); Harding and Swart, *Enforcing European Community Rules*; H. Siedentopf and J. Ziller (eds.), *Making European Policies Work* (London, 1988); M. Cappelletti, M. Seccombe, and J. Weiler (eds.),

and ensured in each of the Member States and there are problems on both fronts.

Problems of Measurement

In order to measure regulatory effects, and to compare regulatory rigour across Member States, attention has to be paid to all stages of the European regulatory process—this includes, in the case of Directive-driven regulation, the stage of transposition into Member State law and the whole enforcement process on the ground.[35] Member States do things in very different ways and this is what makes measurements and comparisons particularly difficult. Major variations are found on the following fronts.[36]

Governmental and legal systems. Some Member States may deal with a regulatory matter (e.g. workplace health and safety) as a matter of criminal law, others as an issue of social insurance. The relationship of regulation to the social security system may also vary, as may the potential impact of civil laws. Member States may also vary widely in their choices of regulatory institution—which may be central government departments, independent agencies, local authorities, trade unions, self-regulatory organizations, or even police departments.

The sanctions and remedies used in enforcement may also cover a wide range—from criminal models to compensation regimes. The manner in which such disparate structures absorb EC rules may be both widely diverging and difficult to analyse without considerable input of resources.

Legal standards and issues of proof. Member States may impose different obligations on regulated parties (some phrased in absolute, some in relative terms) and both modes of proof and standards of proof may vary across Member States.

Enforcement processes. The principles and approaches adopted in taking enforcement action may, again, be widely divergent across Member States—some countries may use prosecutions readily, others may tend always to negotiate compliance. Highly individual strategies may be adopted in using these techniques.

In the face of such variations, the difficulties and costs of evaluating implementation are high. Various approaches to evaluation can be adopted but no easy solutions are to be found. If regulatory rigour is assessed

Integration through Law (Berlin, 1986); European Commission, *The Impact and Effectiveness of the Single Market*, COM (96) 520 final 30 Oct. 1996; *Action Plan for the Single Market* CSE (97) 1 final 4 June 1997.

[35] For Commission acknowledgement of its lack of information on the workings of a regulatory system on the ground see Commission Communication, *Implementing Community Environmental Law* COM (96) 500, (Luxembourg, 1996), 20; and for a response see the Reporting Directive 91/692/EEC of 23 Dec. 1991.

[36] See Baldwin and Daintith, *Harmonisation and Hazard*, ch. 8 for a detailed analysis of variations in Member State systems of regulating workplace health and safety.

with reference to the compliance costs imposed on equivalent industries in different Member States this overlooks the different starting points that are encountered—one Member State's industries may already be operating to a high standard when regulation is introduced, another's industries may have been used to low standards and poor equipment for some time.

If regulatory effectiveness is seen in terms of regulatory *inputs* (e.g. staff devoted to inspection, numbers of inspections and prosecutions) measurements and comparisons have to confront all the variables noted. If *outputs* are looked to (e.g. the level of workplace health and safety achieved in equivalent industries), then much depends on how equivalence is established—similar products may be produced by quite different national methods and work traditions. Comparing examples of regulatory effectiveness by focusing on either actual harms or risks of harms may also be difficult because, for example, different patterns of (actual or risked) injuries and health deficiencies will have to be compared.

Compounding all of the above problems is the vagueness of the mandate that is usually the case in European regulation. A Directive that aims for 'a better level of protection'[37] gives little guidance on how different patterns of protection are to be assessed or compared. It is thus difficult to claim legitimacy on either grounds of effectiveness or evenness of application when clear benchmarks are not available.

Ensuring effective and even implementation. European institutions face a double problem that lies at the core of regulation: how laws and rules can be implemented effectively at Member State level and how implementation can be ensured with *equal* effectiveness and rigour so that there is a level regulatory playing field. It is difficult enough to respond to problems of measurement and comparison but even assuming that rigour and effectiveness can be tested according to agreed yardsticks, steps still have to be taken to ensure that Member States actually do produce the right regulatory results on the ground. The Commission, moreover, is aware of the seriousness of the problem:

Uneven enforcement of EU legislation is often regarded as the most persistent barrier to trade or fair competition within the Single Market because overcoming it entails close scrutiny of national, regional or even local practices. What is needed above all, is mutual confidence between the Member States. Yet enforcement methods are far from harmonised across Member States.[38]

How Euro-regulators have sought to achieve even and effective implementation is best dealt with by considering the development of regulatory strategies in Europe and to this we now turn.

---

[37] See the Framework Directive for the introduction of Measures to Encourage Improvements in Safety and Health of Workers, Directive 89/391, OJ 1989 L183.

[38] See European Commission, *Impact*, 23. On the importance of implementation and enforcement in the environmental field see Commission Communication to the Council and Parliament, *Implementing Community Environmental Law*.

2. The Developing Techniques of European Regulation

Over the last three decades a number of European regulatory strategies have been developed and applied. In outlining these we look to identify the main techniques rather than trace the detailed chronology of regulatory developments.

Legislation: From Old to New Approach

Before 1985 the approach of the Community was very much to adopt specific legislation, laying down detailed rules to be implemented into regulations by each Member State.[39] As a mode of regulatory harmonization this 'old approach' suffered from a number of drawbacks, notably:[40]

- It rigidly imposed common standards rather than allowed for diversity.
- It was slow and by the time Directives were implemented they were outdated.
- Member State regulations swamped the output from Europe.
- Action was difficult in sensitive areas because Article 100 EC demanded unanimity and Member States accordingly enjoyed a veto.
- Failure to link technical harmonization with European standardization led to wasteful duplications, delays, and inconsistencies.
- Implementation problems were encountered in Member States.

By the late 1970s, frustrations with the above difficulties were mounting[41] and a revised strategy was prompted by the European Court of Justice's ruling in the *Cassis de Dijon* case.[42] The Court ruled that goods lawfully marketed in one Member State should not be prevented from entering another in the absence of compelling national policy grounds (such as safety of consumers) known as 'mandatory requirements'. Stress was thus placed on the idea of 'mutual recognition' of Member States' standards and, thus galvanized, the Commission abandoned its programme of detailed regulation in favour of a 'New Approach'. This was set out in

[39] The Treaties constitute the primary legislation of the Community but binding secondary legislation was provided for in Article 189 of the Treaty of Rome. Article 189 EC envisages three kinds of legally obligatory Act: *Regulations*, which are binding in their entirety and are directly applicable and enforceable in courts in all Member States; *Directives*, which are only binding 'as to the result to be achieved' and leave to the Member State 'the choice of form and methods' for implementation; and the *Decision* which is 'binding in its entirely upon those to whom it is addressed'.

[40] See J. Pelkmans, 'The New Approach to Technical Harmonisation and Standardisation' (1986–7) 25 *J. Common Market Studies* 5 249; Baldwin, *Rules and Government*, ch. 9.

[41] Pelkmans, loc. cit. n. 40 above.

[42] Case 120/78 *Rewe-Zentrale* v. *Bundesmonopolverwaltung für Branntwein* [1979] ECR 64.

the Commission's 1985 White Paper[43] which argued that since the objectives of national legislation were 'more often than not identical', the rules and controls developed to achieve such objectives should be recognized in all Member States. This White Paper was accepted in a Council Resolution on 7 May 1985 which endorsed, *inter alia*, the principles that legislative harmonization should be limited to essential safety requirements, that the task of drawing up technical specifications in conformity with the essential requirements of Directives should be entrusted to competent organizations;[44] that those technical specifications should be voluntary, not mandatory; and that national authorities should recognize the presumptive conformity to essential requirements of products complying with harmonized standards.[45] The intention of the New Approach was thus to halt the proliferation of very technical, separate directives for each product and to give producers the option of either operating in accordance with harmonized standards or demonstrating by another means that their products complied with the requirements of the Directive. Broad performance standards and statements of essential requirements were thus to replace detailed specifications. Stress was accordingly placed on distinguishing areas where it was essential to harmonize from those capable of being left to mutual recognition. A central aim was to combine uniformity of objectives with flexibility of means. Harmonization was linked to standardization in the New Approach so as to reduce duplication and the legislative process accelerated by enhancing the unanimity requirement of the old approach through introduction of Article 100A (added by the Single European Act of 1986) which provided for qualified majority voting in the Council on market integrating measures.

A parallel development, directed not at completion of the internal market but at social protection, was the development of the Framework Directive. This device does not lay down old-style detailed prescriptions but a broad set of duties and objectives to be achieved. It may be combined with more detailed 'daughter directives'[46] but it exemplifies differentiated and flexible integration in so far as its terms do not assume uniformity of national response. They allow implementation to be

---

[43] Commission of the EC, *Completing the Internal Market* COM (85) 310 Final. See Pelkmans loc. cit. n. 40 above; N. Burrows, 'Harmonisation of Technical Standards' (1990) 53 *MLR* 711; R. Dehousse, 'Integration v. Regulation? On the Dynamics of Regulation in the European Community' (1993) 30 *J. Common Market Studies* 383.

[44] e.g. CEN or CENELEC—see R. Lauwaars loc. cit. n. 6 above.

[45] See Council resolution of 7 May 1985, *A New Approach to Technical Harmonisation and Standards* (Luxembourg, 1985) OJC 136/1. (Reproduced in S. Weatherill, *Cases and Materials on EC Law* (London, 1992).) For a sociological account of progress towards the single market see N. Fligstein and I. Mara-Drita, 'How to Make a Market: Reflections on the Attempt to Create a Single Market in the European Union' (1996) *Am. J. Sociology* 1.

[46] For details of the Framework Directive in the workplace health and safety area see Baldwin and Daintith, *Harmonisation and Hazard*, and Baldwin, *Rules and Government*, ch. 8.

phased and countenance Member States developing their own rules with minimum requirements more strict than those demanded at the European level.

The New Approach thus offers flexibility but it is not free from political difficulties. Flexibility opens the prospect of different Member States moving at different regulatory speeds; issues of evenness in implementation (such as involve questions of measurement and comparison) are not eased by flexibility; policing the new rules is not facilitated by the greater latitude offered by the New Approach; and self-regulation by industry assumes greater importance than under the old approach.[47]

Legislation: Towards Softer Law

European institutions can encourage greater uniformity of Member State regulation by issuing 'soft laws' such as Resolutions, Recommendations, and Declarations that call for particular steps or approaches to be taken.[48] Soft laws have no legally binding force but they are useful in many ways. They are consistent with a movement (seen in many Member States) away from formal command approaches and towards controls based on persuasion, consent, and information. They are systematic, proactive rather than reactive, allow issues and agendas to be identified, provide 'guidelines for negotiating the effectiveness of community law',[49] set out expectations that Member States, organizations, and individuals will conform to their pronouncements, and operate in the shadow of binding European law.

Institutions: The Commission as Regulator

Centralized regulation and control of enforcement in Member States are both strategies that require levels of resourcing that go beyond anything available to the European institutions. In some selected areas, however, the Commission does exercise a direct regulatory function. Thus, Directorate-General IV (DGIV) of the Commission acts to control competition within Europe in pursuance of Articles 85 and 86 of the Union Treaty and some harmonization Directives envisage the Commission

---

[47] See N. Burrows and H. Hiram, 'The Legal Articulation of Policy in the European Community', in Daintith (ed.), *Implementing EC Law*.

[48] On soft law in Europe see Baldwin, *Rules and Government*, 248–52; K. C. Wellens and G. M. Borchardt, 'Soft Law in EC Law' (1989) 14 *ELR* 267; Snyder, loc. cit. n. 13 above, pp. 31–6; id., *Soft Law and Institutional Practice in the European Community* (EUI Working Paper 93/5 (1993)); Chalmers, *European Union Law*, 161–4.

[49] Snyder loc. cit. n. 13 above, p. 33. In 1996 the Commission announced that it would consider issuing guidelines on environmental inspection for Member States in order to reduce disparity of practice—see Commission Communication, *Implementing Community Environmental Law*, 9.

taking direct implementation measures in limited cases.[50] The EU is unlikely, however, to equip the Commission to control regulation on the ground—it struggles to monitor transpositions into Member State law.[51] Other strategies are, accordingly, being looked to for the purposes of harmonizing regulation.

Institutions, Information, and Networks: The European Regulatory Agencies

Europe might seek to impose even-handed and effective regulation across Member States by direct means—by creating, at the centre of European government, a series of independent regulatory agencies with enforcement powers. This might in some measure make up for the Commission's reliance on Member States to enforce European regulatory rules, it might offer a response to problems of lack of trust between Member States on enforcement issues,[52] and it would hold out the prospect of harmonized and expert regulation across Europe. To date, however, the creation of such agencies has been held back by a number of factors, notably, restrictive readings of Article 4 of the Rome Treaty that rule out the establishment of independent bodies with discretionary powers,[53] and a lack of willingness on the part of Member States to give up their regulatory functions to European agencies.

The Commission can, however, delegate the particular executive functions that it possesses so that committees or agencies, operating to objectives under commission oversight, can assist in the preparation and performance of executive acts.[54]

In some fields the committee route has been followed. Thus a Standing Committee of Experts has been established in the field of discrimination.[55] Such a committee might carry out complaints, monitoring, and reporting functions but it would require substantial administrative support (as might be encountered in an agency structure) in order to monitor implementation properly.

As for agencies, the first two 'satellite bodies' were created in the mid-1970s and a further eight commenced operations in the period 1994–7.

---

[50] For example the General Product Safety Directive (Directive 92/59/EEC OJ No. L.228/24, 11 Aug. 1992)—see Dehousse loc. cit. n. 43 above, p. 252.

[51] Snyder, loc. cit. n. 13 above; Dehousse loc. cit. n. 43 above.

[52] See G. Majone, *Temporal Consistency and Policy Credibility: Why Democracies Need Non-Majoritarian Institutions*, EUI Working Paper RSC No. 96/57 (Florence, 1996).

[53] See M. Everson, 'Independent Agencies: Hierarchy Beaters?' (1995) 1 *ELJ* 180; K. Lenaerts, 'Regulating the Regulatory Process: "Delegation of Powers" in the European Community (1993) 18 *ELR* 23 and Case 9/56 *Meroni* v. *High Authority* [1957–8] ECR 133.

[54] Everson, loc. cit. n. 53 above.

[55] See M. Verwilghen, *Equality of Law between Men and Women in the European Community* (Dordrecht, 1986); B. Hepple, 'The Implementation of the Community Charter of Fundamental Social Rights' (1990) 53 *MLR* 643.

These agencies are specialized administrative authorities, with legal personalities, governed by managerial boards (mainly composed of Member State representatives), and operating outside supranational institutions. Two main categories of function are carried out by these bodies. One group of agencies can be seen as primarily concerned with the collection, analysis, and dissemination of information in particular policy areas (for example, vocational training, living and working conditions, safety and health at work, environment, drugs and drug addiction, medicinal products[56]). The other kind of agency is devoted to the carrying out of particular executive functions and is exemplified by the Office for Harmonization and the Community Plant Variety Office which both implement Community regimes by putting registration procedures into effect.

The 'information' agencies provide a means of bringing some harmonization into European regulation without involving the large resource costs, or raising the political and legal issues, that would be associated with direct central regulation by the Commission or full 'enforcement' agencies. The information agencies can work with national regulators to ensure that actions are based on comparable data; to produce convergence in experts' ideas on regulation and to develop similar procedures. They can provide information on implementation, run exchanges of information and staff, offer common support, and bring stability to intergovernmental contacts on regulatory issues. These pan-European networks pool information, and promote greater uniformity of approaches and action.[57] They can 'Europeanize' the expertise available to Member State regulators. The provision of information by agencies may also encompass policy analysis and the preparation of measures and legislation.[58] Such information agencies, accordingly, may have a degree of input into policy-making in so far as their role in relation to the collection of information and the production of analyses may strongly influence implementation strategies as well as policy developments in European government—agenda setting powers may even be displaced from other European institutions in favour of agencies.[59]

[56] The agencies and starting dates are: European Centre for the Development of Vocational Training (1975); European Foundation for the Improvement of Living and Working Conditions (1975); European Environment Agency (1994); European Training Foundation (1995); Office for Harmonization in the Internal Market (1994); European Monitoring Centre for Drugs and Drug Addition (1996); European Agency for the Evaluation of Medicinal Products (1995); European Agency for Safety and Health at Work (1997).

[57] On agency networking see Dehousse loc. cit. n. 43 above; K. H. Ladeur, *The European Environment Agency and Perspectives for a European Network of Environmental Administrations*, EUI Working Paper No. 96/50, EUI (Florence, 1996). On developments in joint or shared enforcement involving liaison between Community and national officials, see C. Harding, 'Models of Enforcement: Direct and Delegated Enforcement and the Emergence of a "Joint Action Model" ', in Harding and Swart, *Enforcing European Community Rules*.

[58] See Dehousse loc. cit. n. 43 above, p. 255.

[59] See M. Shapiro, 'The Problems of Independent Agencies in the United States and the European Union' (1997) 4 *Journal of European Public Policy* 276.

In the absence of the funding (and the political will) for central enforcement agencies, there is a substantial role for European information agencies to play in coordinating regulation and in creating networks of Member State regulators so that these may work increasingly with shared information, approaches, and strategies in a process of 'administrative integration'.[60] Agencies, however, do raise issues of legitimation.[61] In some respects they might be expected to enhance the legitimacy of European regulation. They may increase efficiency by reducing the tendency to burden Community institutions with multiple, often inconsistent, objectives.[62] They may provide improved transparency by supplying newly consistent forms of data about Member States' regulatory procedures and performance on designated topics and also by moving power from obscure committees of officials into the more open agency domain.[63] Expertise claims might be strengthened by reducing conflicts between national experts and creating a unified European expertise. Both expertise and efficiency gains might be enhanced in so far as networking encourages high levels of performance and reliability on the part of Member State regulators (otherwise they will be excluded from networks and the realms of influence).

Even accountability might be said to be enhanced by substituting agencies for committees of bureaucrats. Such agencies rely on the non-compulsory part of the Community budget for their funding and, accordingly, the European Parliament is in a position to demand a good deal in terms of reporting, participation in hearings, or policy developments before it unfreezes funds.[64]

The less sanguine view is that European agencies, even those restricted to information-related functions, are engaged in politically significant activities that cannot be hidden behind the smoke-screen of claims that they are only engaged in 'technical' or 'information-gathering' activities.[65] The public, on this view, rightly recognizes that information is power and that policies turn on analyses of data.[66] They are, accordingly, liable to be sceptical of attributing legitimacy on the basis of claims to neutral technical expertise. Instead they may demand a political accountability

---

[60] See A. Kreher, 'Agencies in the European Community—A Step towards Administrative Integration in Europe' (1997) 4 *J. of European Public Policy* 225, 238–40.

[61] See Dehousse loc. cit. n. 43 above; Majone loc. cit. n. 52 above.

[62] Kreher loc. cit. n. 60 above, p. 239.

[63] As Dehousse points out (loc. cit. n. 43 above, p. 259): 'the true functional alternative to agency action is not a Parliament–Council dialogue, but decision-making in the framework of comitology committees, which is hardly a model in terms of democracy or transparency'.

[64] Dehousse, ibid. 258–9.

[65] See Shapiro loc. cit. n. 59 above, p. 287: 'If the independent agency argument is that information = technical expertise outside politics = technocracy = a non-democratic legitimacy, the response is that information is not technical but political and that technocracy is, these days, not perceived by the public as legitimate.'

[66] See also Ladeur, 'European Environment Agency'.

that the European agencies do not offer. Present arrangements, it has been added, need to be reformed in order to make claims to accountability carry conviction—for example by setting out statements of objectives for agencies; by setting up an electoral college to appoint agency directors; by the presentation of annual accounts to Parliament and Council; by the publication of agency proceedings; by subjecting the work of agencies to frequent examination by the various committees of the European Parliament; and by making all agencies directly subject to scrutiny by the Court of First Instance and the Court of Auditors.[67]

Claims that European agencies lead to efficient policy-making may also be offset by rejoinders that setting up independent regulatory bodies may produce a lack of coordination and even conflicts of policy at the heart of European government.[68] Nor, it could be argued, do agency-driven networks necessarily increase transparency and access—they may be 'totally opaque to any but the interior players'.[69] Again, suggestions for improving transparency have been put forward—these include proposals that agency decision-making and policy-making processes be made subject to the procedural requirements of a European Administrative Procedure Act and that rights of audience and observer status in agency decision-making be given to public interest groups.[70]

Control via the Courts: Litigation as Regulation

Centralized controls over European regulation demand, as noted, very substantial levels of resourcing and, accordingly, decentralized strategies have proved popular with European policy-makers. One such strategy relies on the production of legislation and subsidiary rules at the centre of European government but leaves matters of monitoring and enforcement to individuals and organizations who are encouraged to enforce their rights under European law. Thus, it has been argued that the Community might rely on the direct applicability of community law by facilitating enforcement proceedings before national courts with resort, where necessary, to preliminary ruling of the European Court of Justice under Article 177.[71] Such a strategy has, indeed, been emphasized by the Commission in relation to the single market programme with Communications being used both to indicate the Commission view of

---

[67] See Everson loc. cit. n. 53 above.

[68] See Shapiro loc. cit. n. 59 above, but cf. Dehousse loc. cit. n. 43 above, pp. 258–9.

[69] Shapiro loc. cit. n. 59 above, p. 287.

[70] See Everson loc. cit. n. 53 above, p. 201.

[71] The obligations that European law places on Member States can be enforced at the instigation of the Commission (Art. 169 EC) or by Member States (Art. 170) in a two-stage process involving negotiation and litigation. To date such enforcement actions have been largely confined to issues of legal transposition—see generally Snyder loc. cit. n. 13 above.

the law and to encourage participants in the market to insist on their Community rights.[72]

For its part, the European Court of Justice has played a role by strengthing the hand of those who enforce rights within European regulatory regimes. Leading with cases such as *Francovich*[73] the ECJ has given individuals and organizations an instrument to use in national courts to enforce community law against their governments—in that case ruling that a State that had failed to protect an individual's rights as instructed by a Community rule was liable for the harm caused to the individual.

Court actions, however, offer only limited potential as a method of ensuring even and effective regulation across Europe.[74] Costs to central government are liable to be reduced by the devolving of enforcement to individuals but the ECJ tends to restrict itself to issues of transposition into law rather than looking at regulatory effects on the ground and the resource constraints that affect individuals, pressure groups, and enterprises may detract from the potential of control through litigation.[75] Jurisprudential difficulties also make it far more difficult for individuals to enforce in cases of misimplementation of regulatory standards than for traders to prise open national markets that are protected in breach of Community Law. As Weatherill argues, it is not easy to envisage judicial recognition (at EU or domestic level) of an individual's legal 'right' to require effective regulation of, say, a factory in another Member State and this is the case whether the claimant acts on behalf of a pressure group or a factory that suffers competitive disadvantage in a

---

[72] See J. Schwarz et al., *The 1992 Challenge at National Level* (1990); The Sutherland Report (p. 41); Siedentopf and Ziller, *Making European Policies Work*; P. P. Craig, 'Once Upon a Time in the West: Direct Effect and the Federalism of EEC Law' (1992) 12 *OJLS*; Snyder loc. cit. n. 13 above.

[73] Joined cases C-6/90 and C-9/90 *Francovich and Bonifaci* v. *Italy* [1992] ECR 1-5357, see E. Szyszczak, 'European Community Law: New Remedies, New Directions' (1992) 55 *MLR* 690 and cases C-46, 48/93 *Brasserie du Pecheur* v. *Germany* [1996] ECR 1-1029; case C392/93 *R* v. *HM Treasury, ex p. British Telecommunications Plc* [1996] ECR 1-1631; case C-5/94 *R* v. *Min. of Ag. Fisheries and Food ex p. Hedley Lomas (Ireland) Ltd* [1996] ECR 1-2553; cases C-178, 179, and 188-990/94 *Dillenkofer* [1996] ECR 1-4845. See also case C-106/89 *Marleasing* v. *La Comercial International de Alimentacion SA* [1990] ECR 1—a case involving private parties in which the ECJ ruled that national courts are required to interpret national legislation so far as possible in accordance with a directive, whether enacted before or after a Directive, and case C-271/91 *Marshall* v. *Southampton and South West Area Health Authority* (No. 2) [1993] ECR 1-4367.

[74] On the limitations of *Francovich* and ensuing case law see C. Harlow, 'Francovich and the Problem of the Disobedient State' (1996) 2 *ELJ* 199 (speaking of the 'illusion of a remedy'); D. Chalmers, 'Judicial Preferences and the Community Legal Order' (1997) 60 *MLR* 164 pp. 191–9; and S. Weatherill, 'Reflections on EC Law's "Implementation Imbalance"', in L. Kramer, H.-W. Micklitz, and K. Tonner (eds.), *Law and Diffuse Interests in the European Legal Order* (Baden-Baden, 1997).

[75] See E. Szyszczak, 'L'Espace Sociale European: Reality, Dreams or Nightmare?' (1991) *GYIL* 284.

conscientiously enforcing Member State.[76] Inadequacies of information and expertise as well as diffusion of interests and losses are also liable to limit the capacity or incentive of individuals, groups, or firms to monitor and control, by resort to court, the enforcement practices or performance of regulators—especially those in Member States other than their own. A further question is whether evenness and effectiveness can be adequately ensured by a system triggered by *ad hoc* sporadic forays in the courts by individuals or groups; by reliance on courts with limited time and resources; and by processes presenting serious evidential and procedural hurdles to potential controllers of regulation. In some areas, moreover, there may be no party with an incentive to go to court to see that the rule of law obtains. The Commission has recognized, in the environmental sector, for instance, that private economic operators do not see their role as being one of supervising other businesses' compliance with environmental legislation and that private interests, in general, are lacking as an enforcement driving force.[77] What may be called for is not only a broad liberalization of the rules on standing to increase the enforcement role of pressure groups and non-governmental organizations but an allocation of powers to Community-level agencies to allow them to pursue enforcement failures through national courts.[78]

3. European and Member State Regulation

European Impact on Member State Regulation

Rules imposed at the European level may constrain domestic regulators in a number of different ways.[79] First, European laws may be introduced into an area and these will prevail over domestic legislation. They may apply European standards to specific issues[80] and may set out to implement broad regulatory strategies that accord with, or differ quite strongly

---

[76] See Weatherill loc. cit. n. 74 above, pp. 47–8.

[77] See Commission Communication, *Implementing Community Environmental Law* COM (96) 500 (1996), 11–13 where the Commission argues that Member States should broaden access to justice for non-governmental organizations (NGOs) and that a possible route to better enforcement of Community environmental law would be to ensure that NGOs recognized by Member States would have standing to bring judicial review actions against public bodies in Member States.

[78] See the proposals at Weatherill, loc. cit. n. 74 above, p. 52.

[79] See F. McGowan and P. Seabright, 'Regulation in the European Community and its Impact on the UK', in M. Bishop, J. Kay, and C. Mayer (eds.), *The Regulatory Challenge* (Oxford, 1995); T. C. Daintith, 'European Community Law and the Redistribution of Regulatory Power in the United Kingdom': Paper to ESRC conference: 'The Evolution of Rules for a Single European Market', Exeter, Sept. 1994.

[80] Since the earliest European involvement in environmental matters the Community has issued legislation establishing quality objectives on e.g. water limit values—see G. Cross, 'Enforcement of Environmental Rules: The UK Experience', in Harding and Swart, *Enforcing European Community Rules*, esp. p. 163.

from, the approaches taken in the Member States. In the health and safety sector, for instance, the Community has become the dominant source of regulatory policy. A key step in the Community's assumption of responsibility in this area was the passing of the Single European Act 1986 which introduced Article 118A of the EC Treaty. This provision called on Member States to pay particular attention to encouraging improvements in the working environment as regards health and safety and 'to set as their objective the harmonisation of conditions in this area, while maintaining the improvements made'. The Council was authorized to take action to such ends on the basis of qualified majority action.

The Community has launched three Action Programmes (the last in 1987), issued a Framework Directive on the Introduction of Measures to Encourage Improvements in the Safety and Health of Workers in 1989,[81] and produced a series of 'daughter directives' to flesh out the general terms of the Framework Directive, with calls for action in relation to a number of specific risks. Both EC steps to complete the internal market and to protect workers by direct legislation have impinged on health and safety regulation. Community Directives now cover a host of hazards and British regulators have had to adjust their strategies in ways that sometimes have strained to accord with European approaches. Some tension, for example, has emerged between the demands of the Framework Directive Article 5 (1) that Member State laws shall provide that: 'The employer shall have a duty to ensure the safety and health of workers in every aspect related to work' and the traditional legal phrasings employed within the Health and Safety at Work Act 1974 which instruct employers to take actions 'so far as is reasonably practicable'.[82] Here we see a clash of legal drafting traditions with potentially serious implications for regulators. European insistence on the imposition of, on the face of it, absolute duties (as opposed to duties to act so far as is reasonably practicable) could have a shattering effect on UK regulators and firms, since enforcing duties to ensure safety absolutely and regardless of cost or difficulty would close down a considerable proportion of British industry.

In the utilities sectors generally the Community has produced little specific legislation but in telecommunications a number of Directives have sought to liberalize and move towards a single market. Thus a Directive was adopted in 1990 on competition in the market for telecommunications services.[83] It provided that all exclusive rights for the supply of telecommunications services, other than voice telephony, had to be withdrawn by Member States before 31 December 1990. A further key

[81] (89/91/EEC) OJL 183/89. See Nielsen and Szyszczak, *Social Dimension*; Baldwin and Daintith, *Harmonisation and Hazard*; and Baldwin, *Rules and Government*, 238–41.

[82] See Sections 2–9 of the Health and Safety at Work Act 1974 (HSWA 1974); on absolute and cost-benefit based standards see Chapter 9 above.

[83] Telecommunications Services Directive, Commission Directive 90/388.

Directive also emerged in 1990, the Open Network Provisions Directive,[84] which outlined the conditions necessary for open and efficient access to telecommunications networks within and between Member States.

Not all European actions necessarily demand new action by Member States. The Telecommunications Services Directive was a case in point since the UK had already opened up access to the telecommunication services market under the Telecommunications Act 1984 and no further legislative steps were deemed necessary in order to implement the Directive. On the whole, however, telecommunications regulation has come to be strongly influenced by the European control framework. Telecommunications is an increasingly international market and there has been a single market in telecommunications in the European Union since January 1998. European legislation on telecommunications is, as the DGT has noted, 'increasingly setting sector specific rules for telecommunications services at EU rather than Member State Level'.[85]

As well as direct European occupation of the regulatory 'space'[86] within which a Member State regulator operates, European-level controls can be of influence on a more general basis. Thus the Community rules on competition and the key Articles 85 and 86 provide a framework within which regulators and regulated firms must work. Where, as in telecommunications, the domestic regulator moves emphasis from regulation to competition-based controls, the significance of European-level competition rules is all the greater.[87]

The Commission has powers to apply Articles 85 and 86 and fines may be imposed for breaches of these provisions.[88] The former Article prohibits agreements and concerted practices which restrict competition and which may adversely affect trade between Member States. Article 86 prohibits the abuse of a dominant position by one or more undertakings, again as this may affect inter-state trade. In enforcing competition laws the Commission has a position that has been compared to that of an independent regulatory agency[89] and, given the supremacy of European law, it is an agency to which Member State regulators must give way.

Commission action is not, furthermore, the only avenue by which Articles 85 and 86 may be enforced. As well as forming the basis for complaints to the Commission, these Articles create rights which the national courts are obliged to protect. Competition rules may thus be relied upon in actions

[84] Council Directive 90/387, OJ L192, 24 July 1990.
[85] OFTEL, *Submission to Review of Utility Regulation* (London, 1997), 2.
[86] On regulatory space see L. Hancher and M. Moran (eds.), *Capitalism, Culture and Regulation* (Oxford, 1989) and T. Daintith, 'A Regulatory Space Agency' (1989) 9, *OJLS* 534.
[87] See e.g. C. Scott, *Competition and Co-ordination: Their Role in the Future of European Community Utilities Regulation* (London, 1995), esp. pp. 21–3.
[88] Council Regulation 17/62.
[89] See L. Laudati, 'The European Commission as Regulator: The Uncertain Pursuit of the Competitive Market', in Majone, *Regulating Europe*.

for damages or injunctive relief brought in the national courts. This means that firms seeking access to networks or infrastructure facilities may potentially challenge decisions denying access where those denials flow from agreements restricting competition and adversely affecting inter-state trade or constituting abuses of dominant positions.

Competition laws from the European level thus have the capacity to affect domestic regimes at all levels. Similarly, other general European laws on such matters as the Free Movement of Goods[90] may impinge heavily on domestic regimes—prohibiting, for instance, national monopolists in energy sectors from maintaining exclusive rights to import.[91]

As will be returned to below, it is the European principle of subsidiarity that holds sway in decisions on whether regulation should be carried out at the Member State or the European level[92] and the principle of proportionality governs the degree of intervention that regulation can involve. Proportionality is called for in Article 3 (*b*) EC which, *inter alia*, states that action by the Community 'shall not go beyond what is necessary to achieve the objectives of this Treaty'. As developed by the European Court of Justice (ECJ) the principle applies generally and to all regulatory levels.[93] Various formulations of the proportionality principle are encountered in the decisions of the ECJ and it may be asked whether regulatory measures are 'the least restrictive that could be adopted in the circumstances'; whether 'the means adopted to achieve the aim correspond to the importance of the aim and are necessary for its achievement';[94] or whether the act is suitable and necessary and 'does not impose excessive burdens on the individual'.[95]

ECJ review on the grounds of proportionality may directly impinge on domestic regulation in a number of circumstances—for instance where a party made subject to a regulation argues that his or her right at European law (e.g. to move goods freely) is prejudiced by the regulation. The ECJ has, for instance, scrutinized with rigour a Member State's argument that action was necessary in order to protect public health.[96] Overall the effect on regulators will be to encourage strategies that can be shown to be the least restrictive consistent with achieving legitimate targets.

On the severity of Member State regulators' actions, Community law imposes restraints other than through proportionality principles. The choice

---

[90] See Articles 30 to 36 EEC.   [91] See Sayer, 'Impact', 8.
[92] See below, pp. 175–6.
[93] See Craig and de Burca, *EC Law*, 340–9; G. de Burca, 'The Principle of Proportionality and its Application in EC Law' (1993) *YBEL* 105.
[94] Case 66/82 *Fromancais SA* v. *FORMA* [1983] ECR 395.
[95] See J. Schwarze, *European Administrative Law* (London 1992), 687.
[96] See for example Case 40/82 *Commission* v. *United Kingdom* [1982] ECR 2793 in which a UK ban on poultry imports was sought to be justified on health grounds under Article 36 of the Treaty. The ECJ felt the measures were really aimed at protecting UK producers from French imports in the pre-Christmas period and rejected the UK's defence.

of penalties to be used in enforcing European laws is not left entirely to the Member State's free discretion.[97] Member State authorities, for instance, are obliged to impose effective and dissuasive sanctions; they have, when penalizing infringements by the award of compensation, to ensure that compensation covers the damage sustained, and their duty is to penalize infringements of Community law under conditions (procedural and substantive) analogous to those applicable in domestic law. The European Court of Justice has also adhered to the view that the Community is competent to instruct Member States on the use of sanctions that have a punitive character without being criminal[98]—this allows considerable central control over regulatory enforcement practices at Member State level. The Community has no formal competence in matters of criminal law[99] but Community law may in reality influence the way in which national criminal law is applied. This is exemplified in the fisheries sector[100] where there has been a Europeanization of enforcement and where, for instance, a Community Regulation lays down detailed prescriptions on the types of sanctions to be imposed by Member States for fishery offences.[101]

The ways in which the Community seeks to harmonize laws have already been discussed but it should be noted that these may have considerable (and complex) effects on the ways in which Member States and their regulators exercise controls. It can be argued, for instance, that the use of Directives tends to produce a bias towards command and control styles of regulation. This is because Member States have to produce laws which have legally binding effects if they are to implement Directives properly. The use of mere 'administrative practices' which might be altered at the whim of the administration is not considered by the European Court of Justice to constitute fulfilment of the duty to implement Directives contained in Article 189 EC[102]. In terms of regulatory technique, such an approach by the ECJ favours the use of binding commands rather than economic incentives in pursuit of regulatory ends.

Where harmonization occurs through the coordination of enforcement approaches—be this under the influence of specialist agencies or the Commission itself—the effects on Member State regulators again may be considerable. In fields such as the environment, health and safety at

---

[97] See B. Swart, 'From Rome to Maastricht and Beyond: The Problem of Enforcing Community Law', in Harding and Swart, *Enforcing European Community Rules*.

[98] See case 14/83 *Von Colson and Kamann* v. *Land Nordrhein-Westfalen* [1984] ECR 1891; Case 68/88 *Commission* v. *Greece* [1989] ECR 2965.

[99] See H. G. Sevenster, 'Criminal Law and EEC Law' (1992) *CMLR* 29; but see Case 240/90 *Germany* v. *Commission* [1992] ECR 1-5383.

[100] See A. Berg, 'Enforcement of the Common Fisheries Policy, with special reference to the Netherlands', in Harding and Swart, *Enforcing European Community Rules*.

[101] Ibid. 68 and Regulation 2847/93, Article 31 (3).

[102] See Case 96/8 *Commission* v. *Netherlands* [1982] ECR 1791; Case 160/82 *Commission* v. *Netherlands* [1982] ECR 4637; [1984] 1 CMLR 230.

work, agriculture or fisheries, national regulators will exchange information or even coordinate action on specific problem areas. As such processes develop, collective views and European strategies can be expected to grow stronger and to substitute for 'home-grown' approaches.[103] A further respect in which Europe may influence Member State regulation is by imposing general requirements for the purposes of social protection or social and economic cohesion. Thus, it increasingly appears that the Community will legislate to require Member States to ensure that Universal Service Obligations are maintained in the utilities sectors.[104] Such a requirement offers a response to fears that smaller and remote consumers of energy, telecommunications, and other services will lose those services as policies of liberalization and transparency of costing drive out the cross-subsidizations necessary to sustain supplies to these consumers.[105] Where the Community acts to protect minimal levels of service, Member State regulators will be required to publish targets, to monitor and publish details of quality of service. In the telecommunications field such action came in 1995 with the Draft Directive on the Application of Open Network Provision to Voice Telephony—the first legislative provision for universal service in that sector.[106]

Finally, it should be noted that Community law may affect a State's ability to determine for itself how to demarcate public functions from private functions and this may affect regulatory structures.[107] In certain areas State supervision of an activity may be called for by Community law and this may rule out the placing of regulatory functions in private hands—States, accordingly, may be compelled to retain a larger area of regulatory responsibility than they would otherwise choose.[108]

Member State Influence on European Regulation

Although European-level controls may affect actions taken by Member State regulators, it would be a mistake to see the process of influence as a one-way street. Member States and their regulators do have an effect

---

[103] On the 'fusion' of public instruments from different state levels and Europeanization see W. Wessels, 'An Ever Closer Fusion? A Dynamic Macropolitical View on Integration Processes' (1997) 35 *J. Common Market Studies* 267.

[104] See Scott, *Competition and Co-ordination*, 29; in e.g. the telecommunications sector see *Communication from the Commission of the European Communities on Universal Service for Telecommunications* COM (96) 73 final and OFTEL, *Universal Telecommunications Services: Proposed Arrangements for Universal Service in the UK from 1997* (London, 1997).

[105] At present in the UK the obligations of utilities to provide universal services have been sustained post privatization—see J. Balogh, 'Any and All? Future of Social Obligations' (1997) 8 *Utilities LR* 109.

[106] See Scott, *Competition and Co-ordination*, 81.

[107] See Weatherill, 'Implementation as a Constitutional Issue', in Daintith, *Implementing EC Law*, 351–2.

[108] Ibid. 352.

on choices of strategy at the European level as well as on implementation. In the rest of this chapter we consider such Member State influences on the centre of European regulation and then look at how choices
can be made concerning the appropriate governmental level of regulation.

Many instances of European-level regulation can be seen as the products of Member State negotiations on policy options, negotiations in which
Member States have sought to impose their own regulatory styles and
preferences on the wider Community.[109] Regulatory proposals within
Europe are often generated by individual Member States with strong regulatory traditions. These initiating Member States seek to transfer their
own regulatory styles to the European level for a number of reasons:[110]

- to minimize the costs of adjusting to an alien regulatory regime;
- to assist their own industries by raising European standards to their
  own level;
- to enhance the market for their own compliance-related products
  (e.g. environmental technology developed in relation to the Member
  State's own standards);
- to sustain the level of their own regulatory standards by not moving to a more lax European standard.

The Commission is the body, on such an account, that chooses from the
regulatory policy options: 'The highly regulated Member States, for their
part, may be regarded as innovative policy entrepreneurs in the European
regulatory market, offering their "products" to the Commission.'[111] From
the Commission's point of view such a gatekeeping role is attractive given
the limited financial resources of the Community and the consequent
difficulty the Commission has in generating its own initiatives. Member
State proposals are not, however, implemented on a 'first come' basis—
they are, if adopted by the Commission, the subject of a complex series
of negotiations in which opposing Member States and coalitions may
attempt to block the adoption of a particular approach. Less stringently

---

[109] See A. Heritier, 'The Accommodation of Diversity in European Policy-Making and
its Outcomes: Regulatory Policy as Patchwork' (1996) 3 *J. of European Public Policy* 149.
As an antidote to Heritier's vision of Member States as unitary, rational influences on
the Community, reference can be made to other explanations of the interaction between
national and supranational government—for example, those that pay more attention to
the processes of fusion (whereby public resources at several levels come to merge—see Wessels
loc. cit. n. 103 above); or which stress cultural and institutional factors (e.g. Fligstein
and Mara-Drita loc. cit. n. 45 above). On functional versus intergovernmental bargaining
explanations and the role of officials as opposed to the 'State' see J. Golub, *Why Did They
Sign? Explaining EC Environmental Policy Bargaining*, RSC No. 96/52 (Florence, 1996).

[110] Heritier, loc. cit. n. 109 above p. 151.

[111] Ibid. 152; see also G. P. Peters, 'Bureaucratic Politics and the Institutions of the
European Community', in A. Sbragia (ed.), *Europolitics: Institutions and Policy Making
in the New European Community* (Washington DC, 1992); F. W. Scharpf, 'Political Institutions, Decision Styles and Policy Choices', in R. M. Czada and A. Windhoff-Heritier (eds.),
Political Choice: Institutions Rules and the Limits of Rationality (Frankfurt, 1991).

regulated states may be particularly keen to obstruct newly rigorous and centrally controlled regimes of regulation since their own lower standards may give them a competitive advantage in the market place. The threatened vetoes may be 'bought off' with compromises as the proposal progresses through the Commission, Council, and European Parliament stages of the legislative process and the particular voting rules applicable in the area will affect such negotiations. Where policies depend on the collection of data by experts and where there is a powerful 'information' agency in the sector, negotiations are likely to be informed and influenced by agency input.

The end product of such regulatory competition is an array of European regulatory styles that owes more to the strength of particular Member States in given sectors and to the interplay of Member State regulatory interests than to the influence of a single style or regulatory approach that can be identified within the Commission. As will be seen in the next chapter, there are differing views on the advantages and disadvantages of such regulatory competition and a key question is whether such policy entrepreneurship leads to the 'best' regulatory mechanisms rising to the surface, to confusion, or to a general depression of regulatory standards.

Choosing the Appropriate Level of Regulation

Whether regulation should be carried out at the Member State or European level is a matter on which there is (or purports to be) legislative guidance in the form of the subsidiarity principle.[112] Any allocation of powers within the EC Treaties must have regard to this principle which is found in Article 3(*b*) EC. The text reads:

In areas which do not fall within its exclusive competence, the Community shall take action, in accordance with the principle of subsidiarity, only if and so far as the objectives of the proposed action cannot be sufficiently achieved by the Member States and can therefore, by reason of the scale or effects of the proposed action, be better achieved by the Community. Any action by the Community shall not go beyond what is necessary to achieve the objectives of this Treaty.[113]

---

[112] See generally: Chalmers, *European Union Law*, 221–33; D. Begg et al., *Making Sense of Subsidiarity* (London, 1993); N. Emiliou, 'Subsidiarity: An Effective Barrier against the Enterprises of Ambition?' (1992) 55 *ELR* 383; M. Wilke and H. Wallace, 'Subsidiarity: Approaches to Power-Sharing in the European Community', RIIA Discussion Paper No. 27 (London, 1990), in Weatherill, *Cases and Materials on EC Law*; D. Lasok, 'Subsidiarity and the Occupied Field' (1992) 142 *NLJ* 1228; A. G. Toth, 'The Principle of Subsidiarity in the Maastricht Treaty' (1992) 29 *CMLR* 1079; D. Z. Cass, 'The Word that Saves Maastricht?' (1992) 29 *CMLR* 1107; A. G. Toth, 'A Legal Analysis of Subsidiarity'; and J. Steiner 'Subsidiarity under the Maastricht Treaty', both in D. O'Keefe and P. M. Twomey (eds.), *Legal Issues of the Maastricht Treaty* (London, 1994).

[113] For the Commission's approach to subsidiarity see *Commission Communication to the Council and the European Parliament*, SEC (92) 1990 final, 27 Oct. 1992.

In other words, for a task falling within concurrent powers to be allocated to the Community level, two conditions must be satisfied; first, that the objectives cannot be sufficiently achieved by the Member States and that they can be better achieved by the Community; and secondly, that the Community acts in a way proportional to the objectives to be achieved.

Leaving aside the issue of proportionality and concentrating on the allocation of regulatory power, it becomes necessary to focus on the words 'sufficiently' and 'better'. Here reference can be made to the guidelines devised by the Edinburgh European Council of 1992 which attempted to flesh out the subsidiarity principle. The conclusions of that Council[114] said that reference should be made to: the transnational aspects of an issue that could not be regulated satisfactorily by Member State action; whether actions by Member States alone, or lack of Community action, would conflict with treaty requirements (such as needs to correct distortions of competition or avoid restrictions on trade, or strengthen economic or social cohesion) or damage Member States' interests; and/or whether action at Community level would produce clear benefits by reason of its scale or effects, as compared with action at Member State level. It remains to be seen, however, whether these guidelines will assist in clarifying a concept marked out by its opacity.

Short of clear guidance from the subsidiarity principle, reference might be made to the five benchmarks set out in Chapter 6 when decisions on the allocation of regulatory power are to be made. It was seen in the first section of this chapter that regulation at the European level gives rise to a number of general problems when legitimation under each of the five headings is considered. A number of more particular considerations should, however, be borne in mind in addition to those general points.

Certain circumstances militate in favour of European-level regulation for the sake of efficiency in control.[115] Thus, where there are cross-border externalities (as where pollution from one Member State crosses

---

[114] See *Conclusions of the Edinburgh European Council, Annex 1 to Part A:* EC Bulletin 12-1992, 14. These can now be found, after the 1997 Treaty of Amsterdam, in the *Protocol to EC Treaty on the Application of the Principles of Subsidiarity and Proportionality*, paras 4 and 5 (any legislative proposal must state why it satisfies the principle). See also *EC Institutional Declaration on Democracy, Transparency and Subsidiarity*, EC Bulletin 10-1993, 118 which stresses the obligation of the Community Institutions to take on board the subsidiarity principle in exercising powers and to justify actions with reference to the principle.

[115] See K. Gatsios and P. Seabright, 'Regulation in the European Community' (1989) 5 *Oxford Rev. of Econ. Policy* 37; M. Cave and P. Crowther, 'Determining the Level of Regulation in EU Telecommunications' (1996) 20 *Telecommunications Policy* 725; D. Helm and S. Smith, 'The Assessment: Economic Integration and the Role of the European Community' (1989) 5 *Oxford Rev. of Econ. Policy* 1; F. McGowan and P. Seabright, 'Regulation in the European Community and Its Impact on the UK', in Bishop, Kay, and Mayer, *Regulatory Challenge.*

to another Member State) one state will be affected by the regulatory decisions of another. If the costs of, say, pollution are spread across Member States but the benefits are concentrated in one home Member State (e.g. where the factory is situated) there will be an incentive for the home Member State regulator to exercise less rigorous control than is in the common interest of all Member States—weak control will bring economic benefits to the home Member State whereas costs will be (at least partially) borne elsewhere. Each Member State will, as a result, tend to be worse off than under a cooperative regime. This is a reason for instituting European-level regulation or putting a system of regulatory coordination into effect.[116]

Regulation at a European level, or regulatory coordination, may also be called for where Member States tend to regulate strategically in order to give home firms a competitive advantage—for example by erecting barriers to the importation of products. (The celebrated *Cassis de Dijon* case concerned such a protectionist action by West Germany.)[117] If Member State regulators cannot coordinate so as to achieve consistent and unbiased results, the case for centralized regulation is the stronger. Such coordination may be difficult for two principal reasons—these concern information and confidence.

On the first point, Member States tend to have limited information about each others' intentions, strategies, and incentives. They will, accordingly, tend to hold out for a solution that favours their own industries rather than seek the general solution that, for informational reasons, they would have problems in identifying. Such holding out makes coordination difficult. As for confidence, the key problem is that Member States recognize each others' incentives to pursue national interests by devising rules that favour their own economic interests or by failing to enforce agreed rules for the same reasons. They, moreover, find it extremely difficult to monitor the manner in which other Member State authorities enforce regulatory rules.

Each Member State, accordingly, would like other Members States to enforce, say, atmospheric pollution controls very strictly while they themselves exercise a lenient regime.[118] In the case of measures aimed at market liberalization there is a particular problem of confidence in so far as Member States will tend not to want to be the first to open up their own markets to greater competition because they fear tardiness of reciprocation on the part of other Member States. The result would be that firms in states early to liberalize would be unfairly exposed.

---

[116] Anti-competitive use of market power may also constitute such an externality—see Gatsios and Seabright, loc. cit. n. 115 above, p. 41.

[117] See Case 120/78, *Rewe-Zentrale AG* v. *Bundesmonopolverwaltung für Branntwein* [1979] ECR 649.

[118] See Gatsios and Seabright loc. cit. n. 115 above, p. 45.

The propensity of firms to comply with regulatory requirements may also be affected by perceptions that other Member States' regulators are not applying rules rigorously—the more that firms doubt the rigour of other Member States' actions, the less they will be inclined to cooperate with their own regulators and, as a result, regulation in all Member States may diminish in effectiveness where there is a lack of confidence.

Uncertainties on the above fronts may favour regulation at the European level and the use of strategies that do not incorporate large Member State discretions or present undue difficulties for those monitoring regulatory performance. European-level regulation may, however, prove especially difficult where large discretions are unavoidable—because of the particular regulatory task at issue (it may be complex and dynamic) or where monitoring demands levels of resourcing that are unavailable to the Commission. Some other particular circumstances will also weaken the case for European-level regulation. Where, for instance, effective regulation requires detailed and up-to-date information about an industry, transferring regulation to an authority more distant from the industry than the Member State may reduce effectiveness. Informational and administrative economies may also be achieved by keeping the decision-maker close to regulated parties.[119]

If there is a wide divergence of Member State policies on a topic this may also render European regulation difficult. Such divergence may be coped with by basing regulation on approaches that are the products of compromises and tit-for-tat trade-offs. The result may be a regulatory strategy that is highly imperfect and low in efficiency. In addition, the absence of a strong, identifiable democratic mandate or agreed line may leave regulators exposed to the dangers of regulatory capture. This may take the form of undue influence by powerful economic interests ('firm capture'); or involve the dominant Member States having an excessive hold over regulatory policies ('government capture'); or be marked by the regulatory body coming increasingly to adopt the aims of its own staff ('bureaucratic capture').[120] A further problem, of regulatory confusion, may arise where there is wide divergence between Member State policies. This may be manifested in conflicts between regulation at the Member State and European levels and in duplications of regulation rather than the substitution of European for Member State controls. Those regulated will, as a result, be faced with complex, and often contradictory, regulatory messages and those regulating at the Member State level may find it hard to sustain their commitments to rigorous enforcement.

Where different governments and electorates hold strong and divergent views on, say, the distributional implications of various regulatory options, democratic considerations may favour action at a lower governmental level.

---

[119] See Helm and Smith loc. cit. n. 115 above, p. 4.   [120] Ibid. 46.

The more localized and stronger such concerns are, the more compelling is the case for Member State rather than European regulation.

Conclusions

Decisions concerning European regulatory strategies and appropriate levels of regulation involve complex trade-offs between various desiderata. This chapter has sought to identify the nature of some of these trade-offs. A constant factor has, however, been identified and that is the limited level of resourcing that is devoted within Europe to monitoring and ensuring the even and effective application of European laws. This limitation in itself imposes a ceiling on the levels of information and confidence that can be generated within European regulation. A premium on transparency within European regulatory processes may, accordingly, be argued for with some force. The way to generate trust can only come through developing information supplies at all possible stages of the regulatory process.

On a final note, it should be cautioned that it is possible to conceive of the choice between Member State and European regulation in terms that are too dramatic. Regulatory actions at different levels do intermesh—for instance under the influence of mutual recognition and other harmonization measures—and it may be useful to seek to identify the *blend* of Member State and European-level actions that merits the highest levels of approval. The right question to ask may be: What is the appropriate level and kind of European input into regulation? In any one given sector what may be required is an analysis of the various regulatory objectives that have to be achieved and the kind of European input into regulation that best furthers these.

13

Regulatory Competition
and Coordination

Regulators can be seen as producing a product and as competing with each other with regard to the rules, processes, and enforcement regimes that constitute that product.[1] They may compete in order to achieve a number of ends—for example, national economic advantage or protections for favoured groupings. Competition may occur between national regulators or at the regional or local level. It may even operate within a sector (e.g. energy or environmental protection).

This chapter commences by considering the nature of regulatory competition, the conditions under which it takes place, and its potential effects. It then looks at issues raised by regulators' attempts to coordinate their actions. The related issue of how the appropriate governmental level of regulation can be decided has been examined, in the European context, in Chapter 12.

1. Regulatory Competition and its Preconditions

Regulatory competition is the competitive adjustment of rules, processes, or enforcement regimes in order to secure an advantage.[2] The end in sight is commonly the attracting of investment or business activity into an area or the promotion of regional or national industries by providing them with a more favourable environment (perhaps with lower compliance costs) than their competitors enjoy.[3] It should not be

[1] See R. Romano, 'Law as Product: Some Pieces of the Incorporation Puzzle' (1985) 1 *J. Law Econ. Org.* 225.

[2] See generally: J. McCahery et al. (eds.), *International Regulatory Competition and Coordination* (Oxford, 1996); C. Tiebout, 'A Pure Theory of Local Expenditures' (1956) 64 *J. Pol. Econ.* 416–24; H. Siebert and M. Koop, 'Institutional Competition Versus Centralisation: *Quo Vadis* Europe' (1993) 9 *Oxford Rev. of Econ. Policy* 15–30; J.-M. Sun and J. Pelkmans, 'Regulatory Competition in the Single Market' (1995) 33 *J. Common Market Studies* 67.

[3] See S. Woolcock, 'Competition among Rules in the Single European Market', in McCahery et al., *International Regulatory Competition*, 298.

assumed, however, that when regulators compete there is necessarily a lowering of standards—such competition, as will be discussed below, may lead to a raising of standards (and compliance costs) which may, under certain conditions, produce advantages for local businesses—for example by offering a system of product quality control that enhances sales.

For regulatory competition to take place a number of conditions have to obtain, notably:[4]

Freedom of Movement

Producers of goods or services must be free to move between the jurisdictions of the regulators if they are to be able to choose between regulatory regimes. This may involve operational flexibility or mobility of workplaces, capital, services, or products. There must, accordingly, be no laws that rule out such cross-jurisdictional changes in supply or production—as would be the case internationally were there to be a prohibition on imports.

Information

Those regulated must be able to gain information concerning alternative regimes of regulation if they are to make comparisons and consider potential moves of jurisdiction. Similarly, regulators must possess information concerning other regimes if they are to respond competitively. It must be possible, also, to compare the effects of different regulatory rules and policies and so information about enforcement and how rules are applied is essential. If choices of regulatory regimes are to be made it must be possible, furthermore, to identify the effects of *regulation* as separate from other factors that impinge on performance (e.g. the state of the economy or the taxation system).

Enforcement

For regulatory competition to exist there must be actual as well as assessable enforcement of the regulations at issue or else those comparing regulatory systems will be uncertain as to the real effects of regulation on the ground.

These three conditions are not always easy to satisfy. Thus, in relation to competition between the regulators found in the Member States of the European Union (EU) it has been argued that there are material problems on each of the fronts discussed.[5] There may be considerable freedom to move capital within the EU but labour is not highly mobile

---

[4] See ibid. 302–3.   [5] See ibid.; Sun and Pelkmans loc. cit. n. 2 above.

and local market characteristics or preferences, as well as regulatory and consumer traditions, will limit producers' freedom of movement. Information on the effects of different national regulatory systems is commonly not available to producers or consumers and it is often difficult to isolate regulatory as opposed to other influences on production, costs, or sales. Finally, levels of enforcement are very difficult to predict in the Member States of the EU. As was seen in the last chapter, the EU has only recently started to come to grips with the problem of ensuring effective enforcement in the various Member States and measuring regulatory rigour and effects is extremely difficult.

2. *The Effects of Regulatory Competition*

The optimistic view of regulatory competition holds that it will prove effective in satisfying citizens' preferences. The argument, as associated with Tiebout,[6] is that just as competition forces producers to manufacture the products that consumers want, so competition will produce the regulatory regimes that consumers and citizens want. This occurs in Tiebout's local government context because individuals can vote with their feet and can move to those jurisdictions with the tax/expenditure balances that meet their preferences. This leads local governments to tailor their tax and spend regimes to the desires of residents[7]—if they do not do so they will be voted out of office or residents will move house out of their jurisdictions.

In short the (optimistic) theory of regulatory competition is that if conditions are competitive these will force regulators to 'race to the top' —where the 'top' involves establishing the combination of regulatory rules, processes, and enforcement practices that citizens/consumers desire. In addition, commentators point to a series of benefits of regulatory competition:[8]

Choice and diversity of regulation—consumers will be able to choose among goods and services controlled by different regimes to different standards. Regulation can be tailored to the needs of specific economies, constituencies, and sectors of demand.

Simplification—allowing diversity avoids complex and expensive efforts to harmonize and centralize regulation.

Regulation is kept in check—consumers and constituents can resist tendencies to over-regulate by shunning products and jurisdictions with

---

[6] Tiebout loc. cit. n. 2 above.
[7] See also F. H. Easterbrook, 'Federalism and European Business Law' (1994) 14 *Int. Rev. Law and Econ.* 125.
[8] See Sun and Pelkmans, loc. cit. n. 2 above, p. 82; Woolcock, loc. cit. n. 3 above, pp. 298–9. R. Winter, 'State Law, Shareholder Protection and the Theory of the Corporation' (1997) 6 *J. Legal Stud.* 251.

excessively strict standards and levels of control or by voting out of office those responsible for excessive regulation.

Regulatory failure is resisted—competition may reduce the dangers of regulating in accordance with bad political compromises and of capture of the central regulator by powerful vested interests. Regulatory competition also provides yardsticks with which to measure the performance of particular regulators and this encourages better regulation.

Innovation—competition between regulatory regimes provides a market-driven process for discovering which modes of regulation lead to the results preferred by consumers. The threats of losses of votes and of exit to other jurisdictions will lead regulators to experiment in search of the best regime.

Local control—regulatory competition is consistent with the retention of local control and accountability. If regulation is centralized it may be removed from local scrutiny.

Such optimism concerning regulatory competition needs, however, to be countered by noting, first, that the Tiebout thesis presupposes that genuinely competitive conditions exist—that there is freedom to move, that adequate information concerning regulation is available to all parties, and that enforcement is predictable. It also assumes that mechanisms of accountability exist and operate in a manner that allows all interested parties and groups to voice their preferences and concerns to the regulators. These parties and groups must also have the expertise to be able to process the information they are given and to make their voices heard. In practice, these heroic assumptions are unlikely to be fulfilled. Second, the optimistic vision incorporates what many would see as a romantic, public interest, notion of regulation (for criticism of which see Chapter 3 above). In fact, it could be contended that regulatory competition may not lead to the efficient serving of the public interest but to capture and the serving of particular private interests.[9] Indeed, whenever there are asymmetries of information, political influence, or mobility (e.g. if capital is more mobile than labour) competitive biases will result as regulators become more responsive to those groupings within their constituencies that are best able to exert pressure through votes or moving jurisdictions. Local councillors or regulators may listen more readily to highly mobile large firms than to residents who are unlikely to move out of the area. Peter Self argues that competition between local authorities is likely to compound problems of wealth inequality as rich citizens will tend to congregate in low-tax, well-serviced areas and poorer individuals will suffer the reverse situation.[10]

---

[9] See McCahery et al., *International Regulatory Competition*, 15, and W. W. Bratton and J. A. McCahery, 'Regulatory Competition as Regulatory Capture: The Case of Corporate Law in the USA', ibid.

[10] See P. Self, *Government by the Market?* (Basingstoke, 1993), 63.

Further limitations of regulatory competition include the following:

Transnational problems—regulatory competition may produce high transaction costs as firms spend time interacting with regulators and then attempt to predict regulatory developments. Uncertainty and informational problems within this process may prove expensive as firms attempt to make plans and investment decisions.

Regulatory drift—regulators as well as those regulated may suffer from uncertainties as regulatory policies 'drift' under the influence of competition rather than develop with a sense of direction.[11]

Externalities—where problems cross jurisdictions (e.g. where cross-border pollution occurs) individual regulators in competition with each other may not be able to respond to such problems adequately and a degree of cooperation maybe called for. A solitary competing regulator may have difficulties in finding out about extra-jurisdictional harms. Citizens of area A may, moreover, have voted for a mode of regulation that allows a high level of pollution but citizens of area B may have to suffer the effects of that pollution and of a system of regulation less rigorous than the one they would have chosen. Where regulation in one area is ill-organized, or slack in other respects, this may, similarly, produce negative externalities—for example, a bank failure in one area might produce trans-jurisdictional effects.[12]

Regulatory rigour and accountability—regulatory competition, where less than perfect, may produce under- or over-regulation and it may be difficult to predict the incidence or extent of this. Levels of regulation and regulatory policies may become set in place by competitive forces rather than political processes and this weakens democratic accountability.

Regulatory collusion—groups of regulators may under certain conditions collude in order to limit rather than promote competition.

Social Policy—regulatory competition may worsen the position of the least well-off in society where, for instance, the influence and mobility of such persons is less than that of high earners. Regulators and governments may respond to this disparity by favouring higher earners and this may make it more difficult to support poorer members of society through regulation, taxation, or welfare mechanisms.[13]

Such difficulties as are noted above may be pointed to by those who are sceptical concerning the benefits of regulatory competition and who take the view that this will lead to a 'race to the bottom' in which regulators apply less rigorous requirements (e.g. allow higher levels of pollution or enforce lower safety standards) and do so in the hope of attracting inward investment or giving certain producers advantages in the market

[11] See Sun and Pelkmans loc. cit. n. 2 above, pp. 85–6.
[12] See Woolcock loc. cit. n. 3 above, p. 300.
[13] See D. Begg, P. Seabright, and D. Nevern, *Making Sense of Subsidiarity: How Much Centralisation for Europe?* (London, 1993).

place.[14] Thus within the EU it has been suggested that under mutual recognition regimes, which guarantee the entry into a Member State (MS) of products complying with the regulations of another MS, each MS has an incentive to set low standards to benefit its own firms.[15] In so far as regulatory competition is imperfect, the argument runs, the race will tend to be towards the bottom or else towards the interests of groupings that have captured the regulator.[16]

Steps can, however, be taken to harness regulatory competition and to counter some of the problems noted. Within the EU, for instance, a number of factors limit the adverse effects that may result from regulatory competition. First, harmonizing measures can set minimum standards for regulation (as found, for example, in the taxation, environmental, and health and safety fields). These put a floor on regulatory levels. Second, the ability of a minority of Member States to block legislation can act to protect minimum standards.[17] Third, national regulators appear to be willing and able to maintain standards above those of the common EC level and to do so in response to local political pressures and national policy objectives. Fourth, consumer preferences may place a floor under standards—as where investors demand a minimum level of protection from financial services regulators before they place funds in a capital market.[18] Finally, regulatory drift and policy uncertainties can be controlled through measures such as Framework Directives which reduce national differences of approach and create greater legal certainty but still allow national regulators a degree of flexibility as to the way in which stated objectives are achieved.

On the European front, accordingly, it can be argued that regulatory competition and harmonizing measures should be seen not as direct alternatives but as modes of influence that can be used in harness so as to limit their individual weaknesses. It is not possible, however, to draw the conclusion that regulatory competition can always be rendered benign, whatever the context. It is clear from the above discussion that much depends on the measures used in association with regulatory competition, on the governmental context within which regulators work, and on a series of factors specific to the instance such as the scope for

---

[14] For an example of a 'race to the bottom' approach see W. Cary, 'Federalism and Corporate Law: Reflections upon Delaware' (1974) 88 *Yale LJ* 663–707; Winter, loc. cit. n. 8 above; Romano, loc. cit. n. 1 above; id., 'Competition for Corporate Charters and the Lessons of Takeover Statutes' (1993) 61 *Fordam LR* 843.

[15] See McCahery et al., *International Regulatory Competition*, 38.

[16] See Bratton and McCahery loc. cit. n. 9 above.

[17] Thus Woolcock (loc. cit. n. 3 above) cites Germany's consistent refusal to accept EC-level legislation that allows MSs to undercut the level of provision in Germany and, in the field of environmental policy, Germany, the Netherlands, and Denmark tend to block EC Directives liable to depress regulatory standards. A counter-argument is that the general need to secure MS agreement to legislation will tend to reduce standards to those levels that the poorest performers are able to meet.

[18] Ibid. 318.

genuine competition, the extent to which all affected parties are able to participate in that regulatory competition, and the responsiveness of regulators to all aspects of the competitive and democratic processes. At the end of the day, however, there will be tensions between these two kinds of process that cannot be resolved.

3. Regulatory Coordination

It can be seen from the discussion in this and the last chapter that responding to a number of problems may call for regulatory coordination across national or sectoral boundaries. Such problems tend to arise when the following are encountered:

- cross-jurisdictional or cross-sectoral harms;[19]
- incentives or inclinations to regulatory bias within states or sectors participating in a market;
- lack of information concerning different regulators' intentions and operations within a common market;
- lack of trust and an inability to monitor co-regulators within a shared market;
- tendencies to delay regulatory liberalization so as not to prejudice regulated firms' competitive positions;
- disinclinations of firms to comply with regulations due to perceptions of slackness by those regulating their competitors;
- high costs for firms when complying with a variety of regulatory regimes;[20]
- the ability of regulated firms to manipulate costs and profits by distributing these between different states or sectors or between regulated and unregulated activities so as to distort regulation in their own favour;[21]
- difficulties in measuring and comparing regulatory rigour in divergent regimes within a shared market.

[19] On the need to coordinate regulation across overlapping sectors, or even to merge regulators see OFTEL, *Second Submission to the Culture, Media and Sport Select Committee: Beyond the Telephone, the Television and the PC—Regulation of the Electronic Communications Industry* (London, March 1988) in which OFTEL argues for the bringing together of telecommunications, broadcasting, and information technology regulation in order to deal with the new converged communications world.

[20] Concerns on this front underpinned the calls, in 1997, from Jean Pierson, President of Airbus Industries, for a single European aviation regulatory authority. See *Financial Times*, 29 Oct. 1997: 'Airbus Chief Calls for Single Regulator'.

[21] Where firms provide services in a number of sectors this may increase the case for regulatory coordination or even fusion. Thus the advent of the super-utility (e.g. the United Utilities company which acts in the water, electricity, and telecommunications sectors in the UK and which started operations in January 1996) presents such a challenge.

Regulatory coordination may also produce positive benefits. Thus, high levels of expertise may be achieved by the pooling of experience and staff and coordination may allow new technical developments and networks to be organized in circumstances where the market or sectoral regulation would not provide for such planning. Greater transparency of regulation can ensue when common statistical and accounting techniques are employed across regulatory boundaries and where procedures are standardized. Monitoring the activities of regulated firms may also prove to be more effective when coordination restricts the ability of firms to manipulate information and financial pictures to their own benefit. Similarly, the danger that regulators will be captured by industrial interests may be reduced where regulation is coordinated since there is a lower incentive for a firm to capture the regulator when the regulator is seen not to be in sole charge of policy- or decision-making.[22] The accountability of both the regulators and those regulated may, in turn, be enhanced if improvements in information flows, transparency, and monitoring flow from regulatory coordination.

Substantive fairness can also be sought through coordination; thus, in the utilities, universal service obligations, and measures to combat discrimination can be imposed at the European level through cooperative strategies.[23] Policies of social and economic cohesion can, additionally, be pursued through coordination where the market would be too short-termist and where fragmented regulation would respond inadequately to such market failure. Thus, in the telecommunications field, there is pressure within the European market that draws high-technology developments towards the centre and to Member States that invest heavily in the sector. This tends to exclude less developed regions. A coordinated response, with provision from central funds where necessary, holds out the prospect of spreading high-technology networks across the breadth of the EU.[24] Such coordinated approaches to European networks and regional interests are to be seen across the energy, telecommunications, and transport sectors.[25] They build on a further benefit of regulatory coordination—its potential to reduce political tensions within or across states and sectors. Perceptions of inconsistent regulation tend to produce such tensions with both speed and force.

Coordinating regulation across sectors or states is not, however, a simple task. Resistance to coordination may stem from political opposition to the substance of policies, to the use of new procedures, or to the

[22] I am grateful to Claire Hall and Colin Scott for this point. (The purposes served by regulation may, however, be difficult to identify when coordination occurs and this may present legitimation problems in itself.)

[23] See Scott, *Competition and Coordination*, 27.

[24] Ibid. 31; see also Commission of the European Communities, *Towards Trans-European Network for a Community Action Programme*, COM (90) 585 (1990).

[25] Ibid.

transfer of powers from one decision- or policy-maker or jurisdiction to another. Bureaucracies may fight to protect their own jobs, areas of responsibility, budgets, or even regulatory traditions.[26] Those regulated and powerful economic interests with influence over 'home' regulators are liable to oppose changes that devalue the regulatory advantages that they presently enjoy and they will resist coordinating measures that decrease their ability to manipulate information or costings to their advantage. Even the less powerful will oppose coordinating measures that involve the increased costs of adapting their compliance techniques to new forms of regulation. Finally, as was clear in the last chapter, those coordinating regulation also face a series of difficulties in measuring rigour in regulation and ensuring that where enforcement lies in the hands of different regulators, there is equivalence in the application of rules.

Nor should it be assumed that regulatory coordination is any less prone to undesirable races to the top, or bottom, than regulatory competition. Within Europe the evidence is said to disclose a heavy preponderance of lowest common denominator outcomes from the processes of harmonization, though there are also some indications that bargaining between Member States can on occasions produce the effect of 'ratcheting' standards to levels higher than those of pre-existing national laws.[27] Low standards tend to be explained with reference to the political need to accommodate poor performers but the possible causes of ratcheting have been said to include:[28] first, the 'California effect', in which a particular state imposes its will on others by threatening to impose high standards and exclude goods or services of lower standards from their markets; second, deals made by national negotiators on an intra-sectoral basis, for example where air pollution car standards are traded for industrial plant standards; third, concessions on particular topics made in return for future benefits (e.g. of being seen to show 'good European will'); fourth, 'slack-cutting'—where national representatives collude in order to escape the constraints of domestic policies; fifth, 'expected non-compliance'—where certain states agree to laws or regulations that they have no serious intention of implementing; and, finally, unanticipated consequences—where higher than anticipated standards are agreed to because negotiators have failed to foresee the consequences of their bargains.

It is one thing to identify possible causes of ratcheting, however, and another to say when ratcheting or a race to the bottom will take place in any given situation. On the latter issue commentators might at least agree that further research needs to be done.[29] As for identifying the right

---

[26] See A. Heritier, 'The Accommodation of Diversity in European Policy-Making and Its Outcomes', (1996) 3 *J. European Public Policy* 149.

[27] See J. Golub, *Why did they sign? Explaining EC Environmental Policy Bargaining*, RSC No 96/52 (Florence, 1996).

[28] Ibid. 10–18.   [29] See ibid. 19.

level of regulatory standards, this will depend on such factors as the quality and quantity of relevant information that is available and the effectiveness of the democratic voice in determining those standards.

Conclusions

The game of regulation is becoming more complex as economic, political, and technical changes force agencies and governments to interact with each other in a host of different ways. Pressures both to compete and to coordinate are imposed on regulators at the domestic and sectoral as well as the international level.[30] Whether regulatory competition is possible and whether it produces more desirable regulation depends, we have seen, on a number of factors. The same can be said of regulatory coordination since, like competition, it can operate beneficially or detrimentally. Where coordination is attempted but fails, it may produce the worst of many worlds with rules that are insipid compromises, with divergencies of enforcement that undermine the apparent consistency offered by the published rules, and with increased costs all round. As with regulatory competition the losses as well as the gains may be considerable and the best way to achieve the gains is to be aware of the conditions under which regulators and producers will deliver the different kinds of benefits that the public seeks and under which the public will be able to make its preferences clear.

---

[30] On the need to coordinate the actions of domestic utility regulators to cope with providers of different and multiple utility services, see the joint paper by the Directors General of Electricity Supply, Gas Supply, Telecommunications and Water Services et al., *Regulatory Issues Associated with Multi Utilities* (London, 1998).

14

British Utilities Regulation:
The Basic Structure

Much of the modern British debate on regulation centres on the privatized utilities. It may be useful, therefore, to give an outline of the structure of utilities regulation before more particular issues are considered in Part II of the book. In this chapter, therefore, we consider:

- the privatized utilities industries;
- the regulators;
- legal frameworks and regulatory processes.

1. The Privatized Utilities Industries

Between the 1940s and 1980s the main utility services were provided by public corporations.[1] Telecommunications were supplied by the Post Office and after 1981, when telecommunications were separated from postal services, by British Telecom (BT). In the gas industry, British Gas was the virtual sole supplier after 1972. In electricity, the Central Electricity General Board (CEGB) generated and transmitted electricity in England and Wales and twelve regional area boards were responsible for distribution. In water, ten water authorities supplied water and sewerage services in England and Wales after 1973 but, in addition, a number of private statutory water companies provided water.

The privatizations of the utilities in the 1980s and early 1990s were controversial and were based on dissatisfactions in some quarters concerning a number of features of the former regimes.[2] Main concerns related

---

[1] See generally: Hansard Society and European Policy Forum, *Report of the Commission on the Regulation of Privatised Utilities* (London, 1996) hereafter 'Hansard Society' and National Audit Office, *Report by the Comptroller and Auditor General: The Work of the Directors General of Telecommunications, Gas Supply, Water Services and Electricity Supply* (HC645 Session 1995–6, London, July 1996) (hereafter 'NAO Report'); J. Foreman-Peck and R. Millward, *Public and Private Ownership of British Industry 1820–1990* (Oxford, 1994).

[2] See Hansard Society, p. 25; on the problems of public enterprise see C. D. Foster, *Privatisation, Public Ownership and the Regulation of Natural Monopoly* (Oxford, 1992), ch. 3 but see also T. Prosser, *Nationalised Industries and Public Control* (Oxford, 1986).

to: the financial constraints on nationalized industries (especially relating to borrowing and investment); efficiency and incentive structures; the lack of clarity of objectives; the excessive interference by ministers in the decisions of public corporations; the imposition of inappropriate objectives by ministers (e.g. employment protection); short-termism and instability in the targets set for utilities; and lack of transparency in decision-making.

With privatization came a new regime which was broadly similar in the case of telecommunications, gas, electricity, and water. It was established by means of a series of statutes:

- the Telecommunications Act 1984;
- the Gas Act 1986;
- the Electricity Act 1989;
- the Water Act 1989;
- the Water Industry Act 1991;
- the Water Resources Act 1991;
- the Competition and Service (Utilities) Act 1992;
- the Environment Act 1995;
- the Gas Act 1995.

Public limited companies replaced the former public corporations and shares were sold to private investors.[3] BT and British Gas were not broken up into smaller units but were privatized as single entities and given monopoly or near monopoly positions.[4] The water authorities were privatized on a regional basis as virtual monopolies but in electricity there was structural reorganization. The CEGB was replaced by three generators: National Power, Power Gen, and Nuclear Electric (still publicly owned) with transmission by the National Grid Company. Supply and distribution involved privatization of the twelve area electricity boards into Regional Electricity Companies (RECs) which were kept separate from generators. In England and Wales there was, accordingly, both vertical separation, between generation and distribution, and horizontal separation.

Since privatization a number of developments have affected the extent of monopoly power within the utilities. In telecommunications BT and Mercury formed a duopoly in the provision of public and private fixed-link network services but the Government ended this in 1991 and by October 1995 there were 141 licensed operators. BT, nevertheless, retained 95 per cent of exchange connections and 82 per cent of industry turnover into 1995.[5] In the mobile telephone sector, competition was

[3] For dates of sale see Hansard Society, p. 27.

[4] For criticism of the failure to break up see J. Vickers and G. Yarrow, *Privatisation and the Natural Monopolies* (London, 1985), 38–9.

[5] See Hansard Society, p. 33 and M. Armstrong, 'Competition in Telecommunications' (1997) 13 *Oxford Rev. of Econ. Policy* 64.

made possible before BT was privatized and since privatization competition has developed to produce four operators and six networks. The last area of monopoly in the telecommunications market disappeared in December 1996 when the first 44 new licences were issued to allow operators to compete with BT and Mercury on the provision of international services. Competition has continued to grow in the telecommunications sector in recent years and at March 1998 the market was served by over 200 public telecommunications operators. Such competition has led to less use of price controls to protect consumers so that overall the proportion of BT's revenue covered by price capping has diminished from 66 per cent to 24 per cent.

In the gas sector the threshold for competition in supply was reduced in 1992 to allow competitors to use the British Gas network to supply customers who were taking more than 2,500 therms a year (a tenth of the prior threshold). In that market British Gas's share had fallen to below 35 per cent by April 1995 and, in 1996, competition was extended to the market for less than 2,500 therms a year (an extension that became nationwide in May 1998). The Gas Act 1995, which effected this liberalization, also encouraged competition in pipeline systems, service pipes, and services ancillary to gas shipping and supply.[6] By March 1998 it could be reported that some seventy new suppliers were active in the industrial and commercial market and had captured 70 per cent of that market. The phased introduction of competition into the domestic market had by that date led more than a million households to switch to new suppliers.

In water, all companies were given effective monopolies but the Water Act 1989 allowed new suppliers to serve greenfield sites in the areas of existing suppliers (these are termed inset appointments). The Competition and Service (Utilities) Act 1992 extended the potential for inset appointments and allowed competition to supply domestic customers. Local water authorities were not, however, obliged to allow competitors to use their pipes and there is no national pipe network. By early 1996, fifteen applications for inset appointments were under consideration by regulators and in April 1997 OFWAT, for the first time, allowed one water company to compete successfully for the customer of a rival.[7]

In the electricity sector there are considerable natural monopoly elements. The National Grid Company is a monopoly provider of the high-voltage electricity transmission network in England and Wales, and at privatization the fourteen Public Electricity Suppliers (PESs) were given

---

[6] See C. Waddams-Price, 'Competition and Regulation in the UK Gas Industry' (1993) 13 *Oxford Rev. of Econ. Policy* 47.

[7] OFWAT allowed Anglia Water to sell water to Buxted Chickens, formerly the customer of Essex and Suffolk Water: see *Financial Times*, 21 Apr. 1997; also S. Cowan, 'Competition in the Water Industry' (1997) 13 *Oxford Rev. of Econ. Policy* 83.

local monopolies of low-voltage supply to customers with peak demands of one megawatt or less (competition was possible in the case of larger customers).

In electricity generation competition was possible at privatization and competition increased from that time onwards so that by 1996 there were three dozen generation licences. Distribution was maintained at privatization in the hands of the fourteen PESs but in 1994 competition was introduced in the over 100kW markets and in connections to the distribution system and from September 1998 competition began to be phased into the domestic electricity supply market.[8]

2. The Regulators

A number of individuals and institutions are involved in regulating the utilities. The main protagonists are the industry regulators, the Secretary of State, and the Monopolies and Mergers Commission (MMC).

The Industry Regulators

There is an individual regulator for each utility sector. This is the Director General who heads a regulatory office and who enjoys a series of statutory powers and responsibilities. The scheme by sector is as follows:

- Telecommunications: the Director General of Telecommunications (DGT) and the Office of Telecommunications (OFTEL).
- Gas: the Director General of Gas Supply (DGGS) and the Office of Gas Supply (OFGAS).
- Electricity: the Director General of Electricity Supply (DGES) and the Office of Electricity Regulation (OFFER).
- Water: the Director General of Water Services (DGWS) and the Office of Water Services (OFWAT).

The functions of the Directors General (DGs) are numerous and do vary in some important respects. Their key powers and functions, however, include:[9]

- enforcing and modifying licence conditions;
- obtaining and producing information, and keeping documents;
- advising the Secretary of State, the Director General of Fair Trading, and the MMC on certain issues;
- setting or overseeing quality of service standards, the terms on which consumers are to be compensated for breaches, and monitoring compliance with standards;

[8] See R. Green and D. M. Newbery, 'Competition in the Electricity Industry in England and Wales' (1997) 13 *Oxford Rev. of Econ. Policy* 27.
[9] The list that follows is based on Hansard Society, p. 29.

- approving equipment and setting standards;
- determining certain disputes and prices;
- a limited role in issuing licences;
- investigating complaints;
- exercising general competition law functions.

The NAO's 1996 report on the work of the DGs reveals, *inter alia*, details of the DGs' appointments[10] as in Table 6.

The offices of the DGs are modestly resourced with staff numbers and gross expenditure, on 1994–5 figures as in Table 7.[11]

TABLE 6. *DGs' offices*

	OFTEL	OFWAT[a]	OFGAS[a]	OFFER
Director General	Mr David Edmonds[a]	Mr Ian Byatt	Mr Callum McCarthy	Mr Callum McCarthy
Date of first appointment	1998	1989	1998	1999
Duration of current appointment	Fixed term, 3 yrs	Fixed term, 4 yrs, 1 month	Fixed term, 5 yrs	Fixed term, 4 yrs, 10 months
Date when current appointment is due to end	2001	2000	2003	2003
Basic salary (£)	120,000	95,000	140,000	140,000
Other emoluments	Use of car	Use of car	Use of car	Use of Car

[a] In July 1998 the Government reaffirmed its commitment to merge OFGAS and OFFER. Mr McCarthy was appointed to head OFGAS from 1 November 1998 and OFFER from 1 January 1999. His salary covers both roles.

TABLE 7. *Staff and expenditure*

	OFTEL	OFGAS	OFWAT	OFFER	TOTAL
Numbers of staff	162	68	178	215	623
Gross expenditure (£000)	9,330	4,481	9,225	9,859	32,900

---

[10] See NAO Report, p. 29.   [11] Ibid. 30.

All DGs employ staff with relevant experience including accountants, economists, engineers, scientists, and lawyers. Consultants are also used to provide advice and expertise, for example, on economic, project management, corporate finance, and engineering issues.

The Secretary of State

The Secretary of State plays an important role in relation to the following functions and powers:

- issuing licences;
- reconsidering licence modifications agreed between licensees and industry regulators;
- enforcing competition laws (with a power to veto);
- appointing the industry DGs.

The Monopolies and Mergers Commission (MMC)

The MMC considers references to it, which may be made by DGs and arise where there is a disagreement between a DG and a licensee on a licence modification, or if the Secretary of State has blocked a modification that has been agreed by the DG and licensee. The Secretary of State can also make references to the MMC concerning takeovers or mergers and the Director General of Fair Training (DGFT) can refer under general competition legislation.

3. Legal Frameworks and Regulatory Processes

Central to utilities regulation in Britain is the notion of the independent, individual regulator.[12] At the time of telecommunications privatization the Government believed that individualized regulation would produce a quicker, more decisive, and less bureaucratic form of control than would be forthcoming from a collegiate regime.[13] The system has been broadly followed in other utilities. The mode of regulation is based on a combination of general legislation (e.g. on fair trading and competition) and the licensing of individual operators in accordance with particular parent statutes. The relevant statutes establish institutional structures and provide for operator licensing but the licences issued to individual operators contain the detailed terms stipulating the services to be provided and, in many cases, the arrangements for the control of prices. The RPI–X price cap is thus imposed on providers as a condition of their licences

---

[12] On regulator independence see Foster, *Privatisation*, chs. 8 and 11.
[13] On individuals as regulators see Chapter 22 below, pp. 323–6.

and changes in the cap constitute licence variations. (For details of price capping see Chapter 17 below.)

The duties of the DGs are set out in specific parent statues. All such duties require the DG to exercise his or her powers in the manner that he or she considers is best calculated to achieve the aims specified in the relevant Act.[14] These aims differ in some respects but include:

- Securing the continued provision of the service or services which define the industry.
- Securing the continued ability of licensed operators to finance this provision.
- In the gas industry, securing effective competition and, in the electricity industry, promoting competition in generation and supply.
- Subject to the above (and some other duties in some cases) protecting customers' interests as regards prices, other terms of supply, and the quality of services and either maintaining and promoting effective competition (in the telecommunications industry) or, in the water industry, facilitating effective competition.

Accountability of the Directors General is provided for in a number of ways.[15] Regulators are liable to judicial review (rather than appeal) on the usual grounds of illegality, irrationality, or procedural impropriety.[16] Parliament, on the other hand, has few specific powers over the DGs—though it does vote appropriations to pay for the regulatory bodies and it may vote to pass a Resolution of the House of Commons to overturn ministerial orders (e.g. on the designation of public telecommunications operators). General parliamentary scrutiny can also be applied by means of both value for money examinations and financial auditing by the Comptroller and Auditor General and the National Audit Office.[17] The Select Committees also have a role to play in scrutinizing DGs who may be called upon to give evidence before them. (In 1995 the DGs of Telecommunications, Gas Supply, and Electricity all appeared before the House of Commons Trade and Industry Select Committee.) The Public Accounts Committee will take evidence and report on matters raised in the Comptroller and Auditor General's reports and the actions of Directors

---

[14] See NAO Report, ch. 2 and Section B2 of Appendices. For discussion of regulatory mandate in the utilities see Prosser, *Nationalised Industries*, ch. 1 and compare this with Foster, *Privatisation*, ch. 9. As noted above (pp. 81–2), Prosser contests the view that utility regulation should be judged with reference principally to efficiency and argues that a mixture of social and economic objectives have to be considered.

[15] For further discussion of accountability see below, Chapter 21. An appeal involves an appraisal of the merits of the initial decision, a judicial review is more narrowly concerned with the legality of that decision.

[16] For discussion of the grounds for judicial review see *Council of Civil Service Unions* v. *Minister for the Civil Service* [1985] AC 74 and the judgement of Lord Diplock; P. P. Craig, *Administrative Law* (3rd edn., London, 1994), Part 2.

[17] See NAO Report.

General are open to review by the Parliamentary Commissioner for Administration (PCA, or ombudsman).

The above controls apart, Parliament has almost no statutory powers with which to control or direct DGs. The OFT has a role in relation to utilities regulation that derives from its responsibility to investigate mergers, monopoly situations, and anti-competitive practices in the public utilities as elsewhere. It also advises the Secretary of State on whether to make references to the MMC.

As already indicated, references on regulatory matters can be made to the MMC (e.g. where the regulator and licensee disagree on a licence modification) and resultant MMC investigations constitute *de facto* a form of qualified appeal by licensees against proposed licence changes (one not available to other parties, such as consumers, who are affected by DGs' decisions).[18] DGs may only amend licences with the agreement of the licensee or following a relevant finding by the MMC subsequent to a reference. This *de facto* appeal is especially important in the telecommunications, gas, and electricity regimes as price controls in those sectors can only be changed by formal licence amendment.[19]

Accountability of a DG to the Government is provided for by means of the appointments process;[20] in requirements that Annual Reports be submitted to relevant Secretaries of State (which must be laid before Parliament); and through the subjection of DGs' offices to treasury financial controls. Ministers, in addition, possess certain powers over the decisions of DGs. They can, as noted, block licence modifications agreed between DGs and licensees so that these have to be referred to the MMC if they are to proceed. The Secretary of State can issue 'general directions' to DGs and has powers to act in special circumstances such as national emergencies.

---

[18] The word 'qualified' is employed because the DGs have a duty to have regard to MMC proposals following a reference but can exercise discretion in acting on these—see *R* v. *Director General of Electricity Supply ex p. Scottish Power*, Court of Appeal 3 Feb. 1997. DGs have to make licence modifications as appear to them to be requisite to remedy or prevent any adverse effects specified in the MMC report—see Electricity Act 1989, section 14 (1); Railways Act 1993, section 15; Gas Act 1986, section 26; Telecommunication Act 1984, section 15; Airports Act 1986, section 46; Water Industry Act 1991 section 16 and C. Graham, 'Regulatory Responses to MMC Decisions', in P. Vass (ed.), *CRI Regulatory Review 1997* (London, 1997).

[19] In the water and sewerage industry the DG can determine price limits without needing formally to amend a licence but a dissatisfied licensee can nevertheless require a DG to refer the matter to the MMC for a determination—which will be final and substituted for that of the DG.

[20] In February 1998 the DG of OFLOT, Peter Davis, resigned following discussions with the Secretary of State for Culture, Chris Smith—the media broadly saw this as a sacking carried out to restore public confidence in lottery regulation. In October 1998 John Prescott, Deputy Prime Minister, announced a 'purge' of rail regulators (deciding to replace John Swift QC as the Rail Regulator at the end of his contract and notifying the early departure of the Franchising Director, John O'Brien. The cause for such action was said to be their failure to take a tough line on poor operators—see *Fiancial Times*, 1 Oct. 1998.

The regulatory process also provides for a degree of accountability to consumers and the public through the mechanisms of consultation. The parent statutes for the utilities sectors make various provisions for bodies representing consumers. In telecommunications, the 1984 Act requires the establishment of four Advisory Committees for Telecommunications (one for each country in the UK). Members are appointed by the Secretary of State and the DG must consider advice from these committees. The Act also requires the DG to establish two further advisory bodies to deal with small businesses and with those over pensionable age or disabled. The DG can also establish such other advisory bodies as he or she sees fit.

In water, the DGWS must established up to ten Customer Service Committees for England and Wales. The DGWS appoints the chairs of those after consulting the Secretary of State and the membership. The chairs of these committees together with the DG form the OFWAT National Customer Council.[21]

In electricity, the DGES must establish a consumer committee for the area of each electricity supplier and, again, the DG appoints the chairs of these after consulting the Secretary of State, and then chooses the membership. The Electricity Act 1989 established a National Consumers' Consultative Committee consisting of the chairs of the consumer committees and chaired by the DGWS.

Gas differs in that the DGGS has no duty to establish consumer committees but there is an independent statutory Gas Consumers' Council (GCC) whose members are appointed by the Secretary of State. Gas also differs from water and electricity in that the GCC is funded not by the DGGS but by the Secretary of State.

The functions of the various consumer committees vary in details but their functions include reporting to and advising the industry DG; reviewing their sector; making representation to the DG and/or service suppliers; and consulting suppliers on matters affecting the interests of consumers.

DGs have a variety of duties to consult and these generally include:

- Consulting publicly, on making licence modifications, by publishing proposed modifications and considering representations or objections made within a specified period.
- Consulting similarly in relation to licence enforcement.
- Considering representations on enforcement and (in electricity, water, and gas) considering matters referred to them by the user committees, or consumers' councils.
- Approving service providers' complaints procedures.

---

[21] See generally C. Graham, 'Consumer Bodies: Practice and Performance', in CRI, *Regulatory Review 1996* (London, 1996).

- On disputes between certain parties, or on certain issues, the DG must consider a representation and then make a decision on a dispute—for example in a dispute between a public electricity supplier and a person seeking connection or in a dispute on the cost of a connection.

Turning from accountability to the decision-making and policy-making processes adopted by the DGs, the general stance of the DGs has been that they favour openness and transparency. All of the DGs who reported to the NAO in 1995–6 stressed that they carried out far more extensive consultations than were required by statute and the NAO found that the trend was towards an increase in the amount of consultation undertaken.[22] Consultation was often initiated by the issue of a consultation paper. Views and responses were considered by DGs and written responses were normally made publicly available unless confidentiality had been requested. The DGs have been issued with very limited statutory obligations to give reasons for their decisions or actions but they told the NAO that they favoured explaining reasons for decisions and gave examples of this.

OFTEL led the way in using hearings within the policy-making process when, in November 1995, it held its first hearing on a proposed new condition to be inserted into BT's and other operators' licences prohibiting anti-competitive practices. Public hearings were also held on the new price control review in April and May 1996 and, more recently, on OFTEL's Work Programme in February 1998.

OFTEL has also established standing and *ad hoc* Working Groups with the industry, representatives of users, and with other relevant interests in order to deal with particular issues. In addition, OFTEL regularly uses one-day or half-day workshops to conduct discussions informally with the industry, consumers, and interested groups. These meetings are used to assist in policy formulation.[23] In order to provide information for participants at such meetings, and for general reasons of transparency, OFTEL makes available information on regulatory methods and publishes accounts, statistics, and comparable performance indicators.

Conclusions

Throughout the 1990s the regulation of the privatized utilities has been the subject of almost constant debate. Central concerns have been the

[22] NAO Report, para. 4.7.
[23] See NAO Report, pp. 64–5. Workshops were held in October 1995 (Anti-competitive practices; Service Providers; Interconnection); November 1995 (Universal Service); January and February 1996 (Price Control; Universal Service).

efficiency, accountability, and fairness of regulatory structures and performance.[24] We review the debates on these issues in Chapters 18, 21, and 22. What is clear from Chapter 6 is that the success or failure of British utilities regulation will depend not merely on its being seen to produce results efficiently, accountably, and fairly but on its being seen to produce the *right* results and to do so in a way that achieves an acceptable distribution of benefits. In this respect utilities regulation is no different from regulation in all other areas.

[24] For reviews of the debate see R. Baldwin, *Regulation in Question* (London, 1995); D. Helm, *British Utilities Regulation* (London, 1995); Hansard Society; M. E. Beesley (ed.), *Regulating Utilities: Broadening the Debate* (London, 1997).

II

PARTICULAR CONCERNS

15

Price Setting in Natural Monopolies

This and the following four chapters are concerned with economic regulation of the utilities sector. This chapter focuses on the nature and implications of natural monopoly—a condition that governs the costs of many activities undertaken by utilities, especially their distribution networks. Natural monopoly can be defined as a situation in which the market can most cheaply be supplied by a single firm. (A gas distribution network is a good example.) A natural monopolist, left to itself, would for reasons discussed below be likely to charge excessive prices and there is accordingly a need for some form of price regulation, and scope for debate about the kind of price regulation that is appropriate.

Not all activities undertaken by utilities are naturally monopolistic, though historically the markets may for policy reasons have been supplied by a single firm, typically a public enterprise. In such cases, decisions have to be made about where, how, and when to liberalize the market and allow competition to enter. It is therefore necessary to discuss how to manage the transition to competition and the implications for regulating entry, prices, and quality of service. These issues are tackled in the following four chapters which deal, respectively, with the complementary roles of competition and regulation (Chapter 16), methods of price control (Chapter 17), the measurement of efficiency (Chapter 18), and regulating quality of service (Chapter 19).

1. What is a Natural Monopoly?

A natural monopoly arises when the market is served most cheaply by a single firm, rather than by a multiplicity of competing firms.[1] In cases where

---

[1] See M. Armstrong, S. Cowan, and J. Vickers, *Regulatory Reform: Economic Analysis and British Experience* (London, 1994), chs. 2–3; S. Berg and T. Tschirhart, *Natural Monopoly Regulation* (Cambridge, 1988); W. W. Sharkey, *The Theory of Natural Monopoly* (Cambridge, 1982); C. D. Foster, *Privatisation, Public Ownership and the Regulation of Natural Monopoly* (Oxford, 1992), ch. 6.

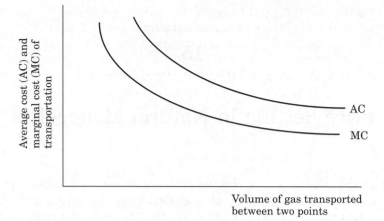

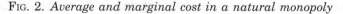

Volume of gas transported
between two points

As the volume of gas transported increases, there is a fall in the average cost (AC) of transportation
—both operating costs and investment or capital costs. This implies that the cost of moving an
additional unit (the marginal cost or MC) always lies below the average cost: what drags the average
down is the (low) additional cost of transporting an extra or marginal unit.

Fig. 2. *Average and marginal cost in a natural monopoly*

the firm is producing a single product or service—for example, transporting
gas between two points, the situation can be represented in Figure 2,
which shows how average cost (*AC*) per unit transported falls as the
volume transported increases.

An implication of declining average cost is that the additional cost
incurred by the pipeline operator on transporting each further unit is
not only falling itself but also less than the average cost. This situation
is shown in Figure 2 by the marginal cost curve (*MC*).

Possible sources of declining unit costs are many.[2] In the case of pipe-
lines, the capacity of the pipe can be increased without a commensurate
increase in investment cost. Firms with a larger scale of operation may
also be able to reduce costs by having proportionately lower overheads
or by being able to employ more specialized and efficient personnel. A
further important consideration in networks for distributing electricity,
gas, telecommunications, and water services to final users is associated
with what are called economies of density. Thus, it is cheaper on a per
household basis for a single distribution company to deliver electricity
to all the houses in an area than to have two competing networks each
serving half of them. This is because the latter arrangement requires
unnecessary duplication of a major part of the distribution network.

[2] See D. A. Hay and D. T. Morris, *Industrial Economics and Organization* (2nd edn.,
Oxford, 1991), ch. 2.

Whether an activity is a natural monopoly of this kind depends not only on engineering factors but also upon management processes and the operation of social and economic factors within the enterprise. It might theoretically be possible for a monopolist to serve a market at a lower unit cost than two or more competing firms can achieve. Incentives to efficiency under a monopoly may, however, be very weak, and as a result, it may in practice be cheaper to have the market supplied by two competitors in spite of the theoretical advantage of the monopoly.

The declining unit costs associated with economies of scale of the kind described above are one aspect of natural monopolies. A second reason for cost reduction arises through economies of scope, which are encountered in many industries when it is cheaper for one firm to provide two or more related products and services together, than for each of them to be provided by a separate firm. A good example from the communications industry is provided by cable television networks which deliver both broadcast entertainment services and telecommunication services. Both telecommunications and cable TV companies utilize much of the same infrastructure—the trenches and ducts which contain the cables. If a single firm provides both services, it can do so more cheaply than two firms can when using separate distribution networks.[3] Economies of scope, which typically arise from the use of common assets to produce separate products, have the effect of reducing the number of firms in an industry.

The tendency towards natural monopoly is most pronounced when economies of scale are combined with economies of scope. The former reduce the number of firms producing each service individually, while the latter encourage each firm in the market to produce a range of services. Acting in combination, they may generate a situation in which a significant number of markets are served by the same monopolist.

Determining whether a particular area of activity is a natural monopoly is a complex process. Natural monopolies are vulnerable to technological development. Thus, the argument that telecommunications, particularly the access network or local loop which connects households and firms to the local exchange, is a natural monopoly has been significantly weakened by the development of new technologies based on wireless distribution. These give customers access to the exchange without the necessity to construct fixed link networks. The natural monopolies of energy and water distribution systems, however, appear to be well rooted.

---

[3] M. Cave and P. Williamson, 'Entry, Competition and Regulation in UK Telecommunications', (1996) 12 *Oxford Rev. of Econ. Policy* 100.

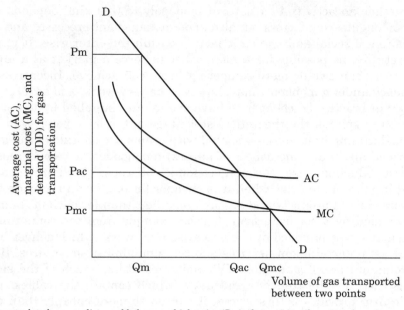

An unregulated monopolist would charge a high price (*Pm*), thus raising the price of gas to consumers. The ideal price would be *Pmc*, where the demand curve (DD) cuts the marginal cost curve (MC). If this price were charged, gas prices would be based on a charge for transportation which reflected the true marginal cost to the economy of transporting the last or marginal unit. However, a price equal to *Pmc* would fail to cover the firm's average cost (AC); hence the firm could not survive in the long run. The lowest price consistent with the firm breaking even is *Pac*. If the regulator must ensure that the firm breaks even, this is the best price available.

FIG. 3. *Pricing options for a natural monopolist*

2. Implications for Pricing

The implications for pricing of services provided by a natural monopoly can be tackled by asking two questions: what price would emerge in the absence of intervention, and what prices should regulators try to attain?

The first question can readily be answered in relation to Figure 3. This reproduces Figure 2, with the addition of a demand curve *DD*, which shows how demand for gas pipeline services varies with the price charged.

If the price of transportation is high, the implied price of gas made available to consumers will be high, and gas consumption will diminish. As gas transport prices fall, this will be reflected in lower prices at the retail level, and demand for gas and for gas transport will rise.

In these circumstances, a monopolist controlling the pipeline will maximize its profits by setting a relatively high price, *Pm*, which lies above average cost and hence delivers a monopoly profit.[4] As a result, gas prices

---

[4] For how that price is determined, see D. Begg, G. Fischer, and R. Dornbusch, *Economics* (4th edn., London, 1998).

paid by consumers will be high, and those consumers will suffer, to the benefit of shareholders in the monopoly who will enjoy excess profits.

This unsatisfactory state of affairs can clearly be mitigated by the regulation of prices, but what price for gas transport should the regulator set? Ideally the prices of goods and services sold in the economy should be set at their marginal costs,[5] whether they apply to final demand such as gas purchased by households or to an intermediate product such as gas transport. This is desirable because at a price where the demand curve cuts the marginal cost curve (*Pmc* in Fig. 3), output has been expanded up to the point where the buyers' willingness to pay for an additional unit of the service provided, shown by the height of the demand curve, exactly equals the marginal cost to the economy of producing that final unit of output. At a price higher than this, the buyers' willingness to pay would exceed the marginal cost of providing an extra unit. At a price lower than this, the marginal cost to the economy of providing the last unit of output is greater than the buyers' willingness to pay for it. The best price for the service is, therefore, a price equal to marginal cost.

As inspection of Figure 3 demonstrates, however, if gas transport services were priced at *Pmc*, then the price charged would fail to cover the average cost of service. As a result, the firm would make a loss.

If it were a public enterprise, that loss could be made up from general taxation. A privately owned single product firm which did not receive state aid or another form of subsidy would, however, go out of business. If the firm is constrained to avoid losses and break even, then the most appropriate regulated price is shown by *Pac* in Figure 3. This is more satisfactory than the monopoly price *Pm*, but less efficient than a price equal to marginal cost, *Pmc*.

The implication is that a regulator who is setting prices for a single product firm which has to break even should seek to drive prices down to average costs. Most regulated firms, however, produce several services, and this gives more flexibility in the pricing process. It is not possible in the case of a multi-product firm to identify individual average costs for the separate services, because those services will typically have common inputs such as capital equipment, and as a result it will not be possible to attribute all costs unambiguously to individual services. It will, however, be possible to establish the marginal cost of each service, by identifying the increases in overall costs associated with increasing the output of any service when the output of other services is held constant.

As before, the most efficient price for each service occurs where the demand curve *Da Da* or *Db Db* crosses the marginal cost curve (*MCa* or *MCb*), as illustrated by *Pmc*^{a} and *Pmc*^{b} in Figure 4.

[5] See Armstrong et al., *Regulatory Reform*, 14–18.

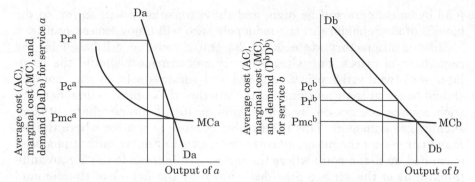

The ideal prices are where the demand curves (Da Da and Db Db) cut the marginal cost curves (MCa and MCb). A firm charging such prices would, however, make losses as both products are produced in conditions of economies of scale. Hence the need for a mark-up over marginal costs. One possibility would be to have an equal mark-up to cover common and fixed costs; i.e. to choose Pc^a and Pc^b. Such prices, though, have different distorting effects on demand for the two services; it falls much more for b than for a. A preferred option is so-called Ramsey pricing, which involves a high proportionate mark-up on service a, where demand is unresponsive to price (Pr^a) and a low proportionate mark-up on b, where demand is more responsive to price (Pr^b).

FIG. 4. *Efficient pricing for a multi-service utility*

We face once again, however, the problem that, if the firm sells each service at a price equal to its marginal cost, the firm will incur losses. In order to break even, it must, therefore, charge a mark-up above marginal costs.

One simple way of achieving this objective would be to fix prices that contain an equal proportionate mark up on each service, of a size which just allows the firm to break even. These prices are shown in Figure 4 as Pc^a and Pc^b respectively. This is the solution consistent with average cost pricing for the single product firm. It is preferable in most circumstances, however, to set a proportionate mark-up over marginal cost for each service which varies from service in accordance with demand conditions.

These preferred prices are illustrated in Figure 4 by Pr^a and Pr^b; they are also known after their inventor as Ramsey prices.[6] The logic behind them is as follows. In the case of service a, demand is relatively unresponsive to price, and a high mark-up can be charged without that mark-up having a major effect on consumption, compared with the case where price is equal to marginal cost. Demand for service b by contrast, falls much more as price rises. A high mark-up on service b will lead to a major distortion of the amount consumed.

[6] See Armstrong et al., *Regulatory Reform*, 47–51; G. T. Brown and D. S. Sibley, *The Theory of Public Utility Pricing* (Cambridge, 1986), 39–44.

To express this principle more generally, when prices are being set for a regulated monopoly which produces a variety of services and which—because it is privately owned—is required to break even, they should embody the minimum mark-ups over marginal costs that are necessary to allow the firm to break even. Services where demand is relatively responsive to price should generally have a lower than average proportionate mark-up, while services where demand is relatively unresponsive to price should have a higher than average mark-up over their marginal costs. This enables common costs to be recovered in a way that reduces to a minimum the harmful effects of distortion in output caused by the mark-up over marginal cost.[7]

Conclusions

This chapter has defined natural monopoly, which occurs when a market is most cheaply served by a single producer. Natural monopolies arise from economies of scale, which mean that the largest firm has a cost advantage over its competitors, and is hence likely to become a monopolist. Where two or more products or services are produced more cheaply by a single firm than separately by two firms, economies of scope are in evidence. A combination of economies of scale and economies of scope is likely to lead to dominance of the market by a single multi-product firm.

Such a firm has the market power to charge prices which generate excessive profit. The natural regulatory response is to control prices. In the case of a single product firm, if the firm is required to break even, the most satisfactory regulated price which can be imposed at any point in time is equal to average cost. In the case of a multi-product firm, a break-even constraint should lead to differential mark-ups on services. Such mark-ups should be greater where demand is relatively unresponsive to price and smaller where it is relatively responsive.

This analysis has allowed us to identify what might be efficient pricing rules for a natural monopoly. Utility regulators in practice have to undertake the prior, and crucial, process of determining whether regulation of price and other aspects is in fact necessary. Our discussion has also assumed that regulators know the costs of the firms they regulate. In practice they do not, and they need to develop incentives for firms to show how they can reduce their costs and keep them down.

[7] For an implementation of Ramsey pricing to the telecommunications sector, see Brown and Sibley, *Public Utility Pricing*, ch. 7.

Regulation versus Competition

1. Competition and its Virtues

Competition involves rivalry among firms for the customer's business across all the dimensions of the service—price, quality, and innovation. Its opposite is a situation in which a single firm can effectively act independently of any competitors and impose a particular offering on the market place. Inevitably, competition is a matter of degree rather than something which is either fully present or absent. Industries differ in their structure, ranging from the situations where there is a multiplicity of small producers, through more concentrated markets with a small number of larger producers (and sometimes a competitive fringe) to the state of monopoly. The degree of rivalry encountered also depends upon firm behaviour, which ranges from out-and-out competition in all dimensions of the service, through more limited forms of competition in which, for example, firms compete in terms of quality but not in terms of price, to openly or tacitly collusive or parallel behaviour in all the dimensions of service provision.

As a method for obtaining the best deal for consumers, detailed regulation is seen by many to be inferior to systems allowing competition subject to the safeguards of general competition law. Thus Steven Littlechild, in his 1983 report for the British Government on price controls for BT, wrote: 'Competition is by far the most effective means of protection against monopoly. Vigilance against anti-competitive prices is also important. Profit regulation is merely a "stop-gap" until sufficient competition develops.'[1]

Hence springs the expression: competition is the best regulator. Underlying this proposition is the belief that firms have the strongest incentives to give customers what they want in terms of price and quality of

---

[1] S. Littlechild, *Regulation of British Telecommunications Profitability* (London, 1983), 1; see also OFTEL's arguments in favour of control via competition and consumer protection rules as opposed to regulation by means of prescriptive licence conditions: OFTEL, *Second Submission to the Culture, Media and Sport Select Committee* (London, Mar. 1998); see also M. Grenfell, 'Can Competition Law Supplant Utilities Regulation' and M. Bloom, 'The Impact of the Competition Bill', both in C. McCrudden (ed.), *Regulation and Deregulation* (Oxford, 1999).

service when they are in competition. In such circumstances firms also have a strong incentive to gain a temporary advantage over their rivals through innovation and the development of new services. Compared with this scenario, the regulation of a monopoly that faces no competition has many disadvantages. If the regulator controls the price of the service, the firm producing it may retaliate by reducing quality. In order to counteract this, the regulator may then become involved in specifying an increasing number of the characteristics of the service, and runs the risk of eventually micro-managing its production and distribution. Perhaps even more importantly, price regulation tends to remove incentives for innovation. Thus, if a firm introduces a cost-saving innovation, a regulator may respond by enforcing a lower price, and the prospect of this will eliminate the incentive to cut costs. For the same reason, a regulated monopoly will have little incentive to meet customers' demands exactly.

A final argument in favour of competition is that it encourages firms to price whatever services they produce more efficiently. Chapter 15 showed how goods and services should ideally be priced in a way that takes account of marginal and incremental costs and of the demand conditions to which the firms are subject. In particular, if common or fixed costs have to be recovered, it is desirable that they be recovered disproportionately on services for which the demand is relatively unresponsive to price. Firms operating in markets subject to competitive entry are drawn to set prices in this fashion, because this tends to maximize their own profits.[2] An unregulated monopolist would set prices higher, and this would reduce consumers' welfare.

Competition is just a means to the end of consumer welfare, and it is necessary that it should be effective in achieving that end.[3] Pinning down precisely what is meant by effective competition is, however, a difficult task, perhaps best attempted by identifying those forms of competition that are ineffective. As well as cases of straightforward collusion, these include situations in which one firm exercises such dominance in the market that it is in practice able to act with a high degree of independence from its competitors. Situations of this kind are likely to emerge particularly where, as in the case of many utilities, a market has just been opened up to competition and the incumbent firms start with a market share of 100 per cent. Another form of ineffective competition can arise when too many firms enter an industry which, because of its cost conditions—manifested in significant economies of scale—is best served by a single firm or a small number of firms. The problem here is that excessive entry involves a needless duplication of fixed costs which are

[2] See W. Baumol, J. Panzar, and R. Willig, *Contestable Markets and the Theory of Industry Structure* (New York, 1988), chs. 2–5, 11, 12, for a proof of this important but difficult proposition.

[3] See J. Vickers, 'Concepts of Competition' (1995) 47 *Oxford Economic Papers* 1–23.

either recovered in prices, to the detriment of consumers, or which leave entrants with losses, borne by their investors. While competition of this type would also be ineffective, there are reasons to doubt that the ordinary operation of the market process would bring it into being, since potential entrants would be aware of the risks of making substantial investments which they would be unlikely to recover.[4] For this reason the dangers of 'excess entry' are likely to be quite small, unless such inefficient investments arise as an unintended consequence of regulation.

2. Where is Competition Possible?

There are thus good reasons for permitting and in some circumstances even encouraging as much competition as is possible in the utilities sector. The scope for competition, however, depends upon a variety of considerations. The chief of these is the cost conditions in the industry —a topic discussed in Chapter 15. The distribution networks that characterize the utilities demonstrate significant economies of scale, which give firms with large numbers of customers cost advantages over their smaller competitors. These advantages arise both from unit cost reductions that are associated with greater throughput and from economies of density. This consideration makes the local distribution network in electricity, gas, and water effectively a natural monopoly, and hampers the development of competition in the access network for telecommunications.

Several economists have pointed out that the presence of economies of scale is not sufficient by itself to eliminate the possibility of some form of competition. They argue, instead, that even in the presence of scale economies a market might be contestable if it were possible for an entrant to gain market share by undercutting the incumbent's prices, and then exit from the market when the incumbent responded with a price cut of its own. In such circumstances the simple threat of competition would be enough to prevent the possibility of excess monopoly profits.[5] If this process is to work, however, the entrant must be capable of leaving the industry without incurring excessive costs when the incumbent responds by cutting its prices. For this to be the case, the technology must be such that the entrant does not have to make irrecoverable investments in order to enter the market. To put it in another way, there must be no 'sunk costs'. It is one of the major characteristics of distribution networks, however, that they do require large and long-lived investments which cannot be recovered if the entrant leaves the industry. For this

---

[4] M. Armstrong, S. Cowan, and I. Vickers, *Regulatory Reform: Economic Analysis and British Experience* (London, 1994), 107–11.

[5] W. Baumol, 'Contestable Markets: An Uprising in the Theory of Industrial Structure' (1982) 72 *Am. Econ. Rev.* 1–15.

reason the role of potential competition in disciplining an incumbent with a monopoly distribution network is very limited.

These technological considerations are not the only factors influencing the scope for competition. Many utilities have pricing structures that embody considerable amounts of cross-subsidy. These stem from their histories within the public sector and from the major impact which the energy, telecommunications, transport, and water industries have on economic and social development and the distribution of income. Utilities, for example, traditionally charge a uniform tariff to all customers of the same category (business or residential) in a service area, even though cost of service differs from one customer to another. BT thus offers the same menu of quarterly rental payments to residential telephone subscribers, whether they live in suburban areas, which are relatively cheap to serve, or in remote and sparsely populated parts of the country, where service is costly. There is also a tradition in the telecommunications industry in Europe and elsewhere for monthly or quarterly rental payments for access to the network to be set below cost, with the deficit being recovered by relatively high and profitable call charges.

When competition is introduced into a market involving cross-subsidies of these kinds, both across customers and across services, there is a risk that it will be distorted. Entrants will naturally seek out profitable markets, leaving the incumbent to serve the unprofitable ones. In the long run, entry of this 'cream skimming' form may undermine the incumbent's capacity to meet its pricing and service obligations. The presence of social as well as economic considerations in the pricing of utility services adds additional complexity to the development of competition, and ways have to be found of accommodating these constraints within a competitive framework (see below).

Table 8 gives an assessment of the scope for competition in five utilities.[6] In particular, Table 8 shows how the potential for competition in each industry varies with each stage of the production process under consideration. One approach to regulating industries with different competitive potential at each stage is to break them up at privatization, and sell the monopolistic and competitive elements as different units. The monopolistic components can then be subject to price control, while the competitive activities can be deregulated. This approach brings the great advantage that it overcomes problems associated with vertical integration, when a monopolist in one area of activity has an opportunity to extend its market power from that area into related competitive markets. The disadvantage of such break-ups, however, is that they prevent the

[6] For a recent review of the situation in all utilities, see the special edition (1997) 13 *Oxford Rev. of Econ. Policy: Competition in Regulated Industries* 1–103; M. Beesley (ed.), *Regulating Utilities: Broadening the Debate* (London, 1997); and D. Helm and T. Jenkinson (eds.), *Competition in Regulated Industries* (Oxford, 1998).

TABLE 8. *Competitive potential in Electricity, Gas, Railways, Telecommunications, and Water*

Industry	Scope for Competition
Electricity	
generation	Good
high-voltage transmission	Nil
regional distribution	Nil
supply	Good
Gas	
extraction	Good
national and regional distribution	Nil
supply	Good
Railways	
track, stations, and signalling	Very limited[a]
services	Moderate[b]
Telecommunications	
local network	Moderate
long-distance and international network	Good
services	Good
Water and Sewerage	
infrastructure	Nil[c]
supply	Moderate

[a] There may be limited competition between alternative routes for certain journeys—for example the East coast and West coast routes between London and Scotland.
[b] Competition in services is only possible on a limited number of more profitable routes—for example between London and Gatwick airport.
[c] Except at the boundaries of two companies' service areas.

realization of those economies of scope that might be available to a firm undertaking several connected activities. A single telecommunications operator running both a local and a long-distance network may, for example, have lower costs than two separate firms operating the networks independently.

In the UK, the successive privatizations of the 1980s and the early 1990s show how the Government's views on this issue changed. British Telecom, in 1984, and British Gas, in 1986, were privatized as integrated firms. The electricity supply industry, by contrast, was privatized in 1989 in the form of three separate activities: electricity generation, which was considered to be potentially competitive and not subject to price regulation; high-voltage transmission, which was carried out by the National Grid Company; and regional distribution and supply, which was carried out by ten regional electricity companies (RECs). Supply of electricity, initially a monopoly of the RECs, was progressively opened up to competition. The National Grid Company was initially jointly owned by the RECs, but has subsequently been floated off as a separately owned entity. The privatization of electricity in Scotland, by contrast, was carried out on the basis of two vertically integrated firms.

The railways industry was also broken up at privatization. The track, stations, and signalling were sold as a single integrated firm, Railtrack. The rolling stock owned by British Rail was divided among three leasing companies, and the running of services was entrusted to twenty-five train operating companies. In the water industry some parts of the country are served by companies providing both water and sewerage services, but in other areas the two functions are carried out by separate firms.

It is noteworthy that British Gas, which was privatized as a whole, has since decided voluntarily to break itself up into two companies through de-merger. This followed an MMC recommendation of compulsory break-up in 1992, which was rejected by the Secretary of State. In 1996, however, British Gas's supply activity, British Gas Trading, was de-merged as a separate company known as Centrica. The company's pipeline business and its exploration and production activities were combined in BG Transco.

Consideration has even been given to introducing competition in water, where the prospects seem least favourable. Where new housing developments are planned near the boundaries of the service areas of two or more companies, there is scope for competition for the right to provide the service. Since 1992, competition has been extended to large customers who can contract with an alternative supplier using a number of possible arrangements, including a direct connection to the new supplier system or the purchase of bulk water supply from the previous supplier at the boundary of the site. By the end of 1997, two such arrangements had been approved using the direct connection method, together with a third, under which a new company acted as a broker, buying water at a price determined by OFWAT from the local water company, and selling it on to a large company.[7] Further proposals are currently under consideration by OFWAT. This demonstrates the potential for the introduction of competition even in apparently inauspicious circumstances.

3. Managing the Transition to Competition

All UK utilities regulators have been given duties relating to the promotion or fostering of competition, although this is normally combined with a duty to ensure that the dominant supplier maintains the capability to

[7] See generally C. Robinson, 'Introducing Competition into Water', in Beesley, *Regulating Utilities: Broadening the Debate*; S. Glaister, 'Incentives in Natural Monopoly: The Case of Water', in M. E. Beesley (ed.), *Regulating Utilities: A Time for Change?* (London, 1996).

finance its functions to meet demand.[8] As the previous section demonstrates, competition takes a variety of forms, which can conveniently be broken down into infrastructure competition (involving the construction of competing distribution networks) and service competition (relying upon a single distribution network). Infrastructure competition is best illustrated by the telecommunications industry, which brings the added complication that the competing networks have to interconnect with one another in order to ensure that a customer on network *A* is able to communicate with a customer on network *B*. This necessitates some kind of interconnection pricing regime, to provide payment for one firm's use of another's network. A similar, but non-reciprocal, pricing regime is necessary for service competition, under which all service providers make payments to the network operator for the transport or transmission of, say, gas or electricity which they supply to final customers. We discuss below the principles which underlie this form of access pricing, and the particular difficulties that are encountered when the network owner is also active in the supply market, and is in competition with other firms to which it sells transport or distribution services. This is just one of a number of complications which arise in managing the transition to competition.

Restrictions on the Incumbent

The first step in introducing competition in utilities is achieved by liberalizing entry into what had formally been a statutory monopoly. Typically, entrants into utilities markets have to acquire a licence from the relevant government department—this being necessary to impose certain conditions relating to consumer protection or the maintenance of the integrity of the network. In each of the industries listed in Table 8, entry has been staggered or controlled. In telecommunications, only one entrant was licensed in the period 1984–91 under the so-called duopoly policy.[9] Even when that restriction was relaxed, competition in international telecommunications was confined to two networks for a further five years. In the electricity and gas industry, competition developed progressively, beginning with the largest customers, as shown in Table 9. In railways, no fully competing companies offering precisely the same routes were permitted at privatization, but the Office of Railway Regulation announced in late 1997 that consideration would be given to introducing more competition among train operators from 1999. Following the review, the Rail Regulator announced that from 1999 new services would

---

[8] Governmental proposals to change regulatory, objectives can be found in DTI Green Paper *A Fair Deal for Consumers: Modernising the Framework for Utility Regulation*, Cm. 3898 (London, 1998) (hereafter DTI Green Paper 1998).

[9] M. Cave and P. Williamson, 'Entry, Competition and Regulation in UK Telecommunications', (1996) 12 *Oxford Rev. of Econ. Policy* 100.

TABLE 9. *Introduction of competition in Electricity and Gas Supply*

		Customers affected	Date of Introduction
A	**Electricity**	1+MW (5,000 sites)	1990
		100+kW (50,000 sites)	1994
		All customers	1998
B	**Gas**	25,000+ therms	1986
		2,500+ therms	1992
		All customers	1997/8
			(region by region)

be permitted where it could be shown that they would benefit passengers without placing undue burdens on the taxpayer. Steps would be taken to prevent the emergence of 'rail' wars.[10]

Where competition is introduced, it initially takes place under highly unusual circumstances, since the incumbent has, to that point, enjoyed a 100 per cent market share. Where the incumbent is vertically integrated, additional problems arise. A competitor in electricity supply, for example, has to use the distribution network of a regional electricity company, which has its own previously monopolistic supply business. A competitor of BT also has to use BT's network, especially to terminate calls made by its subscribers to a BT subscriber. There are thus two linked problems, the first arising from the existence of a highly dominant firm in the market, the second from the dominant firm's frequent vertical integration.

In order to deal with the problem of dominance, regulators typically impose some restrictions on the conduct of the incumbent in the newly liberalized market. One alternative would be to rely entirely on the provisions of ordinary competition law. Governments and regulators in the UK and elsewhere have generally decided that additional restrictions are appropriate in the early stages of the development of competition.

These restrictions have frequently been enshrined in licence requirements, which include a provision that dominant incumbents should not, in fixing tariffs, 'show undue preference to any person or class of persons, and shall not exercise any undue discrimination against any person or class of persons'.[11] This and related licence conditions have been invoked to limit the competitive response which the incumbent can

[10] ORR, *New Service Opportunities for Passengers: A Consultation Document on the Development of the Competitive Framework of Passenger Rail Services* (London, Oct. 1997); ORR, *New Service Opportunities for Rail Passengers: Statement* (London, Mar. 1998).

[11] Gas Act 1986—see C. Waddams-Price, 'Undue Discrimination and Cross-Subsidies: Price Structures in UK Utilities' (1997) 8 *Utilities LR* 191–200.

make in a market opened to competition. In the telecommunications industry, for example, they provided a basis for OFTEL's refusal until 1991 to permit BT to offer quantity discounts to its larger customers, which were specially targeted by Mercury, BT's competitor. Even when such quantity discounts were permitted after 1991, their nature and extent were restricted in complex ways. The prohibition against undue preference and undue discrimination has also survived OFTEL's elimination of many more detailed pricing restrictions, carried out in amendments to BT's licence in 1996, when a new Fair Trading Condition was introduced which prohibits abuse by BT of its dominant position.[12]

The progressive introduction of competition in gas supply has led OFGAS to introduce in the licence of British Gas Trading a system for the progressive relaxation of controls on its competitive response. It still may not show undue preference or undue discrimination, but even as a dominant firm, it is entitled to supply gas on terms which are reasonably necessary to meet competition. In November 1997 OFGAS determined that competition was established in the market for gas supplied to customers paying by direct debit in the South West of the UK and that British Gas Trading's price response was acceptable.[13]

Similar special arrangements for large firms can be found in European regulation of the telecommunications industry. Under the EU Directive on Interconnection and Universal Service, a firm enjoying 'significant market power' (defined as a market share of 25 per cent or above) is subject to restrictions on its pricing, publication, and information disclosure and other forms of behaviour from which firms with a smaller market share are exempt.[14]

These restrictions can be justified as interim measures necessary for the development of competition in markets which had formerly been 'unnatural monopolies'. They are, however, distinct from measures designed explicitly to promote entry, of the kind observed in the regulation of the UK telecommunications market. In 1984–91, this took the form of freeing Mercury (the second licensee) from the threat of further competitive entry under the duopoly policy. Subsequently, OFTEL introduced a regime governing the arrangements under which entrants paid BT for access to its local network which relieved them of obligations to make a contribution to the losses which BT incurred on that network. This limited concession was explicitly acknowledged by OFTEL as being a temporary form of entry promotion, justified by the benefits which

[12] OFTEL, *Pricing of Telecommunications Services from 1997* (London, June 1996).
[13] OFGAS, *Value Plus: British Gas Trading's Pricing to Direct Debit Customers in the South West of England: A Decision Document* (London, Nov. 1997).
[14] Directive 97/33/EC of the European Parliament and the Council of 30 June 1997: Interconnection in telecommunications with regard to ensuring universal service and inter-operability through application of the principles of ONP.

telecommunications' customers would receive as a result of the development of competition. Other regulators have not promoted competition by positive methods to the same extent.

Access Pricing

As noted above, a crucial factor in the costs of any entrant is the price which that entrant has to pay for access to the distribution network.[15] The owner of such a network has two motives for charging high access prices. The first is a simple desire to maximize monopoly profits; the second, which arises if a network owner is also competing in the supply market, is the desire to raise its rivals' costs and maintain a dominant position in that market.

These considerations have meant that regulators are likely to have to intervene in access pricing either by imposing detailed prices for the use of the elements of the network,[16] or by limiting the overall revenues which the network owner can collect to those which are necessary for the recovery of its costs. Either approach involves a detailed analysis by the regulator of the costs incurred by the network.[17]

The problem of access pricing does, however, become more directly intertwined with that of the development of competition as a result of the social considerations which play a part in determining the prices of utilities services. This can best be illustrated by an example in the telecommunications industry. As noted above, in many countries access to the telecommunications network is priced below cost, and the losses made there are recovered through high call charges. Entrants, therefore, find it profitable to seek customers who continue to use the incumbent's access network in order to originate or terminate calls but who rely upon their new supplier for the provision of the long distance or international element of their calls.

There is thus the obvious danger that a new entrant may choose to enter the profitable long-distance market even though it is less efficient at providing long-distance conveyance than the incumbent. This will additionally deny to the incumbent the call revenues that are necessary to cross-subsidize access. One way of eliminating this possibility is by allowing the incumbent to charge new entrants for access to its network at rates which take account of the lack of balance in the tariff structure. The incumbent, for example, could be allowed to make a charge to the entrant for call termination which covers not only the cost of that call

---

[15] For a discussion of access pricing, see M. Armstrong, S. Cowan, and J. Vickers, *Regulatory Reform* (London, 1994).

[16] This is a key issue in the electricity industry, as the structure of pricing on the National Grid can determine where generating plant is located.

[17] See the discussion of price caps in Chapter 17 below.

termination but also includes an additional element comprising the excess profit which the incumbent *would have made* by providing the call at retail prices which it needs in order to cross-subsidize other services such as access to the network.[18] If an interconnection charging regime of this kind were to be introduced, then an entrant would only be able to gain a profitable foothold in the industry if its costs in supplying the services that it provides itself, rather than buys from the incumbent, are less than those of the incumbent. Such a rule would, in consequence, only encourage entry where the entrant is more efficient than the incumbent.

A great deal has been written about access pricing rules of this kind.[19] In practice, however, regulators have generally preferred to set access prices on the basis of the costs of the network service provided, with a uniform mark-up to cover common costs or to recover permitted cross-subsidies.

Universal Service

A further important interaction between competition and pricing objectives arises from the desire of many governments and regulators to maintain 'universal service' in the utilities sector. This means that services must be made available at uniform and affordable prices to all households within a firm's service area.[20] The desire to maintain affordability often leads to prices of particular services which are less than cost. Uniformity of prices in the presence of cost differences imposes a problem in itself, however, because it means that serving customers in high-cost areas may be a loss-making activity. When the sector is open to competition, competitors will have no interest in serving such customers, and the incumbent operator, which has to provide service universally, is left with them. This arrangement might, at the end of the day, cause the whole system of universal service to unravel, as competitors would progressively attract more customers, leaving the universal service operator with a remainder characterized by increasingly high costs; it would then be faced progressively with raising its tariffs to cover these higher costs.

In most utilities markets that are open to competition, the power of the incumbent is such that it is able to deal with this problem fairly painlessly. In telecommunications, however, where competition is best

[18] This approach to access pricing, known as the Efficient Component Pricing Rule or ECPR is set out in W. Baumol and J. G. Sidak, *Toward Competition in Local Telephony* (Cambridge, Mass., 1994).

[19] See, for example, Armstrong, Cowan and Vickers, *Regulatory Reform*, 148–9, 156–7; M. Armstrong, C. Doyle, and J. Vickers, 'The Access Pricing Problem: A Synthesis', 44 (1996) *Journal of Industrial Economics* 131.

[20] On the social dimension of regulation, see DTI Green Paper 1998, pp. 31–9.

developed, arrangements have been introduced for measuring and then sharing the cost of universal service obligations among all firms in the market. Thus the 1997 EU Directive on Interconnection and Universal Service[21] outlines a method of estimating the losses suffered by the incumbent operator in meeting universal service obligations (USOs) and authorizes a procedure for those losses to be shared among all operators in proportion to their revenues, either through the creation of a universal service fund, on which the USO operator draws and to which all operators contribute, or through a payment made by entrants which supplements the interconnection payments which they make to the dominant incumbent. Because the incumbent initially has a very high market share, and hence makes the largest contribution to the costs of providing universal service, the redistribution brought about by such arrangements in the early stages of competition is limited. As market shares evolve, however, this situation may change.

In the UK, the telecommunications regulator (DGT) has determined that the cost of universal service borne by BT is too small to justify such a scheme, especially when account is also taken of the marketing or other benefits which the company receives as a result of being a universal service operator.[22] So far, discussion of how the continuation of universal service obligations can be combined with competition has largely been confined to the telecommunications industry, although it is noteworthy that the current regulatory system for gas supply in the UK also contains a provision for OFGAS to introduce a similar cost-sharing scheme.

Freeing Prices

As competition develops, one of the key issues that a regulator faces is when to remove the system of direct control over charges to customers. If price control is removed prematurely, consumers may suffer from excessive prices being charged. Conversely, price controls which are retained for too long a period are not only redundant in the sense that the process of competition is adequate to 'control' prices itself, but they may do positive harms for a reason discussed more fully in the following chapter—that the dominant firm may be able to use monopoly profits to cross-subsidize those services that it sells in competitive markets and thus may distort the competitive process. This immediately raises the difficult question of how to determine when the market for a particular product is sufficiently competitive for price control to be abandoned.

---

[21] Directive 97/33/EC of the European Parliament and the Council of 30 June 1997 on interconnection in telecommunications with regard to ensuring universal service and inter-operability through application of the principles of ONP.
[22] OFTEL, *Pricing of Telecommunications Services from 1997.*

In order to make a well-founded decision about this, the regulator has, in effect, to undertake a competition analysis of the market in question.[23] This involves analysing market shares and prices (and how they have changed over time) and the key characteristics of the market in question, such as the extent of barriers to entry. After a competition analysis of this kind, OFTEL concluded in 1996/7 that the market for supply of telecommunications services at a retail level to business and residential customers in the UK had developed to such an extent that price control was only required in respect of a subset of residential customers, and that price control for supply of BT's network services was only necessary in respect of approximately half the network services (in value terms) which BT supply. The Director General of Telecommunications further forecast that from 2001 there would be no need for any retail price controls at all.[24]

The UK electricity and gas regulators will face similar decisions concerning when to deregulate retail prices for energy following the opening up of the supply markets in 1998. OFFER's recent supply price control regime for electricity supply only lasts for two years from April 1998, and a decision will be taken about whether a renewal is necessary in the light of developments in the market.

4. Competition in Regulated Industries: The Prospects

It is possible to portray the passage from monopoly to fully competitive markets as involving three phases.[25] In phase one, *pre-competitive* markets, competition is emerging and regulation can be used to prevent any firm monopolizing a distribution network giving an advantage to an affiliated supplier over any other. Price regulation of suppliers, as well as of monopoly distribution elements, is used to protect consumers; and sector specific measures, covering such matters as service standards, are necessary, again to protect consumers. In phase two, *emerging competitive markets*, price regulation can be withdrawn from fully competitive parts of the market (but retained for monopoly network provision) and firms allowed to compete. (Thus price controls are no longer required for large parts of BT's business and other operators are not price-capped.) As competition increases there may be a regulatory retreat from detailed prescriptive controls over such matters as service standards and growing reliance on market pressure to protect consumers. In phase three, *fully competitive markets*, economic regulation becomes largely unneces-

---

[23] The procedures necessary for an analysis of this kind are set out in OFTEL, *Effective Competition Review* (London, Feb. 1998).
[24] OFTEL, *Pricing of Telecomunication Services from 1997*.
[25] See DTI Green Paper 1998, p. 10.

sary and general competition laws can be used to secure the operation of the market. The need to regulate becomes confined to the use of special rules to ensure such matters as the compatibility of networks and the ability of consumers to purchase from a range of suppliers. Limited social objectives (such as universal service) can be achieved through special arrangements which are designed to avoid distorting competition.

This chapter has indicated that in all the regulated industries under consideration there is some scope for the development of competition. In particular, prospects for competition in gas and electricity supply are good, and this is reflected in decisions to open up the whole market from 1998. All telecommunications markets now enjoy a measure of competition. Prospects are the least favourable in the railway and water industries.

Opening up formerly monopolized markets to competition is a challenging task for regulators. Experience in the UK and elsewhere suggests that some kind of transitional regime is necessary, which involves the maintenance of price controls at the start of liberalization and further restrictions (in addition to those imposed by competition law) on the former monopolists at the early stages of market opening.

The pricing of access to distribution networks is also crucial to the development of competition, and requires regulatory intervention. Where prices are also intended to achieve social objectives (universal service or income distribution goals), the rules for introducing competition must take account of these. Despite these problems, the progress already made in UK utilities in developing competition has far exceeded earlier expectations, especially in telecommunications and energy supply. Progress in remaining areas is, however, likely to be slower and more difficult.

Price-Capping Mechanisms

One of the essential features of most utilities is that, at least in respect of some of their functions, the companies providing services are not subject to full competition. Only in exceptional cases do households or firms have a choice over which company is to provide them with water and sewerage service. Everywhere there is only one pipeline system for the distribution of gas, and only one high- and low-voltage electricity transmission and distribution system. Even in cases where competition is developing, for example in telecommunications or in the retailing of electricity and gas, the market power exercised by the former monopolist allows it to set its prices to a considerable extent independently of its competitors or customers. In such circumstances, it is natural for the regulator to respond by introducing some form of price control.

We have argued in Chapter 15 above that, in the case of a privately owned utility, the price control regime must strike a balance between the interests of customers—protecting them from monopolistic exploitation— and the interests of investors, who, when they have sunk considerable sums of money into irrecoverable investments, will be concerned lest the regulator should impose a level of charges that makes it impossible for them to recover their investments. Even the fear of this eventuality may be sufficient to deter them from making the investment in the first place. The twin functions of price regulation are thus to protect consumers from exploitation and to provide investors with the confidence to maintain the infrastructure needed to provide service.[1]

1. Rate of Return Regulation

There are a number of ways in which price control can be achieved. The simplest means is to impose a regime of cost-plus pricing.[2] Under such

---

[1] For a detailed analysis of solutions to this dilemma, see B. Levy and P. Spiller (eds.), *Regulations, Institutions and Commitment* (Cambridge, 1996).

[2] See C. Foster, *Privatisation, Public Ownership and the Regulation of Natural Monopoly* (Oxford, 1992), 186–97 on the American experience of cost-plus regulation.

a regime, the regulator sets prices for the utility in such a way that they cover the utility's costs of production and include a rate of return on capital that is sufficient to maintain investors' willingness to replace or expand the company's assets. (This is why cost-plus regulation is also known as 'rate of return' regulation.) In some cases, the firm is required to set the price for each service equal to its costs. In others, individual services can be sold at either above or below cost, but the regulator constrains prices overall so that total regulated revenues cover costs. This regime, or a version of it, was widely practised in regulated industries in the United States until the last decade or so.[3]

Rate of return regulation is subject to one obvious flaw and one more subtle one. The obvious flaw is that the company in question has no incentive to operate efficiently, as it knows that it will be able to recover increasing costs with a subsequent increase in price. Provided that price reviews take place with sufficient frequency, the firm pays no penalty for inefficiency. The less obvious flaw is that the arrangement may give an incentive for the firm to over-invest in capital equipment. Suppose that the regulator calculates the allowable rate of return on assets at 15 per cent per year, whereas the firm's cost of capital—the return required to keep investors replacing and expanding assets in the firm—is only 10 per cent per year. In these conditions, the regulator's estimate allows the firm's investors to make an excess rate of return of 5 per cent per year on whatever investment they put into the business. If this is so, they will have an incentive artificially to inflate the asset base by adopting very capital intensive techniques and by unnecessary extravagance in designing plant (sometimes known as 'gold plating'). Essentially, the more they invest the greater their excess returns. This phenomenon, known after its discoverers as the Averch–Johnson effect,[4] will skew inefficiency in the direction of excessive use of capital, and it may be difficult for the regulator to identify such extravagance by inspecting investment plans, especially if comparable firms are subject to the same incentives. This consequence is, however, secondary to the sheer lack of incentive to control costs of production that is encountered under rate of return regulation.

One revealing way to describe rate of return regulation is thus as a 'low-powered' incentive mechanism—low-powered because the firm benefits little from any efficiency gain. This arises because if cost savings are made, they will almost immediately be taken from the firm and given to consumers in the form of lower prices. This naturally raises the question of what would amount to a 'high-powered' incentive mechanism. Clearly its distinguishing feature must be that the firm retains, at least

[3] See ibid. and A. E. Kahn, *The Economics of Regulation* (2nd edn. 1988), ii, chs. 2–3, 5.
[4] M. Averch and L. Johnson, 'Behaviour of the Firm under Regulatory Constraint' (1962) 92 *Am. Econ. Rev.* 1052–69.

temporarily, a substantial proportion of the benefits of any greater efficiency. This can be achieved by decoupling the revenues that a firm can generate from the costs that it incurs.

2. Price Capping by RPI–X Mechanism

A very high-powered incentive mechanism would operate by setting a trajectory of prices for the firm's products indefinitely into the future— requiring them, for example, to fall by 2 per cent per year in real terms. In such circumstances, a firm not subject to competition would be able to 'keep' in perpetuity the benefits of any cost savings that it achieved. This is not, however, practical, as setting prices in advance for an indefinite period is likely, within a decade or less, either to drive the firm into bankruptcy, if they are set too low, or to allow profits to grow to a politically unacceptable level, if they are set too high. As a result, regulators have increasingly looked for some intermediate variant under which prices are set in advance for a period of four to five years, allowing the firm to benefit from any cost savings made during that period, but recalculated at regular intervals in order to bring them back into line with underlying costs. This regime is known as price capping or RPI–X regulation. Although a few American precursors can be identified, it was first applied on a large scale in the United Kingdom to British Telecom in 1984, and then extended to other UK utilities as they were privatized.[5] It is now used widely throughout the world in the energy, telecommunications, transport, and water industries, and applied both to privatized utilities and to public sector firms.

In order to take account of unpredictable rates of inflation in an economy, a price-capping regime typically allows a firm to vary its prices in any year by an amount that is linked to the overall level of inflation. The price cap usually permits a utility to increase its overall level of prices by the previous year's rate of inflation in the economy, as measured by

---

[5] For the influential report proposing RPI–X for British Telecom, see S. C. Littlechild, *Regulation of British Telecommunication's Profitability* (London, 1983). See also Foster, *Privatisation*, 205–18; R. Rees and J. Vickers, 'RPI–X Price-Cap Regulation', in Bishop, Kay, and Mayer, *Regulatory Challenge*, 352–85; I. Viehoff, 'Evaluating RPI–X', Topics 17 (London, 1995); J. Hillman and R. Braeutigam, *Price Level Regulation for Diversified Public Utilities* (Boston, 1989); P. Vass, 'The Methodology for Resetting X', in P. Vass (ed.), *CRI Regulatory Review 1997* (London, 1997); M. Armstrong, S. Cowan, and J. Vickers, *Regulatory Reform* (London, 1994), ch. 6; M. Beesley and S. Littlechild, 'The Regulation of Privatised Monopolies in the United Kingdom' (1989) 20 *Rand J. of Econ.* 454; C. Lister, 'Price-Cap versus Rate of Return Regulation' (1993) 5 *J. of Regulatory Economics* 25; D. O'Neill and P. Vass, *Incentive Regulation: A Theoretical and Historical Review*, CRI Research Report 5 (London, 1996). For recent governmental thinking see DTI, *A Fair Deal for Consumers: Modernising the Framework for Utility Regulation*, Green Paper, Cm. 3898 (London, Mar. 1998) (hereafter DTI Green Paper 1998), 18–19; and DTI, *A Fair Deal for Consumers: Modernising the Framework for Utility Regulation. The Response to Consultation* (DTI, London, July 1998) (hereafter DTI White Paper 1998).

TABLE 10. *Implementing a price-cap regime: an illustration*

Price cap: RPI –7.5
Previous year's RPI: 2.5
Permitted weighted average change in nominal prices: 2.5 – 7.5 = –5%

Service	Previous year's revenues (£bn)	Previous year's revenue proportion	Proposed price change (%)
1	8	0.5	–2
2	6	0.375	–10
3	2	0.125	–2

Weighted average price change
= (0.5 × –2) + (0.375 × –10) + (0.125 × –2)
= (–1) + (–3.75) + (–0.25) = –5
Price changes compliant with price cap

the retail price index (RPI), which is then varied by a percentage (the X) that reflects the real cost reduction that the regulator expects. Thus, if the firm were subject to a cap of RPI–5 and if inflation in the previous year were 8 per cent, it could raise nominal prices by 3 per cent. The difference of 5 per cent between that figure and inflation has to be made up by cost savings.

The Form of the Price Cap

How the detailed form of the price control is specified will vary from industry to industry. In the energy industry, for example, the same product, a kilowatt hour of electricity or a therm of gas, is sold to all customers. The price-cap regime can thus require an energy utility to reduce the average price of all the energy it sells by a pre-specified amount. In telecommunications, by contrast, a variety of different services are sold, including access to the network paid for by a monthly or quarterly rental, and local, long distance, and international calls which are charged on a per minute basis. A telecommunications firm subject to a price cap will thus have to demonstrate to the regulator that its proposed price increases for individual services, when weighted by the proportion of revenue accounted for by each service, satisfies the overall price cap. This is known as the tariff basket. In order to demonstrate that the cap is satisfied, the firm will typically have to seek approval from the regulator before it introduces price changes. The calculations required are illustrated in Table 10.

The form of price capping described above gives the firm considerable flexibility in setting prices for individual services, or services sold to different classes of customer such as domestic or industrial users. The firm can, thus, increase significantly the price charged for one service, provided it makes equivalent reductions in prices for other services. Such changes in the structure of prices may bear particularly hard upon particular consumers, and as a result, regulators sometimes introduce side constraints to prevent excessive changes in the balance of tariffs. For example, over the period 1993 to 1997, British Telecom was required to reduce the average prices of all of its regulated telecommunications services by 7.5 per cent per annum after adjustment for inflation, but for much of that period it was also prohibited from increasing the price in real terms of any service, with the exception of a quarterly rental charged to its residential customers, which it could increase by 2 per cent a year in real terms. OFTEL was trying by this means to exercise some control over the structure of prices, as well as their overall level. In other countries, the telecommunications regulator has imposed separate price controls on services sold to residential and business customers with the same end in view.

A price cap is typically set every four to five years, and in calibrating the cap (choosing the value of X in the formula) the regulator will typically try to achieve a balance between costs and revenues over the four- or five-year period as a whole.

This is, however, distinct from cost-plus regulation to the extent that the regulator is not, as in cost-plus pricing, simply allowing the firm to recover whatever costs it has historically incurred. Instead, the regulator is making a projection of costs into the future, and setting overall prices so that they will cover those expected costs. If the regulated firm is able to increase its efficiency and reduce costs further than the regulator anticipates, its profits will go up. If it is less efficient than expected, its profits will go down.

The price cap set for the next period will, however, take account of the level of profits that the firm is earning when that new cap comes into operation. If the regulator takes the view that excess profits are being earned, he or she will adjust prices in the subsequent period accordingly, either by a once-and-for-all adjustment to bring prices back into line with costs (known as a 'Po adjustment'), or by a gradual process of elimination of excess profits over the next period. This means that the benefits that a firm reaps from cost savings in the course of a price cap will depend not only upon the number of years that pass before the cap is revised, but also upon how the regulator takes account of excess profits (or losses) at the end of a period in determining allowable prices in the next period.

Procedures for Setting Caps

The mechanics of setting a price cap have now become fairly well established, and an illustrative timetable of a price-capping process is set out

TABLE 11. *An illustrative timetable for resetting a price cap due to come into operation in October 2000*

April 1998 (–30 months): Regulator publishes first consultation on general issues—form of price control (price caps, profit sharing, etc.); coverage; conceptual basis for asset valuation, cost of capital, etc. Work on financial model begins within the Office.

October 1998 (–24 months): Responses to consultation document received from price-controlled firm, competitors, consumer groups, and others; brief period for respondents to comment on or rebut other responses.

October 1998–April 1999 (–24 to –18 months): Financial model developed and validated; data collected and analysed on comparative efficiency; demand projections prepared.

April 1999 (–18 months): Regulator publishes second consultation document, setting out ranges for assumptions and range of values for X.

April–October 1999 (–18 to –12 months): Assumptions underlying modelling narrowed, in light of responses and latest data; financial modelling continues.

July 1999 (–15 months): Responses received to second consultation document.

October 1999 (–12 months): Regulator publishes third consultation document, proposing value of X and other details.

December 1999 (–10 months): Responses received to third consultation document required.

January 2000 (–9 months): Regulator publishes price cap proposal. Firm accepts associated licence amendment or 'appeals' to MMC.

October 2000: Price cap comes into force.

in Table 11.[6] Essentially, the regulator constructs a financial model of the firm's regulated activities (which normally excludes other activities which the firm undertakes either overseas or in non-regulated, competitive markets). The basic structure of that model is set out in Figure 5. Demand for the firm's output, determined by a variety of factors such as general economic growth, will first be projected. On the basis of the

---

[6] For recent consultation documents and statements from regulators, see: OFGAS, *1997 Price Control Review: British Gas Transportation and Storage: The Director-General's Final Proposals* (London, Aug. 1996); OFFER, *The Transmission Price Control Review of the National Grid Company: Proposals* (London, Oct. 1996); ORR, *The Periodic Review of Railtrack's Access Charges: A Proposed Framework and Key Issues: A Consultation Document* (London, Dec. 1997); OFTEL, *Pricing of Telecommunications Services from 1997: Statement* (London, June 1996); OFTEL, *Network Charges from 1997: Statement* (London, July 1997); OFWAT, *The Proposed Framework and Approach to the 1997 Period Review* (London, June 1997). Reports from the Monopolies and Mergers Commission on Regulators' Price Cap Proposals are: *Gas and British Gas* (Sept. 1993); *Scottish Hydroelectric* (June 1995); *Portsmouth Water* (July 1995); *South West Water* (July 1995); *BAA* (July 1996); *Northern Ireland Electricity* (Apr. 1997); *BG* (June 1997); *Manchester Airport* (July 1997).

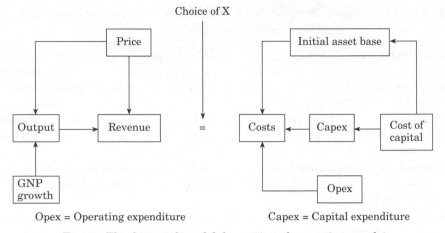

FIG. 5. *The financial model for setting the cap (monopoly)*

anticipated output levels, the regulator projects the costs of the regulated firm, which consist of operating expenditure (Opex) together with capital costs, which comprise depreciation and the allowable rate of return on the value of assets invested in the regulated business. Some of these assets will be inherited at the start of the new price cap; others will be capital expenditure (Capex) made during the period. The task will then be to choose a level of price (hence, implicitly, a rate of change in price) that brings costs into line with revenues.

Figure 5 illustrates the case where the regulated firm is a monopolist. Where the firm subject to the price cap is also subject to competition from entrants, the problem of projecting demand for the regulated firm is more complicated, because it depends upon strategies adopted by competitors. This is illustrated in Figure 6, where the regulator must not only project total output, but also the market share of the regulated firm.

In determining the price cap, the key sensitivities are:

On the demand side: the growth of national income, or of general economic activity over the price control period and (where relevant) the strategy of competitors in terms of their pricing and investment behaviour, which will determine the market share available for the price-controlled firm.

On the cost side: the level of operating expenditure over the price control period, which depends upon an assessment of the scope for efficiency savings in regulated activities.

The amount of capital expenditure the firm has to make over the price control period depends upon how much its output increases, and on what investment is required to meet that extra output. Other key inputs on the cost side are: the valuation of assets inherited from the previous

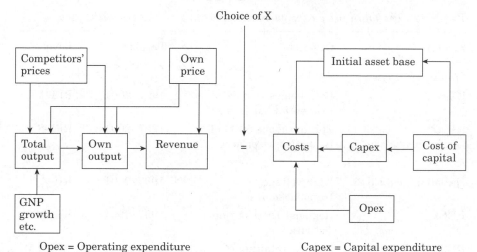

Opex = Operating expenditure   Capex = Capital expenditure

FIG. 6. *The financial model for setting the cap (competitive case)*

period, on which the firm will be entitled to recover a rate of return; the expected depreciation in the course of the current price control period; and the cost of capital or annual rate of return which investors in the regulated activities (as debt or equity holders) require on average to maintain their willingness to invest.

Current price-capping arrangements in the UK are summarized in Table 12. It is important to recall the point made in Chapter 15 above that production in utilities typically involves a series of stages, each of which is subject to different levels of competition. The electricity supply industry, for example, involves the stages of electricity generation, high-voltage transmission, local distribution, and retailing or 'supply' to final customers. Of these, high-voltage transmission and regional distribution are the only two likely to require price control over the longer run, although both generation and supply have been capped because of doubts about the adequacy of existing competition, or because competition is only just being introduced. Where the production processes involve successive stages of this kind, it may be necessary to impose a series of interrelated price caps. For example, there are at present in the gas industry separate caps on British Gas's pipeline or transportation business (Transco), and on the retailing or supply of gas by British Gas Trading (a company formerly part of British Gas which was divested as a separate firm in 1997). Under its price control arrangements, British Gas Trading is entitled to pass on to its customers the charges that it pays to Transco.

In the telecommunications industry, by contrast, BT is subject to a retail price cap that restricts the rate of change in prices for the services that

TABLE 12. *The main price caps currently operating in the UK utilities*

Firm	Coverage	Period	Level
Communications			
BT	Retail sales to 80% of residential subscribers	1997–2001	RPI–4$^{1}/_{2}$
BT	Subset (about 50%) of BT network services	1997–2001	RPI–8
Energy			
National Grid Co.	High-voltage transmission	1997–2001	RII–4
RECs	Regional Distribution Activities	1997–2001	RPI–3[a]
RECs	Supply (retailing of electricity)	1998–2000	RPI–4.5[a]
BG Transco	Transportation and storage of gas	1997–2002	RPI–2
Centrica	Supply (retailing of gas principally to domestic customers)	1997–2000	RPI–4
Transport			
Railtrack	Provision of track and station services to train operators	1995–2001	RPI–2
Train operating companies	Capped passenger fares under franchising agreements	1996–9 1999–2003	RPI–0 RPI–1
BAA	Supply of airport services at Heathrow and Gatwick	1997–2002	RPI–3
Water			
Water and sewerage and water companies	Supply of water and sewerage services	1995–2000	RPI+1.5[a,b] RPI+0.6[a,c]

[a] Averaged value over several companies.
[b] Water and sewerage companies.
[c] Water only companies.

it provides to the majority of residential customers. In markets for other customers, the company is considered to be subject to sufficient competition for price regulation to be unnecessary. The company is, however, also subject to an additional price cap (or, more accurately, a set of three price caps) relating to the wholesale services that it provides on its network either to other telecommunications operators or to its own affiliated retail activity. These cases illustrate the way in which a particular utility sector, or an individual firm, can be subject simultaneously to more than one price cap.

4. Price Caps and Excess Returns

Windfall Taxes

When UK utilities were privatized, the price caps to which they were initially subject were, with one exception, set by the Government. (The exception was Railtrack, the initial price cap for which was set by the Office of the Railway Regulator.) These initial price caps attracted widespread criticism on the grounds that they were too lax, that the companies concerned achieved productivity gains well in excess of those implied by the price caps, and that their share prices, as a result, grew significantly in the first few years after privatization.[7]

The apparent laxity of the initial caps can be put down to a number of factors. In the first place, the Government, as owner of the shares when the first caps were set, may have wished to ensure that the privatizations were successful. This would clearly have been facilitated by setting a lax rather than a tough price cap, since with a lax cap investors would have possessed more confidence in the profit stream of the company being privatized for the first four years or so, and hence have been more prepared to buy the shares. The second, and less transient, reason concerns the information asymmetries that existed between the firm and the organization (government department or regulator) setting the caps. As noted above, when a cap is set, an estimate has to be made of the efficiency savings available in the following years. The management of the firm is likely to have a better grasp of this than the regulator, and will use this advantage to seek to secure a relatively lax cap. As the regulators gather experience over a period of years, however, they collect more information about the performance of comparable firms. Informational asymmetries, accordingly, are likely to diminish, as, in turn, are excess profits.

This process of growth in regulatory intelligence has gradually taken place in the UK, and excess returns to shareholders in privatized utilities have diminished as time since privatization has elapsed. Excess profits

---

[7] See DTI Green Paper 1998, 3.

TABLE 13. *Relative share price growth since flotation*

Sector	Privatization date	Share price growth in % relative to Stock Market average (FTSE All Share Index)		
		First 100 days	First year	First 4 years
BT	11/84	51	52	18
British Gas	12/86	10	22	32
BAA	7/87	43	39	69
Water & Sewerage companies	12/89	31	58	93
Regional Electricity companies	12/90	26	23	124
English generators	3/91	28	27	109
Scottish generators	6/91	2	4	4
N. Ireland Electricity	6/93	32	46	21
Railtrack	5/96	3	15	—
British Energy	7/96	17	21	—

Source: L. Channells, 'The Windfall Tax' (1997) 18 *Fiscal Studies* 281.

in the period immediately following privatization remained a contentious issue, however, and the decision of the new UK Government of 1997 to impose a Windfall Tax was made in order to recapture some of the excess returns earned by shareholders in the early days of privatization.

The extent of these returns is shown in Table 13, which shows, for example, that in the first four years covering privatization, share prices in the water and sewerage companies grew 93 per cent faster than the average of all share prices traded on the London Stock Exchange.[8]

The basis of the Windfall Tax introduced in 1997 was to tax, at a rate of 23 per cent, the difference between the value of a company at privatization and a 'more realistic' valuation based upon that company's after-tax profits for up to the first four years after privatization. That more realistic value was found by averaging profits for the first four years, as set out in the company accounts, and multiplying that average annual profit figure by a price earnings ratio, set at nine. The underlying assumption was that a realistic valuation of a company in the utility

---

[8] From L. Channells, 'The Windfall Tax' (1997) 18 *Fiscal Studies* 281.

TABLE 14. *Payments of the Windfall Tax, by sector*

Sector	Tax payment	
	(£ billion)	(%)
Regional Electricity Companies	1.45	27.9
Electricity Generators	0.65	12.5
Water & Sewerage Companies	1.65	31.7
Others	1.45	27.9
TOTAL	5.20	100.0

Source: Channells, 'Windfall Tax', 284.

sector could be found by multiplying its annual profit stream by nine. On this basis, a Windfall Tax amounting to £5.2 billion was levied on the utilities to yield the distribution by sector that is shown in Table 14.

The Windfall Tax has the effect of transferring to the Government some of the value of the utilities previously belonging to shareholders. The shareholders in question were, however, not necessarily those who enjoyed the substantial increase in profitability of their investments in the four years following privatization, as those may have sold their shares, but those who were holding the shares at the time when it became apparent that the Windfall Tax was likely to be levied.

In terms of its impact on the efficacy of the price-cap mechanism, the key question is whether the Windfall Tax is regarded as a one-off phenomenon associated with excess returns immediately following privatization, or whether the management and shareholders of utilities expect that it may be repeated. If it is regarded as a one-off phenomenon, then it does little to blunt future incentives to increase profits by reducing costs and thus to increase efficiency in the utilities. If, however, it is expected that the tax will be repeated, firms will have reduced incentives to increase profits and efficiency. Should this be the case, a Windfall Tax would have effects similar to the profit sharing arrangements and sliding scale correction mechanisms which we now consider.

Profit Sharing

Under profit sharing regimes, a price-capped utility that earns a rate of return on capital above some specified level has to return a proportion of its excess profits to its customers through lower prices within the period of the price cap. This can also be accompanied by a symmetric arrangement under which, if the firm's profits fall below a certain level, the firm is entitled to raise its prices to recover a proportion of the deficit.[9] The effect of profit sharing is thus to reduce the political dangers that flow from setting X in a manner that would provide unacceptable profits or losses.

Alternatively prices can be linked to dividends paid to shareholders. Thus, rebates can become payable, in some so-called 'sliding scale' mechanisms, when dividends exceed the stipulated levels but prices have not been reduced. The supposed advantage of linking prices to dividends is that companies are less able to manipulate figures on dividends than on, say, profits.[10]

Error Correction Mechanisms

Price caps are set at levels established on the basis of a number of assumptions about rates of economic growth, investment spending by the regulated firm, and other factors. It is possible to fine-tune a price cap within the period of its operation by means of a correction mechanism so that if such assumptions turn out to be mistaken, prices will be adjusted accordingly. For example, if a regulated firm were able to undertake its expected level of investment at a much lower price than that anticipated by the regulator, or if output growth in the economy were higher, then prices would be adjusted downwards automatically to reflect this forecasting error.[11] Again the political costs of setting X in a way that produces unacceptable profits (or losses) are limited. The DTI Green Paper of 1998 endorsed error correction mechanisms as being suitable for further study and the White Paper left action on this front to regulators' discretions.

Both profit-sharing and error correction mechanisms reduce incentives for cost reductions and may lead price-capping closer to rate of return regulation.[12] They do, nevertheless, bring advantages, notably of bolstering the political acceptability of the regulatory system and increasing the level of fairness between consumers and investors. A key question is whether such mechanisms can be put into effect without too much difficulty or

---

[9] See C. Mayer and J. Vickers, 'Profit Sharing: An Economic Appraisal' (1996) 17 *Fiscal Studies* 1; P. Vass, 'Profit Sharing and Incentive Regulation', in P. Vass (ed.), *CRI Regulatory Review 1996* (London, 1996).

[10] P. Burns, R. Turvey, and T. Weyman-Jones, *General Properties of Sliding Scale Regulation*, CRI Technical Paper 3 (London, 1995). See P. Burns, R. Turvey, and T. Weyman-Jones, *Sliding Scale Regulation of Monopoly Enterprises* (London, 1995). R. Turvey, 'The Sliding Scale: Price and Dividend Regulation in the Nineteenth Century Gas Industry', Topics 16 (London, 1996).

[11] Mayer and Vickers, loc. cit. n. 9 above, pp. 13–14; error correction mechanisms are encountered in the system of RPI–X price capping applicable to charges at BAA's South East Airport—see R. Baldwin, *Regulation in Question* (London, 1995), 69.

[12] Such grounds led the Directors-General of Telecommunications, Water Services, Electricity Supply, and Gas Services to oppose profit sharing in their 1997 submissions to the DTI Review of Utility Regulation.

whether they complicate regulatory arrangements, increase administrative costs, and are liable to manipulation by firms which are in a position to choose when profits are recognized, and hence to control the profits recorded in any year. The DTI Green Paper of 1998 stopped short of proposing full-scale profit-sharing—following Treasury arguments that this would blunt efficiency incentives unacceptably.[13] What the DTI proposed (and endorsed after consultation) was that regulators should distinguish between the income that companies earn through their own efforts and that which results from other factors. Companies should be able to retain the profits they have rightly earned, said the DTI, but should not keep the profits they have gained either by factors beyond their control or where they have deliberately misled the regulator by providing incomplete or inaccurate information in the process of setting the price cap.

The case for the DTI approach is that incentives for efficiency are enhanced by allowing companies to retain profits that result from their efforts, but that 'unearned' or improperly earned profits should flow to the benefit of consumers. The residual difficulty is that the complete problem is not solved—profits generated internally and properly might still prove to be unacceptable to some sectors of the public and potential political difficulties would not automatically disappear. The case for allowing profits to be retained would, however, be easier to make where companies can argue that they have genuinely earned them.

5. Conclusions

Price capping has two often cited advantages over traditional cost-plus methods of price control, notably rate of return regulation:

Incentives for greater efficiency. This is not merely a theoretical proposition, but one which is sustained by comparisons of the productivity increases that are found in the various states of the USA that regulate their utilities using different methods of price control. There is now persuasive evidence that forms of incentive regulation do promote greater cost reductions.[14]

Administrative convenience. A four- or five-year price cap involves intensive periods of work in the period before it comes into effect, when the level of the cap is determined using methods described above. Once established, however, regulation is confined to the relatively simple arithmetic task of checking that price changes prepared by the regulated

---

[13] DTI Green Paper 1998, 18–19; DTI White Paper 1995, 10–12; On the Treasury 'victory' see D. Gow and C. Weston, 'Beckett Beaten over Utility Profit Caps', *Guardian*, 3 Mar. 1998.

[14] For example, D. Sappington and D. Weisman, *Designing Incentive Regulation for the Telecommunications Industry* (Cambridge, 1996).

firm do in fact satisfy the constraint (see Table 10). This annual process requires just a few days of work. This contrasts with the substantial workload required under cost-plus regulation when a price change is sought—often on an annual basis.

Productive efficiency and administrative convenience are not, however, the only relevant criteria. It is also necessary to examine whether price capping does in practice avoid the excess profits and resulting ineffi-ciencies that arise from utility services being priced too highly. If price capping is carried out badly, moreover, it may carry the seeds of its own destruction. Excessive profits may generate political pressures that require a regulator to intervene before the announced period of the price cap has expired. The expectation of this occurrence will diminish the incen-tive properties of the regime, and may call into question the viability of the regulatory contract itself. If revisions of the price cap increase in frequency, RPI–X comes to resemble rate of return regulation more and more closely. UK regulators have hitherto, however, resisted pressure for changes within the periods set for caps, despite the high returns that have been earned by some regulated companies.

Measuring Efficiency: Benchmarking, Yardsticking, and Performance

Our discussion of how price caps are set and reset has emphasized the importance of reliable estimates of the efficiency potential of the regulated firm. The price cap is set to allow an efficient operator to break even over the course of, or at the end of, a price control period. If the regulator overestimates that efficient level of costs, then either the firm may drive costs down to the efficient level and earn excess profits, or it may choose to conceal some or all of its efficiency potential, thus gaining higher prices in the next price control period. Under the former policy, the efficient level of costs is soon disclosed, and the regulator has a more secure basis for setting the next price cap. Under the latter policy, inefficiencies can be maintained over an extended period. As explained in Chapter 17, the asymmetry of information between the regulator, who often can only observe the actual level of costs of the firm, and the firm itself, which is likely to have a fairly, if not perfectly accurate view of what it can achieve, works to the disadvantage of consumers.

Regulators can remedy these problems by securing better information about the firm's productive potential. This chapter describes how this might be done, by the use of benchmarking or with reference to comparative competition. It also discusses the record of some utilities in improving efficiency in recent years.

1. Benchmarking

Benchmarking involves collecting and analysing data on a number of firms in order to draw conclusions about what is a realistic 'target' cost level for an efficient firm. The regulator in effect uses the data to establish a 'benchmark' cost level which the firm might reasonably meet, and then bases the price control on those benchmark costs.

The greatest use of comparative analysis has been made in the electricity supply and water and sewerage industries in the UK. This is because they are organized regionally, with each regional electricity company

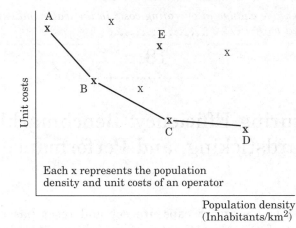

Each *x* represents the population density and unit costs of an operator.

FIG. 7. *The efficiency frontier for a group of water companies*

or water company serving a specified area.[1] Other regulators such as OFTEL, which have attempted to apply the same procedures, have had to rely upon foreign comparators, but this involves the difficulty of collecting accurate data on comparative costs.

In the electricity and water industries, benchmarking has been used at the time of periodic price reviews. Essentially, the regulator has sought to identify, on the basis of comparative cost observations, and after adjustment for environmental factors, which firms are relatively efficient and which are relatively inefficient.

This can be done in various ways. Figure 7, for example, shows information which might be collected about the average costs of supplying water to different areas, characterized by different population densities. The minimum cost, known as the efficiency frontier, is shown by the line in Figure 7, and is found by connecting the lower envelope of cost observations. Other operators can then be graded on the basis of the proximity of their cost observation to the frontier. Firm E, for example, is far from the frontier, suggesting the possibility for considerable 'catch-up' in efficiency. The regulator would, therefore, be justified in assigning to firm E a relatively high value of X in the price control formula. Operator B, by contrast, is on the frontier and might be assigned a value of X which reflected only the trend in cost reduction available to an efficient operator, ignoring 'catch-up'.

---

[1] See, for example, OFWAT, *1996/97 Report on Water and Sewerage Service Operating Costs and Efficiency* (London, Dec. 1997).

TABLE 15. *Percentage change in operating costs in the water industry in 1996–7 compared with 1992–3*

	Water % change since 1992–3	Sewerage % change since 1992–3	Total % change since 1992–3
Water & sewerage companies			
Anglian	–10	–2	–6
Dwr Cymru (Welsh)	–6	6	–2
North West	8	0	5
Northumbrian	–16	–27	–21
Severn Trent	–1	–7	–4
South West	–5	5	–1
Southern	0	–3	–2
Thames	–7	–15	–21
Wessex	–18	–23	–21
Yorkshire	–2	–6	–4
Weighted average	–4	–8	–6

Source: OFWAT.

These, or similar techniques have been employed by both OFWAT and OFFER in their respective price control reviews for water and sewerage companies and for regional electricity companies.[2] OFTEL has periodically carried out efficiency studies on BT, using data from overseas telecommunications companies, notably those in the United States.[3] The results have provoked considerable controversy, especially from firms judged to be relatively inefficient. The latter have complained that the inclusion or exclusion of particular environmental variables has a significant impact upon the distance from the frontier that each firm finds itself at, and have questioned the statistical procedures involved. The regulators concerned appear nonetheless to be satisfied that comparative data are of value in choosing values of X in the RPI–X formula for individual firms which reflect comparative efficiency.

As an illustration, Table 15 shows an evaluation by OFWAT of how successful water companies in England and Wales have been in achieving reductions in their operating costs from 1992/3 to 1996/7. This approach —comparing changes in costs rather than levels of costs—overcomes the

[2] OFWAT, *Modelling Water Costs 1992/93* (London, Dec. 1994).
[3] OFTEL, *BT Comparative Efficiency Study* (London, 1995).

TABLE 16. *Relative efficiency in 1992/3 and reductions in operating costs 1995/6 to 1996/7 of Water and Sewerage companies*

Savings against target	Less efficient: target 2.6% to 3.5% per annum	Around average: target 1.7% to 2.6% per annum	More efficient: target 0.5% to 1.1% per annum
Well above average	Mid-Kent	Northumbrian, Wessex, Wrexham	
Above average	South East, Folkestone & Dover	Mid-Southern Tender, Anglian, South West Thames, Bristol, South Staffs, Three Valleys	Sutton & East Surrey
Average			
Below average	Welsh	Southern Trent, Yorkshire, Bournemouth & West Hants.	York
Well below average		Southern Essex & Suffolk	North West, Chester

Source: OFWAT, *1996/97 Report on Water and Sewerage Service Operating Costs and Efficiency* (London, 1997).

problem of environmental differences. It does, however, fail to take account of differences in efficiency at the starting point. But because OFWAT was forced to make a judgement concerning the relative efficiency of water and sewerage companies in 1992/3 in terms of operating costs, it is able to combine its estimates of the position in 1992/3 with performance since, as shown in Table 16.

In the case of the water industry, the issue of benchmarking spills over into decisions about mergers. Any significant merger is evaluated by OFWAT and by the MMC, and one of the factors to be taken into consideration is the impact that loss of a comparator would have on the effectiveness of regulation. Various efforts have been made to estimate how large this impact would be. A recent adverse MMC decision on a merger proposal has suggested that the effect on regulation of losing another comparator has now reached such a level that further merger proposals are likely to be viewed with great scepticism.[4]

[4] MMC, *Wessex Water Plc and South West Water Plc*, Cm. 3840 (London, Oct. 1996).

2. Comparative or Yardstick Competition

Yardstick competition involves the regulator in placing similar firms in competition with one another with respect to their cost levels, even if they are not competing in the same services market. It thus represents a more formalized implementation of benchmarking.

To explain how it works, we construct a hypothetical (and unrealistic) example of 100 identical towns served by identical water companies. Clearly a regulator could try to establish the efficient costs of a representative company, and set prices on that basis. However, this comes up against the problem of informational asymmetry noted in Chapter 17, and fails to exploit the fact that many observations are available. As an alternative, therefore, the regulator could proceed as follows.[5]

   (i) Collect information on the actual cost of providing water by each of the 100 companies.

  (ii) Allow each company to charge a price for water equal to the average cost of the other 99 companies.

The beauty of this arrangement is that each operator is set a price which depends not on its costs but upon the costs of the other operators. Its revenues are thus detached from its costs, in the manner of the high-powered incentive schemes discussed in Chapter 17. If the company is unusually efficient, its costs will beat (i.e. be lower than) the average of the rest, and it will make excess profits. If its costs are above average, it will make a loss. Its revenues do not depend in any way upon its own costs and so it has the maximum incentive to reduce them. The process should thus drive all operators down to the most efficient costs, with prices set accordingly.

Unfortunately, a number of difficulties lie in the way of implementing this regime. The first arises because prices normally have to be set before the cost observations are made. This can be overcome by introducing a lag, so that this year's prices are based upon last year's average costs, possibly adjusted to take account of expected productivity gains.

Second, there is the risk of collusion. If the operators organize together and agree to maintain their costs at an unnecessarily high level, each will be entitled to a correspondingly higher price, and will be spared the effort of producing efficiently. If the number of firms involved is small, then this will be a serious danger, but, as in other contexts, the risk of collusion diminishes as the number of firms grows.

---

[5] This approach was first formalized by A. Shleifer, 'A Theory of Yardstick Competition' (1985) 16 *Rand J. of Econ.* 319–27. See also M. Armstrong, S. Cowan, and J. Vickers, *Regulating Reform: Economic Analysis and British Experience* (London, 1994), 74–7.

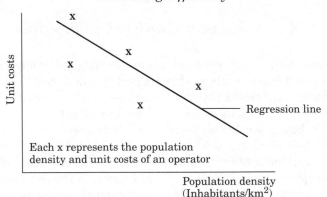

Each *x* represents the population density and unit costs of an operator.

FIG. 8. *Regression analysis of water company costs*

Third, there is the obvious problem that regulated firms typically do not provide their services in identical circumstances. The areas they serve differ in terms of topography, factors such as climate and soil, and the level and structure of demand: both the size of the population and the breakdown of demand between business and residential users of services will vary from place to place. These factors will influence unit costs in ways which should be taken into account in setting prices.

As with the adjustment of benchmarks to accommodate environmental differences, there are statistical procedures capable of dealing with such problems. Suppose that a key feature of the environment that affects costs is population density. Data on observed unit costs and population density can then be graphed as in Figure 8, where each cross represents an observation. A regression line can be drawn through the observations, as shown in the figure. Each firm would then be entitled to charge a price given by the regression line, which reflects the population density-adjusted unit cost of production in that area. Clearly, if the number of environmental factors is large, the process of adjustment will become more complicated. The outcome, moreover, will depend upon the precise method of statistical regression adopted, in particular whether the relationship is assumed to be a straight-line one as in Figure 8, or to take a more complicated form.

UK regulators have not utilized yardstick competition in its pure form—by determining prices with reference to the average costs of a large number of similar firms. Where comparative cost data have been used to estimate efficient cost levels, the 'benchmarking' approach described above has been employed.

3. Productivity Growth: The Record

The level of productive efficiency of the utilities has attracted a good deal of attention, especially on the part of those investigating the impact either of changes in ownership (nationalization/privatization) or changes in the regulatory regime (particularly the introduction of price caps).[6] In this section we discuss some of the studies which bear on these questions.

It is worth emphasizing that there is little prospect of reaching firm conclusions on the effects on productivity of changing ownership or regulation on the basis of observations of a small number of firms over a limited run of years. The problem is that so many other changes are occurring within the firm or within the economy as a whole that it is impossible to isolate the impact of any ownership or regulatory change. There is a well-known tendency, for example, for productivity to rise above trend during a boom and to fall below it during a recession. As a result, the apparent impact of privatization may be distorted by its timing within such a cycle. A firm's productivity will also be affected by management changes. New managerial teams were appointed, for example, to a number of nationalized industries before privatization, with a brief to prepare the companies for sale by eliminating inefficiencies. In such cases, major changes in efficiency associated with privatization took place before the privatization itself.

As far as the impact of changes in the regulatory regime is concerned, UK utilities have all been subject to the price-cap version of price control. It is impossible, accordingly, to gauge the effects on productivity of switching from rate of return regulation to price caps. Evidence from the United States, where many utilities are regulated at the State level (generating significant numbers of observations), and where there has been a progressive transfer from rate of return regulation to price caps, suggests that that change has enhanced efficiency.[7]

A firm's productivity can be measured in various ways. The simplest method is to construct a time series of labour productivity, by dividing the value of the firm's output, adjusted for inflation, by the average number of employees. This may, however, give a misleading impression for a number of reasons.

First, labour productivity may apparently rise simply as a result of the firm contracting out some of its activities to an outside supplier. Adjustments must be made to account for this. Second, in capital intensive industries such as utilities, increases in labour productivity

---

[6] D. Sappington and D. Weisman, *Designing Incentive Regulation for the Telecommunications Industry* (Cambridge, 1996).

[7] Ibid., ch. 11.

TABLE 17. *Productivity growth in selected UK utilities, 1970–1990*

	Labour Productivity (%)		Total factor Productivity (%)	
	1970s	1980s	1970s	1980s
BAA	0.6	2.7	4.8	0.3
British Telecom	4.3	7.2	4.6	3.2
Electricity Supply	3.7	2.5	2.3	1.4
British Gas	4.9	4.9	4.2	1.0

Source: M. Bishop and D. Thompson, 'Regulatory Reform and Productivity Growth in UK's Public Utilities', (1992) 24 *Applied Economics* 1181–90.

may be gained not through improvements in efficiency but through the substitution of capital for labour. This suggests that a more appropriate measure of productivity should take account of both capital and labour inputs. This measure is known as total factor productivity and it involves constructing a measure of total factor inputs, by combining capital input and labour input, and dividing total output by this number. One of the problems with measuring capital is that it involves the valuation of a large number of varied assets. The particular convention adopted to measure capital (notably the question of whether current or historic cost valuations are employed) may thus have a significant impact on the outcome.

Despite these difficulties, a large number of studies have been undertaken to evaluate productivity changes in UK utilities since the 1970s. We cite two of them here. The first is a study comparing productivity growth in a range of UK public enterprises between the 1970s and 1980s, carried out by Bishop and Thompson.[8] Some of their data are shown in Table 17. The experience of the four firms was quite different. While labour productivity grew at least as fast in the 1980s as in the 1970s in the cases of three of them, growth in total factor productivity declined uniformly, probably as the result of substantial investments in the period which increased the capital base.

A more recent study, covering a smaller number of utilities, shows the annual percentage changes in labour productivity and total factor productivity over a variety of periods—a nationalization period, a pre-privatization period, a post-privatization period, a recession period (between 1988 and 1992), and the period between 1992 and 1995. As far as possible, each period was chosen to be at least three years. (See

[8] M. Bishop and D. Thompson, 'Regulatory Reform and Productivity Growth in the UK's Public Utilities' (1992) 24 *Applied Economics* 1181–90.

TABLE 18. *Total factor productivity growth before and after privatization in selected UK utilities*

	Public Ownership Period	Pre-privatization Period	Post-privatization period	Recession Period (1988–92)	Latest Period (1992–5)
BAA	1.5	2.2	(4.9)[a]	(4.3)[a]	5.8
British Gas	0.8	4.2	0.1	(0.1)[a]	(1.3)[a]
British Telecom	7.1	4.8	2.9	2.8	4.7

[a] Parentheses denote negative figure.

Source: S. Martin and D. Parker, *The Impact of Privatisation: Ownership and Corporate Performance in the UK* (London, 1997), 100.

Table 18.) Apart from poor performance in the recession and significant improvements in 1992, the data show no clear pattern. This is consistent with other analyses which suggest that a transfer of ownership by itself may not have a significant impact on productivity and efficiency. The introduction of competition may, however, have such an effect—whether on enterprises in private or in public ownership.[9]

3. Conclusion

Efficiency and cost reduction are the major objectives of regulation. However, regulators must contend with a deficit in their information concerning the true productive potential of the firms they regulate. Benchmarking and comparative competition are two ways of making up part of this deficit, but they are imperfect devices and regulators have to rely, in making projections of productivity growth, on the accumulation of a variety of disparate data and, ultimately, on judgement.

Available data on the productivity performance of regulated utilities suggest that performance has been respectable rather than outstanding in the period since privatization, in comparison with earlier periods. This may improve as competition takes hold in an increasing number of areas.

[9] M. Bishop and M. Green, *Privatisation and Recession: The Miracle Tested* (London, 1995).

Regulating Quality

1. The Need for Regulation and Current Techniques

The various statutes governing the regulation of utilities in the UK create different frameworks for the regulation of quality. In the case of rail services, for example, the Office of the Rail Regulator (ORR) has the power to impose fines following a failure on the part of a train operating company to achieve a pre-specified degree of accuracy in the provision of information on fares and timetables. At the same time, the franchise contracts entered into between train operating companies and the Office of Passenger Railway Franchising (OPRAF) entitle the latter to impose a contractual penalty if an operator fails to meet its obligations relating to scheduling and punctuality as specified in the franchise contract. These general provisions are in addition to arrangements providing entitlements to refunds for individual passengers who have suffered from delayed train services.

The arrangements for the regulation of distribution and supply of electricity give the Director General of Electricity Supply (DGES) and other regulatory bodies considerable powers to impose and enforce standards. Under the Electricity Act, the Director General is entitled to lay down guaranteed standards and if the company fails to provide this level of service it must make a payment to the customer affected (see Table 19). These standards concern such matters as failure to restore supply within a specified period and failure to keep appointments at the customer's premises.

The DGES also has the power to set overall standards of performance. These cover such dimensions of quality of service as the minimum percentage of supplies to be reconnected within the three hours following a fault and the minimum percentage of all customers' letters to be responded to within ten working days (see Table 20). Such standards are set individually for the regional electricity companies. The targets and performance of the individual companies are collated in an annual

TABLE 19. *Guaranteed standards of performance in electricity supply 1996/7*

Service	Performance level	Penalty payment
Respond to failure of a supplier's fuse	Within 4 hours of any notification during working hours*	£20
Restoring electricity supplies after fault	Must be restored within 24 hours	£40 (domestic customers) and £100 (non-domestic customers) for not restoring supplies within 24 hours plus £20 for each further 12 hours.
Providing supply and meter	Arrange an appointment within 3 working days for domestic customers (and 5 working days for non-domestic customers)*	£20 to £100
Notice of planned supply interruptions	Customers must be given at least 2 days notice*	£20 domestic customers. £40 non-domestic customers
Investigation of voltage complaints	Visit or substantive reply within 10 working days*	£20
Responding to meter problems	Visit within 10 working days* or substantive reply within 5 working days	£20
Responding to customers' queries about charges and payment queries	Substantive reply within 5 working days	£20
Making and keeping appointments	Companies must offer and keep a morning or afternoon appointment, or a time appointment if requested by the customer	£20
Notifying customers of payments owed under standards	Write to customer within 10 working days of failure	£20

Notes: Companies may not have to make payments if failure is caused by severe weather or other matters outside their control. But this depends on the particular circumstances and companies must make all reasonable efforts to meet the standards. The standards apply to tariff customers and those marked* vary between customers.

Source: OFFER.

TABLE 20. *Overall standards of performance for Eastern Electricity 1996/7*

1. 93% of supplies to be reconnected following faults within 3 hours and all within 24 hours.

2. 97% of voltage faults to be corrected within 6 months.

3. Connecting new tariff customers' premises to electricity distribution system. 99% of domestic customers to be connected within 30 working days and all non-domestic customers to be connected within 40 working days.

4. All customers who have been cut off for non-payment to be reconnected before the end of the working day after they have paid the bill or made arrangements to pay.

5. Visiting to move meter when asked to do so by customers within 15 working days in all cases.

6. Changing meters where necessary on change of tariff within 10 working days of domestic customers' requests in 98% of cases.

7. Ensuring that the company obtains a firm reading for customers' meters at least once a year in 99% of cases.

8. 99% of all customer letters to be responded to within 10 working days.

Source: OFFER.

report published by OFFER.[1] Other regulators, including OFGAS, OFTEL, and OFWAT possess similar powers. These provisions reflect the concern that, especially in areas not subject to the discipline of competition, there is a continuing risk that, in the absence of strict regulation, quality of service will be degraded by firms seeking to maximize profits by cutting corners on quality.

Regulators generally find it easier to regulate price than quality. Price has the great advantage of being (in certain markets at least) both one-dimensional and objectively measurable. Quality, on the other hand, is harder to pin down. It has many dimensions, some of which typically rest upon subjective evaluations by the purchaser or consumer; and in many cases the true quality of a product only comes to light some time after it has been consumed. In some cases it never comes to light.

This is unfortunate, since in many markets customers appear to attach more importance to quality than to price. This is as true of regulated industries as of other markets. In many regulated sectors, such as gas

[1] OFFER, *Report on Customer Services 1996/97* (London, Sept. 1997). See also OFWAT, *1996–97 Report on Levels of Service for the Water Industry of England and Wales* (London, Nov. 1997); OFTEL, *Telecommunications Companies: Comparable Performance Indicators: Business and Residential* (London, 1998); data on levels of customer complaints in the gas industry are provided by Gas Consumers' Council, which is separate from OFGAS. The gas regulator has the power to impose monetary penalties on companies to secure compliance with overall service standards. The Government has announced its intention to legislate to give all utilities regulators such powers: DTI White Paper: *A Fair Deal for Consumers: The Response to Consultation* (London, July 1998).

or electricity, quality has an important safety dimension. In others, such as telecommunications, commercial users need continuous and reliable services in order to transact their business, and residential customers need such services in order to meet domestic emergencies. Quality issues have understandably, therefore, been a prime concern of regulators.

This chapter first summarizes some results which relate to quality and its regulation; it then identifies certain ways in which quality can be regulated, drawing a distinction between those quality attributes which are individual or private, in the sense that different customers can experience or suffer different levels of service, and those which are general or public in the sense that quality is uniform for all consumers in a particular area. Finally, we discuss possible ways in which optimal levels of quality of service can be established by directly eliciting customers' willingness to pay for increased quality or to trade off one attribute of quality against another.

2. The Simple Economics of Quality Regulation

A number of factors give rise to the difficulties encountered in regulating quality.[2] Consider first the case of an unregulated monopolist supplying a product of uniform quality to its captive market. In pricing output of a given quality, its route to profit maximization is clear: raise prices up to the point where any further increase will reduce demand so much as to lower profits. When quality is a choice variable, however, what are the monopolists' incentives? The answer is that the unregulated monopolist will either undersupply or oversupply quality;[3] the departures from the optimum arising because the monopolist chooses the quality level with an eye to the preference of the marginal consumer, who, at the price charged, is just on the margin of buying or not buying the product. The welfare of all others is ignored.

Suppose now that the firm is subject to rate of return regulation (see Chapter 17). Consumers are likely to benefit chiefly because the price of output of a given quality is controlled. In addition, the quality of output may rise if rate of return regulation encourages capital intensity and if capital is normally required to increase service quality, the result may be excessive quality. An electricity generation network, for example, may contain far more excess capacity to deal with the risk of supply interruptions than customers would ideally like to pay for.

Now replace rate of return regulation with a price cap. The situation becomes less ambiguous, as the regulated firm with a given price cap

---

[2] See L. Rovizzi and D. Thompson, 'The Regulation of Product Quality in Public Utilities', in M. Bishop, J. Kay, and C. Mayer (eds.), *The Regulatory Challenge* (Oxford, 1995).

[3] See M. Spence, 'Monopoly, Quality & Regulation' 16 (1975) *Bell J. of Econ.* 417–29.

will be able to make extra profits by degrading the quality of service. In other words, quality degradation is a means of evading the price cap.

As Chapter 17 has shown, regulation in the United Kingdom typically contains elements both of rate of return and of price capping (because price caps are reset in the light of observed and expected rates of return). There are, as a result, risks of both oversupply of quality (through gold plating) and of undersupply. These opposite risks will apply in varying proportions, depending on the nature of the industry and the regulatory timetable. There is thus a strong case for believing on *a priori* grounds that quality regulation is likely to be a major issue, if a privatized utility is maximizing its profits without being exposed to much competition.

It is worth emphasizing, however, that privatization may be replacing an earlier quality problem with a new one. Thus it is quite plausible to argue that nationalized industries exhibited the worst possible form of quality distortion (because of asymmetric information). Managers had substantial discretion over expenditure and had little personal interest in good financial results. They were thus tempted to gratify their own preferences, which often ran to substantial expenditure on gold plating the engineering and design aspects of capital expenditure, while allocating little time or resources to the quality attributes which were of interest to their customers. The challenge of regulating quality in a privatized industry is thus to convert the cost-cutting behaviour of the firms to the public good, by appropriate forms of intervention.

3. Individual and Overall Quality Standards

Where quality of service can be differentiated *ex ante* or *ex post* across customers, the natural solution is to offer customers a choice of tiered levels of service, and to require compensation to be paid for failure to deliver these as due to individual customers. Such arrangements exist in the telecommunications industry, where customers can pay a higher quarterly payment in return for the guarantee of a quicker repair service.

The issues then arising are how the gradations of service or conditions of eligibility for compensation should be set and how prices for each should be determined. On compensation levels, damages should ideally equal losses borne by the representative consumer divided by the probability that compensation will be sought. This will give firms an appropriate deterrent against breaching standards which takes account of the problem that not everyone will complain. (Thus, if only half complain, the payment will have to be twice the actual damage imposed, in order to give the operator a strong incentive to maintain service standards). In practice, however, some conventional figure tends to be chosen (see Table 19 above).

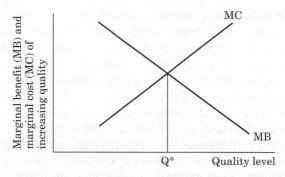

As quality increases it becomes more and more expensive to raise it further: hence the marginal cost of quality improvement (MC) rises as quality rises. In contrast, as quality rises the extra benefit consumers get from a further increase (MB) declines. These two factors determine an optimal level of quality (Q*), where marginal benefit and marginal cost are equal.

FIG. 9. *Determining the optimal level of quality*

Tiered service charges could either be cost-based or reflect demand factors as well, as in Ramsey pricing (see Chapter 15). It is likely that service levels and prices will require regulatory scrutiny, to ensure that they match the range of consumers' preferences.

Where the quality attribute is public (such as the taste of tap water or the probability of a call failure in a telecommunications network), one superficially attractive means of combining price and quality regulation is to incorporate quality measurements directly into the price-cap. This could be achieved by simply appending an extra term to the RPI–X formula—turning it into *RPI–X+a∆Q* where *∆Q* is the improvement in quality. Thus a regulated company that increased its quality of service (and hence raised its quality index Q) would be allowed to raise its prices faster than it might if quality levels remained constant. Equally, any decline in service quality would be accompanied by a decline in the real price of output. In principle, the coefficients in the formula should be set in such a way as to achieve optimum levels of service quality in each dimension under consideration.

Let us suppose that the cost of increasing levels of service quality rises as the quality level rises: that is that there is an increasing marginal cost of quality (see Figure 9). Consumers' marginal benefit of quality is likely to decline as quality increases. There will thus be a determinate optimum. The firm could be given an incentive to aspire to that optimum by setting the coefficient (*a*) in the price-cap formula *RPI–X+a∆Q* at the appropriate level. This happy state of affairs is exhibited at *Q** in Figure 9. But it is equally obvious from Figure 9 that a mis-estimate in either the marginal cost or the marginal benefit of quality, leading to incorrect choice of the quality coefficient in the price cap, would have unfortunate consequences, leading to the considerable oversupply or undersupply of quality.

A further, more obvious, problem, arises from the multidimensional nature of quality and the troubles encountered in measuring it objectively. Even in a relatively simple industry such as water and sewerage, it is not difficult to think of a very large number of different quality attributes. Each of these should be reflected in a dedicated coefficient in the price-cap formula, since omitting any attribute might lead to a serious quality deterioration in that respect. Quality levels would also have to be measurable by objective, or at least agreed, methods, but the difficulties of making measurements would almost certainly mean that many quality attributes would not be covered in the formula. As with all performance indicators, there will be a tendency for the measurable to drive out the unmeasurable. For these reasons, quality of service has not been incorporated in the price cap of any of the regulated industries in the United Kingdom, although regulators have indicated that they will be prepared to revisit an existing price cap if long-term reductions in quality of service are encountered within a control period.

What regulators have used instead of the above approach is a mixture of steps to develop competitive pressure where this is possible; to publish comparative quality data where a number of suppliers are in operation (the electricity and water regulators now publish tables in their Annual Reports that show the performance of the monopoly companies that they regulate against service standard targets);[4] to criticize regulated firms publicly when service standards have fallen; and to use the standard-making powers referred to above. Thus the 'command and control' method of setting standards has generally been adopted in preference to the price-guided method. In terms of Figure 9, the regulator determines Q^* and then enforces it as a minimum standard.

4. Ways of Establishing Customers' Valuations of Quality

There remains, however, the question of how the optimal standard should in practice be determined. As OFWAT has emphasized, quality is not costless and can be over-provided as well as under-provided.[5] The Competition and Services (Utilities) Act requires the public consultation of affected parties about standards, but unless such consultation is carried out skilfully, there is a danger that consumers in particular will opt for higher standards without giving proper weight to the possible cost (and tariff) implications.

[4] On the potential to move from a command approach to quality to one based on the supply of information on comparable quality of service performance and prices (a strategy for more competitive markets) see DTI, *A Fair Deal for Consumers: Modernising the Framework for Utility Regulation*, Green Paper, Cm. 3898 (London, Mar. 1998), 21.

[5] OFWAT, *The Cost of Quality* (Birmingham, 1992).

The obvious way to find out how strongly customers value quality is to ask them directly. This has been practised relatively rarely, although in the 1994 periodic review of price control in the water industry, the Director-General of Water Services instructed companies that their business plans should contain provisions for gauging the strength of consumers' demand for higher standards. OFWAT also commissioned research into householders' willingness to pay for improvements in the taste of tap water, reductions in the risk of hose-pipe bans, or lower chances of their homes being flooded by sewage.

There are a number of well-known difficulties in eliciting reliable information about households' willingness to pay for public services.[6] There is, moreover, a now well-established but worrying finding that consumers typically exhibit a willingness to pay (WTP) for an increment in the level or quality of a public good which is a fraction (often about one half) of the sum of money they would require in compensation for the loss of the same quantity or quality—their willingness to accept, or WTA. The sources of bias arise for a number of reasons, including the following:

Market inexperience—households used to monopoly supply on a 'take it or leave it' basis may find it difficult sensibly to answer questions about variations in the quality of services.

Difficulties in understanding probabilities—when the quality variable is a proportion such as the percentage of telephone boxes in operation or the probability of a hosepipe ban, consumers may have difficulty in understanding the question. Problems of this kind arise in estimates of the willingness to pay for a lower probability of death or injury, but may also bedevil WTP for service quality in utilities.

Strategic or policy bias—consumers may state their preferences falsely in order to influence the outcome. If they are concerned, for example, about the current level of water bills, they may disclaim any interest in improvements in service quality, for fear that the bills will rise even further.

Spill-over effects—these occur when responses are coloured by general political or social attitudes towards such issues as privatization.

There are also obvious difficulties in validating WTP responses. Ideally, an experiment would be contrived in which stated willingness to pay was tested against actual behaviour or revealed preference. This sort of experiment has been carried out in some transport applications, but such situations are difficult to arrange, and validation is often restricted to demonstrations of consistency of responses or showing that responses appear to be systematically related to other socio-economic variables such as income.

[6] See R. C. Mitchell and R. T. Carson, *Using Surveys to Value Public Goods: The Contingent Valuation Method* (Washington, 1989).

Finally, decisions about overall quality standards have important distributional consequences. Even if accurate willingness to pay responses are available, a decision still has to be made about ways of averaging them in order to set the overall standard, which will be too high for some and too low for others. A simple arithmetic average normally gives greater weight to the preferences of those with higher incomes who are able to pay for higher quality levels.

Given the difficulties noted above, it is natural to look for alternative techniques with which to elicit households' valuations. One possibility is a technique frequently used in transport studies (where it is known as stated preference) and in market research (where it is known as conjoint analysis).[7] Under this technique, respondents are asked to choose between alternative packages of attributes. A journey, for example, may be described in terms of its duration, the comfort of the seating, the cleanliness of the environment and, possibly but not necessarily, its price. By ranking the chosen sets of alternatives, individuals show their preferences for particular attributes, either in terms of a willingness to pay (if monetary cost is included), or in terms of willingness to trade. This approach has certain advantages. It offers the respondent concrete alternatives; it makes it harder to exhibit strategic bias; and it focuses the individual upon his or her own preferences. Sample sizes can be diminished, moreover, because each respondent generates a number of observations. This is an appropriate tool for deriving valuations of improvements in the quality of services that are provided by utilities. Final decisions about appropriate quality levels will emerge from a partly political process, but in almost all cases, it is desirable that information about users' preferences should be collected and employed as a major input into the decision-making process.

Conclusions

We have argued that regulating the quality of those services that are provided by the utilities is essential. The natural way to deal with individual or private quality attributes is by offering tiered levels of service, probably with regulated price differences. Overall or public service quality attributes present more serious problems, which are most naturally resolved by eliciting information about consumers' valuations of quality improvement, and comparing them with the costs of improvement. The experience of regulatory UK utilities shows that quality of service can be improved considerably, compared with pre-privatization levels, by a combination of regulation and more customer-focused management. Further improvement is, however, possible.

[7] See M. Cave et al., *Measuring Changes in the Quality of Public Services* (London, 1994).

Franchising and its Limitations

The current importance of franchising as a policy option demands that its virtues and vices be understood. This chapter looks at different types of franchising arrangement, the key difficulties encountered in franchising, and the potential of franchising as a tool of government.[1]

1. Commercial Franchising

The essence of franchising is the allocation (subject to conditions) of a protected or exclusive right to exploit or carry out an activity.[2] In the commercial world franchising is known as a form of marketing or distribution in which one party, the franchiser, allows another, the franchisee, to exploit a trade name, trademark, process, or other resource in return for a fee.[3] The franchise agreement typically allows this exploitation to be carried out in a prescribed manner, over a certain period of time, and within a specified location. The objective of both parties to a commercial or 'private' franchise is likely to be the maximizing of profits. Within the United Kingdom public sector, the closest approach to commercial franchising to be found is the Post Office, where Post Office Counters franchises certain stores to provide retail post office services to the public.

2. Governmental Franchising

Governmental franchising may resemble commercial franchising closely but can be distinguished by its 'public' purpose. The aim of the franchiser

---

[1] For a more detailed discussion see R. Baldwin and M. Cave, *Franchising as a Tool of Government* (London, 1996) on which this chapter draws.

[2] See H. Demsetz, 'Why Regulate Utilities?' (1968) 11 *J. Law and Econ.* 55; S. Domberger, 'Regulation through Franchise Contracts', in J. Kay, C. Mayer, and D. Thompson (eds.), *Privatisation and Regulation: The UK Experience* (Oxford, 1986); O. Williamson, *The Economic Institutions of Capitalism* (New York, 1985), ch. 13; A. Ogus, *Regulation: Legal Form and Economic Theory* (Oxford, 1994), ch. 15.

[3] J. Adams and K. V. Prichard Jones, *Franchising* (London, 1987); C. L. Vaughan, *Franchising* (Lexington, Mass., 1989); C. Joerges (ed.), *Franchising and the Law* (Baden-Baden, 1991); A. W. Dnes, *Franchising: A Case Study Approach* (Aldershot, 1992).

is not to maximize profits but to deliver to consumers or the public an advantage—for example, an efficiently produced and competitively priced utility service.

As a tool of government influence franchising is seen by proponents as particularly useful in a number of respects. It is said to avoid the restrictiveness associated with classical command and control regulation while, nevertheless, allowing some degree of control to be retained. It provides a means of using competition *for* a market as a substitute for competition *within* the market (where this is not possible), and thereby of inducing monopolists to behave as if subject to competitive pressures. (Such competition is generally achieved by allocating franchises according to a bidding mechanism.) It respects managerial freedoms and allows managers rather than bureaucrats to devise responses to preferences within markets. It increases market contestability by allowing firms to bid for rights to supply before they have committed resources to the enterprise. It provides the franchiser with information about the competitiveness of potential suppliers and the costs of servicing the market. It offers an effective sanction for poor performance, namely the threat of franchise termination, suspension, or non-renewal and it reduces the dangers of regulatory capture by minimizing agency discretions.

In Britain franchising has been most notably employed in the broadcasting sector but the privatization process has created extensive new areas of private service provision within which franchising may have or has been given a role. One such important area is railway passenger services where a franchising regime was established under the Railways Act 1993.[4]

Systems of franchising may combine and overlap with other modes of government or service provision, notably with licensing, competitive tendering/contracting out, and contracts for exploitation or concessions. Model forms of the different devices can be contrasted thus:

Franchising—the course of operation is tendered by the franchisee in a competitive context. The regime is based on market incentives with the franchisee bearing at least some of the revenue risk.[5] (The extent of revenue risk a franchise bears may vary widely and as it decreases the franchise resembles a normal commercial contract.) The franchiser and franchisee have a continuing relationship with the franchiser monitoring performance quality. (The prospect of renewal or non-renewal of the franchise operates as a control.)

Licensing—operators are free to compete in the market provided that they have obtained permission to do so. Permission is granted on the satisfaction of certain requirements and may be subject to conditions.

---

[4] See Comptroller and Auditor-General, *Office of Passenger Rail Franchising (OPRAF): The Award of the First Three Passenger Rail Franchises* (HC 701, 1995/6) (London, 1996).
[5] That is, the franchisee's returns vary according to the revenue yielded from sales rather than being set at a fixed sum.

Competitive tendering/contracting out—the service is rendered by the provider to the contracting body, not directly to the public as in franchising. Revenue risks are borne by the contracting body, not the service provider and, because one of the contracting parties also consumes the services, the issue of service variation is often less acute than in franchising and performance monitoring tends to be less problematic than with franchising.

Contracts for exploitation—the state allows a private operator to exploit a public good in return for making a capital investment and paying taxes on profits. A high degree of security is offered by a contract with a period of duration so long that the prospect of renewal or non-renewal does not operate as a control.

3. Modes of Franchise Allocation

All franchising allocation processes involve comparisons of bids. These may be single or a multidimensional processes.

Bidding on Price Per Unit

One option is to introduce bidding on price per unit so that the franchise is awarded to the competitor willing to supply the service to the public at the lowest prices. This is the scheme recommended by Demsetz.[6] Under the assumptions that the auction is vigorously contested, there is a single output, and information asymmetries play no part in determining the spread of bids, bidders will bid their average costs at each stipulated output level. With these assumptions, price per unit auctions identify the firm with the lowest average cost.

The advantages of this type of auction are that the process extinguishes monopoly rents; it identifies the most efficient producer (assuming bidders are not asymmetric); where the output is a clearly identifiable single product it makes for easy identification of the franchise winner. On the debit side, however, it has been argued that a price equal to average cost does not result in a welfare optimizing level of pricing or output.[7] Where, moreover, a variety of services or products is to be provided, it becomes much more difficult to judge which bidder is offering the best deal. The price

---

[6] See Demsetz, loc. cit. n. 2 above, and A. W. Dnes, 'Bidding for Commercial Broadcasting: An Analysis of UK Experience' (1993) 40 *Scottish J. of Pol. Econ.* 104.

[7] See L. G. Telser, 'On the Regulation of Industry: A Note' (1969) 77 *J. Poli. Econ.* 937. The game theoretic literature on regulation suggests that the auction winner should then be paid a subsidy in exchange for price and quantity levels indicated by P_3 and Q_f (see, for example, D. Baron and R. Myerson, 'Regulating a Monopolist with Unknown Costs' (1982) *Econometrician* 911. This, however, requires that the authorities know the firm's marginal cost.

rigidity implied by a price per unit franchise may also become inefficient as demands and technologies change over time.

Bids can be for an average price or a weighted index of temporally viable tariffs, such as exist in the RPI–X price control baskets used to regulate many privatized UK utilities. The advantage of controlling a weighted index instead of actual prices is that it enables more price flexibility and thereby addresses one of the key criticisms of the price per unit form of franchise bidding. However, such bidding may make unrealistic assumptions about potential franchisees' understandings of demand conditions.

Bidding by Lump Sum Payment

In an industry where scale economies are such that least cost production is by a single firm, awarding a franchise to the firm that bids the highest sum will not correct for the inefficiencies of monopoly pricing and output decisions and so consumers will suffer from higher prices and lower outputs than is optimal. Without additional controls on prices, this form of franchise bidding has only a distributional effect as the expected stream of monopoly rents would be capitalized and paid to the franchiser.

As a rule, bidding in the form of lump sum payments should be based on known regulated prices. However, this form of franchising suffers from price inflexibility just as bidding on price per unit does. Bidders would want to know the regulated prices before they determined their lump sum bids. If regulated prices were uncertain, bids would be discounted accordingly. Moreover, if prices are to be specified prior to the auction, the franchiser will have to do this without the very bidding information that would provide a basis for assessing the likely winner's production costs.

Bidding for the Lowest Lump Sum Subsidy

If, before franchising, the market has already been supplied by a public enterprise, the regulator/franchiser may decide that those prices must be maintained. The initial controls on price can, however, be eased in return for improvements in service quality. Bids can be accepted or rejected according to the quality of their business plans, as well as levels of subsidies demanded. If potential franchisees know they will be taking over existing pricing structures they can plan more securely on the revenue side. Franchising may, indeed, be conducted by requiring the winner to begin operating as close to existing publicly operated arrangements as is possible. In this case, lump sum subsidy bidding is probably preferable to price per unit bidding. Price changes can then be left to unfold according to market pressures and stated regulatory strategy.

Marginal Return Bidding

This form of franchise is only suitable where franchisees have to erect their own infrastructures, such as might occur for new rail or underground links. Given that the franchiser has an approximate knowledge of the cost of the project, a rate of return schedule is constructed for capital invested which will eventually fall short of the cost of capital to the franchisee.

It is the marginal return schedule for a given investment for which franchisees bid. With incomplete contracts, which is always the case in utility franchising, the successful franchisee will almost always have room to manœuvre within the original franchise contract. Particularly in government procurement contracts there is a history of cost overruns arising once contracts are under way. Marginal return bidding discourages operators from inflating these costs. In cases where potential franchisees are bidding to take over the operation of existing state-subsidized services (and possibly assets), the bidding could involve a marginal annual subsidy schedule.

Menu Auctions

The franchiser may choose to allow competitors to specify their bids in terms of more than one dimension—typically in terms of price and quality of service.[8] The franchiser then makes a choice from among the combinations on offer, and the quality and price conditions embodied in the franchise contract.

Allowing multiple bidding on a mix of quality of service and price/lump sum variables can provide useful information to the franchiser/regulator, which can be used if renegotiation becomes necessary once the franchisee begins operations. The main drawback of this type of franchise is that it proves more difficult for the franchiser to identify the winning bid than in other auctions. The auctioning process may as a result lack transparency. This has been a problem with bus franchising in London and, unless carefully managed, menu bidding may provide greater gaming opportunities to bidders. Auction theory suggests, however, that where relevant information is dispersed amongst bidders, introducing multiple factors as variables in an open auction reduces uncertainty, as private information is made public.[9]

---

[8] The term 'menu auction' for such procedures was introduced by Bernheim and Whinston—see B. Bernheim and M. Whinston, 'Menu Auctions, Resource Allocation and Economic Influence' (1986) *Quarterly J. of Economics* 1.

[9] The franchiser's revenue may, as a result, rise—see P. Milgrom and R. Weber, 'A Theory of Auctions and Competitive Bidding' (1982) 50 *Econometrica* 1089; R. McAfee and J. McMillan, 'Auctions and Bidding' (1987) 25 *J. of Econ. Lit.* 699. On varying the sequence of bidding and making information available to bidders see M. L. Cripps and N. Ireland, 'The Design of Auctions and Tenders with Quality Thresholds: The Symmetric Case' (1994) 104 *Economic Journal* 316.

Conduct of the Auction

Auctions can be carried out by a number of methods. These include 'public' or 'oral' auctions, in which the auctioneer successively announces prices until a buyer is found, and 'sealed bid' tenders. Public auctions may be either English—in which prices are successively raised until only one bidder remains—or Dutch—in which the price is successively lowered until the object is bought by the first bidder. Sealed bid tenders award the object to the highest bidder either at the price offered by that bidder (a first-price tender) or—more rarely—at the price offered by the second highest bidder (a second-price tender).

In deciding how to auction a franchise the regulator will normally seek to devise a procedure which maximizes revenue, subject to any constraints on quality. One of the major findings of auction theory is that in the private values case (where the object of the bid is valued differently by bidders), all four models yield the same price on average (assuming risk-neutrality) and hence the method of auctioning makes no difference. (It may seem paradoxical that the first- and second-price auctions produce the same result on average, but clearly bidders' behaviour will be different in each case.) In addition, the more bidders there are, the higher the expected revenue, as bidders are led by the pressure of competition to bid right up to their own true valuation of the object on sale. With few bidders, by contrast, each company will bid the least it feels it can win with.

As we have seen, however, franchises are not usually examples of the private values case. Bids are not determined exclusively by their private tastes but depend upon (possibly different) judgements about potential revenues and costs. This may lead to the phenomenon known as the 'winner's curse' whereby the highest bidder realizes as soon as he or she wins that he or she has placed a higher value on the franchise than anyone else, and may thus have overestimated its value. A sophisticated bidder would, however, anticipate this danger and bid less aggressively, though, as before and for the same reasons, the more bidders there are, the higher the expected price will be. The seller can reduce anxieties about the winner's curse by publicizing any information available about the franchise. This reduces bidders' uncertainty and encourages them to bid closer to their true expected value than would be the case if they had poorer information and were more anxious about overbidding.

The key result from the common value model, provided the bidders are risk-neutral, is that the various forms of auction produce different average levels of revenue, because they yield different information to each bidder about other bidders' valuations. The English auction yields the most information, and hence the highest expected revenue, because any bidder can observe all other bidders' behaviour. Next is the second-price tender, which exploits the valuation of at least one other bidder. Finally, the first-price tender and Dutch auction furnish no information, and thus leave bidders most fearful of the winner' curse. When bidders are risk-averse, however, the ranking is less clear cut. The English auction can still be expected to yield more revenue than a second-price tender, and the equivalence of Dutch and first-price tenders is preserved. The first-price tender may, however, now yield higher revenue than an English auction.[10]

Integration Versus Separation

Franchises may be used to divide industries vertically so that separate operations are made of, for example, infrastructure establishment, maintenance, operation, marketing, etc. Alternatively, franchising may involve high levels of integration.[11]

Franchises may also achieve horizontal separation, with each franchisee serving a particular area. The combination of these two forms of separation is particularly appropriate where the franchiser undertakes an activity characterized by economies of scale, while franchisees carry out locally based activities at a different cost-minimizing scale. Much commercial franchising exploits this distinction, with the franchiser providing the brand name and franchisees operating local outlets. The system of rail regulation operating in the UK is of the same kind, with track separated from train operation—although in this case franchising is undertaken by a third party.

Operating Franchises

With an operating franchise the responsibility for maintenance and investment in infrastructure remains with the franchiser, or perhaps some other appointed government body, and the franchisee bears the operating cost risk and all, or a proportion of, the revenue risk.

Operating contracts can prove useful when it is appropriate for the franchiser to carry the investment risk, or when the economies associated with the infrastructure diverge from those associated with its

---

[10] See S. Matthews, 'Comparing Auctions for Risk Averse Buyers: A Buyer's Point of View' (1987) *Econometrica* 633.

[11] Thus in the French water industry, two types of franchise contract are distinguished —the 'concession de service public', in which the franchisee finances initial establishment of the infrastructure, and the 'affermage contract' in which a public authority finances the initial establishment.

operation. This is frequently the case with utility networks, where the natural monopoly component is the infrastructure (and possibly also its operation) while downstream operations (running rolling stock), involve fewer scale economies. In such cases the 'efficient' split is not to divide the utility into several vertically integrated companies but to maintain the network infrastructure in larger blocks than the operational aspects —as in the case of the railways.[12]

Where the expected future investment and maintenance cost of infrastructure are very uncertain, it is usually desirable for the franchiser to bear a significant portion of the associated risk. This is especially so in long-term franchising where the rules for valuing assets at the end of the franchise period are open to doubt. Some form of operating franchise may also be preferable when the sheer size of the infrastructure and expected investment are so large that few, if any, qualified bidders will be attracted to the auction.

Operating franchises enable the scale of each franchise to be smaller, thus increasing the number of franchises. This can facilitate 'yardstick competition'. It also increases the likelihood that an operating firm will have more than one franchise. This brings into play a 'reputational' effect. Parties holding numbers of franchises are, it is suggested, likely to behave more responsibly than holders of single franchises because poor performance on one franchise may have undesirable consequences in relation to renewals of other franchises.[13]

Investment Franchises

The investment franchise assigns a higher level of 'ownership' of the facilities to the operator than does the operating franchise. Problems arise, however, because 'ownership' of the facilities only lasts as long as the franchise contract. As the end of the contract period approaches, the franchisee's incentive to invest declines. Investment in infrastructure is, therefore, likely to be cyclical, rising during the early years of a franchise, and declining as the contract period comes closer to its end.

Several strategies can be employed to limit the variation in the cycle. Punishment clauses for declines in quality of service can have this effect. The problem is also mitigated if franchisees believe that the franchiser is committed to valuing the franchised facilities 'fairly'.[14]

---

[12] Similarly, it has been suggested that divergent economies of scale exist between sewerage and water delivery and argues on this basis for the franchising of water delivery —see J. W. Sawkins, *Water and Sewage in Scotland: A Response*, Univ. of Aberdeen Discussion Papers (1993).

[13] See M. A. Zupan, 'Cable Franchise Renewals: Do Incumbent Firms Behave Opportunistically?' (1989) 20 *Rand J. of Econ.* 473.

[14] See D. Baron and D. Besanko, 'Commitment and Fairness in a Dynamic Regulatory Relationship' (1987) 54 *Rev. Econ. Stud.* 413.

Progressive Versus 'Big Bang' Franchising

Industries may be moved from public to private sector by means of incremental franchising, or the whole sector may be put out to tender at the one time. The arguments mostly favour progressive franchising. Present British experience (for example, in London Bus operations) suggests that one advantage of the incremental approach lies in the increasing ease with which overbidding can be identified as franchising progresses. The franchiser, rather than having to cope with a flood of applications on the basis of little experience, has the opportunity to deal with smaller numbers of tenders and to do so while developing a feel for the credible set of proposals and promises. Renewals are, moreover, staggered (if franchises are of standard duration) and incrementalism thus eases administration and makes for continuity.

Progressive franchising also offers a response to problems of uncertainty. At the time that a franchise system is introduced, there are likely to be few, if any, firms which have had direct experience of operating a complete utility or network of the type being put to tender. The sheer financial size of the individual franchises will tend to restrict the number of serious bidders. There is uncertainty about demand and cost factors and also about regulatory and governmental commitments.

Such factors are likely to lead to a restricted number of franchise bidders. A key task of the franchiser is, therefore, to reduce the level of uncertainty amongst potential bidders. Letting franchise contracts out gradually can greatly reduce bidder uncertainty. The first franchises let will almost certainly be heavily discounted. Once operations begin, uncertainty declines. An operator starts to gain a better understanding of cost and demand conditions, and of the mind of the regulator, and it becomes apparent to the market that the franchisee has obtained a good deal. Bidders for subsequent franchises will suffer less uncertainty, and—other things being equal—the bidders will be larger in number and their bids significantly less cautious. Where at least one of the bidders already operates an existing franchise it will bring valuable and private information to the auction. An open auction can provide useful information to the other bidders, with the outcome that the auction is more competitive and on average bids are higher. Even *post hoc* disclosure of bids will have a similar educational effect.

A contrary argument applies, however, where there are significant complementarities and/or economies of scale or scope between franchised operations, with the result that allocating one franchise at a time may prove to be inefficient. To allow bidders to gain bundles of franchises in order to capture these scale advantages, franchises should be auctioned together.[15]

---

[15] On allowing flexibility in 'bundling' franchises see J. McMillan, 'Selling Spectrum Rights' (1994) 8 *J. of Econ. Perspectives* 145; P. C. Crampton, 'Money out of Thin Air: The Nationwide Narrow Bend PCS Auction' (1995) *J. of Econ. and Man. Strategy*.

4. Franchising: Problems to be Overcome

The literature on franchising indicates that success on four key fronts is essential if franchisers are to achieve designated objectives in an acceptable manner.[16] These fronts concern:

- specification of the franchised service;
- allocating franchises competitively;
- enforcement of franchise terms;
- terminating contracts and refranchising.

Service Specification

Adequate service specification is important in franchising, first, as a basis for competition in the bidding process and, second, to set down benchmarks for evaluating bids. If the franchiser fails to specify the subject matter of the bid with precision then uncertainties will result, costs of bidding will be increased, and applicants will be discouraged. Similar problems will arise if the franchiser defers specification until after the franchise is awarded or retains discretion to alter the specification post the award.

Problems of specification diminish in so far as variations in the quality of service are absent or are deemed to be immaterial and are accordingly discounted. Where, on the other hand, service variation is extreme and extends across a wide range of aspects of the service, difficulties might be expected to be the greater.

Practical experience of service specification suggests that in some sectors this has proved less of an issue than others. The Radio Authority (RA) franchises Independent Local Radio (ILR) services under the Broadcasting Act 1990 but operates without a detailed specification of quality of service. The RA advertises locally, asking for tenders to provide ILR services for a particular area with a designated coverage and characteristically for an eight-year period. Allocations are not uncompetitive, however. The Radio Authority looks for the applicant best able to satisfy the criteria set out in Section 105 of the Broadcasting Act 1990. Attention is thus paid to: the ability of the applicant to maintain the service for the period of the licence; the satisfaction of local tastes and interests; the meeting of interests uncatered for by existing services; and local support for the application. Successful applicants subsequently set down a 'promise of performance' stipulating the programming profile to be offered during the franchise. Such promises may be very short and some examples occupy half an A4 page.

[16] See e.g. O. Williamson, 'Franchise Bidding for National Monopolies: In General and with Respect to CATV' (1976) 7 *Bell J. of Econ.*; 73; Domberger, loc. cit. n. 2 above.

London Transport bus service tendering under the London Regional Transport Act 1984 has also involved relatively unproblematic service specification. (Tendering, as already indicated, differs from franchising but transfer of the revenue risk to the service provider—now being practised on some LT services—does establish a franchising system and the specification functions are similar.) Those agreeing to offer a service to London Regional Transport under the 1984 Act were offered a contract with schedules on service and vehicle specification. These schedules were fairly simple, laying down, for example, requirements on frequencies of service, running times, vehicle types to be used, and displays of route numbers.

Franchising in transport sectors generally might be expected to involve comparatively few specification difficulties because such services are not highly dimensional. The Secretary of State's 1994 guidance to the Director of Passenger Rail Franchising (the Franchising Director) indicated that service levels specified in franchises should look to: frequency and capacity; service availability (throughout the seven-day week); provision of through services by fast trains; intermediate stations served; and journey time. Some complications may be anticipated, however, in sectors such as rail, where separation of the industry is pronounced and high levels of coordination between different participants in providing the service have to be provided for in specifications.

Similarly, the degree of competition a franchisee faces may affect the precision appropriate in the service definition. As the Secretary of State's 1994 Guidance to the Franchising Director put it:

Service quality for railway passenger services and station services operated by franchisees should be specified in a degree of detail that is appropriate for the particular franchise. For some franchises, particularly those conferring monopoly power, you should ensure that the franchise agreement provides an effective substitute for market pressures. For other franchises, where market pressures are present to a greater extent, you should impose such service quality requirements as are necessary to ensure that the taxpayer obtains good value for money.[17]

Experience in television franchising offers a contrast with the above areas and demonstrates that, even where allocation is by highest cash bid, specification is problematic if there is a minimum quality of service to be stipulated. (This is the case with, say, Channel 3 services but not with Cable and Satellite operations.) The Independent Television Commission (ITC) franchises regional Channel 3 licences under the Broadcasting Act 1990 and in its Invitation to Apply for Regional Channel 3 Licences describes the threshold in 63 paragraphs. These paragraphs, moreover, involve the making of a number of potentially contentious judgements on programming issues and, accordingly, specification is far from cut and dried.

---

[17] Secretary of State for Transport, *Guidance to the Franchising Director* (London, 1994).

Where service specification involves the making of judgements, the advantages of franchising may be called into question. A supposed strength of franchising lies, as noted, in its allowing private sector providers, rather than regulating bureaucrats, to be the judges of consumer and market preferences. In so far as service specification involves the making of judgements by franchise authorities, and in so far as the franchise authority selects the best menu of services for the consumer, this advantage of franchising diminishes and franchising approximates to a system of classical-style regulation.

Specification, flexibility, and change
A general difficulty in service specification arises from tensions that exist between the need to lay down a precise description of the service to be provided by the successful bidder and the need to allow for flexibility and scope for innovation and responsiveness to consumer demands after the award of the franchise.

Where, in a sector, there is the prospect of a technical innovation that will demand, within the franchise period, substantial adaptations by franchisees, this may call for a service specification that allows for such flexibility.[18] (Thus difficulties for the franchiser arose in the ILR sector with the prospect of Digital Audio Broadcasting (DAB, which became an issue when planned for adoption by the BBC in 1995/6 in order to offer a higher quality of service). A series of uncertainties thus can arise in relation to costs and transmission arrangements and pressure to adjust franchise specifications and periods is to be expected.

As Armstrong, Cowan, and Vickers argue, franchising works best for straightforward products that involve low sunk costs, such as supplying licence plates for taxis, but in sectors such as the utilities, conditions are very different:

A complete contract would be immensely complex and extremely difficult to write, monitor and enforce. . . . Indeed it would be very hard for the government to commit not to vary some contract terms as events unfold. Much more likely, then, is some kind of incomplete contract that leaves a number of aspects to be resolved. . . . But this is effectively just what regulation involves—a continuing task of contract monitoring, enforcement and renegotiation. Thus in circumstances of any complexity, franchising does not do away with the need for regulation.[19]

---

[18] See J. Dallas, 'Effective Franchising: A Legal Perspective', in CRI, *Franchising Network Services: Regulation in Post, Rail and Water* (London, 1993). The arrival of Digital Audio Broadcasting (DAB) thus gave rise to a series of uncertainties in independent local radio franchising in the mid-1990s and indicated that in periods of rapid technological change the role of the franchiser may also have to change—from acting in a hands-off role it may have to become an instigator, organizer of change, and regulator.

[19] M. Armstrong, S. Cowan, and J. Vickers, *Regulatory Reform: Economic Analysis and British Experience* (London, 1994), 126.

Specifying the regulatory regime
Uncertainties in specifying regulatory regimes will affect franchise allocation processes since applicants will look for predictability of regulation.
Problems may arise, therefore, where regulators retain large discretions
as to quality of service to be provided; where changes in regulatory policy
may be made and where regulatory authority is diffused or uncertain.
Particular difficulties are to be expected in a sector such as rail where
a number of agencies and operators are interdependent and will, in addition, be perceived to be subject to political pressures.

Risk allocation
Risk allocation is a difficulty of specification that increases with the
separation of an industry. Thus, problems have been encountered in the
rail industry. It was clear from the Rail Regulator's July 1994 Consultation Document, *Framework for the Approval of Railtrack's Track Access
Charges for Franchised Passenger Services*, that, in the period leading
up to the first round of franchise allocations, a host of uncertainties
remained on such matters as the extent of industry risk to be borne by
Railtrack, the appropriate rate of return for Railtrack and even whether
private sector rate of return criteria should be applied to an assessment
of Railtrack's charges. The privatizations of Railtrack, the Rolling Stock
Leasing Companies (ROSCOs), and the Infrastructure Services Companies
have also created uncertainties of risk allocation. The Rail Regulator
acknowledged, in the above consultation paper, that 'Railtrack's longer
term revenue requirements will remain subject to continuing uncertainties'
(para. 1.31). A system of periodic review of charges (as familiar in other
utilities) has been instituted in rail, but, as the Rail Regulator conceded,
such a system may involve 'some uncertainty over the future levels of
costs for franchisees' (para. 1.34).

The designers of franchising regimes have to seek to allocate risks fairly
and in a manner optimizing incentives, but also in a way that allows the
locus of risk taking to be identified and the risks made capable of estimating. If franchisees are fearful of risks, their bids will reflect this and consumers or taxpayers will suffer since higher prices or subsidies will result.

A further consideration in allocating risks is the degree of control over
costs that a franchisee enjoys. Franchisees may be wary if asked, as in rail,
to bear revenue risks (with regulatory constraints) yet have high proportions of their costs fixed by mechanisms beyond their control. In terms
of incentives (to bid and operate) it may be appropriate to allocate risks
with an eye to those who are able to affect the relevant costs and risks.

Integration and separation
As noted, problems of specification increase in so far as an operation is vertically separated. Within an integrated system problems of coordination

are dealt with through a central command structure. Where there is vertical separation, a complex network of contracts substitutes for the command structure. Such contracts, in an efficient system, have to force providers to internalize the costs of their own sub-optimal performance. This can be done by providing, for example in a rail context, that the infrastructure company would compensate the train operating franchisee for track failures according to a pre-specified scale that is based on service disruption and losses of revenue. The terms of such contracts can, in theory, provide full compensation and create optimal incentives throughout the system. In practice there may be high costs involved in writing, monitoring, and enforcing contracts that cover all contingencies (where these cannot be anticipated added uncertainties affect the system). Where such contracts are used, providers, moreover, may adopt rigid, rule-bound, practices that lead to inefficiencies. Again, bidders who anticipate such problems might be expected to reduce their bids accordingly. The costs to consumers or the public purse (depending on the mode of franchise allocation) will be greater in a system of franchising that is based on vertical separation than one in which an integrated operation is franchised. The case for franchising a vertically integrated system may also be strong where there is a need to encourage a franchisee to make complementary investments in infrastructure and operating equipment.

Vertical separation, nevertheless, has been employed in complex utilities, for example, in the Swedish railway industry, and is said to bring a number of advantages. First, it allows identification of those parts of an operation that can be made the subject of effective franchising regimes. Second, it paves the way for developing a stable of potentially competing operators and, third, it reduces the difficulties faced by potential competitors to a vertically integrated incumbent where the latter controls access to (and the quality of) the infrastructure or network.

In the final analysis, the competitive advantages of vertical separation have to be balanced against the superior coordination and incentives to invest that are associated with integrated systems. In effecting this balance, the costs of the uncertainties and contractual controls encountered in vertical separation should not be underestimated—particularly in a complex sector such as rail. Vertical separation also brings potential problems of network coordination. Thus, a criticism of rail franchising in Britain has been that operators have been slow to provide route or ticketing information concerning the services of other operators.[20]

Price controls and competition
Specifying the regime of price control may be approached in a number of ways. Pricing freedom may be allowed in a competitive market (for

---

[20] For critical comment see C. Woolmar, *The Great British Railway Disaster* (London, 1996). The Rail Regulator has responded to such tardiness—*inter alia* by imposing fines on train operators for failing to meet targets on answering calls to the National Rail Enquiry Service promptly.

example, Channel 3 TV franchisees may charge for advertising as the market will bear). Prices may be fixed by the franchiser, or pricing limits may be imposed. Where, as in rail, different regulators control access charges and fares structures, a level of regulatory coordination is required.

Much depends here on the franchising philosophy adopted and the priority given to encouraging competition. The following broad approaches to franchising can be contrasted:

Competition for the market—consumer benefits are gained by offering an exclusive market and by using a system of competitive bids to serve this. Promises made in bidding are then enforced and detailed service specifications used to protect consumers.

Competition for and within the market—competitive bids to serve are employed and promises of service are enforced but the service may be defined flexibly and the right to serve the market is not exclusive. Guarantees concerning protection from competition are limited or absent. An incremental approach to competition may be adopted.

Examples of the first approach are encountered in the UK water industry and of the second approach in ILR and rail. In ILR franchising no guarantees are offered on freedom from competition within a geographic area (the Radio Authority's objective is to obtain the most services and greatest consumer choice within a band width). The Railways Act 1993 (Section 4) seeks also to combine franchising with competition but the Franchising Director may give exclusive use of the infrastructure to a franchisee if he judges this to be necessary for expeditious franchising of the service.[21]

The general problem of uncertain specification of potential exposure to competition has been summarized by the Rail Regulator:

At the time at which they make bids, franchisees are unlikely to have reliable information about the extent of the competition they might face and the impact of competition on the finances of their franchise. In such circumstances, they are likely to err on the side of caution, discount the risk excessively and thus reflect less than the full value of the franchise in their bids.[22]

---

[21] The Secretary of State's 1994 guidance to the Rail Regulator indicated that it was the Government's policy to moderate competition on routes to be franchised to the extent necessary to ensure the successful launch of the first generation of franchises.

[22] Rail Regulator, *Competition for Railway Passenger Services* (London, 1994), 12; also D. Kennedy, *Competition in the British Rail Industry* (London, 1996). Such uncertainties can cost taxpayers huge sums. In March 1998 the National Audit Office (NAO) reported on the Conservative Government's sell-off of the British Rail leasing companies. The NAO concluded that the companies had been worth £2.9 billion but had been sold for £1.8 billion (within two years, indeed, the initial buyers had sold at a profit of £850 million) and that uncertainties about the privatization and regulatory processes for rail had reduced numbers of bidders for the companies and the prices they were prepared to offer (see *Financial Times*, 5 Mar. 1988).

The franchise term
The duration of a franchise affects, amongst other things, the incentive to bid for the franchise, the continuity and quality of the service offered, infrastructure investment, and the effectiveness with which the franchiser holds the franchisee to promises given during the competition for the franchise.[23] In specifying the term two main issues arise, first, the extent of the term itself and, second, whether there should be provision made for adjusting or 'rolling' the franchise term.

On the term itself, it is usual to effect a trade-off between factors such as saleability, continuity, and investment-enhancing on the one hand, and quality of service enforcement on the other. Where large sunk investments are involved in an operation, a long-term franchise may be necessary to combat incentives to under-investment. Under-investment in infrastructure would not be a problem if a displaced incumbent could be accurately compensated for investments made during the franchise term (for example, by providing that the franchiser will repurchase assets at fair market value). Some investment activities, however, are not readily measurable. Accounting choices (for example, asset depreciation rates) are contentious and there may be considerable sunk costs involved in planning and implementing large-scale investment projects. This suggests that where franchise terms are short (in comparison with the lives of relevant assets) these will prove expensive in terms of subsidy even if there is competition in the bidding process. The disadvantage of long-term contracts (as indicated in the French water industry) is that incumbents become difficult to remove, new entrants are discouraged, and franchising turns into a scheme of regulation. Against this, the long-term contract may encourage service innovation by offering a longer period in which to recoup the costs of innovation.

London Bus contracts normally last three years; in ILR franchising, as noted, the usual term is eight years; the ITC's Channel 3 franchises run for ten years; and rail operator franchises are likely to be offered for seven years or a little longer. In the rail industry around the world franchise terms vary from one year up to thirty years.

Experience to date indicates that franchisers in some sectors put a high premium on continuity and are happy to roll franchise contracts. Foster has argued that franchise renewal has tended to become automatic, as was generally the case with public utility franchises throughout most of the nineteenth century, and as has been the case with cable television franchises in the United States.[24]

---

[23] See Williamson, loc. cit. n. 16 above: Domberger loc. cit. n. 2 above; Kennedy, *Competition in the British Rail Industry*.

[24] See C. D. Foster, *Privatisation, Public Ownership and the Regulation of Natural Monopoly* (Oxford, 1992), 202; J. Vickers and G. Yarrow, *Privatisation: An Economic Analysis* (1988), 110–15; M. A. Zupan, 'The Efficiency of Franchise Bidding Schemes in the Case of Cable Television' (1989) 32 *J. Law and Econ.* 401.

The ITC Channel 3 franchising system, for instance, gives considerable security to franchise holders. Although a franchisee receives a ten-year contract, one or more applications for a ten-year renewal period may be made during the last four years of the contract and may only be refused by the ITC where the Commission is not satisfied that the licensee would provide a service in compliance with the conditions in the existing licence or with legislative requirements on types of programme to be offered; or where the ITC intends to grant a new licence on the basis of a different regional map or division of the broadcasting clock; or where it appears to the ITC that the franchisee's sources of funds are such that renewal would not be in the public interest. The ITC may, however, fix new financial terms where it grants a renewal—it may thus determine a sum that it considers would have been payable in a cash bid had it been granting a fresh licence under competitive tendering conditions.[25]

In Channel 3 franchising the original idea was to use ten-year contracts and then have new competitions. The decision to move to rolling contracts (taken at Cabinet level) was based partially on the view that controls through the market for corporate control were more appropriate in this sector than controls imposed by the franchiser. Such a strategy places, however, a low priority on enforcement of promises made in franchise applications, on controlling quality of service, and on competition for the market as a provider of incentives to efficiency.

Transfers of the franchise
Two major problems may arise under this heading. First, the franchise may be assigned to another party, second, the ownership of the franchise may change in a substantial manner.[26] On the first issue, transfers are usually not allowed without permission. Thus the ITC, for example, makes it a condition of Regional Channel 3 licences that the licence should not be transferred except with the prior consent in writing of the Commission. London Transport imposes a similar condition upon successful tenderers as does the Radio Authority in relation to ILR franchising. As for changes in the composition of the franchisee, the Radio Authority not only reserves the right to revoke licences on changes occurring which 'affect the nature and characteristics' of the licensee (a power the ITC also possesses) but it also requires prompt notification to the Authority of any change in ownership of shares carrying 30 per cent or more of voting rights.

---

[25] The ITC's proposed method for doing this is set out in ITC, *Channel 3 Licence Renewal: Methodology and Procedure* (London, Jan. 1998).

[26] Windfall gains may give rise to controversy on changes in ownership. In March 1998 the Deputy Prime Minister, John Prescott, criticized the 'excessive profits' made by directors of privatized rail companies and hinted that he was considering ways to curb these. During that month the directors of Great Western Holdings (a franchised operator) were considering selling their business and multi-million pound personal profits for directors were being discussed—see *Financial Times*, 4 Mar. 1998.

Competition for Franchises

Franchise bidders will only undertake to behave in the manner that they would adopt in a competitive market if there is effective competition in the process of allocating franchises. Such competition calls for sufficient numbers of adequately informed parties who are keen to obtain franchises and who are not deterred by undue costs or uncertainties. A good deal has been said above on the uncertainties that flow from problems of specification or from regulatory, governmental, or operational and technical unknowns.[27] A further factor that may affect numbers of competitors in a franchising round is the imposition of a pre-qualification requirement—one that restricts entry into the franchise competition to 'approved' categories.

Pre-assessment may reduce bidding numbers but it can be seen as a means of achieving greater precision in the franchise allocation criteria in so far as all bidders will have passed a worthiness hurdle. Such a process is used to establish bidders' credentials. Only those that can show sound financial backing and an array of skills which appear likely to enable the firm to operate the franchise within the contract specification will be permitted to bid.

A particular worry in utility franchising is that bidding numbers may be so small that real competition is not possible. In London bus franchising, for example, it was quite common for there to be only two or three interested bidders.[28] The National Audit Office has, however, noted that a good level of competition was achieved for the first three passenger rail franchises.[29]

In general terms, the best way to encourage bidders is to reduce the associated uncertainties. The greater the uncertainties felt by potential bidders, the smaller the expected number of bidders will be, the lower the final contract price will be and the more likely it will be that post-contract renegotiation problems will arise. Another key variable determining the number of bidders, as indicated, is the cost of bidding. Typically, bidders will bear their own costs. The more complex the franchising process, the fewer the number of bidders in equilibrium.[30] Actual reckonings of bidding costs are hard to come by, but estimates range from

---

[27] On ITC practice see Section 2 of the Broadcasting Act 1990.

[28] See S. Glaister and M. Beesley, *Bidding for Tendered Bus Routes in London* (mimeo, 1990). In the case of CATV in the United States, the average number of bidders per franchise was four or five (Zupan, loc. cit. n. 24 above). The 1991 Channel 3 television allocation round has been said to have involved aggressive rivalry, with collusion not a problem) but some incumbents were unopposed and some successful bids were notably small, for example, in the case of television areas Central, Scotland, and Border: A. W. Dnes, 'Bidding for Commercial Broadcasting' (1993) 40 *Scottish J. of Pol. Econ.* 104.

[29] See Comptroller and Auditor-General, *Office of Passenger Rail Franchising*.

[30] See M. Canoy and M. Waterson, *Tendering, Auctions and Preparation Costs*, Discussion Paper No. 31, Univ. of Reading (1991).

between US $5 and US $15 (1984 prices) per home served to obtain a cable television franchise.[31] Some Channel 3 television licence bids in the UK in 1991 are said to have cost £1 million.

Enforcement

Holding franchisees to their promises is essential if franchise allocations are to be seen as fair and if the virtues of competing for the market are to be reaped. Since, however, franchise specifications may incorporate flexibility and may grant franchisers a degree of discretion in the enforcement function, franchisers will commonly fulfil regulatory as well as purely enforcement roles. (It was, for example, upon the ITC's insistence in 1993 that the idea of moving News at Ten to 6.30 or 7.00 p.m. was dropped.)

Information

A first aspect of enforcement is the collection of information by the franchiser. Present franchise contracts in the UK radio, television, and transport industries routinely impose conditions concerning the supply of data on issues that are relevant in evaluating the quality of the service delivered and the extent to which promises of performance are being fulfilled.

Monitoring

Franchisers routinely monitor service quality rather than simply trust the data supplied by the franchisee. Thus London Transport engages in comprehensive revenue collection and control monitoring (involving uniformed and plain clothes staff). On-vehicle spot checks are conducted and service performance reporting is continuously carried out. Qualitative appraisals and specific complaints investigations are also conducted and standardized reporting on, for example, accidents and health and safety issues occurs.

In transport franchising, the monitoring of quality might be expected to be less problematic than in some sectors since performance and service quality is to a significant extent measurable in terms of quantitative data (on, for example, volumes, revenues, services not operated, punctuality, lost mileage, and reliability). Some problems have, nevertheless, been encountered. Thus, in February 1988 the National Audit Office (NAO) called on the rail Franchising Director, John O'Brien, to tighten procedures for verifying the train performance information provided by operators. The system under review involved Railtrack collecting much of the relevant data but the NAO stated that the Franchising Director ought

---

[31] M. A. Zupan, 'Non-price Concessions and the Effect of Franchise Bidding Schemes on Cable Company Costs' (1989) 21 *Applied Economics* 305.

to obtain independent auditing and verification of the systems and data involved.[32] Where service quality assessments are more complex and involve the judgements of the franchiser—as in Channel 3 television franchising by the ITC—then in addition to the information collecting and monitoring techniques already described, franchisers may find it useful to carry out more formal periodic reviews.[33]

Sanctions

Presently established franchising schemes give franchisers a number of sanctions for potential use. The following are common:

- powers to give directions;
- notices of non-compliance and warnings;[34]
- regulatory powers;
- fines;[35]
- reductions in the franchise term;
- suspensions;[36]
- revocation.

Franchisers are sometimes alleged by commentators to be in a weak position to sanction franchisees because there is a danger of lack of continuity of service (the 'blank screens' problem).[37] Experience in the broadcasting field indicates that where substitutability is high this problem can be exaggerated. Thus, ITC staff suggest that there would be little danger of blank screens on Channel 3 following a franchise

---

[32] See *Financial Times*, 6 Feb. 1988.

[33] ITC's annual performance reviews (from 1993/4 onwards) are publicly available.

[34] The rail Franchising Director employs a system of warnings. The first stage involves a franchisee being 'called in' to the Director's office to explain a service failure. Three call-ins within a three-year period, or a single, more serious failure, will trigger a 'breach' in the regulations which is then made public and can lead to a penalty being levied. Very serious failures to meet performance targets, know as 'defaults', can lead to the loss of a franchise. In the ten months to February 1998 eleven operators were called in a total of 20 times to explain service failures (compared to five operators being called in 8 times in the previous year). After three call-ins the Director usually negotiates packages of improvements rather than imposes fines. National Express agreed in January 1998 to provide an extra £500,000 of passenger benefits as compensation for missing its deadline on introducing new trains to the Gatwick Express franchise. In March 1997 the Franchising Director threatened to fine South West Trains £1m. if the company failed to satisfy him that the previously encountered level of train cancellations would not recur.

[35] In 1994 Granada Television was fined £500,000 by the ITC. The Rail Regulator has imposed fines on licence holders and employed a 'sliding scale' to punish very poor performance more heavily than performance that has just missed the target—see his Submission to the Department of Trade's 1997 *Review of Utility Regulation*, 4. In the autumn of 1997 the Rail Regulator imposed fines totalling £350,000 on train operators for failing to meet the target for promptly answering calls to the National Rail Enquiry Service. The Rail Regulator has, however, noted that fines, unlike compulsory rebates, do not compensate consumers for poor service delivery.

[36] See Broadcasting Act 1990 S. 110 (1) (c).   [37] See Foster, *Privatisation*, 202.

revocation since present technology would allow programmes from other franchisees to be transferred across to fill gaps. In some sectors potential entrants to the market may be waiting in the wings, eager to show their mettle.

Cross-subsidization

In the absence of problems of overbidding most franchisers do not worry unduly concerning the extent to which a franchisee is fulfilling service promises by effecting cross-subsidies from non-franchised to franchised operations. Franchisers tend to take the view that the relevant markets will regulate the extent of such cross-subsidies quite effectively.

Non-renewal as a control

As noted above, franchisers, when setting the term of the franchise, effect a balance between creating incentives to invest and increasing the enforceability of contracts. The shorter the term, the greater the enforcement leverage becomes (providing that a pool of potential competitors exists and incumbent advantages do not insulate the present franchisee). A cited danger of franchising is a form of capture in which renewals of franchises become automatic (cable television franchises in the USA are cited as an example).[38] Designers of franchising systems might, accordingly, be advised to instruct franchisers to make explicit any undertakings concerning continuity that are relied upon.

Enforcement, regulation, and change

As indicated, bodies such as the ITC and Radio Authority have had to engage in extensive negotiations with franchisees concerning not merely the specification of contractual conditions but also the adaptation of those conditions to changed circumstances. Changes may even necessitate regulatory responses from the franchisers and occur under a number of headings:

The market. This may provide varying degrees of competition for the franchisee and, in turn, the appropriate levels of franchise specification and regulation may change.

Access. If the conditions and prices of access to networks vary over time then the franchiser may have to act to control such variations (if this is possible) or may have to make allowances in holding the franch-isee to promises made in a different context.

Regulatory/governmental changes. Enforcement has to adjust to both changes in demands made of franchisees by regulators and variations in governmental constraints.

Technological changes. These, as noted above, may demand a change of role in the franchiser from enforcer to organizer/regulator in so far as

---

[38] Ibid.

new advances change the nature of operations and have to be responded to in a coordinated fashion.

Legal innovations. New statutes or judicial rulings may alter market and regulatory conditions. Enforcement activity, again, may have to adjust.

Franchisees will often seek to renegotiate contractual terms, fees paid, or subsidies given—because they have overbid, made erroneous calculations, or suffered genuine changes in their costs. In a sector such as rail, where the costs of franchisees are to a large degree a product of regulatory decisions, the case for renegotiating may be strong and relatively easily evaluated. Where costs are market-determined, the franchiser may refuse to make concessions on the grounds that franchisees must bear the risks of miscalculation rather than shift these to taxpayers or consumers.

Interdependency

Enforcing franchisee promises becomes more difficult in so far as the franchisee is not responsible for all aspects of service provision or where service deficiencies flow from the actions of others. Thus, if several franchisees were to run trains on the same track, the trains of efficient operator A might be delayed by the breakdowns of inefficient operator B's trains on the track ahead. (If one franchisee operates all the trains the costs and revenue effects of such breakdowns fall fully on that provider.) Similar problems arise when there is separation of train operation, track, signalling, etc. Franchise contracts in such situations have to provide a complex network of compensatory provisions if all parties in separated operations are to bear the costs of their own failings. The administrative costs associated with such compensation schemes may be considerable.

Enforcement and incentives to efficiency

Franchisers who possess discretion, for example to control price boundaries, may wish to impose incentives to efficiency on franchisees. Thus a system of RPI–X price controls might be adopted with X growing incrementally. This would inject a strong regulatory dimension into franchising and, as noted, would affect bidding. The negative effects of such a pursuit of incentives may, however, be reduced in so far as the limits of such devices are set out clearly in advance (for example, by stipulating a ceiling for X or a maximum increase within a specified period). Franchisees are discouraged not so much by rigour in controls as uncertainty.

As for incentives to invest, these will be greatest where the incumbent enjoys a high level of security in the franchise. If enforcement considerations demand a lack of security because there exist, for example, important variations in service quality, the appropriate response may lie in the approach to separation of the industry that is taken. The solution may be to retain infrastructure provision in one set of hands, organized according to certain timescales, and to franchise out operational matters according to a shorter time frame. This is the strategy seen in rail franchising at present.

Termination and Refranchising

A claimed strength of franchising is that repeating tendering processes can reduce dangers of malperformance.[39] Williamson, however, has argued that the incumbent advantages at refranchising are so considerable that no real competition can take place; that, since both the incumbent and franchiser understand these advantages, the incumbent is afforded a good deal of leeway before the franchiser will terminate the contract for malperformance.[40]

Williamson identified two aspects of termination costs which, he predicted, would lead to contract performance problems. First, psychological costs on the part of publicly accountable officials—who would not want to attract attention to performance problems and so cast doubts on their own roles. Secondly, he pointed to the costs of gathering and interpreting information including auditing costs, together with the expenses of the quasi-judicial hearings and appeals that would need to take place prior to termination. These would provide a disincentive on the part of officials to represent consumers' interests vigorously.

It can be responded, however, that franchisees do bear some potential costs of malperformance. Most utility franchising will involve the franchisee making highly specific investments for which there is a wholly inadequate second-hand market. These investments may be partially stranded by disciplinary actions on the part of the franchiser.

Franchisees do, nevertheless enjoy certain incumbency advantages. Thus, on-the-job experience provides the franchisee with information not available to other (new) bidders. This informational asymmetry also applies between incumbent and franchiser.

In long-term utility franchise contracts the incumbent operator is usually expected to undertake a programme of investment to maintain the long-term viability of the utility. Depreciation methods designed to yield valuations at the end of a franchise period are notoriously difficult to define with exactitude, especially in industries characterized by changing technology, and maintenance expenditure undertaken during contract fulfilment is unobservable and open to manipulation.[41]

Such incumbent advantages obtain both during the term of the franchise and when it comes to franchise renewal. In expectation of these

---

[39] R. Posner, 'The Appropriate Scope of Regulation in the Cable Television Industry' (1972) 3 *Bell J. of Econ.* 98.

[40] Williamson, loc. cit. n. 16 above.   [41] Zupan, loc. cit. n. 31 above.

advantages, bidders will enhance their bids in anticipation of being able to renegotiate the contract once operations are underway. However, as noted above, where a franchisee has more than one franchise, or is interested in acquiring other franchises, it will have horizontal reputational concerns. In industries with a large number of franchises, the evidence suggests that track records are important to franchisers when assessing bids.

At the stage of contract renewal, the incumbent advantage centres on the superior information held by the incumbent and the real advantages associated with learning by doing. The result may be that the level of competition is limited. Where investment is fully transferable, any cost savings resulting from investment by the incumbent are transferred to the replacement operator which leaves the incumbent with insufficient incentive to invest. It then becomes optimal for franchisers to favour incumbents at refranchising so as to improve their incentives to invest.

In addition to the normal requirements for the regulation of a utility, asset valuations must be determined whenever refranchising occurs. Asset valuation problems derive from the inadequacy of formal accounting to provide values that will be accepted by all sides. The root cause of the problem is that information is imperfect and asymmetric, and thus affords the players room to influence the version of 'accounting' reality adopted. Investment in infrastructure and maintenance is not perfectly observable or verifiable and companies' accounts are not designed with franchising and regulation in mind.

Conclusions: Circumstances Favourable to Franchising

We have defined franchising as an arrangement whereby a course of operation is tendered by a franchisee in a competitive context and in which the franchisee bears at least some of both cost and revenue risks. Moreover, the franchiser and franchisee have a continuing relationship, with the former monitoring the latter in respect of quality of performance. The prospect of renewal also acts as a form of control. As a consequence, the franchisee must operate for a finite period—not so long that the present value of any activities after its termination is negligible.

What characteristics of an activity suggest that franchising will produce desired objectives effectively? The above discussion points to the following factors.

Openness to competition for the market. The service in question must be such that a number of firms are available to supply it and thus constitute potential franchisees. Without this characteristic, there will be no prospect of competition for the market. Franchising, accordingly, would not be an option where a proprietary technology necessary to operate the franchise is exclusively available to one firm.

Restrictions on competition in the market. If a franchise is to have any value, it must be possible to impose a limitation on entry by unfranchised rivals.

Duration. The activity must be such that a franchise contract can be formulated for a period of time which allows further competitions for new franchises.

Specification of the service. The activity to be undertaken by the franchisee has to be capable of specification in advance if it is to form the basis of a competitive franchising process. Similarly, the uncertainties attaching to the activity have to be acceptable to those competing for the franchises and must not result in excessive costs to the public purse or excessive prices to consumers. Major uncertainties are likely to relate to markets, access prices, regulatory constraints, and governmental influences. However, the activity need not be fully specified *ex ante*. If the allocation process is to be a multidimensional one, then other aspects, apart from price, need not be fully specified.

Allocation of risks. The contract must allocate cost and revenue risks explicitly between franchisee and franchiser.

Observability. It must be possible for the franchiser, at reasonable cost, to monitor adherence to the franchise agreements in respect of those attributes which are recorded in the contract.

Enforceability. The franchiser must be able to hold franchisees to their promises. This demands that alternative providers be available and can be substituted without unacceptable service interruption or transaction costs.

Transferability of assets. It must be possible for the franchiser to transfer, or to arrange the transfer of, relevant assets to each successive franchisee.

Valuation. In cases where payments are made in respect of the franchise, it must be feasible to establish its value. Monetary transfers may, however, be in either direction and accordingly franchising is quite practicable for loss-making operations, as well as for extracting positive rents.

Market failure. In some areas unconstrained competition may lead to market failure. Franchising may overcome this by appropriate specification of the service.

The case for franchising weakens, and arguments for regulating strengthen, when these preconditions for effective franchising are so poorly established that the benefits of a competition for the market cannot be achieved. In such circumstances the franchiser is likely, in any event, to be forced to adopt strong regulatory methods to achieve its designated objectives.

Combining franchising and regulation, it should be borne in mind, may produce the worst of both worlds. Competing for the market may be pointless where uncertainties exceed a certain level. The effect will be to regulate after selecting the regulatee in a highly inefficient manner. Thus, the unknowns attaching to anticipated regulatory actions may combine with other uncertainties and may distort bids in a way that imposes unacceptably high costs on the public or consumers of services. Under conditions of high uncertainty, the regulation of service providers who are selected by a method other than by competitive bidding may prove more appropriate than franchising.

When should franchising be seen as the first-choice mode of governmental influence? The case for franchising is at its strongest when limitations on market entry are justified and when the above preconditions for successful franchising are encountered. As for types of franchise, the key considerations relevant to the choice of owning versus operating franchises are the following. In favour of an operating franchise it can be noted that the short franchise duration implies frequent rounds of competition and that there should be few problems with asset transfer. Against this, however, operating franchises may involve weak incentives both to look after assets and to choose cost minimizing input combinations.

Factors in favour of ownership franchises are their tendency to promote efficient choices of technique and avoid inefficient modes of production. Counting against ownership franchises are, however, the excessive incumbent advantages that may be found at renewal, the relative infrequency of renewals, and the difficulties of asset valuation. These considerations suggest that, broadly speaking, an operating franchise is likely to be more appropriate when: limited technical choices are available; the franchisee's use of the assets can be monitored, and negligence penalized; idiosyncrasy of assets makes valuation difficult and the activity is relatively unintensive in the use of capital. An ownership franchise, by contrast, is likely to be more desirable when the industry is capital intensive; substantial variation in choice of techniques makes efficient, well-informed investment decisions crucial; and when assets are general purpose, facilitating valuation at franchise termination.

In the right circumstances, franchising is capable both of extracting monopoly profits, otherwise seen in the form of excess returns or inefficiency, and of encouraging the efficient use, and in some cases, the efficient development, of infrastructure.

One of the great merits of franchising is its flexibility, in particular, the ability to match the form and duration of the franchise contract to the particular conditions in operation. As more experience of franchising is accumulated, and as its effects come to be analysed, we anticipate that it will become easier to match the form of franchising with the particular circumstances encountered. Whether franchising is appropriate in any particular set of circumstances will depend on whether the preconditions set out above can be satisfied. It should be emphasized, however, that franchising does not solve at a stroke the difficulties that are commonly associated with traditional command and control styles of regulation (for example, setting appropriate standards, overcoming legal complexities, informational and enforcement issues). In so far as the preconditions for effective franchising do not obtain, any franchising regime employed may rapidly come to manifest the characteristics of less successful versions of command and control regulation.

Turning from the efficient pursuit of legitimate objectives to considerations of accountability, due process, and expertise, it should be noted that franchising regimes are to be judged on these criteria as much as command and control or other regulatory mechanisms. Thus, franchising authorities should be expected to be as accountable as any other regulatory bodies (or Directors General) and the processes whereby the terms of franchises are set and enforced should be designed to be as transparent, accessible, and fair as other regulatory mechanisms. This demands, for instance, adequate disclosures and consultations on draft franchise contracts. (Proper scope for the exercise of expert judgements by franchisers should, however, be allowed within such regimes.) Franchising normally operates as a competition to offer a defined service but resort to a competitive allocative process should not be seen as a substitute for accountability and openness concerning the nature of the service to be offered or the steps taken to ensure delivery.

TABLE 21. *Allocating franchises*

Modes of franchise allocation	Advantages	Problems
Bidding on price per unit	Identifies most efficient producer.	Limited usefulness when variety of products is to be provided.
		Price rigidity may restrict responsiveness to demand and technological change.
Bidding by lump sum	Raises funds for Treasury.	Consumers suffer from inefficiencies of monopolistic pricing and output levels.
		Monopoly rents remain.
		If prices specified in advance, responsiveness will be low.
Bidding for lowest lump sum subsidy	Reduces costs to public purse.	Price specification produces rigidity difficulties.
		Initial controls on price may have to be relaxed in return for higher service quality.
Marginal return bidding	Useful when franchisee erects infrastructure.	Franchisee may enjoy considerable room for manœuvre within the franchise contract.
	Limits cost inflation problems in procurement contracting.	
Menu auctions	Bids can be made on a mix of quality and price.	Identifying winning bid raises contentious issues.
	Renders a stock of private information available for franchiser's use and this reduces uncertainties.	Less transparency than in e.g. price per unit bidding.

TABLE 22. *Franchising problems*

General problem	Particular difficulties
Service specification	Poor specification produces uncertainties which raise costs to consumers.
	Wide service variation makes specification especially difficult.
	If judgements are involved, bureaucrats become judges of market preferences.
	Tension between specification for bidding purposes and catering for flexibility to respond to market demands and changes or technological advances.
	Specifying regulatory regimes and price restrictions for extended periods.
	Stating how risks are allocated.
	Indicating potential exposure to competition.
	Vertical separation increases specification problems.
	Fixing a franchise term that facilitates enforcement but encourages bidding and investment.
Allocating franchises competitively	Is there a pool of potential bidders?
	Will uncertainties deter bidders?
	Collusion and secrecy of bidding.
	Costs of bidding.
	Overbidding to discourage competitors.
	Incumbency advantages.
Enforcement of franchise terms	Information on performance.
	Need to monitor and collect information directly.
	Can sanctions be exercised?
	Tension with need to encourage bidding by giving security and long terms in franchises.
	Distinguishing 'genuine' renegotiations (due to changes in the market) from manipulative franchisee behaviour.
	Where difficult to locate cause of poor performance (e.g. because of interdependency of operations).
Termination and refranchising	Incumbent advantages (e.g. information asymmetry).
	Valuation of assets.
	Creating incentives to invest and maintain long-term viability.

Accountability

Regulatory accountability is particularly important when clear legislative mandates are hard to identify and when the divergent interests of various groups of consumers and producers have to be balanced. Accountability matters all the more when there are fundamental disagreements about the purposes of regulation—whether, for instance, economic efficiency should be the sole aim of utilities regulators or whether social objectives should be taken on board.[1]

This chapter concentrates on the utilities but raises points of relevance to other sectors. The main focus will be the accountability of the regulators and proposals for reform on that front. The direct holding to account of the providers of regulated utility services will, however, also be considered. Questions of due process and fairness, though at points closely linked with issues of accountability, will be examined in Chapter 22.

1. Regulators and their Accountability

In recent years there have been numerous calls for the regulators, and particularly the utilities regulators to be made more accountable.[2] The

---

[1] Compare the efficiency-based approach of C. D. Foster, *Privatisation, Public Ownership and the Regulation of Natural Monopoly* (Oxford, 1992), ch. 9, with the 'social' approach of P. Hain, *Regulating for the Common Good* (London, 1994); or T. Prosser, *Law and the Regulators* (Oxford, 1997), ch. 1, and 'Privatisation, Regulation and Public Services' (1994) 3 *Judicial Review* 3 at 8–17. On accountability generally see A. Ogus, *Regulation: Legal Form and Economic Theory* (Oxford, 1994), ch. 6; Foster, *Privatisation*, ch. 8.2; C. Graham, *Is there a Crisis in Regulatory Accountability?* (London, 1996); N. Lewis, 'Regulating Non-governmental bodies', in J. Jowell and D. Oliver (eds.), *The Changing Constitution* (2nd edn., Oxford, 1989). For recent governmental discussion see the DTI Green Paper, *A Fair Deal for Consumers: Modernising the Framework for Utility Regulation*, Cm. 3898 (London, Mar. 1998) (hereafter DTI Green Paper 1998) and DTI, *A Fair Deal for Consumers: Modernising the Framework for Utility Regulation: The Response to Consultation* (DTI, London, July 1998) (hereafter DTI White Paper 1998).

[2] Suggestion for reform have come from all quarters of the political spectrum—see e.g. C. G. Veljanovski, *The Future of Industry Regulation in the UK* (London, 1993); Adam Smith Institute, *Who Will Regulate the Regulators?* (London, 1992); Hain, *Regulating for the Common Good*; Centre for the Study of Regulated Industries, *Regulating the Utilities: Accountability and Processes* (London, 1994); D. Helm, 'Reforming the Regulatory Frameworks', paper presented to OXERA Conference on Regulatory Reform (17 June 1993); National Consumer Council, *Paying the Price* (London, 1993) and *Regulating the Public*

most forcefully stated concerns and proposals have related to accountability to the following institutions or groups:[3]

- Parliament;
- Government;
- monitoring or appeal bodies;
- super-agencies;
- the judges;
- consumers.

Accountability to Parliament

As seen in Chapter 14, parliamentary control of utilities Directors
General and other regulators is not markedly strong.[4] Ministers do not
tend to answer to Parliament for regulators and, although regulators can
be called before departmentally organized Select Committees of the House
of Commons,[5] their annual reports provide the only regular focus for potential parliamentary scrutiny. Improvements are possible. A number of
commentators have advocated the establishment of a House of Commons
Select Committee on Regulated Industries (or Utilities) to resemble the
former Select Committee on Nationalized Industries.[6] The regulators might
be required to report annually to such a Committee and be examined
publicly. Such scrutiny would enhance democratic accountability and

Utilities (London, 1997); John Baker (National Power), 'Re-think of the Regulator's Role',
Observer, 6 Apr. 1994; Sir Iain Vallance (British Telecom), 'Time is up for this Regime of
Regulators', *Evening Standard*, 10 Mar. 1995; Hansard Society; Confederation of British
Industry, *Regulating the Regulators: A C.B.I. Discussion Paper* (London, Oct. 1996); Report
of the HC Select Committee on Trade and Industry, March 1997; National Audit Office,
*The Work of the Directors General of Telecommunications, Gas Supply, Water Services and
Electricity Supply*, HC 645, Session 1995–6 (London, July 1996). For a general review see
Graham, *Is there a Crisis in Regulatory Accountability?* and for a specific sector A . McHarg,
'Accountability in the Electricity Supply Industry' (1995) 6 *Utilities LR* 34.

[3] For regulators' responses to reform proposals see the submissions to the President of
the Board of Trade's 1997 *Review of Utility Regulation* from the Director General of Water
Services (Sept. 1997); Director General of Telecommunications (Sept. 1997); Director
General of Electricity (Oct. 1997); Director General of Gas Supply (Nov. 1997); and the
Rail Regulator (Oct. 1997). (These Submissions will hereafter be cited as OFWAT, OFTEL,
OFFER, OFGAS, and Rail Regulator Submissions, respectively.) See also OFTEL, *Improving Accountability* (London, 1997). Arrangements for accountability to those regulated may
be met with suspicion by those who fear capture, but they are not unknown in November
1998; Howard Davies of the Financial Services Authority (FSA) said that the FSA was to
set up a practitioners' forum so that it would be accountable to regulatees who would 'tell
us if we are imposing unreasonable burdens', *Financial Times* 11 Nov. 1998.
[4] See the works noted at n. 2 and generally R. Baldwin and C. McCrudden, *Regulation
and Public Law* (London, 1987).
[5] Utilities Directors General have given evidence, for example, to the Trade and Industry Committee; the Employment Committee; the Public Accounts Committee.
[6] See e.g. R. Baldwin, *Regulating the Airlines* (Oxford, 1985), 272–3; Veljanovski, *Future
of Industry Regulation*, 85; Graham, *Is there a Crisis in Regulatory Accountability?*, 45; id.,
'Accountability and the Regulators' (1992) 3 *Utilities LR* 46; P. Hain, 'Regulating for the
Common Good' (1994) 5 *Utilities LR* 90, 93; Baker, loc. cit. n. 2 above; editorial, *Financial
Times*, 10 Mar. 1995; NCC, *Regulating the Public Utilities*, 27.

enable a Select Committee to accumulate regulatory expertise and assist in opening out the regulatory process. It could do so in a more comprehensive, coordinated and consistent approach than is now possible with a number of Select Committees sharing the oversight of regulation. The Director General of Water Services has argued in favour of a Select Committee of both Houses of Parliament with specific responsibility for the water industry.[7] Such a single utility committee would not, however, be so well equipped to draw lessons across sectors as would a Regulated Industries Committee and parliamentary resources might not stretch to dedicated committees for all the important regulated sectors.

Oversight by a general Select Committee on Regulated Industries would operate without imposing a second decision-making layer over and above the regulator (as is the case with an appeals structure). A second voice on regulatory issues would be provided, while second-guessing the regulator would be avoided. It would improve accountability by allowing the regulators to explain their activities to Parliament and the public within an easily identified forum.[8] The potential rigour of scrutiny by Select Committee, should not, however, be exaggerated. Limitations on parliamentary time and Select Committee influence are considerable and such a committee would only be able to investigate particular sectors at relatively infrequent intervals.

A further way to improve periodic parliamentary scrutiny might be provided, it has been said,[9] if regulators were required to submit regular rolling plans of action to ministers who would approve these and draw up appropriate guidelines. Those guidelines would then be subject to parliamentary approval.[10] This system would enhance democratic accountability while avoiding day-to-day Whitehall interference. It would allow regulatory regimes to be assessed against performance targets and would prevent regulators from pursuing their own personal, ideological, or bureaucratic agendas.

There are precedents for ministerial policy guidance systems, most notably encountered in civil aviation regulation in the 1970s and in the railways and environmental fields in the nineties.[11] As experience in

[7] See OFWAT Submission, 14.

[8] See DTI Green Paper 1998, 52, which suggests that Parliament might take further steps to coordinate committees when dealing with regulation. The DTI White Paper 1998, 30, notes, however, 'little support' for a new Select Committee.

[9] See Hain, *Regulating for the Common Good*, 22; NCC, *Regulating the Public Utilities*, 16–19.

[10] See also Chapter 22 below for a discussion of policy statements and the clarification of mandates.

[11] The National Enterprise Board also operated under guidelines—see Industry Act 1975 s. 7 (1). On civil aviation guidance see Baldwin, *Regulating the Airlines*, ch. 14 and P. Reid, 'Regulating Airlines: Why the Arms-Length Approach has Failed', in T. Harrison and J. Gretton (eds.), *Transport UK* (London, 1985). On forms of policy control see R. E. Cushman, *The Independent Regulatory Commissions* (New York, 1941), 730 and on the railways and environmental powers see Railways Act 1993, s. 4 (s) and Environment Act 1995 s. 4 (2)–(9).

the aviation sector showed, however, guidance systems do bring difficulties. Guidance may take so long to develop and agree that it may be out of date by the time it is finalized. It may increase levels of litigation concerning regulators' decisions;[12] uncertainties may result from conflicts between agency and department policies and ministers may use guiding powers to constrain regulators too tightly.

Such difficulties led to the abandonment of the ministerial guidance system for the civil aviation sector in 1980.[13] It was replaced by a statutory requirement that the regulator itself should publish periodic plans. This is not to say, however, that a guidance system, particularly one giving the main drafting role to the regulator, could not be devised to improve both accountability and openness.[14]

The majority of the regulators themselves have recognized the need for democratic decision-making on social issues but have produced different proposals on this front.[15] The Director General of Telecommunications (DGT) has suggested that issues that are properly for Ministers and Parliament to determine include those which relate to social or environmental public policy objectives—'defined as activities which require either a net increase in costs to all consumers taken together and/or some material market distortion away from cost related prices resulting in more customers paying, through higher prices for services, for benefits derived by others'. The Director General of Electricity Supply (DGES) has expressed a similar view[16] as has the Director General of Water Services[17] (DGWS). The Director General of Gas Supply (DGGS), however, argued to the 1997 DTI Review of Utility Regulation that regulation should be confined to economic matters and that a broadening of the remit of regulators might exacerbate concerns over the legitimacy of unelected regulators. The DGGS did not favour any increase in ministerial powers of direction over regulators on the grounds that this might destroy the regulators' independence by effectively subjecting regulatory decisions to day-to-day political pressures or by producing 'backdoor' taxation if the guidance, for instance, called for prices to be raised to protect the environment or subsidize particular groups of consumers.[18]

On how democratically legitimate guidance might be introduced, the DGT has recommended that the telecommunications regulatory regime should be modified to allow a framework for public policy issues to be set periodically by means of a Statutory Instrument made by Ministers

---

[12] See *Laker Airways Ltd* v. *Dept of Trade* [1977] QB 643; *R* v. *Director of Passenger Rail Franchising ex p. Save Our Railways and Others* CA 15 Dec. 1995.

[13] See R. Baldwin, 'A Quango Unleashed: The Abolition of Policy Guidance in Civil Aviation Licensing' (1980) 58 *Pub. Admin.* 287.

[14] See Prosser, *Law and the Regulators*, 294–5.

[15] See OFTEL, OFFER, and OFWAT Submissions.   [16] OFFER Submission, 11.

[17] See OFWAT Submission, 10, though this states that responsibility should be that of ministers, rather than the Government and Parliament.

[18] See OFGAS Submission, 6–7, 22–3.

and subject to affirmative resolution of both Houses of Parliament.[19] Alternatively, it has been suggested, the Secretary of State could have a limited power of licence modification by Statutory Instrument. The DGT would be expected to give published advice on these issues and Ministers would have to bear in mind the constraints on such advice that European regulatory and competition frameworks would impose.

In the water sector, the DGWS has advocated that his legal duties should be extended more generally 'to take into account, in particular the interests of disadvantaged customers'[20] and that he should be required to seek approval from ministers on how to meet these duties. The procedure leading to ministerial decisions, at least on environmental matters, would involve a quadripartite process involving the companies, OFWAT, the quality regulators, and the DoE and would aim at providing Ministers with the full array of relevant information.[21]

In electricity, the DGES has warned that although social objectives should be decided by Government and Parliament,[22] governmental guidance to regulators might bring the Government into central issues of regulatory decision-making and this could be perceived as undermining the independence of the regulator from government.[23]

For its part, the DTI has proposed in its 1998 Green and White Papers that Ministers should issue statutory guidance on social and environmental objectives, including energy efficiency objectives, that are relevant to regulation for each utility sector. Such guidance would not constitute mandatory instruction but regulators would be obliged (as a secondary duty) to have regard to it in the exercise of their functions. It would be subject to 'full consultation, including consultation with Parliament' and would last for a set duration (e.g. the length of a Parliament or the usual duration of a price control period). It remains to be seen whether Parliament will have a power to approve or disapprove such guidance.

In the case of governmental wishes to implement social or environmental measures (including energy efficiency steps) which have 'significant financial implications' for consumers or for regulated companies, the 1998 Papers propose that these should be decided by Government and furthered by primary or secondary legislation rather than through guidance to the regulators.[24] The reasoning was that this would give a higher degree of transparency and predictability together with assurance for investors.

---

[19] OFTEL Submission, 16–17.   [20] OFWAT Submission, 11.

[21] On environmental issues similar arrangements already exist and the regulator receives guidance from the Secretary of State on environmental obligations appropriate for the next periodic price review exchanges between the regulator, the Environment Agency, the industry, and the Government. The Secretary of State gives non-statutory guidance to the regulator which is published.

[22] OFFER Submission, 11–12.   [23] DTI Green Paper 1998, 12–13.

[24] Ibid. 13, this proposal was confirmed in DTI White Paper 1998, 8.

There does seem a strong case for ministerial guidance, subject to approval by Parliament, for all regulators who are asked to pursue social or environmental rather than purely economic objectives. The DGES, Professor Littlechild, point out with some force that tempering economic with 'social' objectives brings the Government more closely into regulation but if elected governments responsible to Parliament do decide that regulators should act to protect certain vulnerable interests, such closer involvement is unavoidable. An approved policy guidance mechanism might provide the mode of influence that best protects regulatory independence and encourages transparency. The use of legislation for measures with significant financial implications might offer more certainty and transparency than is the case with guidance but quantifying 'significant' in this context could itself give rise to difficulties and uncertainties and certain approaches could well negate the value of a guidance system. The danger is that if regulated parties protest loudly and frequently about financial implications, the matters at issue will not be dealt with in guidance. Ministers will find legislating time-consuming and a framework on social and environmental matters will be slow to develop.

Parliament might also speak with a clearer voice concerning the duties of the regulators. In the utilities the Directors General have primary duties—to ensure the financial viability of providing companies to see that reasonable demand is met and to promote competition[25]—and secondary duties to protect the interests of consumers. Some regulators have contended that the precise ordering of duties is irrelevant but the NCC has argued that there is a lack of clarity in the statutory priorities that leaves too much to the regulator's discretion and does not give the consumer interest enough weight. Recent emphasis on competition as an end in itself is said to have produced adverse effects for groups of consumers.[26] The solution favoured by the NCC and echoed in the recommendations of the DGWS, DGT, DGES, Rail Regulator, and DTI Green and White Papers of 1998, is to clarify regulators' duties by making the protection of consumer interests a primary duty.[27] It cannot be expected that Parliament could ever write a blueprint for detailed regulation by means of statements of statutory objectives but it could avoid fundamental confusions concerning priorities.

---

[25] The exact wording and ranking of duties varies in the parent legislation.

[26] NCC, *Regulating the Public Utilities*, 20.

[27] Ibid.; OFWAT Submission, 6, OFTEL Submission, 26, OFFER Submission, 3. Rail Regulator Submission, 2; DTI Green Paper 1998, 14–15; DTI White Paper 1998, 8. The then DGGS, Clare Spottiswode, argued to the 1997 DTI Review that regulation was already directed at consumer protection and a change in statutory duties was unnecessary (OFGAS Submission, 6). The DTI Green Paper states that all other duties should be subject to the single primary duty to protect consumers' interests and that the primary duty should make it clear that where possible the route to consumer protection should lie through promoting effective competition.

Accountability to Government

Policy guidance systems increase regulators' accountability to government as well as to Parliament but a further way to increase accountability to government is to subject new regulatory rules to more rigorous cost-benefit analysis (CBA) to the satisfaction of a central secretariat.[28] As seen in Chapter 7 above, proponents of CBA claim that it increases agency rationality and efficiency, gives greater oversight, improves access to rule-making, and strengthens accountability by making regulatory rule-making more transparent.[29] Sceptics respond that pursuing economic efficiency may be at odds with the distributional concerns of statutory objectives. They contend that CBAs diffuse and weaken accountability; reduce openness and accessibility by translating policy issues into complex technical analyses; are beset with imponderables; are far from value-neutral in the assumptions they make; and are highly prone to manipulation. The primary effect of CBA testing, sceptics contend, is to increase regulators' costs and slow down regulatory processes. Even if there is merely *some* truth in the sceptics' contentions, it is difficult to see CBA as a solution to problems of regulatory accountability.

Governments themselves can, of course, increase the accountability of regulators by instituting governmental reviews of regulation. In June 1997, Mrs Margaret Beckett, the President of the Board of Trade, took such a step when she announced the review of regulation that resulted in the March 1998 Green Paper.[30]

Governments can also hold regulators to account by bringing overt political pressure to bear on them. This can be achieved by making public demands in the media. Thus, in November 1997, the press reported that the Government might force the rail regulator, John Swift, to resign after he refused to publish a league table of train companies which had charged excessive fares.[31] 'Whitehall sources' relayed ministerial anger that Mr Swift had delayed publication of the league table for three months and a representative of the regulator was quoted as indicating that publication was forthcoming. More dramatic still was the departure of the Director General of the Office of the National Lottery, Peter Davies, on 3 February 1997. This followed a libel action between Richard Branson and Guy Snowden, Chairman and Chief Executive of G-Tech Corporation, one of the largest shareholders in National Lottery operator Camelot. The

---

[28] See generally, Chapter 7, above, and T. O. McGarity, *Reinventing Rationality: The Role of Regulatory Analysis in the Federal Bureaucracy* (Cambridge, 1991); R. Baldwin, *Rules and Government* (Oxford, 1995), ch. 7; G. Bryner, *Bureaucratic Discretion* (New York, 1987), chs. 3 and 4; R. Pildes and C. R. Sunstein, 'Reinventing the Regulatory State' (1995) 62 *Univ. of Chicago LR* 1.

[29] See e.g. Bryner, *Bureaucratic Discretion*.

[30] See Mrs Beckett's speech to the Utilities 2000 conference on 30 June 1997.

[31] See *Guardian*, 3 Nov. 1997: 'Rail Regulator Angers Prescott over Excessive Fares Table'. In October 1998, Mr Prescott announced that Mr Swift's contract would not be renewed.

jury in that action decided that Mr Branson had told the truth in stating that Mr Snowden had attempted to bribe him. That finding precipitated a good deal of media criticism of Peter Davis's own performance and the Director General's resignation followed shortly after he was invited to meet with Chris Smith, the Secretary of State for Culture, Media, and Sport. The letter reported that the resignation had been a 'joint decision' between Mr Smith and Mr Davis and had been taken to uphold public confidence in the lottery system. Many media outlets described the event as a sacking.

Finally, the powers that were set down in the Deregulation and Contracting Out Act 1994 should not be forgotten. This Act gave broad ministerial powers to remove certain statutory burdens on business and did so by allocating much criticized 'Henry VIII' powers that allowed such a minister to amend, modify, or repeal primary legislation. This could be done where, in the ministerial opinion, an item of legislation imposed a burden on business and where repeal would not affect necessary protections. Such action could be taken by the minister passing a Statutory Investment and without need for primary legislation (though some scrutiny would be provided by a new select committee, the Deregulation Committee).[32] By the end of 1996, forty-four deregulation measures had been introduced by the Deregulation Unit of the Cabinet.

Regulatory enforcement procedures were also subjected to control by section 5 of the 1994 Act which created ministerial powers to issue orders to regulatory enforcers and agencies requiring them to employ business-friendly enforcement procedures. The effect of this provision was most noticeable in the health and safety, environment, and food safety sectors where revisions of enforcement procedures were carried out so as to give greater priority to the minimization of regulatory costs to business.[33] During the last weeks of the Major Government it became clear that enforcers of regulation were almost universally opposed to the introduction of business-friendly procedures and that there was far from complete support for such procedures from those regulated.[34] The new Labour Government has indicated that it will no longer use section 5 of the 1994 Act but it does favour business-friendly enforcement. The emphasis is now on developing informal links between regulators and businesses and on the use of an informal enforcement concordat.[35]

[32] See C. Harlow and R. Rawlings, *Law and Administration* (2nd edn., London, 1997), 166.

[33] See e.g. Health and Safety Commission, *Enforcement Policy Statement* (London, 1995) Environment Agency, Management Statement OP/OP/008 Version 1 (05/96) Deregulation (Improvement of Enforcement Procedures) (Food Safety Act 1990) Order 1996, SI 1996 No. 1683 (in force 19 July 1996). For discussions see N. Burrows and C. Woolfson, 'Business Friendly Procedures and Enforcement in an Era of Deregulation' (1998, mimeo).

[34] The Deregulation Unit surveyed opinion: 94% of regulators and 30% of the regulated were broadly opposed—see Burrows and Woolfson, loc. cit. n. 33 above.

[35] The Labour Government is committed to developing Local Business Partnerships, to bring together businesses, local authorities, and regulators. The Access Business Group

Accountability to Monitoring or Appeal Bodies

The performance of regulators might be subjected to increased scrutiny by extending the remit of the National Audit Office (NAO). Regulation could then be assessed with regard to procedural outputs (e.g. in consulting, or disclosing information) as well as operational efficiency. The NAO might compare the performance of different regulators, consider the relevance of different performance measures, and encourage consistency of approaches between regulators. Such scrutiny might involve the NAO in more contentious appraisals than are presently conducted but a continuing form of regulatory audit would be provided by such an extension of NAO's remit.

More radical proposals involve extending the role of the Monopolies and Mergers Commission (MMC) to provide more widely available or 'short form' appeals from regulators' decisions.[36] Alternatively, the MMC, rather than the regulator, could decide all utilities licence modifications and adjudicate generally on regulatory disputes.[37] At the moment only a regulated company can appeal against a regulator's decision to the MMC, but in April 1995 the gas regulator, Clare Spottiswode, canvassed the idea that the Government might be given an equivalent power and has seen merit in principle in allowing third party appeals to the MMC.[38]

The Competition Act 1998 strengthens utility regulation by giving the utility regulators concurrent powers with the DGFT to apply the new prohibitions introduced in the Act against cartels, anti-competitive agreements, and abuses of market power. Under the Act an appeal to an independent Competition Commission is possible in the case of many decisions of the DGFT, the DGT, or the regulators relating to the prohibitions established in the Act. Such a right of appeal extends to third parties. The Act also makes it possible for consumers and consumer representatives to challenge decisions made. The Competition Commission will take on the existing functions of the MMC in relation to, for instance, references concerning licence conditions. When exercising the appellate function it will be known as the 'tribunal'. The Act also allows the

has been charged to develop an enforcement concordat and a draft was produced in January 1998. This set down 'Principles of Good Enforcement' under the headings: Standards; Openness; Helpfulness; Complaints; Proportionality; and Consistency. It calls on enforcers *inter alia* to put advice clearly and simply; to confirm this in writing; and to discuss cases with businesses before formal enforcement action is taken. Some regulators fear that, in a continuation of the Conservative deregulation agenda, they will be expected to be business friendly at the expense of consumers or other intended beneficiaries of statutory regimes of regulation—see Burrows and Woolfson, loc. cit. n. 33 above.

[36] See CBI, *Regulating the Regulators*; C. Foster, 'Natural Monopoly Regulation: Is Change Required?', in CRI, *Regulating the Utilities* (London, 1993). See generally: T. Prosser, 'Appealing to the MMC: Or Elsewhere?' (1996) 7 *Utilities LR* 2. Under the Competition Act 1998 the Competition Commission takes over the MMC's functions from April 1999.

[37] Veljanovski, *Future of Industry Regulation*, 84.

[38] See *Financial Times*, 18 Apr. 1995: 'Watchdog Stirs up a Storm over Reform of Regulation', and OFGAS Submission, 34–8.

Competition Commission to review cases on their merits but objectives or parameters are not set for the competition tribunal. Instead the Act gives wide powers to the Competition Commission to set its own rules and regulate itself, subject to the supervision by the Secretary of State. The decisions of the tribunal are subject to appeal to the High Court on points of law and levels of penalties.

Appeals procedures are often viewed as useful safeguards but caveats should be entered. First, appeals mechanisms may increase delays and costs and, as the gas regulator has pointed out, they may weaken the capacity of the first instance decision-maker to make sustainable policies.[39] To allow governmentally instituted appeals might expose regulators to political interference and undermine their authority. Second, a divergence between policies adopted at first instance and on appeal may be produced and lead to confusion, amid the delays and uncertainties of a two-tier process. Third, if appeals involve legalistic arguments before generalist decision-makers, these may prove less timely and less expert than decisions by specialists. Finally, an appeals procedure may not always provide a second opportunity for a fair decision. It may offer an avenue to the 'real' decision-maker that is delayed by a kind of mock examination before the first-instance body.[40] This is especially the case where appeals proliferate. For such reasons the DGWS has argued that if rights of appeal against OFWAT decisions were extended to consumer interests, the right should be limited to regional Customer Service Committees and grounds of appeal should be limited to the DGWS's failure to have proper regard to representations concerning price limits for companies within its remit.

As for extending the MMC role as first instance decision-maker, questions about the MMC's own accountability and transparency may then arise (evidence to the MMC is submitted on a confidential basis and MMC hearings are held in private but reports set out conclusions in full).[41] Appeals, for their faults, at least allow decisions at one level to be tested at another. This would not be the case if regulators' decisions were simply given over to the MMC and specialist regulators became 'at best

[39] See OFGAS Submission, 35. For an example of such incapacitation in 1960s civil aviation regulation, see Baldwin, *Regulating the Airlines*, ch. 4. The DGGS has, as an alternative, suggested that the regulator might be required both to consult parties explicitly on the need to refer a decision to the MMC and to explain the reasons for accepting or rejecting such a request.

[40] Baldwin, *Regulating the Airlines*, 41–7. Helm has argued that the MMC is not appropriate as an appellate body in individual cases—see D. Helm, 'Regulating in the Public Interest', in D. Corry (ed.), *Profiting from the Utilities* (IPPR, London, 1995), 21; see also Prosser, *Law and the Regulators*, 301–3. The DGGS was reported (*Financial Times*, 11 Nov. 1997) as favouring appeals to the MMC but retaining in regulators' hands the discretion to reject or modify MMC rulings 'to protect customers' interest'.

[41] See OFTEL Submission, 30; Rail Regulator Submission, 9; DTI Green Paper 1998, 53–4. In the DTI White Paper 1998, 31, it is argued that the MMC should experiment with the introduction of 'open hearings' into its procedures, and should increase the disclosure of written evidence.

prosecutors'.[42] On a final note, few rights of appeal are provided in monopsonistic sectors such as pharmaceuticals. It can be argued that equivalent rights should apply across regulated sectors, monopsonistic or not.

Accountability to Super-Agencies

Increased accountability for regulators can be established by grouping their activities together and providing for control by the central board of a super-agency. Some commentators from both left and right have argued that the utilities regulators should be amalgamated by sector or even brought together under one roof.[43] This would make officials controlling particular sectors accountable to the single board of a super-agency and would encourage regulators to take account of: similarities in the issues regulated; competition and arbitrage between products such as gas and electricity; and the breakdown of old industry demarcations.[44] Amalgamation would also help to end jurisdictional confusions;[45] promote consistency of policy across sectors; encourage common approaches to such issues as calculating the costs of capital and defining the capital on which returns are calculated; allow industrial policies to be implemented; and bring economies of scale.[46]

The DGES has conceded that there is a case for closer coordination of gas and electricity regulation and perhaps for merging OFFER and

[42] Foster, loc. cit. n. 36 above, 105. See also the arguments of OFGAS (Submission, 36–7) in favour of retaining the regulator's discretion following an MMC reference (the regulator merely has to 'have regard' to the MMC recommendations). The DTI Green Paper 1998, 55–6 canvassed opinion on proposals for (*a*) requiring regulators to consult the MMC on proposed licence modifications (following references to the MMC) before moving to statutory consultation; and (*b*) making MMC recommendations binding but after the MMC has published preliminary findings and invited, and considered, comments on these. The DTI White Paper 1998, 31, reported the Government's intention to legislate to require regulators to gain MMC.

[43] See e.g. Hain, *Regulating for the Common Good*, 23, Veljanovski, *Future of Industry Regulation*, 83.

[44] Veljanovski, *Future of Industry Regulation*, 83; D. Helm, 'Regulating in the Public Interest', presentation to IPRR Conference 'Regulating in the Public Interest', 16 May 1995. Amalgamations of regulatory bodies may thus be advocated on efficiency-enhancing grounds also—see Helm, loc. cit. n. 40 above. On the challenges presented by firms providing services across a number of utilities see the joint paper by the Directors General of Electricity Supply, Gas Supply, Telecommunications, Water Services et al., *Regulatory Issues Associated with Multi-Utilities* (London, 1998) hereafter 'Joint Paper on Multi-Utilities 1998'.

[45] In October 1997 the Rail Regulator, John Swift QC, told the Select Committee on Transport that confusion between his role and that of the Franchising Director often arose and should be ended. The Committee subsequently recommended that a single new strategic railway authority should take over the roles of the Rail Regulator and the Franchising Direction—see HC Select Committee on Transport, *The Proposed Strategic Rail Authority and Railway Regulation* (London, Mar. 1998).

[46] P. Hain, D. Corry, S. Souter, and M. Waterson, *Regulating our Utilities* (IPPR, London, 1994).

OFGAS while the DGGS has advocated early merger.[47] There are increasing interactions between gas and electricity markets; with gas an increasingly important fuel for electricity generation; with many companies aiming to supply in both markets; with 'dual fuel' options being offered to customers; and with the possibility that positions of market dominance in one market may be used to secure advantages in the other.[48] A development manifesting closer coordination was indeed taken in January 1998 when, in an unprecedented joint statement, the DGES and DGGS issued a pronouncement asking the regional electricity companies to stop offering to supply gas to their customers until their own electricity markets were open to competitors.[49] The DTI Green and White Papers of 1998 accepted that the convergence of the electricity and gas markets called for the replacement of the separate regulators with a single energy regulator operating with a single office.[50] It was proposed that the change be made as soon as possible, with interim measures to ensure collaboration. OFTEL, for its part, has recommended that in the new merged world of electronic communications (where the barriers between telecommunications, broadcasting, and information technology activities are falling away ever faster), there is a need to exert control over economic and social issues by means of a single electronic communications regulator if overlaps and convergencies are to be responded to adequately.[51]

One model of umbrella agency—a utilities commission—has been seen as fulfilling a role in overseeing the whole field of utilities regulation. It would comprise a board made up of expert advisers (appointed by the Secretary of State); have powers of scrutiny and subpoena based on those of a Select Committee; supervise individual regulators; advise governments on regulatory policies and strategies; and resolve disputes between regulators and industries.[52]

---

[47] See OFFER Submission, 19–20; OFGAS Submission, 26.

[48] The advent of the super-utility, in the form of the United Utilities Company, combining water, electricity, and telecommunications provision, which commenced operations on 1 Jan. 1996, brings a new urgency to discussions of regulatory coordination—see the Joint Paper on Multi-Utilities 1998, n. 44 above. At OFTEL's public meeting on its future work programme, held on 10 Feb. 1998, Don Cruickshank, the Director-General of OFTEL, stressed that 'mega mergers' between telecoms operators, computer groups, and entertainment and information providers were inevitable, leading to new kinds of companies that were not catered for by existing regulatory regimes.

[49] See *Financial Times*, 22 Jan. 1998; OFGAS later amended its request to allow electricity companies to market gas contracts but not to make 'dual fuel' offers in which electricity and gas prices are tied together—see *Financial Times*, 28 Jan. 1998.

[50] DTI Green Paper 1998, 26; DTI White Paper, 18. See also DTI, *Public Consultation Paper on the Future of Gas and Electricity Regulation* (DTI, London, Sept. 1998).

[51] See OFTEL, *Second Submission to the Culture, Media and Sport Select Committee: Beyond the Telephone, the Television and the PC: Regulation of the Electronic Telecommunications Industry* (London, Mar. 1998). A separate, single, regulator for content and cultural matters is now advocated: the Electronic Communications Standards Authority.

[52] Ibid. In Britain there is no equivalent to the Administrative Conference of the USA in the shape of a body that can take a systematic view of regulatory strategies and procedures.

Alternatively, there seems a strong case for establishing a new, independent body—a standing Regulatory Review Commission—the sole function of which would be to review regulatory strategies and procedures across all sectors. The DGWS has proposed that regulators, as a group, could be required to report annually on the work they do—in order to develop good practice and consistency[53]—but an independent Regulatory Review Commission might take the kind of distanced view of regulation that existing bodies, wedded to particular strategies, cannot and which an umbrella agency involved in regulation itself could not.

The value of umbrella agencies in, say, the energy, communications, financial services, and transport fields, depends to a great degree on the extent of interactions, similarities, and needs to coordinate approaches across sectors. Super-agencies may, however, not be problem free. They may, in broadening their range of activities, produce excessive burdens for their senior staff, and as a result, less effective scrutiny; their size may dilute rather than increase accountability where the focus of that accountability is reduced; they may find it difficult to sustain reputations when increased numbers of regulatory failures flow from increased responsibility; and they may be attacked for excessively concentrating power.[54]

There is no necessary reason why coordination between separate regulators could not produce the consistency of approach that super-agencies would bring and different sectors may be marked by highly specific characteristics that are dealt with by highly focused regulatory institutions. As for the *supervisory* model of agency in particular, this may fall foul of the same criticism that was directed at NEDO's 1976 idea for nationalized industries' policy councils. Objectors then argued that placing a 'buffer' agency between the Minister and a corporation would add a layer of bureaucracy and an extra source of policy confusion and delay, without resolving real tensions between Ministers and agencies.[55]

Accountability to the Judges

The architects of the 1984 Telecommunications Bill have been said to have been determined to keep law and the courts out of the new system of utilities regulation and, to date, British regulators in general have been remarkably free from judicial interventions.[56] This is in spite of the

---

[53] See OFWAT Submission, 15.

[54] See M. Taylor, *Peak Practice: How to Reform the UK's Regulatory System* (Centre for the Study of Financial Innovation No. 23, Reading, 1996).

[55] National Economic Development Office, *A Study of UK Nationalised Industries* (London, 1976).

[56] See Foster, Privatisation, 267. On the courts and regulatory agencies generally see Baldwin and McCrudden, *Regulation and Public Law*, ch. 4; Harlow and Rawlings, *Law and Administration*, ch. 10; and J. Black, P. Muchlinski, and P. Walker, *Commercial Regulation and Judicial Review* (Oxford, 1998).

considerable resources that are possessed by many regulated companies and their competitors as well as the substantial finances that are at stake in regulatory decisions. There may, however, be increasing inclinations to litigate. Calls for more rigorous structuring of regulatory processes and discretions, may, if put into effect, add to the likelihood of litigation and there is pressure within Europe to see court action as a primary means of enforcing rights within regulatory regimes that are covered by European rules.[57] The legal frameworks of the utilities, moreover, do provide lawyers with a high level of involvement in the drawing up of contracts and licences and in interpreting the legal limits of the regulators' powers.[58]

Are the judges willing to scrutinize regulators rigorously? Would this be desirable? On the first point, judges have, on different occasions, shown tendencies both to defer to the expertise and special role of regulators[59] and a willingness to enter into scrutiny in spite of the regulator having argued that judicial intervention was inappropriate.[60] It is clear that the principles of administrative law apply to the activities of regulators and that judicial review will avail in accordance with those principles.[61] Secretaries of State, the MMC, and self-regulators are similarly subject to judicial control.[62] What is less clear is whether the regulated utilities providers, such as British Gas or BT, are liable to review on public law principles. Some commentators have suggested that the courts might be prepared to exert control on 'private' bodies exercising monopoly powers that are conferred by statute[63] and a past Director General of Fair Trading has argued for this approach.[64] European law might also be relevant since those utilities that provide public services under state control and

[57] See Chapter 12 above.

[58] See J. McEldowney, 'Law and Regulation: Current Issues and Future Directions', in M. Bishop, J. Kay, and C. Mayer (eds.), *The Regulatory Challenge* (Oxford, 1995). On the case for controlling regulators' discretions in order to reassure private investors in regulated industries see B. Levy and P. T. Spiller, *Regulations, Institutions and Commitment* (Cambridge, 1996). On why regulatory discretion may not always be undesirable see R. Baldwin and K. Hawkins, 'Discretionary Justice: Davis Reconsidered' [1984] *PL* 570.

[59] See *R* v. *Independent Television Commission, ex p. TSW Broadcasting Ltd* (1992) *Independent*, 27 Mar. 1992. In *R* v. *Secretary of State for Trade and Industry ex p. Lonrho* (1989) 1 WLR 525 Lord Justice Watkins recognized the danger of the court substituting its view for that of the body designated by Parliament as having authority in an area—see McEldowney, loc. cit. n. 58 above.

[60] *Mercury Communications Ltd* v. *Director-General of Telecommunications and Others* (1995) *Financial Times*, 10 Feb. For comment see A. McHarg, 'Regulation as a Private Law Function' [1995] *PL* 539.

[61] See generally P. P. Craig, *Administrative Law* (3rd edn., London, 1994), 239–40.

[62] See *R* v. *Panel on Takeovers and Mergers ex p. Datafin* [1987] 1 QB 815 (applying judicial review to bodies, albeit set up privately, that exercise powers with a 'public' element). See also *R* v. *ICSTIS ex p. Firstcode* 24 Feb. 1993 (Court of Appeal, Lexis, discussed by C. Scott, 'The Juridification of Regulatory Relations in the UK Utilities Sector', in Black et al., *Commercial Regulation*); R. Cranston, 'Reviewing Judicial Review', in G. Richardson and H. Genn (eds.), *Administrative Law and Government Action* (Oxford, 1994); J. Black, 'Constitutionalising Self-Regulation' (1996) 59 *MLR* 24.

[63] Craig, *Administrative Law*, 240.

[64] Sir G. Borrie, 'The Regulation of Public and Private Power' [1989] *PL* 552, 560–1.

have special powers might be regarded as 'emanations of state' and, accordingly, treated as liable, like states, to comply with European law.[65]

An examination of applications for judicial review of regulators' actions in recent years fails to reveal a high level of consistency in judicial approaches.[66] The Divisional Court has generally been disinclined to interfere with regulators' discretions on licence enforcement issues[67] but rulings have been given on the DGES's obligation to make a determination on connection charges.[68] In relation to licence modifications, judicial review has been resorted to as an alternative to the triggering of an MMC review but the Divisional Court has taken a non-interventionist approach.[69] In contrast, the Court of Appeal has at least once overturned the Divisional Court's decision and found a DGES decision not to modify a licence to be based on reasons that were not valid.[70]

Judicial reviews of regulation in certain sectors has been characterized by an express unwillingness to adapt an interventionist position. In relation to franchising by the Independent Television Commission (ITC) Lord Templeman has stressed in the House of Lords that where Parliament has not provided for an appeal mechanism the courts must not invent one.[71] The Divisional Court echoed such an approach when unsuccessful applicants for Channel 5 licences applied for judicial review against the ITC's award decision on the ground that the successful bidder had been allowed unfairly to enhance its bid after the application had been made. The Court stated that the ITC's decisions were not in any sense readily reviewable judicially because 'matters of judgement were entrusted to an expert body by Parliament'.[72] Such decisions are noteworthy as clear examples of institutional deference based on rationales combining mandate and expertise-based arguments.

---

[65] See Case C-188/89 *Foster* v. *British Gas* [1990] ECR 1-3313; C. Scott, 'The Juridification of Regulatory Relations in the UK Utilities Sector', in Black et al., *Commercial Regulation* (hereafter 'Scott'); and L. Woods, 'Quasi-Public Bodies: The European Dimension' (1996) 6 *Utilities LR* 220.

[66] For reviews focusing on particular sectors see Scott (telecommunications) and M. Hopper, 'Financial Services Regulation and Judicial Review: The Fault Lines', in Black et al., *Commercial Regulation*.

[67] See *R* v. *Director General of Telecommunications ex p. Let's Talk (UK) Ltd* QBD 6 Apr. 1992.

[68] *R* v. *Director General of Electricity Supply ex p. Redrow* 21 Feb. 1995 (QBD), discussed Scott.

[69] See *R* v. *Director General of Telecommunications ex p. British Telecommunications Plc, Divisional Court* 20 Dec. 1996 unreported, discussed Scott.

[70] *R* v. *Director General of Electricity ex p. Scottish Power* Court of Appeal 3 Feb. 1997, unofficial transcript, discussed Scott.

[71] See *R* v. *Independent Television Commission ex p. TSW Broadcasting Ltd Independent* 27 Mar. 1992, [1996] EMLR 291; see Prosser, *Law and the Regulators*, ch. 9 and 'The House of Lords and Channel 3 Licences: The TSW Decision' (1992) 3 *Utilities LR* 47–50.

[72] *R* v. *Independent Television Commission ex p. Virgin Television Ltd* [1996] EMLR 318; see Prosser, *Law and the Regulators*, 261.

Consistent with concerns that institutions do not usurp each others' functions are those cases in which the courts have protected regulators from undue political interference. Thus, in the *Skytrain* case involving Laker Airways, the Court of Appeal, in 1977, found that Peter Shore, the Secretary of State for Trade, had acted *ultra vires* in issuing policy guidance to the Civil Aviation Authority, which had the effect of negating Laker's licence to operate Skytrain to New York. Lord Denning found, *inter alia*, that the guidance instructions given to the CAA were too stark or peremptory to constitute guidance—they were more akin to directions but they had not been issued in accordance with the parent statute's provisions for giving directions and the Court was unwilling to see the CAA licensing system overridden by the Secretary of State.[73] The courts, moreover, have continued to police binding policy guidance mechanisms to ensure that, where these are used, regulators act consistently with their terms. Thus, in 1995, the pressure group Save Our Railways argued in the Court of Appeal that the Franchising Director had erred in law by setting minimum service levels (MSLs) on a number of passenger rail franchises that departed substantially from those established by British Rail (BR).[74] Central to the case was the set of Objectives, Instructions, and Guidance that were issued by the Transport Secretary to the Franchising Director in March 1994 under section 5 of the Railways Act 1993. This guidance called for the MSLs stipulated in passenger rail franchises to be 'based on' former levels of BR provision. The Court of Appeal accepted the Save Our Railways arguments and the MSLs had to be redrafted for the franchises at issue.

On the issue of judicial interventionism, it should, finally, be noted that it may be possible to set up certain legal challenges as either commercial issues or matters of judicial review. The key case here was decided in 1995 and involved Mercury Communications Ltd's challenge to the basis of BT's charges to it for interconnection.[75] Mercury attacked OFTEL's interpretation of BT's licence in relation to such charges and might have done so by way of judicial review. Instead, the issue was pursued as a matter of commercial contract. OFTEL and BT sought to have the proceedings struck out on the basis that such an action should have been brought as an application for judicial review and that the procedural protections that judicial review procedures offered to public bodies (for example, on time-limits) would be bypassed if legal action by the commercial route

---

[73] See R. Baldwin, 'A British Independent Regulatory Agency and the "Skytrain" Decision' [1978] *PL* 57.

[74] *R* v. *Director of Passenger Rail Franchising ex p. Save Our Railways* Independent, 20 Dec. 1995, The Times, 18 Dec. 1995. See J. Goh, 'Privatisation of the Railways and Judicial Review' (1996) 7 *Utilities LR* 42–3; Prosser, *Law and the Regulations*, 197.

[75] *Mercury Communications Ltd* v. *Director-General of Telecommunications* HL [1996] IWLR 48; Scott; and see A. McHarg, 'Regulation as a Private Law Function' [1995] *PL* 539.

were to be allowed.[76] The House of Lords, nevertheless, allowed the commercial legal process to be used on the grounds that the substance of the dispute concerned the effect of the terms of a contract. The ruling thus eases the path of those wishing to challenge regulators' decisions (at least where those decisions fall to be considered as collateral issues in determining private law rights). Regulators are, as a result, more exposed to challenge by litigation than formerly—perhaps more exposed than the House of Lords anticipated in the *Mercury* case.[77]

Turning now to whether more activist review would be desirable in the field of regulation, it is necessary, first, to consider the limitations of judicial interventionism.[78] Trial-type procedures are not tailored to the decision of polycentric issues in which judgements have to be made simultaneously on a number of interconnected issues.[79] Nor do trials, which involve sporadic (often unpredictable) sallies that impose high costs on regulators and regulatees, offer ideal conditions for developing regulatory policies. They produce not merely an increase in the judicialization of processes and a greater use of lawyers but defensiveness in regulation and consequently regulatory lag. Judicial review may also distort regulatory processes by inducing a bias towards less reviewable modes of operation. This may be manifest in a movement towards the use of informal pressures and negotiations and may involve a drift towards less transparent and accessible regulatory procedures.[80]

Trial-type processes also involve choices between the arguments of competing parties rather than continuing and rational approaches to the development of strategies for sectors and industries. Judges, moreover, may possess limited expertise in specialist sectors.[81] They may see problems, procedures, and solutions in legalistic terms, and they offer

---

[76] See *O'Reilly* v. *Mackman* [1983] 2 AC 237 on the balance of protections and entitlements in the procedure for applications for judicial review.

[77] See Scott; McHarg, loc. cit. n. 75, 550. On the taking into account of regulatory frameworks when deciding private law issues (and the regulatory impact of this) see Scott, and *Timeload* v. *British Telecommunications Plc* Court of Appeal 30 Nov. 1993 (Lexis).

[78] On judges and regulators see Baldwin and McCrudden, *Regulation and Public Law*, ch. 4; Cranston, loc. cit. n. 62 above; Scott; and on review in the USA see S. Breyer and R. Stewart, *Administrative Law and Regulatory Policy* (3rd edn., Boston, 1992), 363–94; I. Harden and N. Lewis, *The Noble Lie* (London, 1986), 275–8. On British administrative law generally see Craig, *Administrative Law*.

[79] See L. L. Fuller, 'The Forms and Limits of Adjudication' (1978) 92 *Harv. LR* 353; B. B. Boyer, 'Alternatives to Trial-Type Hearings for Resolving Complex Scientific, Economic and Social Issues' (1972) 71 *Mich. LR* 111; J. L. Jowell, *Law and Bureaucracy* (Dunellan, 1975); Baldwin, *Regulating the Airlines*.

[80] For an account of such an effect on a regulatory body see C. McCrudden, 'The Commission for Racial Equality: Formal Investigations in the Shadow of Judicial Review', in Baldwin and McCrudden, *Regulation and Public Law*. On juridification as an inducement to less democratic decision-making see Cranston, loc. cit. n. 62 above, and, more broadly, G. Teubner, 'Juridification—Concepts, Aspects, Solutions', in G. Teubner (ed.), *Juridification of Social Spheres* (Berlin, 1987).

[81] See Baldwin and McCrudden, *Regulation and Public Law*, 63–8.

representation to the parties involved in the court case rather than to the array of parties that stands to be affected by a decision or policy.

Accountability to Consumers

British regulators are obliged to protect the interests of consumers by controlling product standards and prices where the market fails to do this.[82] The interests of different consumer groups may, however, diverge. Where a regulator encourages competition, for example, this may benefit large industrial and commercial customers, who can shop around, but it may prejudice domestic and small business consumers. The increasing emphasis on competition in the utilities tends also to heighten differences between large and small consumers.[83] The consumer voice has been said to be weak in British regulation because information and expertise may be limited and because access to important processes (e.g. licence modification negotiations in the utilities) may be incomplete.[84]

It has been argued, furthermore, that a structurally independent voice for the domestic consumers of each industry is generally absent in British regulation and more organizations modelled on the Gas Consumers' Council should be set up.[85] On this point there are divergent opinions. One school of thought stresses the advantages of consumer committees set up by regulators in so far as they have direct access to the Director General and possess an accepted status within the regulatory scheme. In their submissions to the Review of Utility Regulation of 1997 the DGT, DGES, and DGWS stressed the merits of integrating consumer representation within the regulatory body (as in their own regimes). In favour of such arrangements it is suggested that with integration:

---

[82] On regulators and consumers see M. Purdy and P. Cullum, 'Utility Regulation: A Consumer Perspective' (1997) 8 *Utilities LR* 138; C. Graham, 'Consumers and Privatised Industries' (1992) 3 *Utilities LR* 38; C. Hicks (ed.), *Utilities and their Consumers* (London, 1993).

[83] See NCC, *Regulating the Public Utilities*, 31.

[84] See generally Purdy and Cullum loc. cit. n. 82 above; C. Graham, 'Consumer Bodies: Practice and Performance', in CRI, *Regulatory Review 1996* (London, 1996). For a particular study see OFTEL, *Meeting Customer Needs in Telecoms: The Role of Consumer Representatives* (London, 1996).

[85] See NCC, *Paying the Price*, ch. 9; Purdy and Cullum, loc. cit. n. 82 above; and Graham, *Is there a Crisis in Regulatory Accountability?* Graham points out that utilities regulators have generally sought to consult the consumer interest by a variety of formal and informal procedures (e.g. the Public Utilities Access Forum) but much of this activity is discretionary and consistency of practice is lacking. On arguments for a dedicated Telecommunications Consumer Council see C. Scott, C. Hall, and C. Hood, 'Regulatory Space and Regulatory Reform', in P. Vass (ed.), *CRI Regulatory Review 1997* (London, 1997), 242–4. OFTEL (*Second Submission*, 28) has also argued that in its proposed new scheme for regulating electronic communications there should be a statutory Electronic Communications Consumer Council with its own independent resources and 12–15 members appointed by the Secretary of State following open 'Nolan-type' procedures.

- Consumer complaints and representations feed directly into the regulatory mechanism and inform the DG's policy deliberations.
- Consumer representation assists the monitoring of performance.
- DGs can obtain consumer feedback on any issue very rapidly.
- Consumer committees can advise the DG on policy issues.
- Consumer protection is made part of regulation rather than set up in an antagonistic relationship with the regulator.
- DGs may rely on consumer committees to help implement policies and the taking into account of local issues is facilitated.
- Consumer committees have access to information and expert advice that would not be available otherwise.
- Consumers have better notice of forthcoming developments and policies and this allows feedback at an early date.
- Access to the DG places consumer issues high on the agenda.

The counter-view is that placing the consumer body within the regulatory office potentially compromises its independence; creates a skewed information source; restricts its ability to speak its mind; and makes it unduly dependent on the willingness of the regulator to provide the necessary resources and access.[86] The DTI Green and White Papers of 1998[87] stress the Government's belief that statutory independent consumer councils with their own dedicated staff and resources, defined functions, and rights to information are better placed to argue the consumer's case with authority than are non-independent bodies. Separating consumer representation from the regulatory offices would also, the DTI said, encourage more open debate on regulatory decisions and raise the profile of consumers in the regulatory process. The intention, accordingly, is that independent statutory consumer representative bodies will be established, with rights of access to information held by regulators and regulated companies, that the regulators would have specific duties to consult these bodies, and that consumer representative bodies should advise regulators, handle complaints, disseminate information of interest to consumers, and keep issues of consumer concern under review.[88] There may also be a case for combining utilities consumers' councils. Thus, OFGAS argued to the DTI that, in the light of developing competition in the supply of domestic utility services and the emergence of multi-utilities, there could be advantages in establishing a single statutory

---

[86] The DGWS (OFWAT Submission, 9) suggests that the danger that integration compromises independence is more apparent than real—a sentiment echoed by the DGES (OFFER Submission, 21).

[87] DTI Green Paper 1998, 16–17; DTI White Paper 1998, 9.

[88] Ibid. A further DTI public consultation paper, *Consumer Councils*, was published in Sept. 1998. It detailed the functions, powers, and organization of the utilities consumer councils and invited comment on a number of propositions.

independent Consumers' Council to provide a single focus and consistent form of domestic consumer representation across the utilities.[89] The DTI does not propose a body to cover all the utilities but it is in favour of a single energy consumers' council in line with its proposals to merge gas and electricity regulation.[90]

Suggested ways to improve the consumer voice other than by setting up fully independent bodies include:

• increasing the resources of consumer organizations and the National Consumer Council;

• increasing the extent to which key figures in consumer organizations are appointed by the Secretary of State rather than by the regulator;[91]

• opening access to regulatory processes and increasing the quantity and quality of information available to consumers (on which see Chapter 22);

• giving consumers powers to contest regulators' decisions by instituting references to the MMC on public interest grounds. (The Competition Act gives consumers and consumer representatives the right to challenge the decisions of the DGFT and the DGT, concerning an anti-competitive agreement, cartel, or concerted practice, as well as in the case of alleged abuse of a dominant market position.)

To extend the consumer voice on a generic basis might, however, be to overlook the differences between large and small, or industrial and domestic, consumers. The danger is of strengthening the hand of the powerful at the expense of the weaker, less well-organized consumers. Aware of such dangers, the NCC has argued that the Government should set up independent bodies for each utility sector to represent the interests of domestic and small business consumers, with each consumer body completely independent of the regulator and with sufficient resources to provide information, carry out research, lobby, and handle complaints.[92]

2. The Accountability of Service Providers

It might be argued that the deficiencies of regulator accountability can be remedied by the direct accountability of service providers. Thus, the

[89] OFGAS Submission, 27–8.
[90] DTI Green Paper 1998, para. 3.17; DTI White Paper 1998, 9.
[91] See OFWAT Submission, 8.
[92] See NCC, *Regulating the Public Utilities*, 32 and Purdy and Cullum, loc. cit. n. 82 above, 141.

large utility companies can be said to be held to account by a variety of mechanisms that supplement the regimes of regulation and regulators' accountability that apply in their sectors. Here we review those mechanisms, focusing on accountability to markets and consumers, shareholders and government.

Accountability to Markets and Consumers

Competitive markets for products and services can be expected to control providers and offer a degree of consumer protection.[93] Governments, for their part, can plan and structure those markets by use of competition laws and through the allocation of funds and permissions to enter the market. If competition within the market place is not possible then devices such as franchising can be resorted to so that competition for the market can be used as a substitute for competition within the market (see Chapter 20).

In some sectors, however, it has to be accepted that service or product competition can at best be achieved only partially. In the British utilities, regulators have sought to remove entry barriers and introduce competition as a substitute for regulation in a number of areas (see Chapter 16) but, in a host of market sectors, virtual monopolies of supply remain and are likely to stay in place. Competition has developed through the telecommunications industry and in large parts of the gas and electricity industries but direct competition in water and sewerage has been minimal to date.[94]

Such market weaknesses can be compensated for by regulatory efforts to boost the influence of the consumer voice. Thus, during the 1980s and early 1990s the Government, under the Citizens' Charter programme, imposed duties of compensation on the public utilities and imposed relations between providers and consumers that involved clearer specifications of quasi-contractual or contractual rights and remedies, greater use of performance indicators, and compulsory performance standards set by the regulators.[95] Whether 'charterism' offers an adequate substitute

[93] See C. Scott, 'Privatisation, Control and Accountability', in S. Picciotto, J. McCahery, and C. Scott, *Corporate Control and Accountability* (Oxford, 1993).

[94] See National Audit Office, *The Work of the Directors General of Telecommunications, Gas Supply, Water Services and Electricity Supply*, 5; DTI Green Paper 1998, ch. 4; OFWAT Submission, 22—only one inset appointment was made by the date of the Submission. This contrasts with the OFTEL Submission (p. i), which describes the telecommunications market as 'an increasingly competitive market, not a utility'.

[95] See the Competition and Service (Utilities) Act 1992; Chapter 19 above on quality controls and on the Citizens' Charter; A. Barron and C. Scott, 'The Citizens' Charter Programme' (1992) 55 *MLR* 526; White Paper, *The Citizens Charter: Raising the Standard*, Cm. 1599 (London, 1991); G. Drewry, 'Mr Major's Charter: Empowering the Consumer' [1993] *PL* 248. N. Lewis, 'The Citizens' Charter and Next Steps: A New Way of Governing?' (1993) *Pol. Q.* 316.

for healthy markets or vigorous regulatory mechanisms is, however, a matter subject to considerable doubt.[96]

In such discussions it should not be forgotten that some service providers do themselves take steps to ensure a degree of accountability to consumers. British Telecom (BT), for example, has a Consumer Relations team and has also established consumer liaison panels which are neither research panels nor external consumer or regulatory bodies but are 'forums which enable consumers to participate in corporate decision-making'.[97] The stated aims of such panels are *inter alia* to:[98]

- promote effective two-way communication and feedback between BT and its customers;
- identify and manage consumer issues;
- influence policies, attitudes, and behaviours;
- use feedback to change working practices;
- provide a means whereby the company can listen effectively and objectively to consumers;
- develop a climate where the implications of strategies and decisions for consumers are always given equal consideration with technological and commercial factors;
- maintain the appropriate balance between commercial imperatives and human values.

Recruitment to liaison panels is organized by independent individuals rather than BT but BT does pay the administrative costs. As for the impact of such arrangements, BT claims that panels have made a major contribution to BT policy at all levels, from the siting of the new payphones and dealing with malicious calls to developing policies on the environment and consumers with special needs.

With liaison regimes as outlined, the extent of the influence or accountability that results will depend to a great extent on the information made available to panels, the goodwill of management, and the attention that managers pay to the consumer voice. Where such arrangements work well they achieve a good deal and often do so in areas over which regulators might struggle to exert control.

At a more general level, however, the National Consumer Council (NCC) has complained that consumers and their representative organizations face severe difficulties in obtaining the information necessary both to hold service providers to account and to scrutinize the work of regulators.[99] Information concerning companies' accounts and how they relate to consumer charges is often left out of the consultation documents produced

---

[96] For scepticism concerning the Citizens' Charter see Drewry, loc. cit. n. 95 above.
[97] See BT, *Putting Consumers on the Agenda* (London, 1996), 4.
[98] Ibid.   [99] See NCC, *Regulating the Public Utilities*, 11–13.

by regulators for price reviews, says the NCC.[100] The regulated businesses have to send 'regulatory' accounts to their regulator and these must be publicly available. The non-regulated parent companies also have to publish annual accounts in line with general company law duties. It is, however, extremely difficult to compare the accounts of the regulated businesses with those of parent companies and of associated businesses. This makes it very hard for consumer groups to track the inflows and outflows of money. Such problems are compounded by the convergencies, mergers and takeovers that have served to cloud the financial picture in recent years, especially in the case of the new cross-utility companies. Increasingly complex ownership and accounting arrangements place hurdles in the way of consumer investigations. A further problem is said to be the 'climate of commercial confidentiality' which extends through the utilities and is detrimental to consumer interests. The NCC argues that the regulators should issue clear and public criteria on when commercial confidentiality is justified and that the onus should be on the companies to prove the need for confidentiality and non-disclosure to the public. As for the financial reporting system, the suggestion is that the main governmental departments that oversee regulation, as well as the regulators, should revise the financial reporting rules to ensure that the accounts of the regulated businesses and their parent companies are transparent and comparable.[101]

The DTI does acknowledge the above difficulties and proposes that information on the utilities held by the regulators should be disclosable in line with the Freedom of Information White Paper[102] and that regulators should require monopoly businesses to publish accounts and financial information in a more standardized format. The Government has also indicated that there may be value in taking steps to increase understandings in relation to multi-utilities by seeking ways to apply a common format for regulatory accounts and financial information across the utility sectors.

Accountability to Shareholders

A supposed advantage of privatization is that the managers of service-providing companies will become accountable to their shareholders.[103] Governmental stress on using privatization to create a large class of small shareholders also brings the idea that consumer concerns and interests

---

[100] OFTEL is exempted from this criticism—it publishes more information on BT's financial performance than previously.

[101] Ibid. 13.

[102] See DTI Green Paper 1998, 48–51; DTI White Paper 1998, 26; White Paper, *Your Right to Know*, Cm. 3818 (London, Dec. 1997).

[103] See T. Prosser and C. Graham, 'Privatising Nationalised Industries: Constitutional Issues and New Legal Techniques' (1987) 50 *MLR* 16.

will be recognized by that extensive body of shareholders who also happen to be consumers. A problem with such a vision, however, is that shareholder control over management is subject to a number of limitations familiar in corporate law literature.[104] These tend to be the more serious as the body of shareholders becomes more extended. Such limits on shareholder power flow from restrictions on resources; lack of information concerning managerial policies or actions; limited expertise in the relevant sphere of corporate activity; poor incentives to take action within the company rather than 'exit' from it by selling their shares;[105] and an inability to bring strong pressures or sanctions to bear on corporate managements in the face of considerable directorial power to control general meetings, information supplies, and the proxy machinery for voting.[106]

As for the market for corporate control, this is supposed to act as a control on inefficient managers in so far as the capital markets monitor corporate activity and takeovers and managerial changes will take place where failures to maximize share values and returns to shareholders are identified.[107] Unfortunately, however, a number of factors militate against the effective operation of this market—not least the wide share ownership that has resulted from privatization policies. If such companies are not seen as purely private but are subject to governmental or regulatory constraints, obligations and incentives, the market for corporate control may again be suppressed. Where governments have held 'golden shares' (discussed below) the free transferability of shares within providing companies is compromised and this substitutes negotiations with the Government for the operation of the capital market.

Even if shareholder controls operate efficiently, however, this may not ensure that consumer or public interests will be furthered. A service-providing firm that enjoys a degree of monopoly power may do well for its shareholders whether it satisfies its customers or not. Regulatory accountability through shareholder power is, accordingly, a misguided enterprise unless private shareholder interests are congruent with public interests.

[104] See e.g. V. Finch, 'Company Directors: Who Cares about Skill and Care?' (1992) 55 *MLR* 179 at 180–9; M. Stokes, 'Company Law and Legal Theory', in W. Twining (ed.), *Common Law and Legal Theory* (Oxford, 1986).

[105] On 'exit' from firms see H. G. Manne, 'Mergers and the Market for Corporate Control' (1965) *J. Pol. Econ.* 110, Hetherington, 'When the Sleeper Wakes: Reflections on Corporate Governance and Shareholder Rights' (1979) 8 *Hofstra LR* 183.

[106] See T. Eisenberg, 'Access to the Corporate Proxy Machinery' (1970) 83 *Harv. LR* 1489; P. Davies (ed.), *Gower's Principles of Modern Company Law* (6th edn., London, 1997).

[107] See generally, Stokes, loc. cit. n. 104 above; C. Bradley, 'Corporate Control: Markets and Rules' (1990) 53 *MLR* 170; Franks and C. Mayer, 'Capital Markets and Corporate Control: A Study of France, Germany and the UK' (1990) 10 *Economic Policy* 191. T. Jenkinson and C. Mayer, 'The Assessment: Corporate Governance and Corporate Control' (1993) 8 *Oxford Rev. of Econ. Policy* 1.

One way to link shareholder and consumer interests is, however, provided in the notion of the 'customer corporation'.[108] In such a corporation dividends paid to shareholders are connected with charges to consumers, and there is an alignment of the interests of customers, investors and regulators. Professional managers committed to consumer interest will, it is said, protect consumer interests more effectively than mechanisms of consumer representation allow.

Why, though, would investors want to put money into a company in which consumers' interests come first? The reason, argues John Kay, is that they offer low-risk returns. Investments would be made in an environment containing fewer uncertainties than are found at present —for example relating to the evolution of the relevant regulatory regime —and, as a result, customer corporations could be expected to carry considerably more debt in their balance sheets than do the existing utility-providing companies.[109]

In regulatory terms, a sea-change is allegedly involved in a move to such corporations. Instead of a contest being fought between a consumer-representing regulator and a team of shareholders representing managers, both parties would pursue broadly similar objectives. Regulation would supposedly be more light-handed and better informed than at present and, in addition, it would protect consumer interests while diminishing the need for political second-guessing of managerial decisions.

Residual issues concern the extent to which the hand of regulation really would be lightened in such a system—different classes of consumer interests would still have to be balanced and it could be said that the difference between such a technique and current RPI–X regulation may be undramatic. Regulators would have to produce a formula to link shareholder returns and prices to consumers yet this is already involved, at least implicitly, within RPI–X mechanisms. The anticipated death of adversarial relations between managements and regulators might be said to have been greatly exaggerated.

Accountability to Government

Governments can use residual shareholdings in privatized companies to hold service providers to account but, although the Government possessed minority shareholdings in over thirty companies after the privatizations of the 1980s and 1990s, it was the stated policy not to exercise influence through this mechanism.[110] What the Government did do was retain its right to use such shares to vote against unacceptable takeover bids. A degree of uncertainty, however, surrounded such shareholdings since

---

[108] See J. Kay, 'The Future of UK Utility Regulation', in M. Beesley (ed.), *Regulatory Utilities: A Time for Change?* (London, 1996).
[109] Ibid. 168.   [110] See Prosser and Graham, loc. cit. n. 103 above, 33.

governmental assurances concerning their use were unenforceable and speculation concerning possible governmental interference hung in the air.[111] Virtually all such shares have since been sold off by the Treasury. The vast bulk of retained government shares in BT were sold in 1992–3 and other residual shareholdings were sold off in 1995–6 and 1996–7 to contribute over £1.2 billion to privatization proceeds targets.[112] In later privatizations, such as that of British Gas, no such residual shareholding was provided for.

Resistance to unwanted takeovers might also be achieved by the use of a 'golden share'. This is a special rights redeemable preference share provided for in the articles of association of the company and held by the Government.[113] Certain courses of action are then specified as constituting a variation in the rights of the Special Shareholder and can only be effective with the written consent of the Special Shareholder. This allows controls over shareholdings and such matters as the nationality of senior staff to be exercised. Thus, after the privatizations involving Amersham International, Cable and Wireless, Jaguar and Rolls-Royce, the disposal of a material part of the company (defined as 25 per cent) was deemed to be a variation of rights of the Special Shareholder.[114] As noted above, government shareholdings do constitute a significant impediment to the disciplines of the capital market. The Government does, however, own Special Shares in British Gas, National Grid, National Power, and Powergen (such shares in the regional water and electricity companies expired in March 1995 and the special share in British Telecommunications Plc was redeemed in the autumn of 1997).

Such share ownership can also be used to appoint a Government director to the board of a service provider in order to exert influence and ensure that the firm serves public as well as private interests.[115] Governmentally appointed directors have to date, however, only played a limited role in regulated companies' operations. They are said to have been largely chosen in the past on the basis of external commercial expertise but it has been envisaged that they will discuss company affairs with the Government.[116] The core problem is that present company law restricts the power of a director to act other than in the interests of the

---

[111] Ibid.

[112] See National Audit Office, *Report by the Comptroller and Auditor General: Sales of the Government's Residual Shareholdings* (HC 265, 1996/7) (London, 1997). By 1998 the Government retained only small (*c.* £60m.) residual shareholdings in BT and the Mersey Docks and Harbour Company.

[113] See C. Graham and T. Prosser, 'Golden Shares: Industrial Policy by Stealth?' [1988] *PL* 413. In June 1998 the Government announced that it would hold a golden share on the sale of air traffic control services.

[114] Graham and Prosser, loc. cit. n. 113 above, 414.

[115] See Hain, *Regulating for the Common Good*, 22.

[116] Prosser and Graham, loc. cit. n. 103 above, 34.

company as a whole.[117] Until this position is changed, the government director is perhaps best viewed as, at most, a potential source whereby governments can be supplied with information concerning the providers' operations and as a means of representing governmental views to the board.[118]

A further way in which governments can exercise influence over service providers is through contractual relationships and the exercise of the state's economic power.[119] The Government enjoys some freedom in its contracting practices[120] but European law does exert control over public procurements in certain respects (in an attempt to prevent such practices as discrimination according to nationality) and the Coordination Directives attempt to lay down common procedures.[121] These Directives constrain governments by calling for competitive contracts to be awarded to lowest tenderers and for criteria relevant to awards to be set out openly in contract documentation.[122] Domestic law also places limits on government control by contract.[123] Judicial review will be exercised where administrators stray from awarding contracts on proper commercial grounds[124] and UK law, under European influence, now imposes strict constraints on the range of considerations that public bodies can take into account when awarding contracts.[125] These restrictions do not do away with governmental influence, but they limit the extent to which service providers can be said to be held to account by governments through contractual mechanisms other than those encountered in franchising programmes or imposed through specific contracting-out regimes.[126]

---

[117] See Finch, loc. cit. n. 104 above; *Boulting* v. *Association of Cinematographic, Television and Allied Technicians* [1963] 2 QB 606, 626–7; *Kuwait Asia Bank EC* v. *National Mutual Life Nominees Ltd* [1991] 1 AC 187.

[118] See the Public Accounts Committee's discussion of the role and responsibilities of nominee directors (HC 33, 1985–6) and the Treasury response (Cmnd. 9755, London, 1985–6).

[119] On control through economic power ('dominium') as opposed to influence through legal commands ('imperium') see T. C. Daintith, 'Regulation by Contract: The New Prerogative' (1979) *Curr. Leg. Prob.* 41; T. C. Daintith, 'The Techniques of Government', in J. Jowell and D. Oliver (eds.), *The Changing Constitution* (3rd edn., Oxford, 1994); C. C. Hood, *The Tools of Government* (London, 1983). On government by contract generally see I. Harden, *The Contracting State* (Buckingham, 1992); Prosser and Graham, loc. cit. n. 103 above, 41–9; C. Turpin, *Government Procurements and Contracts* (Harlow, 1989); M. Freedland 'Government by Contract and Public Law' [1994] *PL* 86.

[120] See Daintith, loc. cit. (1979) n. 119 above, 59.

[121] See Craig, *Administrative Law*, 686–9.

[122] See the Public Works Directive 71/305 and the Public Supplies Directive 77/62 as supplemented by Directive 89/665. Directive 90/531 deals specifically with the utilities sector. See also the Public Services Directive 92/50.

[123] See e.g. Craig, *Administrative Law*, ch. 15 and pp. 697–8.

[124] See e.g. *R* v. *Lewisham B.C. ex p. Shell UK Ltd* [1988] 1 All ER 938; *R* v. *Enfield L.B.C. ex p. Unwin* [1989] COD 466; S. Arrowsmith, 'Judicial Review and the Contractual Powers of Public Authorities' (1990) 106 *LQR* 277.

[125] Deregulation and Contracting Out Act 1994. EC Directives on procurement have been given effect to in UK secondary legislation—see e.g. the Public Works Contracts Regulations 1991 and Craig, *Administrative Law*, 687.

[126] On the contracting out of public services see Harden, *The Contracting State*; Craig, *Administrative Law*, 108–13.

Conclusions

Improvements in the accountability of regulators and regulated industries can be suggested—the formation of a Select Committee on Regulated Industries and the issuing of approved guidelines for regulators, for instance, seem sensible steps—but it would be a mistake to assume that any improvement in accountability that can be devised will always be in the public interest. As is usually the case in regulation, trade-offs are at issue. The abilities of regulators to develop and apply their expertise, to operate efficiently in pursuit of their mandate, and to function in a transparent and accessible manner, may all be prejudiced by ill-judged moves to increase accountability. Where, for instance, review procedures allow other institutions (be they ministers, courts, or specialist review bodies) to second-guess regulators, there may be a holding to account but there may also be: decisions by officials who are less expert than the specialist regulators being reviewed; duplications and confusions of policy; delays in processes; and the removal of real decision-making power to bodies less transparent and accessible in their operations than those under review.

Accountability in regulated industries will continue to be a focal issue—too many competing interests are at stake for the topic to drift off-stage. The trick for reformers will be to devise and implement improvements in accountability that are consistent with overall gains in legitimacy.

Procedures and Fairness

To claim that a regulator's procedures are appropriate and fair is to claim a number of things.[1] A first matter that may be referred to is the quality of the processes used to make policies, rules, or decisions. In evaluating these processes, questions fall to be asked about their openness, transparency, and accessibility to various groupings or individuals. In contrast with such purely procedural concerns, a second relevant matter is the quality of outcomes of regulatory procedures and whether the actual policies, rules, and decisions that regulators arrive at are coherent, intelligible, and fair between different parties. This second issue thus relates to the substantive dimension of fairness.

This chapter begins with the first set of issues and reviews a number of proposals designed to improve openness, transparency, and accessibility. (Again, the utilities will provide a central focus.) The second part of the chapter considers the quality of outcomes and suggested reforms on that front.

1. Procedural Fairness

As with accountability, it is especially important for regulators to be able to legitimate themselves with strong claims to operate fair procedures when there are uncertainties about mandates and regulatory ends.[2] In recent years, however, British utilities regulators, in particular, have been heavily criticized with regard to their procedures and one commentator has suggested that many participants in regulatory processes 'feel they

---

[1] On fair procedures generally see D. Galligan, *Due Process and Fair Procedures* (Oxford, 1996), esp. ch. 1, and for recent governmental views, DTI, *A Fair Deal for Consumers: Modernising the Framework for Utility Regulation*, Green Paper, Cm. 3898 (London, Mar. 1998) (hereafter DTI Green Paper 1998); DTI, A Fair Deal for Consumers: *Modernising the Framework for Utility Regulation: The Response to Consultation* (DTI, London, July 1998) (hereafter DTI White Paper 1998).

[2] For regulators' views on their own processes see the Submissions to the President of the Board of Trade's *Review of Utility Regulation* from the Directors General of Water, Telecommunications, Gas Supply and Electricity Supply dated September, September, and October 1997 respectively (hereafter referred to as OFWAT, OFTEL, OFGAS and OFFER Submissions).

are subject to the justice of a kangaroo court'.[3] Proposals for regulatory change have addressed concerns on a number of fronts and consideration of these may be of relevance to sectors beyond the utilities.

Reason-giving

It has been argued that regulators should have a legal duty publicly to state their reasons for major decisions—for instance on licence modifications.[4] In combination with published strategic plans, reason-giving is likely to render actions more intelligible to affected parties than would otherwise be the case. Such reason-giving does not, moreover, have to be legalistic in nature or set precedents in stone. Its purpose can be seen as explaining and rationalizing regulation.

Thus, there is a case in, say, price reviews,[5] for imposing duties on regulators to publish:

- the criteria upon which the review is based;
- the options under consideration;
- the anticipated consequences for various types of affected party (e.g. domestic consumers);
- adequate data to allow informed comment;
- detailed reasons for the decision;
- the conclusions of reviews of the social obligations attached to suppliers of services.

In evaluating proposals on reason-giving it should be borne in mind, however, that utilities regulators publish reasons widely on a voluntary basis[6] and that placing legal procedural requirements upon regulators may not only increase costs and delays within the regulatory process, but may also involve a shift in power away from regulators. Procedural requirements may make it more easy to mount legal challenges to regulators' actions and may make regulators more vulnerable to capture by those who are adept at manipulating such challenges. The effective pursuit of legitimate regulatory objectives may have to be traded off against the more effective protection of regulatee and consumer interests.

---

[3] C. G. Veljanovski, *The Future of Industry Regulation in the UK* (London, 1993), 81.

[4] See e.g. ibid. 84; DTI Green Paper 1998, 47–8; DTI White Paper 1998, 25. The utilities statutes call for reasons for *proposed* modifications to be given to affected parties but there is no duty to give reasons for decisions after representations on a proposal have been made and considered—see e.g. Telecommunications Act 1984, s. 12; Gas Act 1986, s. 23; Electricity Act 1989, s. 11; Water Act 1989, s. 15. The courts have recently shown a greater willingness to imply a duty to give reasons: see *R* v. *Secretary of State for the Home Department ex p. Doody* [1994] 1 AC 531.

[5] See National Consumer Council (NCC), *Paying the Price* (London, 1993) and NCC, *Regulating the Public Utilities* (London, 1997), 8–15. The DTI Green Paper 1998, 47, proposes a requirement to give reasons for 'key decisions'—'which will need to be defined' but would include decisions on price reviews and new service standards.

[6] See e.g. OFTEL Submission ch. 5; OFWAT Submission, 16.

Openness of reasoning can also be enhanced, suggest some commentators, by taking regulatory decisions away from the first regulator for
determination before an independent body—for example the Monopolies
and Mergers Commission (MMC).[7] Within such a process the regulator
would have to make out a case in public before such a body and would have
to engage in open justification of its position or proposals. Questions might
then arise, however, concerning the openness and accountability of the
MMC itself; the potential of such a system to duplicate bureaucracies
and create confusions and conflicts of policy; the delay and expense involved; and the demotion of the specialist regulator in favour of decision-
making by a less expert, more generalist body.[8]

Information Disclosure

At present it is often said to be unclear why some regulators are acting
in a particular manner or how they see the arguments or select and weigh
evidence. More open access, it is urged in many quarters, is needed in
the form of new rules on disclosure. Greater use of open committees and
public hearings to consider evidence and arguments, and granting to
consumers, competitors, and affected parties greater rights of participation in regulatory policy and decision-making are suggested means of
improving access.[9] On disclosure, there do seem strong arguments in principle for maximizing access to the information that is held by regulators.
Local authorities, after all, have been subjected to extensive disclosure
rules[10] and regulators, it has been said,[11] could publish, or make available, *inter alia*:

---

[7] See Veljanovski, *Future of Industry Regulation*, 258–9.   [8] See also Chapter 21.

[9] See J. Baker (National Power), 'Re-think of the Regulator's Role', *Observer*, 6 Apr. 1994;
Sir I. Vallance (British Telecom), 'Time is up for this Regime of Regulators', *Evening Standard*,
10 Mar. 1995; Veljanovski, *Future of Industry Regulation*; NCC, *Paying the Price*. (OFTEL
and OFGAS do hold workshops, seminars, and other meetings to discuss policy—these
are not formal public meetings but do offer access to representatives of some sectors of
the public.) The Competition and Services (Utilities) Act 1992 does provide statutory consultation and publication procedures on certain issues in the Telecommunications, Gas,
Electricity, and Water industries, notably: when Directors General make regulations setting standards of performance, when complaints procedures are established by operators,
and when ministers draw up regulations on billing disputes. For a regulator's view see
John Swift QC, 'Transparency, Consistency, and Predictability as Regulatory Objectives',
in C. McCrudden (ed.), *Regulation and Deregulation* (Oxford, 1999).

[10] See Local Government (Access to Information) Act 1985.

[11] NCC, *Paying the Price*, 111–12 and M. Purdy and P. Cullum, 'Utility Regulation:
A Consumer Perspective' (1997) 8 *Utilities LR* 138. It should be noted that the utilities
regulators do take some voluntary, though not necessarily uniform, steps to disclose
material: general practice (led by OFTEL) involves disclosing responses to consultation
documents (unless authors stipulate otherwise) and the DGWS publishes letters to the finance and regulatory directors of the water companies—see C. Graham, *Is there a Crisis in
Regulatory Accountability?* (London, 1996).

- information on trends in average household bills;
- estimates of the impact on different groups of policy changes or decisions;
- explanations of discrepancies in trends between different industries;
- letters to operating companies of a non-commercially confidential nature (OFWAT has provided a lead in this area);
- information allowing consumers to compare the performances of different companies on price and quality of services;[12]
- comparative information on a cross-utility basis on issues arising generally (e.g. on customer care complaints handling, and billing arrangements).

The utilities regulators have made considerable advances on disclosure in recent years and have endorsed policies favouring openness.[13] Current powers, however, do not allow maximum disclosure. Thus, the DGT cannot disclose commercially confidential information to other regulators, such as the Independent Television Commission, and the Telecommunications Act is silent on the publication of information in the interests of competition. The DGT, accordingly, has called for legal changes and endorsed the view that the more market power a player has, the higher the hurdle should be before publication is disallowed.[14] On the burden of proving the need to keep information confidential, the DGGS has argued that this should be reversed so that the regulated firm has to substantiate why there is such a need.[15]

In electricity, the DGES does not have the power to disclose, without consent, information on particular business for the purposes of giving reasons for decisions and the DGES's duty[16] to supply information for the benefit of customers excludes commercially confidential information and is not mirrored by a duty to inform other parties such as potential market entrants, investors, or commentators. The DGES has suggested that reforms on these fronts might be considered.[17]

As for consumer access to information, the NCC has argued that consumer bodies should have a legal right of access to regulatory and to company information.[18] Alongside this right should be legal standing, says the

[12] A point now accepted at the governmental level. The DTI expects regulators to require financial information in a more standardized format that will facilitate consumer understanding and comparisons (White Paper 1998, 27).

[13] See e.g. OFTEL Submission, 27–33 and *Consultation Procedures and Transparency* (London, 1995); National Audit Office, *The Work of the Directors General of Telecommunications, Gas Supply, Water Services and Electricity Supply* (HC 645, Session 1995–6) (London, 1996) (hereafter NAO Report), 64; T. Prosser, *Law and the Regulators* (Oxford, 1997), ch. 3.

[14] See OFTEL Submission, 31; the Competition Act 1998 allows publication of information unless this will cause 'significant harm'.

[15] See OFGAS Submission, 32.   [16] Electricity Act 1989, s. 48.

[17] OFTEL Submission, 24. OFWAT takes the view that the burden of proof should rest on those arguing for restrictions on disclosure (OFWAT Submission, 17).

[18] NCC, *Regulating the Public Utilities*, 33.

NCC, to make representations to government, regulators, and companies. Given that issues of confidentiality could be dealt with, there seems no strong case for denying such entry into regulatory processes or data to consumer bodies, and restricting the right of access to particular designated organizations would do much to counter claims that excessive or vexatious intrusions would result.

The proposal placed on the table by the DTI is that records and information on the utilities held by regulators should be disclosable in line with the Freedom of Information White Paper[19] unless the company involved can demonstrate that disclosure will cause 'substantial harm'.

Trials and Public Hearings

The potential use of public hearings, or even trial-type procedures, in British regulation is an issue that has been considered in recent years by regulators as well as politicians, pressure groups, and other commentators.[20] The legitimacy of regulatory decisions, it is stated by advocates of reform, would be increased by processes involving participation by affected interests, the giving of reasons and explanations, and raising the potential for judicial review. Openness in such forms offers a response, moreover, to criticisms of over-personalization in regulation. At present the utilities regulators employ public hearings to canvass views (these were pioneered by OFTEL[21]) but the movement towards formal, trial-type procedures has not been made.

Prosser has suggested that thought should be given across the utilities to the use of Civil Aviation Authority style trial-type hearings and to *ex parte* rules that restrict communications from government to regulators.[22] (The reasoning here is that if formal guidance is given to regulators by governments—a step Prosser favours—there is little justification for less formal contacts.)

---

[19] DTI Green Paper 1998, 48; DTI White Paper 1998, 26; White Paper, *Your Right to Know*, Cm. 3818 (London, Dec. 1997).

[20] See e.g. Prosser, *Law and the Regulators*, 296. On 1 May 1995, Shadow Chancellor Gordon Brown stated that Labour wanted 'public hearings on prices, service standards and profits before price decisions are made'—for comment see *Financial Times* leader, 'Labours of the Market', 2 May 1995. In October 1993 OFTEL led the way and conducted an 'Industry Workshop' for consulting on interconnection—this was not a formal public hearing but was a movement in that direction—see C. Scott, (1994) *Utilities LR* 53.

[21] See OFTEL Submission, 29. The first OFTEL public hearing was in November 1995 and concerned a proposed variation of British Telecom's licence to prohibit anti-competitive practices; hearings on the price control review followed in April and May 1996. In a more ambitious effort to increase transparency, OFTEL held an open meeting on its future work programme at King's College London on 10 Feb. 1998. The Rail Regulator has made extensive use of hearings in approving access agreements but these have not been open to the public and transcripts are unpublished—see Submission to *Review of Utility Regulation* 1997 pp. 5–6.

[22] See Prosser, *Law and the Regulators*, chs. 8 and 10 and R. Baldwin, *Regulating the Airlines* (Oxford, 1985).

That trial-type hearings have their limitations has, however, been shown by experience in the USA,[23] where critics have stressed that trials are poor at dealing with multifaceted, polycentric, issues;[24] that the independence of decision-making necessary to give legitimacy to trials is difficult to reconcile with the governmental influence that almost inevitably impinges upon regulatory activity; that systems of precedent may prove unduly restrictive in times of market change; that issues may not recur frequently enough to allow general rules to be applied in trials; that disputes may arise from restrictions on access to trials; and that trials can prove slow and expensive modes of decision-making.[25]

The Civil Aviation Authority experience has shown that trial-type procedures can serve useful regulatory purposes, notably in improving openness,[26] but it cannot be assumed that in all regulated sectors the conditions for successful trial use will be found. (In some sectors, for instance, issues will not recur with a sufficient frequency or similarity of components as to allow systems of precedent or guiding rules to be developed.)

Trials may have a role in regulation but they are not the best way to improve access to consumers and competitors in all contexts. Different kinds of tailor-made hearings may, however, combine breadth of access with effective evidence collection and lay the basis for policy-making. An increased role for inquiry-types of process and a flexibility of procedural design thus seem ways forward.

Rules on Rules

An alternative to the inquiry-type of process can be offered by the use of statutory rule-making processes—perhaps modelled on the 'notice and comment' procedures contained in the US Administrative Procedure Act 1946.[27] Such procedures would, on designated topics, involve the regulator in: giving notice of the proposed rule in a national register; allowing an opportunity to interested persons to comment in writing; issuing a statement setting out the basis and purpose of the rules; and providing a period of post-promulgation delay before rules are effective.

Such requirements might enhance regulators' claims to be acting with (and to be bound to act with) proper fairness and accountability. Issues

[23] See C. Foster, 'The Future of Regulation' (1993) *Utilities LR* 110.

[24] On the limits of trials and polycentricity see e.g. L. L. Fuller, 'The Forms and Limits of Adjudication' (1978) 92 *Harv. LR* 353; B. Boyer, 'Alternatives to Trial-Type Hearings for Resolving Complex, Scientific, Economic and Social Issues' (1972) 71 *Mich. LR* 111; J. L. Jowell, *Law and Bureaucracy* (Dunellan, 1975); Baldwin, *Regulating the Airlines*.

[25] See the comments to this effect of the Rail Regulator: Submission to *Review of Utility Regulation* 1997, 6.

[26] See Baldwin, *Regulating the Airlines*; Prosser, *Law and the Regulators*, ch. 8.

[27] Section 553—see S. Breyer and R. Stewart, *Administrative Law and Regulatory Policy* (3rd edn., Boston, 1992), 536–648; G. Bryner, *Bureaucratic Discretion* (New York, 1987), ch. 2; I. Harden and N. Lewis, *The Noble Lie* (London, 1986), 235–7, 275–7.

would arise as to the rules to be covered by such processes; the definition of exemptions from notice and comment procedure;[28] the distinction
between rules and decisions; the dangers of legalism and defensiveness;
and the prospect of regulatory biases in favour of well-organized parties
who are adept at working with such procedures. These difficulties are
not, however, insurmountable and, on balance, there does seem a case
for notice and comment requirements being applied at least to certain
types of major regulatory rule.

At present, the utilities statutes require that regulators who intend to
modify licences: give reasons for the proposed modification; specify a period
(of at least 28 days) for making representations or objections; and consider any representations or objections. In contrast to the position in US
law, British utilities statutes do not, however, demand that regulators
give reasons for modifications *after* representations and objections have
been considered.[29] The force behind the requirement to consider is thus
less than it might be.

It would be unfair to accuse British regulators of an unwillingness to
open out their procedures. The first Director General of Telecommunications promised openness in his first Annual Report and, in many
respects, his successor Don Cruickshank offered a lead to other regulators, not to say bureaucrats generally.[30] Thus, in the telecommunications
sector the Director General has issued consultation documents; invited
representations on these; called meetings of representatives from industry and other groups; made public the representations made; and published his advice to the Secretary of State. A site on the World Wide Web
has set out consultative documents, responses to these, and other information. An annual operating plan has been published since 1995 disclosing objectives, priorities, and a work programme and this has been
said to resemble a US-style annual regulatory plan.[31]

As for notice and comment rule-making, the telecommunications price
review of 1995–6 did operate along such lines with an initial sixty-eight-
page consultation document, a two-month period for comments, a second
(ninety-page) document setting down proposals on the price formula and
responding to comments, and a further consultation period followed by
two weeks for comments on submissions made. Five open hearings were
also held on the price review with opening statements from OFTEL, British
Telecom, other suppliers, and consumer organizations as well as comments
from the floor. A summary record of the hearings was published as an
annex to the next consultation document upon which further comments
and submissions were invited before final proposals were put to BT.[32]

[28] Which include, in the USA, general statements of policy.
[29] See Telecommunications Act 1984, s. 12; Gas Act 1986, s. 23; Electricity Act 1989,
s. 11; Water Act 1989, s. 15.
[30] See Prosser, *Law and the Regulators*, 83–6 and OFTEL Submission, 29–34.
[31] Prosser, *Law and the Regulators*, 84.   [32] Ibid. 85.

The procedure has been replicated by OFTEL on other topics but it is important to note that much of what OFTEL does to enhance transparency is done on a voluntary basis and it cannot be assumed that this will be replicated in all regulatory sectors or even sustained under all Directors General.

The DTI argued in 1998 that a greater degree of formality should be introduced into regulatory procedures and proposed that each utility regulator should be placed under a statutory duty to consult on and then to publish and follow a code of practice governing their consultation and decision-making processes.[33] Such codes of practice, it was envisaged, would cover consultation on forward priorities, procedures, and timetables or taking key decisions, the publication of decision-making criteria, arrangements for third party representations, the use of hearings, and various ways of offering views to regulators.

Even if statutory structuring of processes is not forthcoming, an option for regulators in a wide variety of sectors is to come together, voluntarily or in a manner coordinated by government, and undertake to apply a shared and clear set of procedures to common contexts and issues.[34] Such procedures, again, might be employed to create opportunities for third parties, consumer bodies, and others to make their views known.[35] The virtue of voluntary guidelines would lie in enhancing access to regulation and countering charges of 'personalized' processes, without running into the greatest dangers of legalism. The counter-argument is that, without statutory structuring, transparency (and coordination on transparency) may depend on the approaches of the individuals in post as Directors General. It may be feared that not all of these will share the enthusiasm for transparency demonstrated by Don Cruickshank, when DGT, and that some may see their sectors as having characteristics that do not allow the adoption of a standardized procedure.

2. *Substantive Fairness*

It is difficult to claim to be operating procedures consistent with satisfactory outcomes if there is a lack of clarity concerning the objectives of

---

[33] DTI Green Paper 1998, 47; DTI White Paper 1998, 25.

[34] The NCC has argued (NCC, *Regulating the Public Utilities*, 22–5) that 'the government should formulate a common framework of principles and rules for regulatory processes, following public consultation'.

[35] The NCC (*Regulating the Public Utilities*) urges that common procedures should flow from a governmentally imposed duty for regulators to carry our public consultations before taking decisions and that the procedures should involve: consulting consumer organizations at an early stage, and during the consultation process as a whole; producing plain-language consultation documents; statements about impacts on consumers; proper time for consumer responses; public availability of background information; public availability of all responses to consultations and criteria governing exemptions for confidentiality; and supply of details of the outcome of consultation to all who have participated.

regulation, or if procedures tend to produce vacillations and inconsistencies of policies; or if the procedures used seem to allow interference, capriciousness, or personal whims to intrude. The proposals under consideration in this section seek to deal with these problems.

Regulatory Objectives and Guidelines

One way to make the meaning of statutory mandates more clear and to set out the social as well as the efficiency objectives of regulators, comes via the production of guidelines and objectives. There are a number of ways to do this. First, the regulators may, themselves, publish statements setting out their visions of their objectives. In some sectors (e.g. water and telecommunications) the DGs have already moved in this direction from their own accord and the Civil Aviation Authority publishes policy statements under a statutory duty.[36] Such arrangements may, again, depend on the goodwill or philosophy of the individual Director General and cannot be assumed to last over time or new appointments.[37] The DTI, in its Green and White Papers of 1998, stops short of advocating mandatory publication of plans.[38] It argues that the predictability of regulation could be improved by regulators consulting on and publishing work programmes and priorities for a period of perhaps three years and expects regulators to engage in such consultation and publication of programmes.

Regulators' own visions of their mandates have little democratic authority in themselves, since they are produced by unelected individuals. A second mode of producing guidelines does, however, address this point. Thus, as noted in Chapter 21, it has been suggested that regulators should be required to submit rolling plans of action to Ministers who would approve these and draw up appropriate guidelines which would then be subjected to a process of parliamentary approval.[39]

The strengths and weaknesses of ministerial policy guidance systems were noted in the last chapter and will not be repeated here. It should be stressed, however, that if it is seen as particularly important to set down the social objectives of regulators and to make it clear that regulators are to pursue more than efficiency-enhancing ends, the case for democratically legitimate guidelines may be difficult to counter. Recent

[36] See Civil Aviation Act 1982 s. 69 as amended by the Licensing of Air Carriers Regs. SI 2992/1992. The most recent statement was issued in May 1993—see Prosser, *Law and the Regulators*, 231–2.

[37] See Prosser, *Law and the Regulators*, 84–5 on the part played by Director General Don Cruickshank in rendering OFTEL procedures transparent.

[38] DTI Green Paper 1998, 47 and proposal 7.4; DTI White Paper 1998, 25.

[39] P. Hain, *Regulating for the Common Good* (London, 1994), 22; Prosser, *Law and the Regulators*, 294–8; D. Corry, D. Souter, and M. Waterson, *Regulating Our Utilities* (IPPR, London, 1994), 80; A. McHarg, 'Accountability in the Electricity Supply Industry' (1995) 6 *Utilities LR* 34.

precedents for the use of guidelines are to be found in the rail and environmental fields[40] and broad support for such a development seems, moreover, to be growing not merely on the part of academic commentators but also from within the Government,[41] the Confederation of British Industry,[42] consumer organizations,[43] and the body of regulators.[44]

Consistency and Predictability: From Personal to Collegiate Regulation

Regulatory uncertainty tends to provoke strong attacks from shareholders, managers, and potential entrants to regulated industries. These parties place a high premium on being able to plan investments and predict developments and regulators themselves have stressed the value of stability. Thus the Director General of Telecommunications has argued for the continued institutional independence of his office on the basis that this conduces to the 'secure climate' which is necessary for ongoing shareholder investment and, in turn, better service quality, value for money, and choice for consumers.[45] In early March 1995, the electricity regulator, Stephen Littlechild, came under heavy media fire after deciding to reopen the regional electricity companies' pricing formula, which had been expected to run for five years, and had been set only months before in August 1994. He took such steps because Northern Electricity's response to a hostile takeover bid from Trafalgar House made manifest the excessive generosity to shareholders that was built into the 1994 formula. His action was not the only interim adjustment carried out by regulators. There has been a tendency across regulated industries to shorten intervals between reviews and extend the scope and complexity of pricing formulae (see Chapter 17). It was, however, Professor Littlechild's action of March 1995 that most dramatically prompted a host of media calls for reforms aimed at making regulation more consistent and predictable.[46]

A proposal, possibly more commonly put forward than any other, involves replacing the individual utilities regulator with a board, committee, or tribunal or establishing panels of knowledgeable persons (perhaps along the lines of non-executive directors) to assist the regulator.[47]

---

[40] See Railway Act 1993, s. 4 (5) (ministerial guidance to Rail Regulator); Environment Act 1995 s. 4 (2)–(9) (ministerial guidance to Environment Agency).
[41] DTI Green Paper 1998, 13; DTI White Paper 1998, 7.
[42] Confederation of British Industry, *Regulating the Regulators* (London, 1996), 24–5.
[43] See NCC, *Regulating the Public Utilities*, 16–19.
[44] See, in particular OFTEL Submission, 16–17.   [45] See OFTEL Submission, 13.
[46] See e.g. M. Smith, 'Littlechild has Robbed us All', *Observer*, 12 Mar. 1995; the *Financial Times* leader 'Reforming the Regulators', 10 Mar. 1995; and D. Nicholson-Lord, 'Just who are the Regulators?', *Independent*, 10 Mar. 1995.
[47] See e.g. Baker, loc. cit. n. 9 above; Vallance, loc. cit. n. 9 above; Veljanovski, *Future of Industry Regulation* 60–2; *Financial Times* leader, 10 Mar. 1995; H. McRae, 'The Regulators Must Go by the Board', *Independent*, 23 Feb. 1995; Smith, loc. cit. n. 46 above.

Proponents of reform argue that a board or committee structure will avoid the placing of weighty political pressures upon a single pair of shoulders; reduce the danger that regulators will feel vulnerable and behave defensively; create a sense that decisions follow internal debate; reduce unpredictable behaviour; and avoid the impression that individual whims have a place in regulation. A move to collegiate regulation, furthermore, is said to be liable to reduce any potential for corruption; to increase legitimacy and accountability; to quell the 'cult of personality' and stop personality clashes prejudicing discussions between regulators and regulated firms; to encourage continuity and stability of policy across changes in governments and regulators; to bring diversified experience to bear; and to spread the workload involved in regulating complex industries. Finally, such a reform, it is contended, replaces the 'rule of man' with the rule of law; and introduces the possibility of more transparency through the use of open deliberations at which interested parties may attend.

Don Cruickshank, when DGT, argued for individual regulators to be replaced by Commissions made up of a small number of people with relevant expertise, not representatives of particular interest groups.[48] An analogue of collegiate decision-making has, indeed, been established in telecommunications regulation through the appointment of a number of expert advisory panels who are free to publish their advice to the DGT. Similarly, the Rail Regulator has reported that in practice he operates collegiate forms of decision-making through a monthly Council whose membership includes non-executives as well as senior managers.[49]

In other utilities sectors, more serious reservations concerning collegiate decision-making have been voiced and submissions of the DGES and DGGS to the 1997–8 DTI Review[50] warn that: conflicting views within Commissions may lead to poor quality or inconsistent decisions; a greater consistency of decision-making can be expected from an individual than from a panel whose composition may change; commissions may find it difficult to take decisions quickly (especially if members are part-time) and hard to maintain a grasp of detail as well as broad policy,

---

The House of Commons Trade and Industry Select Committee recommended replacing the telecommunications Director General with collegiate decision-making in its report *Telecommunications Regulation* (HC 254, London, 1997). On 16 May 1995, Tony Blair endorsed regulatory panels in his address to the Institute for Public Policy Research (IPPR) Conference on *Regulating in the Public Interest*. In April 1995, Clare Spottiswoode, the gas industry regulator, canvassed the proposal that regulators adopt panels of advisers and formalize such arrangements; see Labour Party, *Vision for Growth* (London, 1996). On personalization and the British constitutional tradition see T. Prosser, 'Privatisation, Regulation and Public Services' (1994) *Juridicial Review* 3, at 7–8.

[48] OFTEL Submission, 33–4.   [49] See Rail Regulator, Submission, 5.
[50] OFFER Submission, 17–18; OFGAS Submission, 23–4.

whereas single regulators can take quick and decisive action when necessary; and commissions may find it difficult to sustain continuity of relations with parties affected by regulation and to participate in meetings, conferences, and interviews. They caution, also, that: some clarity of responsibility might be lost in moving to Commissions; the composition of the Commissions would need careful consideration and might prove contentious; individual Commissioners might develop their own staffs and their own bilateral relationships with the individual chairing the Commission; and the nature of regulation might change with a move to Commissions—for example, on the balance between active and reactive stances. This would have implications for incumbents versus entrants.

Both the DGES and the DGWS have suggested that steps short of moving to Commissions might be worth formalizing. Thus, the regulator might be required to act on the instructions of a Board—the relationships being similar to that of a company Chief Executive and the company board. Alternatively, as suggested by the DGGS, regulators might be required to appoint advisory panels or boards who would meet regularly to advise on business plans, general policies, or particular issues. The DGWS has argued that there is no reason why the relevant Secretary of State should not be involved in appointments to such boards or why these bodies should not be given statutory recognition. On the appointments issue, however, the opinions of the DGES and DGGS differ from those of the DGWS— the two energy regulators favour the appointment of panels by the regulators themselves, on the grounds that it is important that the regulator has full confidence in those giving advice. They warn that, if appointments were made by the Secretary of State, the board would be supervisory, not advisory, and, as such, would itself have to be accountable to Parliament and Select Committees.

The DTI Green Paper of 1998 did not propose any particular avenue of reform. It stated that there were risks in concentrating too much discretion on individuals—namely: of lack of accountability to any board of directors or equivalent; of unpredictable decision-making; and of discontinuities when new appointments are made. Following consultation, however, the DTI White Paper took a stronger line and concluded that small executive boards of three full-time members should take the place of individual regulators in the energy and telecommunications fields.[51] On balance, the arguments for boards or Commissions seem to carry more force than the objections lodged—many such objections might be catered for by heading boards or Commissions with single individuals able to communicate for the institution as a whole and take emergency

[51] DTI Green Paper 1998, 44–5; DTI White Paper 1998, 24.

actions.[52] What is clear is the weight of demand that there be depersonalization at the top of the regulatory hierarchy.

An alternative way both to improve consistency and predictability and to depersonalize regulation might, of course, be provided by bringing the various regulators together into super-agencies on the commission model. As noted in the last chapter, this might enable common issues, such as costs of capital, to be dealt with more uniformly; raise the quality of support staff; and lend greater consistency and coherence to regulation.[53]

Whether such proposals have merit turns, in part, on how the causes of regulatory uncertainties are analysed. If excessively frequent adjustments to price formulae are put down to the individual regulator being too prone to the vagaries of political pressures (and Professor Littlechild did acknowledge that public concern had influenced his decision to reopen the REC's price formula in March 1995)[54] then there may be a case for sharing burdens between Commissioners. It should be pointed out, however, that the history of US regulation is full of accusations that Boards and Commissions have succumbed to political pressures of various kinds and sanguinity concerning collegiate decision-makers can be exaggerated.[55] To counter-balance a number of worries about the power of Directors General, or perceptions of this, it should, moreover, be pointed out that the formal statutory position of the Director General may disguise the extent to which decisions are in reality taken in a collegiate fashion. In the telecommunications sector, for instance, it has been pointed out by researchers with enviable access to OFTEL's processes, that senior staff other than the Director General often provide leadership in some areas or apply brakes to the Director General and that much of the framing and policy analysis that underpins both major and less important decisions is carried out by more junior staff.[56] If regulatory functions are, in this way, seen as quite widely dispersed through the regulatory system, the debate about Directors General versus Commissions is placed in a more realistic, perhaps less dramatic, context.

Controlling the Incidence of Reviews

Price formula problems might, however, be thought to stem from sources other than the individual Director General, such as the difficulties

---

[52] On the board versus commission issue a relevant factor may be the need to have larger numbers of members (and so a commission model) where a wide range of specialization and expertise is required—for example where a regulator has a very broad spread of functions as would be the case with a general energy regulator—see DTI Green Paper 1998, 45.

[53] See Baker, loc. cit. n. 9 above.

[54] See S. Littlechild, 'Better to Grasp the Nettle Now', *Financial Times*, 9 Mar. 1995.

[55] For a review of capture theories see B. Mitnick, *The Political Economy of Regulation* (New York, 1980), ch. 2 and above, Chapter 7.

[56] See C. Scott, C. Hall, and C. Hood, 'Regulatory Space and Regulatory Reform', in P. Vass (ed.), *CRI Regulatory Review 1997* (London, 1997), 246.

regulators face in gaining adequate and timely information on the cost structures of utilities, or the problems of attempting to sustain price formulae for five years in fast moving markets. If such analyses of regulatory problems are embraced, then the solutions perhaps do not lie in changing the nature of the regulator. Instead they may be found in reformed approaches to information collection or the development of methods to limit the damage caused by setting price caps at levels that prove no longer (or never to have been) appropriate (for discussion of which see Chapter 17). It has been suggested that there is a need to clarify the occasions on which regulators may change formulae between reviews (e.g. when figures differ from forecasts or a company has misled the regulator). A further idea is that where there is a prima-facie case for review, the regulator ought to be obliged to appeal to another body—probably the MMC—for the right to change a determination.[57] Such a process would involve the MMC not in substituting its judgement on the price cap for that of the regulator but in acting as a gatekeeper to the process of price-cap adjustment by the regulator.

Consistency of Regulatory Methodologies

It has been suggested that regulators' actions would be rendered more consistent, and would be seen as more consistent, if common approaches to fundamental regulatory issues were developed.[58] Similar ways of treating such matters as cost of capital and rates of return, as well as parallels in ways of conducting price reviews, supplying information, and carrying out consultations, could be worked towards. Indeed, such steps might reduce the scope for argument and negotiation at periodic reviews. The NAO's comparative study of the work of the utilities regulators identified areas where more consistency of approach might be needed (e.g. approaches to the valuation and depreciation of assets and the cost of capital and the treatment of efficiency gains).[59] Over the last three years, however, the utilities regulators have developed arrangements for discussion and consultation (now formalized with quarterly meetings) in order to identify 'best practice' and so a degree of movement towards

[57] See leader, *Financial Times*, 10 Mar. 1995. In its consultation paper 'Price Control Review: British Gas Transportation and Storage', 8 June 1995, OFGAS notes three possible new approaches to price controls: shortening review periods to three years; allowing interim reviews where figures differ from forecasts; and sharing excess profits between consumers and shareholders.

[58] See e.g. NCC, *Paying the Price*, 110, and *Regulating the Public Utilities*, 11–15. DTI Green Paper 1998, 48–9 and D. Helm, 'Reforming the Regulatory Frameworks', paper to OXERA conference, 17 June 1993 (Helm emphasizes that common methodologies might reduce inefficient capital market substitution effects since different treatments of financial variables such as asset valuation and cost of capital can lead to regulatory arbitrage in the supply of capital).

[59] NAO, *Work of the Directors General* paras. 3.34–3.46.

consistency is in train. The DGWS has suggested that regulators as a group might be required 'to report annually on the work they do to develop good practice and secure consistency where appropriate'.[60] Such a requirement would help to sustain the development of consistent approaches. As for consistency of procedures, the CBI proposed in 1996 that the MMC (perhaps reconfigured as a Competition Commission) could issue a code of conduct governing all consultation and decision-making processes in the variety of regulatory fields. Again, the regular meetings of the utilities regulators are in tune with working towards common or core procedures on such matters as price control decisions. The DGWS has suggested that consistency and comparisons between regulatory processes, as well as commitments to good procedures, would be enhanced by a requirement on each sectoral regulator to publish a Code of Conduct on process.[61] Such a step would encourage transparency in processes without committing regulators in different fields to a single set of procedures. In this respect it would pay heed to the virtues of approaches being tailored to particular regulatory contexts. In relation to some issues or types of decisions it may, nevertheless, be feasible to produce genuinely common procedures and to set these down.

The Government view, as expressed in 1998, is that action is needed to remedy deficiencies in arrangements for formal debate of issues of common regulatory interest.[62] The intention is to place the regulators under a duty to give collective consideration to matters of common interest. This duty will be supported by formal procedures to ensure transparency, and regulators will be required to consult on and publish a collective forward work programme. The duty to consider would, in essence, place current voluntary procedures on a statutory basis and would, in addition, involve a collective duty to review regulatory practice on specific issues where requested to do so by the Secretary of State.

Fairness between Interests and Social Policy

Regulators have to balance the divergent interests of shareholders, potential industry entrants, the public, different consumer groupings and third parties.[63] In doing so they will be influenced by the importance they attach to encouraging competition in the market. In the eyes of some commentators,[64] heavy emphasis on competition creates incentives on incumbents to maximize profits and 'cherry-pick'—i.e. serve those markets that are most lucrative (and prone to competition from new

---

[60] OFWAT Submission, 15.   [61] Ibid.

[62] DTI Green Paper 1998, 49; DTI White Paper 1998, 28.

[63] Thus the NCC (*Paying the Price*, 91) asked the DGWS in 1993 'to consider the share of [water] industry costs that should be borne by the industry, by external finance and by polluters as well as by water consumers'.

[64] Hain, *Regulating for the Common Good*, 12.

entrants). As a result, poorer communities and those more difficult to serve (because, for example, of geographical dispersion) will be discriminated against. Their positions will be aggravated because they have an unequal bargaining position compared with larger users. Increased competition and the cost-related pricing that regulation tends to encourage may thus have undesired consequences. The National Consumer Council has expressed particular concern in relation to the increasing number of households struggling to pay for the basic essentials of water and sewerage and has recommended that benefit levels should take on board actual, not notional, bills for water and sewage; that these sums should be added in full when housing costs are calculated; and that disconnections of water and sewage services should be outlawed.[65]

Regulators have to decide how to balance the pursuit of efficiency against the social objectives that statutes, political parties, and commentators designate as appropriate. At present, however, social responsibilities tend to fall between three stools—the companies, the regulators, and Government:

The privatised companies are commercial bodies: their first allegiance is to their shareholders. The regulators are bound by specific statutes and terms of reference and take the view that any other or extra social policy objectives are the responsibility of government. But government departments now point to the regulators, not government, as shouldering the overall responsibility for these essential service industries.[66]

This brings the discussion back to the case for a system of approved guidelines for regulators—a case that may rest as much on considerations of substantive fairness as on needs to clarify mandates. Setting social responsibilities involves inherently political decision-making and arguably should not be left to regulators without guidance from accountable political sources. It can, furthermore, be contended that to rely on a number of separate, unguided, and uncoordinated regulators to develop key industries is a negation of planning. The British utility industries, in particular, need to act within the framework of industrial policies for say, energy, communications, and transport sectors. In each major sector, it can be urged, broad objectives should be laid down by elected governments and regulators' guidelines should have parliamentary approval. This implies also that ministers should not simply rubber-stamp the draft statements of objectives that regulators produce.

---

[65] NCC, *Paying the Price*, 135–7.

[66] Ibid. 133; the Director-General of Water Services, Ian Byatt, has argued that regulators should not be given social duties since these are properly for governments to decide —see 'A Balancing Act that has to Provide Benefits for All Players', *Evening Standard*, 10 Mar. 1995. See also Corry, Souter, and Waterson, *Regulating Our Utilities*, 33, 95, 97; C. D. Foster, *Privatisation, Public Ownership and the Regulation of Natural Monopoly* (Oxford, 1992), ch. 9 and C. McCrudden, 'Social Policy and Economic Regulators', in C. McCrudden (ed.), *Regulation and Deregulation* (Oxford, 1999).

A further reason for laying down social objectives is to clarify issues concerning the respective duties of incumbments and of new entrants to a sector—such as relate to obligations of universal supply and the terms of entry for new entrants.

Fairness between Interests: Executive Pay

A strong current of public and press opinion has, during recent years, held that the managers of regulated industries have been lining their pockets with excessive salaries and share options and has urged that the gravy train has to be stopped.[67] Commentators have argued that regulatory capture 'has not been avoided: it has been endemic'.[68] One response to the problem might be thought to lie in linking changes in the rewards of managers and staff, as well as shareholders, to changes in the prices paid by consumers.[69] This is an approach that might be applied to all of the staff of the utilities, not merely to top executives, but this may add considerably to regulatory burdens.

Alternatively, the issue of reasonable managerial and staff rewards might be met not with a regulatory but with a corporate governance reform.[70] Such issues have been considered by the Cadbury, Greenbury, and Hampel Committees.[71] Cadbury advocated the principle of openness, recommending disclosure of the salaries of the company's chairman and highest-paid UK director together with the appointment of remuneration committees consisting wholly or mainly of non-executive directors.[72]

---

[67] See e.g. 'Fat Cats Get Fatter', *Financial Times*, 20 Apr. 1993. On 14 May 1995 the *Observer* headlined with a report that directors of the privatized electricity, water, and gas companies had used cheap share schemes to 'award themselves more than £40 million', with twelve individuals becoming millionaires and the average director collecting £350,000. On 31 May 1995, 4,500 British Gas shareholders, at the company AGM, 'poured abuse' on British Gas directors with accusations of greed and deceit—see 'Fury Fails to Burst Gas Bubble', *Independent*, 1 June 1995. In 1995 the Labour Party claimed that, in the electricity industry alone, 72 top executives had awarded themselves £72 million in share options since privatization in 1990 (*Financial Times*, 18 July 1995, p. 15). See also DTI Green Paper 1998, 21; DTI White Paper, 1998, 13.

[68] Helm, loc. cit. n. 58 above.

[69] On shareholder to consumer linkage see the discussion of the 'customer corporation' at p. 310 below and J. Kay, 'The Future of UK Utility Regulation', in M. Beesley (ed.), *Regulating Utilities: A Time for Change* (London, 1996). The DTI White Paper 1998, 13, urged regulators to take account of levels of consumer service and satisfaction when setting new price caps.

[70] See R. A. Chandler, 'Disclosure of Directors' Remuneration: Public Accountability or Public Relations?' (1996) 7 *Utilities LR* 92; DTI White Paper 1998, 13 (urging regulators to notify remuneration committees of levels of consumer service).

[71] See *Report of the Committee on Corporate Governance* (Chair: Sir A. Cadbury) (London, 1994); *Report of the Greenbury Study Group on Directors' Remuneration* (Chair: Sir R. Greenbury) (London, 1995); *Preliminary Report of the Committee on Corporate Governance* (Chair: Sir R. Hampel) (London, Aug. 1997, Final Report Jan. 1998).

[72] Cadbury Report, para. 4.42; see V. Finch, 'Corporate Governance and Cadbury: Self-Regulation and Alternatives' (1994) *JBL* 51.

Cadbury was, however, against shareholder involvement in directors' remuneration on the basis that it could not sensibly be reduced to a vote in favour of, or against, a motion.[73] Greenbury did not think that remuneration should be a standard agenda item at a company's annual general meeting (AGM) but argued that remuneration committees should determine the packages for Executive Directors and should consist exclusively of non-executives. Discounted share options should be banned, said Greenbury, and all long-term incentive schemes and share option plans should be approved by shareholders. Annual Reports should contain greater detail on pay, pensions, and perks; the chair of the remuneration committee should answer to the AGM on pay-offs; and huge pay-offs for poorly performing directors should be ended. As for the utilities, Greenbury urged that the privatized water and energy companies should review existing remuneration packages and that in future privatizations no share options should be granted for at least six months. In response to Greenbury the London Stock Exchange, on 12 October 1995, published amendments to its *Listing Rules* to require companies to report in their annual financial statements on the amount of each element in the remuneration package of each director by name. Further amendments, effective from 30 September 1996, demanded advance shareholder approval for long-term incentive schemes to which directors are eligible.

The broad thrust of the Hampel Committee's report of January 1998 was to steer the corporate governance debate away from accountability and in the direction of business profitability. Hampel agreed with Cadbury and Greenbury that remuneration committees of non-executive directors should develop pay policies for executive directors but Hampel urged that such committees should make recommendations on pay to the board, not take decisions on the board's behalf. As for shareholders, Hampel recommended that long-term incentive plans, but not all remuneration packages, should require shareholder approval and that shareholder approval of the remuneration report should be left to the individual company and not be mandatory.

On the latter point, press reports in November 1997 indicated that the Labour Government favoured more rigorous controls than Hampel and was considering legislation to compel directors to win shareholder approval for their remuneration packages at each annual general meeting and to make it compulsory for all substantial shareholders to vote on all the resolutions put forward at AGMs.[74] Four months later, the DTI Green Paper noted that public confidence in the utilities, and in regulatory fairness, had been undermined by excessive boardroom pay.[75] The

---

[73] Ibid., paras. 4.43, 4.44.   [74] See e.g. *Guardian*, 8 Nov. 1997.
[75] DTI Green Paper 1998, 20.

Government was said to be attracted to ensuring a closer link between directors' remuneration and the achievement of rigorous customer service standards, particularly for companies operating in monopoly and pre-competitive markets. It repeated its concern that shareholders should have a role in approving the policies set out in boards' annual remuneration reports and urged that best corporate practice be adopted by the utility companies. It warned the business community that if it wished to prove that there was no need for further action on directors' pay it was 'up to them to ensure that there is no further abuse or excess'.[76]

To legitimate directors' pay levels in regulated industries by resort to control via remuneration committees, shareholder endorsements, and rules on disclosure is, however, a difficult task. The boards to which remuneration committees report are controlled by the directors whose pay is at issue; non-executive directors face severe problems in controlling insiders because they are highly dependent on the board for information;[77] they lack in-depth knowledge of directors' performance; they have limited time and resources at their disposal; and their expertise may not lie in the relevant area. Non-executive directors may also be poor controllers of executive directors' pay because they may share the same professional and social milieu as executive directors and they may be disinclined to be seen as being a nuisance.[78]

As for deficiencies of shareholder control, these were discussed in Chapter 21 and they would be encountered as much in controlling executive pay as in influencing policy directions more generally. All in all, corporate governance mechanisms are not likely to provide high levels of legitimation for those seeking to assure consumers about levels of executive pay in regulated sectors.

It might be commented that recent clamour on rewards may divert attention from the more serious, structural defects of British regulation[79] but this may be to underestimate the importance of the rewards issue. The media's appetite for stories on executive greed is considerable and public perceptions of unfair rewards may affect the credibility of regulatory regimes in no small way. If public acceptability is a precondition of effective and legitimate regulation, the public's sensitivities have to be borne in mind.

---

[76] DTI Green Paper 1998; DTI White Paper 1998. In March 1998 the Government announced that it would conduct a major long-term review of company law to culminate in a White Paper in March 2001—see DTI, *Modern Company Law for a Competitive Economy* (London, 1998).

[77] See V. Finch, 'Company Directors: Who Cares about Skill and Care' (1992) 55 *MLR* 179; Institute of Chartered Accountants, *Report of Study Group on the Changing Role of the Non-executive Director* (ICA, London, 1991).

[78] Finch, loc. cit. n. 77 above, 199; C. S. Axworthy, 'Corporate Directors: Who Needs Them?' (1988) 51 *MLR* 273.

[79] See Helm, loc. cit. n. 58 above.

Conclusions

As with accountability it is the issue of trade-offs with values such as efficiency and expertise that lies at the heart of debates on procedures and fairness. This, however, is no simple matter of deciding the trade-offs that are appropriate (if that could be deemed simple). Real difficulties are involved in predicting the effects of procedural developments and the nature of resultant trade-offs. Would, for instance, giving consumers a right to appeal regulators' decisions to the MMC produce a strong shift in regulatory policy-making power from the expert regulators to the less specialist MMC? Would ministerial guidelines for regulators produce unwarranted levels of 'lay' interference in regulators' decisions or would this free regulators from making decisions on which they are vulnerable?

Most such issues have to be judged with reference to particular contexts although some general conclusions are suggested in the discussion above. (Ministerial guidance for regulators on social obligations does seem, on balance, to be desirable.) What can be drawn from the broad debate on procedures and fairness are, nevertheless, a few caveats. First, it may be right to bear in mind issues of competence and to be wary of steps that take effective decision-making power away from those regulators who have developed considerable levels of specialist expertise and place such power in less expert hands. Wariness should be the greater where the gains from a reform are uncertain or where the 'new' decision-makers present similar problems of accountability or transparency as the old. Second, it should be remembered that multi-tiered decision-making almost inevitably produces problems of delay, duplication, conflict, and confusion of policy. Again, it is advisable to be certain of the gains to be achieved before multiple tiers are created. Third, the dangers of undue influence and capture should be kept constantly in mind. Before new procedures are established it is appropriate to consider who will best be able to work those procedures to their own advantage and the extent to which this will lead to problems of capture and defensiveness. This is especially the case when increased legalization of a process is a possibility.[80] Finally, the costs of uncertainty and of delays should be attended to. Placing emphasis on 'acceptable' procedures and 'correct' results can blind one to the price that has to be paid for these (especially perhaps, if one is a lawyer). On occasions it may be better to have a timely decision than to wait for a decision that offers the chance of a marginally higher level of procedural acceptability or correctness.

[80] See the warnings of the DGGS in OFGAS Submission, 30–1.

....

23

....

Conclusions

Regulation often appears to be a game in which the rules are uncertain, the method of scoring is in dispute and the distinction between players and spectators is unclear. This is because regulators' mandates tend to be imprecise; identifying good regulation involves contention and rights of participation are often subject to debate. Regulators, moreover, carry out a number of functions that are not always compatible. They not only exercise control—over, for example, monopoly power—but they also act to organize and enable the development of competitive markets. They seek to encourage efficiency but often have to take on board a variety of different social objectives.[1] Regulators, furthermore, have constantly to balance various interests and to perform trade-offs of different values. Balances have to be made between providers and consumers; different service providers; commercial and domestic consumers; incumbents and potential new entrants; infrastructure suppliers and operators of services; and a host of other sets of divergent interests.

As for trading-off values, each of the benchmarks discussed in Chapter 6 may have to be weighed against the others in any given context. Should more accountability be established at a given cost in efficiency? Should greater freedom to exercise expert judgements be given in spite of the loss of accountability involved? Should more efficient regulation be sought by reducing access to the regulatory process? These and similar questions have to be faced by regulators on a daily basis.

Nor are there any easy answers. The arguments presented in this book suggest that we should be highly sceptical of regulatory solutions or designs that are couched in terms of single values—notions, for instance, that certain strategies will be efficient and therefore are justifiable and should be pursued without further debate.

It also follows that in such an uncertain and politically contentious world, any regulator will live a precarious existence. No claim to legitimacy that a regulator makes will ever be recognized as clear-cut or beyond argument and, to render life more difficult, no set of regulatory conditions or even public expectations of regulation is liable to remain static.

---

[1] See T. Prosser, *Law and the Regulators* (Oxford, 1997), 304.

The regulator's world is also, we have seen, one in which it is difficult to deal with issues in isolation—it is a world of overlaps, interactions, and blurred boundaries. Regulation, for example, is difficult to tease apart from self-regulation; 'public' actions, decisions, policies, and rules are difficult to separate from 'private' ones; regulated spheres are not easy to distinguish from those that are unregulated; domestic systems of regulation interact with supra-national regimes; different regulatory mechanisms operate in coordination as well as in competition; and questions of enforcement cannot be completely disentangled from those concerning policies and rules. As for understanding regulatory origins and developments, we saw, in Chapter 3, that an array of different, often competing, approaches to explanation is readily uncovered in the literature.

Not only, therefore, is regulation a politically contentious activity, it is one that presents a host of technical and intellectual challenges. Does such a catalogue of difficulties, however, offer a counsel of despair? Does it imply that since any regulatory action will give rise to contention, anything goes? The answer to both questions is definitely 'no'. We have suggested that regulatory activities be judged according to the five benchmarks of Chapter 6 and we have sought to consider how various strategies tend to measure up to those different benchmarks in a variety of settings. To recognize that judgements about regulation will give rise to contention, even if it is assumed that everyone in society agrees on the five benchmarks, is not to counsel despair but to recognize that the choices made in regulation are inevitably political ones. Being clear about those benchmarks that are relevant in evaluating regulation, and discussing regulation with reference to these yardsticks, brings clarity to the regulatory debate rather than imposing any particular political vision on participants in that conversation. Not only does it help to identify certain pitfalls of regulatory analysis (such as single benchmark evaluations) but it also assists in identifying the trade-offs that have to be considered when, for example, assessing reforms.

As for the search for 'better' regulation, a number of proposals have been reviewed in the pages above and certain of these have found their way into the present Government's plans. The Labour Government, furthermore, has demonstrated from its earliest days an awareness of the need for clear benchmarks. When the President of the Board of Trade, Margaret Beckett, announced the Government's review of utility regulation in June 1997 she stated that her aim was to establish a framework to deliver value, quality, and choice to customers and encourage managers to innovation and efficiency. The existing framework, she said, would be updated in a manner guided by the principles of 'transparency, consistency and predictability with enhanced accountability'. Another theme from this book suggests, however, that new laws in themselves can only provide part of any answer to the perceived deficiencies of regulation—even if agreement is assumed on deficiencies and political objectives. This is the theme that regulatory systems should be seen in the round—as comprising not merely sets of laws and rules but also: institutional frameworks; policy and governmental settings; sets of procedures; enforcement, monitoring, and information-using strategies and approaches; clusters of ideas and assumptions about how things are to be done; configurations of regulated firms and individuals; levels of resourcing; and groups of persons with their backgrounds, preferences, cultures, disciplines, ideas, incentives, and expectations.

Viewing regulation as a whole in this way implies that changes in laws and rules, no matter how sophisticated, are unlikely to come to grips with all of the aspects of a regulatory system that are of potential concern. Reforms, for example, to increase accountability and place newly powerful enforcement powers in regulators' hands may well fail to address problems that stem from, say, the culture, personnel, accepted practices, or resourcing levels that are encountered in the regulatory system. Changes, it follows, may be required on a huge variety of fronts and may require not so much new laws as, for example, new ideas, staff, training methods, enforcement philosophies, modes of organization, informal procedures, or levels of financial support.

As for the future of regulation, what is clear is that the political dimension of the regulators' work will not disappear. Not only that, it may prove increasingly to be the case that direct democratic influence will be demanded not merely with respect to the decisions, actions, and policies of regulators but also with regard to those of the 'private' firms that provide regulated or public services. It has been seen already that firms such as BT can no longer assume that they are in all respects private and accordingly outside the scope of such concerns. Difficult political judgements will remain and will be the proper province of democratically-legitimated bodies.

The main hope for improving regulation lies not in taking such judgements away from legitimate institutions but in developing our understandings on two fronts. First, concerning the array of choices between various goals that different regulatory arrangements present us with. Second, about the potential of new regulatory arrangements to provide us with more attractive ranges of choice. It is on these fronts that we hope to make a contribution with this book.

Bibliography

ABEL, R., *The Legal Profession in England and Wales* (Oxford, 1988).
ADAMS, J., and PRICHARD JONES, K. V., *Franchising* (London, 1987).
—— and THOMPSON, M., *Risk Review* (London, 1991).
Adam Smith Institute, *Who Will Regulate the Regulators?* (London, 1992).
ARMSTRONG, M., 'Competition in Telecommunications' (1997) 13 *Oxford Rev. of Econ. Policy* 64.
—— COWAN, S., and VICKERS, J., *Regulatory Reform: Economic Analysis and British Experience* (London, 1994).
—— DOYLE, C., and VICKERS, J., 'The Access Pricing Problem: A Synthesis' 44 (1996) *Journal of Industrial Economics* 131.
AVERCH, M., and JOHNSON, L., 'Behaviour of the Firm under Regulatory Constraint' (1962) 92 *Am. Econ. Rev.* 1052–69.
AXWORTHY, C. S., 'Corporate Directors: Who Needs Them?' (1988) 51 *MLR* 273.
AYRES, I., and BRAITHWAITE, J., *Responsive Regulation: Transcending the Regulation Debate* (Oxford, 1992).
BAGGOT, R., 'Regulatory Reform in Britain: The Changing Face of Self-Regulation' (1989) 67 *Pub. Admin.* 435.
—— and HARRISON, L., 'The Politics of Self-Regulation' (1986) 14 *Policy and Politics* 143.
BAILEY, S., 'Economic Incentives for Employers to Improve the Management of Workplace Risk', paper to W. G. Hart Legal Workshop, London, 4 July 1995.
BAKER, C. E., 'The Ideology of the Economic Analysis of Law' (1975) 5 *Philosophy and Public Affairs* 3.
BALDWIN, R. (ed.), *Law and Uncertainty* (London, 1996).
—— *Regulating Legal Services* (Lord Chancellor's Department, London, 1998).
—— *Regulating the Airlines* (Oxford, 1985).
—— *Rules and Government* (Oxford, 1995).
—— *Regulation in Question* (London, 1995).
—— 'A Quango Unleashed: The Abolition of Policy Guidance in Civil Aviation Licensing' (1980) 58 *Pub. Admin.* 287.
—— 'A British Independent Regulatory Agency and the "Skytrain" Decision' [1978] *PL* 57.
—— and CAVE, M., *Franchising as a Tool of Government* (London, 1996).
—— and DAINTITH, T., *Harmonisation and Hazard* (London, 1992).
—— and HAWKINS, K., 'Discretionary Justice: Davis Reconsidered' [1984] *PL* 570.
—— and McCRUDDEN, C., *Regulation and Public Law* (London, 1987).
—— SCOTT, C., and HOOD, C. (eds.), *A Reader On Regulation* (Oxford, 1998).
—— and VELJANOVSKI, C. C., 'Regulation by Cost-Benefit Analysis' (1984) 62 *Pub. Admin.* 51.
BALOGH, J., 'Any and All? Future of Social Obligations' (1997) 8 *Utilities LR* 109.

BARAM, M. S., 'Cost-Benefit Analysis: An Inadequate Basis for Health, Safety and Environmental Regulatory Decisionmaking' (1980) 8 *Ecology LQ*.

BARDACH, E., and KAGAN, R., *Going by the Book: The Problem of Regulatory Unreasonableness* (Philadelphia, 1982).

BARKER, R., *Political Legitimacy and the State* (Oxford, 1990).

BARON, D., and BESANKO, D., 'Commitment and Fairness in a Dynamic Regulatory Relationship' (1987) 54 *Rev. Econ. Stud.* 413.

—— and MYERSON, R., 'Regulating a Monopolist with Unknown Costs' (1982) *Econometrician* 911.

BARRON, A., and SCOTT, C., 'The Citizens' Charter Programme' (1992) 55 *MLR* 526.

—— —— *The Citizens' Charter: Raising the Standard*, Cm. 1599 (London, 1991).

BARROW, M., 'Public Services and the Theory of Regulation' (1996) 24 *Policy and Politics* 263.

BAUMOL, W., 'Contestable Markets: An Uprising in the Theory of Industrial Structure' (1982) 72 *Am. Econ. Rev.* 1–15.

—— 'On Taxation and the Control of Externalities' (1972) 62 *Am. Econ. Rev.* 307.

—— PANZAR, J., and WILLIG, R., *Contestable Markets and the Theory of Industry Structure* (New York, 1988).

BECK, U., 'The Politics of Risk Society', in J. Franklin (ed.), *The Politics of Risk Society* (Cambridge, 1998).

—— *Risk Society* (London, 1992).

—— *The Reinvention of Politics* (Cambridge, 1997).

BECKER, G., 'Crime and Punishment: An Economic Approach' (1968) 76 *J. Pol. Econ.* 161.

—— 'A Theory of Competition among Pressure Groups for Political Influence' (1983) 98 *Quarterly J. of Economics* 371.

BECKERMAN, W., *Small is Stupid: Blowing the Whistle on the Greens* (London, 1995).

BEDER, S., 'The Fallible Engineer' (1991) *New Scientist* 38.

BEESLEY, M. E. (ed.), *Regulating Utilities: A Time for Change?* (London, 1996).

—— (ed.), *Regulating Utilities: Broadening the Debate* (London, 1997).

—— and LITTLECHILD, S., 'The Regulation of Privatised Monopolies in the United Kingdom' (1989) 20 *Rand J. of Econ.* 454.

BEETHAM, D., *The Legitimation of Power* (London, 1991).

BEGG, D., FISCHER, G., and DORNBUSCH, R., *Economics* (4th edn., London, 1998).

—— SEABRIGHT, P., and NEVERN, D., *Making Sense of Subsidiarity: How Much Centralisation for Europe?* (London, 1993).

BERG, A., 'Enforcement of the Common Fisheries Policy, with Special Reference to the Netherlands', in C. Harding and B. Swart, *Enforcing European Community Rules* (Aldershot, 1996).

BERG, G., and TSCHIRHART, T., *Natural Monopoly Regulation* (Cambridge, 1988).

BERGMAN, M., and LANE, J., 'Public Policy in a Principal-Agent Framework' (1990) 2 *J. of Theoretical Politics* 339.

BERNHEIM, B., and WHINSTON, M., 'Menu Auctions, Resource Allocation and Economic Influence' (1986) *Quarterly J. of Economics* 1.

BERNSTEIN, M. H., *Regulating Business by Independent Commission* (New York, 1955).

BISHOP, M., and GREEN, M., *Privatisation and Recession: The Miracle Tested* (London, 1995).

—— KAY, J., and MAYER, C. (eds.), *Privatisation and Economic Performance* (Oxford, 1994).

—— —— —— (eds.), *The Regulatory Challenge* (Oxford, 1995).

—— and THOMPSON, D., 'Regulatory Reform and Productivity Growth in the UK's Public Utilities' (1992) 24 *Applied Economics* 1181–90.

BLACK, D., *The Behavior of Law* (New York, 1974).

BLACK, J., 'An Economic Analysis of Regulation: One View of the Cathedral' (1997) *OJLS* 699.

—— *Rules and Regulators* (Oxford, 1997).

—— 'Constitutionalising Self-Regulation' (1996) 59 *MLR* 24.

—— 'New Institutionalism and Naturalism in Socio-Legal Analysis: Institutional Approaches to Regulatory Decision-Making' (1997) 19 *Law and Policy* 53.

——, MUCHLINSKI, P., and WALKER, P. (eds.), *Commercial Regulation and Judicial Review* (Oxford, 1998).

BLANCHARD, C., 'Telecommunications Regulation in New Zealand: How Effective is "Light-Handed" Regulation?' (1994) 18 *Telecommunications Policy* 154.

BODDEWYN, J. J., *Global Perspectives on Advertising Self-Regulation* (Westport, Conn., 1992).

BORRIE, G., 'The Regulation of Public and Private Power' [1989] *PL* 552.

BOYER, B., 'Alternatives to Trial-Type Hearings for Resolving Complex, Scientific, Economic and Social Issues' (1972) 71 *Mich. LR* 111.

BRADLEY, C., 'Corporate Control: Markets and Rules' (1990) 53 *MLR* 170.

BRAITHWAITE, J., 'Enforced Self-Regulation' (1982) 80 *Mich. LR* 1461.

—— *To Punish or Persuade* (Albany, NY, 1985).

—— 'The Limits of Economism in Controlling Harmful Corporate Conduct' (1982) 16 *Law and Society Review* 481.

—— 'Enforced Self-Regulation: A New Strategy for Corporate Crime Control' (1982) 80 *Mich. LR* 1466.

BRATTON, W. W., and McCAHERTY, J. A., 'Regulatory Competition as Regulatory Capture: The Case of Corporate Law in the USA', in J. McCahery et al. (eds.), *International Regulatory Competition and Coordination* (Oxford, 1996).

BRAYBROOKE, D., and LINDBLOM, C. E., *A Strategy of Decision* (New York, 1963).

BRENNAN, G., 'Civil Disaster Management: An Economist's View' (1991) 64 *Canberra Bulletin of Pub. Admin.* 30–3.

BREYER, S., *Breaking the Vicious Circle: Toward Effective Risk Regulation* (Cambridge, Mass., 1993).

—— *Regulation and its Reform* (Cambridge, Mass., 1982).

—— and STEWART, R. B., 'The Discontents of Legalism: Interest Group Relations in Administrative Regulation' (1985) *Wisconsin LR* 685.

—— and STEWART, R., *Administrative Law and Regulatory Policy* (3rd edn., Boston, 1992).

BROWN, G. T., and SIBLEY, D. S., *The Theory of Public Utility Pricing* (Cambridge, 1986).

BROWN, R., 'Theory and Practice of Regulatory Enforcement: Occupational Health and Safety Regulation in British Columbia' (1994) 16 (1) *Law and Policy* 63.

BRYNER, G., *Bureaucratic Discretion* (New York, 1987).

BURCA, G. DE, 'The Principle of Proportionality and its Application in EC Law' (1993) *YBEL* 105.

BURNS, P., TURVEY, R., and WEYMAN-JONES, T., *Sliding Scale Regulation of Monopoly Enterprises* (London, 1995).

—— —— —— *General Properties of Sliding Scale Regulation*, CRI Technical Paper 3 (London, 1995).

BURROWS, N., 'Harmonisation of Technical Standards' (1990) 53 *MLR* 711.

—— and HIRAM, H., 'The Legal Articulation of Policy in the European Community', in T. C. Daintith (ed.), *Implementing EC Law in the United Kingdom* (Chichester, 1995).

—— and WOOLFSON, C., 'Business Friendly Procedures and Enforcement in an Era of Deregulation' (1998, mimeo).

BURROWS, P., *The Economic Theory of Pollution Control* (Oxford, 1979).

BUTTON, K., and SWANN, D., *The Age of Regulatory Reform* (Oxford, 1989).

Cabinet Office, *Building Business, Not Barriers*, Cmnd. 9794 (London, 1986).

—— *Checking the Cost of Regulation: A Guide to Compliance Costs Assessment* (London, 1996).

—— *Lifting the Burden*, Cmnd. 9571 (London, 1985).

—— *Releasing Enterprise*, Cm. 512 (London, 1988).

—— *Regulation in the Balance: A Guide to Regulatory Appraisal Incorporating Risk Assessment* (London, 1996).

CADBURY, A., *Report of the Committee on Corporate Governance* (Chair: Sir A. Cadbury) (London, 1994).

CALABRESI, G., *The Cost of Accidents: A Legal and Economic Analysis* (New Haven, 1970).

—— and MELAMED, A., 'Property Rules, Liability Rules and Inalienability: One View of the Cathedral' (1972) *Harv. LR* 1089.

CALCUTT, SIR D., *Review of Press Self-Regulation*, Cm. 2135 (London, 1992–3).

CALVER, R. L., McCUBBINS, M. D., and WEINGAST, B. R., 'A Theory of Political Control and Agency Discretion' (1989) 33 *Am. J. Pol. Sci.* 588.

CANOY, M., and WATERSON, M., *Tendering, Auctions and Preparation Costs*, Discussion Paper No. 31, Univ. of Reading (1991).

CAPPELLETTI, M., SECCOMBE, M., and WEILER, J. (eds.), *Integration through Law* (Berlin, 1986).

CARSON, W. G., 'Some Sociological Aspects of Strict Liability and the Enforcement of Factory Legislation' (1970) 33 *MLR* 396.

—— *The Other Price of Britain's Oil* (Oxford, 1982).

CARY, W., 'Federalism and Corporate Law: Reflections upon Delaware' (1974) 88 *Yale LJ* 663.

CASS, D. Z., 'The Word that Saves Maastricht?' (1992) 29 *CMLR* 1107.

CAVE, M., and CROWTHER, P., 'Determining the Level of Regulation in EU Telecommunications' (1996) 20 *Telecommunications Policy* 725.

—— and WILLIAMSON, P., 'Entry, Competition and Regulation in UK Telecommunications' (1996) 12 *Oxford Rev. of Econ. Policy* 100.

CAVE, M. et al., *Measuring Changes in the Quality of Public Services* (London, 1994).

Centre for the Study of Regulated Industries, *Regulating the Utilities: Accountability and Processes* (London, 1994).

CHALMERS, D., *EU Law and Government* (Aldershot, 1998).

CHANDLER, R. A., 'Disclosure of Directors' Remuneration: Public Accountability or Public Relations?' (1996) 7 *Utilities LR* 92.

CHANNELLS, L., 'The Windfall Tax' (1997) 18 *Fiscal Studies* 281.

CLARKE, L., *Acceptable Risk* (Berkeley, Calif., 1989).

CLARKSON, C., 'Kicking Corporate Bodies and Damning their Souls' (1996) 59 *MLR* 557.

COASE, R., 'The Problem of Social Cost' (1960) 3 *J. Law and Econ.* 1.

COFFEE, J. C., 'No Soul to Damn, No Body to Kick' (1981) 79 *Mich. LR* 386.

Comptroller and Auditor-General, *Office of Passenger Rail Franchising (OPRAF): The Award of the First Three Passenger Rail Franchises* (HC 701, 1995/6) (London, 1996).

Confederation of British Industry, *Regulating the Regulators: A C.B.I Discussion Paper* (London, 1996).

COOTER, R., and ULEN, T., *Law and Economics* (Glenview, Ill., 1988).

CORRY, D., SOUTER, D., and WATERSON, M., *Regulating Our Utilities* (IPPR, London, 1994).

CRAIG, P. P., 'Once upon a Time in the West: Direct Effect and the Federalism of EEC Law' (1992) 12 *OJLS*.

—— *Administrative Law* (3rd edn., London, 1994).

—— and BURCA, G. DE, *EC Law* (London, 1995).

—— and HARLOW, C. (eds.), *Lawmaking in the European Union* (Dordrecht, 1998).

CRAMPTON, P. C., 'Money out of Thin Air: The Nationwide Narrow Bend PCS Auction' (1995) *J. of Econ. and Man. Strategy*.

CRANOR, C. F., *Regulating Toxic Substances* (New York, 1993).

CRANSTON, R., *Regulating Business* (London, 1979).

—— *Consumers and the Law* (London, 1984).

CRAWFORD, S., and OSTROM, E., 'A Grammar of Institutions' (1995) 89 *Am. Pol. Sci. Rev.* 582.

CREW, M. A. (ed.), *Deregulation and Diversification of Utilities* (Dordrecht, 1989).

CRIPPS, M. L., and IRELAND, N., 'The Design of Auctions and Tenders with Quality Thresholds: The Symmetric Case' (1994) 104 *Economic Journal* 316.

CROSS, G., 'Enforcement of Environmental Rules: The UK Experience', in C. Harding and B. Swart (eds.), *Enforcing European Community Rules* (Aldershot, 1996).

CROUCH, C., and DOVE, R. (eds.), *Corporatism and Accountability* (Oxford, 1990).

CULYER, A. J. (ed.), *Economic Policies and Social Goals* (London, 1974).

CUSHMAN, R. E., *The Independent Regulatory Commissions* (New York, 1941).

DAINTITH, T., *Law as an Instrument of Economic Policy* (Berlin, 1988).

—— 'A Regulatory Space Agency' (1989) 9 *OJLS* 534.

—— 'Regulation', in International Association of Legal Science, *International Encyclopaedia of Comparative Law*, vol. xvii (Tübingen, 1997).

—— 'European Community Law and the Redistribution of Regulatory Power in the United Kingdom', Paper to ESRC Conference, Sept. 1994.

—— 'Regulation by Contract: The New Prerogative' (1979) *Curr. Leg. Prob.* 41.

—— 'The Techniques of Government', in J. Jowell and D. Oliver (eds.), *The Changing Constitution* (3rd edn., Oxford, 1994).

DALLAS, J., 'Effective Franchising: A Legal Perspective', in CRI, *Franchising Network Services: Regulation in Post, Rail and Water* (London, 1993).

DAVIES, P. (ed.), *Gower's Principles of Modern Company Law* (6th edn., London, 1997).

DAVIS, K. C., *Discretionary Justice* (Chicago, 1969).

DAWSON, S., WILLMAN, P., BAMFORD, M., and CLINTON, A., *Safety at Work: The Limits of Self-Regulation* (Cambridge, 1988).

DEHOUSSE, R., 'Integration v Regulation? On the Dynamics of Regulation in the European Community' (1993) 30 *J. Common Market Studies* 383.

—— et al., *Europe after 1992*, EU1 Working Paper 92/31 (Florence, 1992).

DEMSETZ, H., 'Why Regulate Utilities?' (1968) 11 *J. Law and Econ.* 55.

DE MUTH, C., *A Fair Deal for Consumers: Modernising the Framework for Utility Regulation: The Response to Consultation* ('White Paper') (London, July 1998).

—— *Public Consultation Paper on the Future of Gas and Electricity Regulation* (London, Oct. 1998).

—— *Public Consultation Paper on Consumer Councils* (London, Sept. 1998).

—— and GINSBERG, D., 'White House Review of Agency Rule-Making' (1986) 99 *Harv. LR* 1075.

DERTHICK, M., and QUIRK, P., *The Politics of Deregulation* (Washington, 1985).

Director-General of Telecommunications, *Submission to Review of Utility Regulation* (London, 1997).

DIVER, C. S., 'The Optimal Precision of Administrative Rules' (1983) 93 *Yale LJ* 65.

DNES, A. W., 'Bidding for Commercial Broadcasting: An Analysis of UK Experience' (1993) 40 *Scottish J. of Pol. Econ.* 104.

—— *Franchising: A Case Study Approach* (Aldershot, 1992).

—— 'Bidding for Commercial Broadcasting' (1993) 40 *Scottish J. of Pol. Econ.* 104.

DOMBERGER, S., 'Regulation through Franchise Contracts', in J. Kay, C. Mayer, and D. Thompson (eds.), *Privatisation and Regulation* (Oxford, 1996).

—— and SHERR, A., 'The Impact of Competition on Pricing and Quality of Legal Services' (1989) 9 *Int. Rev. Law and Econ.* 41.

DOUGLAS, M., 'Risk as a Forensic Resource' (1990) 119 *Daedalus* 1.

—— *How Institutions Think* (London, 1986).

—— *In the Active Voice* (London, 1982).

—— *Risk and Blame* (London, 1992).

—— *Risk: Acceptability According to the Social Sciences* (London, 1985).

—— and WILDAVSKY, A., *Risk and Culture* (Berkeley, Calif., 1982).

DOWNS, A., *An Economic Theory of Democracy* (New York, 1957).

DRAKE, C. D., and WRIGHT, F. B., *Law of Health and Safety* (London, 1983).

DREWRY, G., 'Mr Major's Charter: Empowering the Consumer' [1993] *PL* 248.

DTI, *Cutting Red Tape for Business* (London, 1991).

—— *A Fair Deal for Consumers: Modernising the Framework for Utility Regulation*, Green Paper, Cm. 3898 (London, Mar. 1998).

—— *Burdens on Business* (London, 1985).

—— *Checking the Cost to Business* (London, 1992).

—— *Counting the Cost to Business* (London, 1990).

—— *Cutting Red Tape* (London, 1994).

—— *Thinking about Regulation* (London, 1994).

DUNLEAVY, P., *Democracy, Bureaucracy and Public Choice* (London, 1991).

DURANT, J., 'Once the Men in White Coats Held the Promise of a Better Future', in J. Franklin (ed.), *The Politics of Risk Society* (Cambridge, 1998).

DUXBURY, N., *Patterns of American Jurisprudence* (Oxford, 1995).

DWORKIN, G., BERMONT, G., and BROWN, P. (eds.), *Markets and Morals* (Washington, 1977).

DWORKIN, R., 'Is Wealth a Value?' [1980] 9 *J. Legal Stud.* 191;

—— *A Matter of Principle* (Cambridge, Mass., 1986).

EASTERBROOK, F. H., 'Federalism and European Business Law' (1994) 14 *Int. Rev. Law and Econ.* 125.

EFILWC, *Catalogue of Economic Incentive Systems for the Improvement of the Working Environment* (Dublin, 1994).

EISENBERG, T., 'Access to the Corporate Proxy Machinery' (1970) 83 *Harv. LR* 1489.

ELIASSEN, E., and KOOIMAN, J., *Managing Public Organisations: Lessons from Contemporary European Experience* (London, 1993).

EMILIOU, N., 'Subsidiarity: An Effective Barrier against the Enterprises of Ambition?' (1992) 55 *ELR* 383.

European Commission, *The Impact and Effectiveness of the Single Market*, COM (96) 520 final 30 Oct. 1996.

—— *Action Plan for the Single Market* CSE (97) 1 final 4 June 1997.

EVERSON, M., 'Independent Agencies: Hierarchy Beaters?' (1995) 1 *ELJ* 180.

FANTONI, B., *Private Eye's Colemanballs* (London, 1982).

FEATHERSTONE, K., 'Jean Monnet and the "Democratic Deficit" in the European Union' (1994) 32 *J. Common Market Studies*, 149.

FELDMAN, D., and MEISEL, F., *Corporate Commercial Law: Modern Developments* (London, 1996).

FENN, P., and VELJANOVSKI, C., 'A Positive Economic Theory of Regulatory Enforcement' (1988) 98 *Economic Journal* 1055.

FERGUSON, R., 'Self-Regulation at Lloyds' (1983) 46 *MLR* 56.

—— and PAGE, A., 'The Development of Investor Protection in Britain' (1984) 12 *Int. J. of Sociology of Law* 287.

FINCH, V., 'Company Directors: Who Cares about Skill and Care? (1992) 55 *MLR* 179.

—— 'Corporate Governance and Cadbury: Self-Regulation and Alternatives' (1994) *JBL* 51.

—— 'Personal Accountability and Corporate Control: The Role of Directors' and Officers' Insurance' (1994) 57 *MLR* 880.

FIORINO, D. J., 'Citizen Participation and Environmental Risk: A Survey of Institutional Mechanisms' (1990) 15 *Science, Technology and Human Values* 226.

FISCHHOFF, B., *Improving Risk Communication* (Washington, 1989).

—— SLOVIC, P., LICHTENSTEIN, S., REID, S., and COMBS, B., 'How Safe is Safe Enough?' (1978) 9 *Policy Sciences* 127.

—— WATSON, S., and HOPE, C., 'Defining Risk', in T. S. Gluckman and M. Gough (eds.), *Readings in Risk* (Washington, 1993).

FISSE, B., 'Sentencing Options against Corporations' (1990) *Criminal Law Forum* 211.

—— and BRAITHWAITE, J., 'The Allocation of Responsibility for Corporate Crime' (1988) 11 *Sydney LR* 468.

—— —— 'Accountability and the Control of Corporate Crime', in M. Findlay and R. Hogg (eds.), *Understanding Crime and Criminal Justice* (Sydney, 1988).

FOREMAN-PECK, J., and MILLWARD, R., *Public and Private Ownership of British Industry 1820–1990* (Oxford, 1994).

FOSTER, C., 'Natural Monopoly Regulation: Is Change Required?', in CRI, *Regulating the Utilities* (London, 1993).

—— *Privatisation, Public Ownership and the Regulation of Natural Monopoly* (Oxford, 1992).

FOSTER, C., 'The Future of Regulation' (1993) *Utilities LR* 110.

FOSTER, H. D., *Disaster Planning* (New York, 1979).

FRANCIS, J., *The Politics of Regulation* (Oxford, 1993).

FRANKLIN, J. (ed.), *The Politics of Risk Society* (Cambridge, 1998).

FRANKS, and MAYER, C., 'Capital Markets and Corporate Control: A Study of France, Germany and the UK' (1990) 10 *Economic Policy* 191.

FREEDLAND, M., 'Government by Contract and Public Law [1994] *PL* 86.

FREEDMAN, J. O., *Crisis and Legitimacy* (Cambridge, 1978).

FRIEDLAND, M. L. (ed.), *Securing Compliance* (Toronto, 1990).

FROUD, J., BODEN, R., OGUS, A., and STUBBS, P., 'Toeing the Line: Compliance Cost Assessment in Britain' (1994) 24 *Policy and Politics* 4.

—— and OGUS, A., ' "Rational" Social Regulation and Compliance Cost Assessment' (1996) 74 *Pub. Admin.* 221.

FRUG, G. E., 'The Ideology of Bureaucracy in American Law' (1984) 97 *Harv. LR* 1277.

FULLER, L., *The Morality of Law* (New Haven, 1964).

—— 'The Forms and Limits of Adjudication' (1978) 92 *Harv. LR* 353.

GALLIGAN, D., *Due Process and Fair Procedures* (Oxford, 1996).

GATSIOS, K., and SEABRIGHT, P., 'Regulation in the European Community' (1989) 5 *Oxford Rev. of Econ. Policy* 37.

GELLHORN, E., and KOVACIC, W., *Antitrust Law and Economics* (St Paul, Minn., 1994).

—— and PIERCE, R. J., *Regulated Industries* (St Paul, Minn., 1982).

GIBBONS, T., 'The Utility of Economic Analysis of Crime' (1982) 2 *Int. Rev. Law and Econ.* 173.

GIDDENS, A., 'Risk Society: The Context of British Politics', in J. Franklin (ed.), *The Politics of Risk Society* (Cambridge, 1998).

—— *Beyond Left and Right* (Cambridge, 1994).

GLAISTER, S., *Deregulation and Privatisation: British Experience* (World Bank, Washington, DC, 1998).

—— 'Incentives in Natural Monopoly: The Case of Water', in M. E. Beesley, *Regulating Utilities* (London, 1996).

—— and BEESLEY, M., *Bidding for Tendered Bus Routes in London* (mimeo, 1990).

—— KENNEDY, D., and TRAVERS, T., *London Bus Tendering* (London, 1995).

GOH, J., 'Privatisation of the Railways and Judicial Review' (1996) 7 *Utilities LR* 42–3.

GOLDSTEIN, J., and KESHANE, R., *Ideas and Foreign Policy: Benefits, Institutions and Political Change* (Ithaca, NY, 1993).

GOLUB, J., *Why did they Sign? Explaining EC Environmental Policy Bargaining*, RSC No. 96/52 (Florence, 1996).

GORZ, A., *Critique of Economic Reason* (London, 1989).

GOULD, L., et al., *Perceptions of Technological Risks and Benefits* (New York, 1988).

GOWER, L. C. B., *Review of Investor Protection*, Cmnd. 9125 (London, 1984).

—— *Review of Investor Protection: A Discussion Document* (London, 1982).

GRABOSKY, P. N., 'Counterproductive Regulation' (1995) 23 *Int. J. of Sociology of Law* 347.

—— and BRAITHWAITE, J., *Of Manners Gentle: Enforcement Strategies of Australian Business Regulatory Agencies* (Melbourne, 1986).

GRAHAM, C., 'Consumer Bodies: Practice and Performance', in CRI, *Regulatory Review 1996* (London, 1996).

—— *Is there a Crisis in Regulatory Accountability?* (London, 1996).

—— 'Consumers and Privatised Industries' (1992) 3 *Utilities LR* 38.

—— and PROSSER, T., *Privatising Public Enterprises* (Oxford, 1991).

GRANTHAM, R., 'Corporate Knowledge: Identification or Attribution?' (1996) 59 *MLR* 732.

GRAY, T. (ed.), *UK Environmental Policy in the 1990s* (Basingstoke, 1995).

GREEN, R., and NEWBERY, D. M., 'Competition in the Electricity Industry in England and Wales' (1997) 13 *Oxford Rev. of Econ. Policy* 27.

GREENBURY, R., *Report of the Greenbury Study Group on Directors' Remuneration* (Chair: Sir R. Greenbury) (London, 1995).

GUNNINGHAM, N. and GRABOSKY, P., *Smart Regulation: Designing Environmental Policy* (Oxford, 1998).

HADDEN, S. G., *A Citizen's Right to Know: Risk Communication and Public Policy* (Boulder, Colo. 1989).

HADLEY, A. T., *Railroad Transportation: Its History and Its Laws* (London, 1985).

HAIN, P., *Regulating for the Common Good* (London, 1994).

—— 'Regulating for the Common Good' (1994) 5 *Utilities LR* 90.

HALL, P. A., 'Policy Paradigms, Social Learning and the State: The Case of Economic Policy-Making in Britain' (1993) 25 *Comparative Politics* 275.

HALL, P. G. (ed.), *The Political Power of Economic Ideas* (Princeton, 1989).

HAMPEL, R., *Preliminary Report of the Committee on Corporate Governance* (Chair: Sir R. Hampel) (London, Aug. 1997, final report Jan. 1998).

HANCHER, L., '1992 and Accountability Gaps' (1990) 53 *MLR* 669.

—— and MORAN, M. (eds.), *Capitalism, Culture and Regulation* (Oxford, 1989).

HANDMAN, J., and PENNING-ROWSELL, E. C. (eds.), *Hazards and the Communication of Risks* (Aldershot, 1990).

Hansard Society, *Making the Law* (London, 1992).

—— and European Policy Forum, *Report of the Commission on the Regulation of Privatised Utilities* (London, 1996).

HARDEN, I., *The Contracting State* (Buckingham, 1992).

—— and LEWIS, N., *The Noble Lie* (London, 1986).

HARDING, C., 'Models of Enforcement: Direct and Delegated Enforcement and the Emergence of a "Joint Action Model"', in C. Harding and B. Swart (eds.), *Enforcing European Community Rules* (Aldershot, 1996).

—— and SWART, B., *Enforcing European Community Rules* (Aldershot, 1996).

HARLOW, C., 'A Community of Interests: Making the Most of European Law' (1992) 55 *MLR* 331.

—— and RAWLINGS, R., *Law and Administration* (2nd edn., London, 1997).

HARRIS, D., et al., *Compensation and Support for Illness and Injury* (Oxford, 1984).

HARRIS, R. A., and MILKIS, S. M., *The Politics of Regulatory Change* (2nd edn., New York, 1996).

HAWKINS, K., 'Compliance Strategy, Prosecution Policy and Aunt Sally' (1990) 30 *BJ Crim*. 144.
—— 'Enforcing Regulation: More of the Same from Pearce and Tombs' (1991) 31 *BJ Crim*. 427.
—— *Environment and Enforcement* (Oxford, 1984).
—— (ed.), *The Human Face of Law* (Oxford, 1997).
—— and THOMAS, J. (eds.), *Enforcing Regulation* (Boston, 1984).
HAY, D. A., and MORRIS, D. T., *Industrial Economics and Organization* (2nd edn., Oxford, 1991).
HAYEK, F., 'The Use of Knowledge in Society' (1945) 35 *Am. Econ. Rev.* 519.
Health and Safety Commission, *Plan of Work for 1990/1 and Beyond* (London, 1989).
HELM, D., *British Utilities Regulation* (London, 1995).
—— 'Reforming the Regulatory Frameworks', paper presented to OXERA Conference on Regulatory Reform, 17 June 1993.
—— *Reforming the Regulatory Framework* (Oxford, 1993).
—— and JENKINSON, T. (eds.), *Competition in Regulated Industries* (Oxford, 1998).
—— and SMITH, S., 'The Assessment: Economic Integration and the Role of the European Community' (1989) 5 *Oxford Rev. of Econ. Policy* 1.
HEPPLE, B., 'The Implementation of the Community Charter of Fundamental Social Rights' (1990) 53 *MLR* 643.
HERITIER, A., 'The Accommodation of Diversity in European Policy-Making and its Outcomes: Regulatory Policy as Patchwork' (1996) 3 *J. of European Public Policy* 149.
HETHERINGTON, 'When the Sleeper Wakes: Reflections on Corporate Governance and Shareholder Rights' (1979) 8 *Hofstra LR* 183.
HICKS, C. (ed.), *Utilities and their Consumers* (London, 1993).
HILLMAN, J., and BRAEUTIGAM, R., *Price Level Regulation for Diversified Public Utilities* (Boston, 1989).
HM Treasury, *The Setting of Safety Standards* (London, 1996).
—— *Economic Appraisal in Central Government* (London, 1991).
HOOD, C., *Administrative Analysis: An Introduction to Rules, Enforcement and Organisations* (Brighton, 1986).
—— *Explaining Economic Policy Reversals* (Buckingham, 1994).
—— 'Keeping the Centre Small' (1978) 26 *Pol. Stud.* 30.
—— *The Tools of Government* (London, 1983).
—— and JONES, D., *Accident and Design* (London, 1997).
HOPPER, M., 'Financial Services Regulation and Judicial Review: The Fault Lines', in J. Black, P. Muchlinski, and P. Walker (eds.), *Commercial Regulation and Judicial Review* (Oxford, 1998).
HORLICK-JONES, T., *Acts of God?* (London, 1990).
HORN, M. J., *The Political Economy of Public Administration* (Cambridge, 1995).
—— and SHEPSLE, K. A., 'Commentary: Structure, Process, Politics and Policy' (1989) *Va. LR* 499.
HORWITZ, R., *The Irony of Regulatory Reform: The Deregulation of the American Telecommunications Industry* (Oxford, 1989).
HOWARTH, W., 'Self-Monitoring, Self-Policing, Self-Incrimination and Pollution Law' (1997) 60 *MLR* 200.

HUTTER, B. M., *Compliance: Regulation and Environment* (Oxford, 1997).
—— *The Reasonable Arm of the Law* (Oxford, 1988).
Interdepartmental Liaison Group on Risk Assessment (ILGRA), *The Use of Risk Assessment in Government Departments* (London, 1996).
JACOBSEN, J. K., 'Much Ado about Ideas' (1995) 47 *World Politics* 283.
JAFFE, L. L., 'The Independent Agency: A New Scapegoat' (1956) 65 *Yale LJ* 1068.
JASANOFF, S., 'The Misrule of Law at OSHA', in D. Nelkin (ed.), *The Language of Risk* (Beverly Hills, Calif., 1985).
JENKINSON, T., and MAYER, C., 'The Assessment: Corporate Governance and Corporate Control' (1993) 8 *Oxford Rev. of Econ. Policy* 1.
JOERGES, C. (ed.), *Franchising and the Law* (Baden-Baden, 1991).
JORDAN, A. G., *Engineers and Professional Self-Regulation* (Oxford, 1992).
JORDAN, W. A., 'Producer Protection, Prior Market Structure and the Effects of Government Regulation' (1992) 15 *J. Law and Econ.* 151.
JOWELL, J. L., *Law and Bureaucracy* (Dunellan, 1975).
—— and OLIVER, D., *The Changing Constitution* (3rd edn., Oxford, 1994).
KAGAN, R. A., 'Should Europe Worry about Adversarial Legalism?' (1997) 17 *OJLS* 165.
KASPERSON, R. E., et al., 'The Social Amplification of Risk: Progress in Developing an Integrative Framework', in S. Krimsky and D. Golding (eds.), *Social Theories of Risk* (Westport, Conn., 1992).
—— et al., 'The Social Amplification of Risk: A Conceptual Framework' (1988) 8 *Risk Analysis* 177.
KATZMAN, M. T., 'Pollution Liability Insurance and Catastrophic Environmental Risk' (1988) *Journal of Risk and Insurance* 75.
KAY, J., 'The Future of UK Utility Regulation', in M. E. Beesley (ed.), *Regulating Utilities* (London, 1996).
—— MAYER, C., and THOMPSON D. (eds.), *Privatisation and Regulation: The UK Experience* (Oxford, 1986).
KEELER, T. E., 'Theories of Regulation and the Deregulation Movement' (1984) *Public Choice* 103.
KELMAN, S., *Regulating America, Regulating Sweden* (Cambridge, Mass., 1981).
—— 'Cost-Benefit Analysis: An Ethical Critique' (1981) 5 (1) *Regulation* 33.
KENNEDY, D., 'Cost-Benefit Analysis of Entitlement Problems: A Critique' (1981) 3 *Stanford LR* 387.
KENNEDY, D., *Competition in the British Rail Industry* (London, 1996).
KING, M., 'The Truth about Autopoiesis' (1993) 20 *J. of Law and Society* 218.
KOELBLE, T. A., 'The New Institutionalism in Political Science and Sociology' (1995) *Comparative Politics* 231.
KOHN, M. (ed.), *Cross-National Research in Sociology* (London, 1988).
KOLKO, G., *Railroads and Regulation* (Princeton, 1965).
—— *The Triumph of Conservatism* (New York, 1965).
KRIMSKY, S., and GOLDING, D. (eds.), *Social Theories of Risk* (Westport, Conn., 1992).
—— and PLOUGH, A., *Environmental Hazards: Communicating Risks as a Social Process* (Dover, Mass., 1988).
KRONMAN, A., 'Wealth Maximisation as a Normative Principle' (1980) 9 *J. Legal Stud.* 227.
LACEY, N., and WELLS, C., *Reconstructing Criminal Law* (2nd edn., Clandon, 1998).

LADEUR, K. H., *The European Environment Agency and Perspectives for a European Network of Environmental Administrations*, EUI Working Paper No. 96/50 (Florence, 1996).

LANDES, W., and POSNER, R., 'The Private Enforcement of Law' (1975) 4 *J. Legal Stud.* 1.

LANDIS, J. M., *The Administrative Process* (New Haven, 1938).

LANE, J. E. (ed.), *State and Market* (London, 1985).

LASOK, D., 'Subsidiarity and the Occupied Field' (1992) 142 *NLJ* 1228.

LAUDATI, L., 'The European Commission as Regulator: The Uncertain Pursuit of the Competitive Market', in G. Majone (ed.), *Regulating Europe* (London, 1996).

LAUWAARS, R., 'The Model Directive on Technical Harmonisation', in R. Bieber et al., *1992: One European Market* (Baden-Baden, 1988).

Law Commission, *Legislating the Criminal Code: Involuntary Manslaughter* (London, 1996).

LEIGH, L. H., *The Criminal Liability of Corporations in English Law* (London, 1969).

LENAERTS, K., 'Regulating the Regulatory Process: "Delegation of Powers" in the E.C.' (1993) 18 *ELR* 23.

LEVINE, M. E., and FORRENCE, J. L., 'Regulatory Capture, Public Interest and the Public Agenda: Toward Synthesis' (1990) *J. Law Econ. Org.* 167.

LEVY, B., and SPILLER, P. (eds.), *Regulations, Institutions and Commitment* (Cambridge, 1996).

LEWIS, N., 'The Citizens' Charter and Next Steps: A New Way of Governing?' (1993) *Pol. Q.* 316.

—— 'Regulating Non-governmental Bodies', in J. Jowell and D. Oliver (eds.), *The Changing Constitution* (2nd edn., Oxford, 1989).

—— and GOH, J., *The Private World of Government* (Sheffield, 1998).

LISTER, C., 'Price-Cap versus Rate of Return Regulation' (1993) 5 *J. of Regulatory Economics* 25.

LITTLECHILD, S. C., *Regulation of British Telecommunications Profitability* (London, 1983).

LOUGHLIN, M., *Local Government in the Modern State* (London, 1986).

LOWI, T. J., *The End of Liberalism* (2nd edn., New York, 1979).

LUHMANN, N., 'Law as a Social System' (1989) 83 *NWULR* 136.

MCAFEE, R., and MCMILLAN, J., 'Auctions and Bidding' (1987) 25 *J. of Econ. Lit.* 699.

MACAVOY, P., 'The Federal Power Commission and the Co-ordination Problem in the Electrical Power Industry' (1973) 46 *S. Cal. LR* 661.

MCBARNET, D., 'Law, Policy and Legal Avoidance' (1988) *JL Soc.* 113.

—— and WHELAN, C., 'The Elusive Spirit of the Law: Formalism and the Struggle for Legal Control' (1991) 54 *MLR* 848.

MCCAHERY, J., BRATTON, W., PICCIOTTO, S., and SCOTT, C. (eds.), *International Regulatory Competition and Coordination* (Oxford, 1996).

MACCRIMMON, K. R., and WEHRUNG, D. A., *Taking Risks* (New York, 1982).

MCCRUDDEN, C., 'The Commission for Racial Equality: Formal Investigations in the Shadow of Judicial Review', in R. Baldwin and C. McCrudden, *Regulation and Public Law* (London, 1987).

—— (ed.), *Regulation and Deregulation: Policy and Practice in the Utilities and Financial Services Industries* (Oxford, 1999).

McCubbins, M. D., Noll, R. G., and Weingast, B. R., 'Administrative Procedures as Instruments of Political Control' (1987) 3 *J. Law Econ. Org.* 243.

MacDonagh, O., 'The Nineteenth-Century Revolution in Government: A Reappraisal' (1958) 1 *Historical J.* 52.

McEldowney, J., 'Law and Regulation: Current Issues and Future Directions', in M. Bishop, J. Kay, and C. Mayer (eds.), *The Regulatory Challenge* (Oxford, 1995).

Macey, J. R., 'Organisational Design and Political Control of Administrative Agencies' (1992) 8 *J. Law Econ. Org.* 93.

McGarity, T. O., *Reinventing Rationality: The Role of Regulatory Analysis in the Federal Bureaucracy* (Cambridge, 1991).

McGee, A., and Weatherill, S., 'The Evolution of the Single Market: Harmonisation or Liberalisation?' (1990) 53 *MLR* 578.

McGowan, F., and Seabright, P., 'Regulation in the European Community and its Impact on the UK', in M. Bishop, J. Kay, and C. Mayer (eds.), *The Regulatory Challenge* (Oxford, 1995).

McHarg, A., 'Accountability in the Electricity Supply Industry' (1995) 6 *Utilities LR* 34.

—— 'Regulation as a Private Law Function' [1995] *PL* 539.

McLean, I., and Foster, C., 'The Political Economy of Regulation: Interests, Ideology, Voters and the UK Regulation of Railways Act 1844' (1992) 70 *Pub. Admin.* 313.

McMillan, J., 'Selling Spectrum Rights' (1994) 8 *J. of Econ. Perspectives* 145.

Majone, G., *De-Regulation or Re-Regulation?* (London, 1989).

—— *Regulating Europe* (London, 1996).

—— 'The Rise of the Regulatory State in Europe' (1993) 17 *West European Politics* 77.

Makkai, T., and Braithwaite, J., 'The Limits of the Economic Analysis of Regulation: An Empirical Case and a Case for Empiricism' (1993) 15 (4) *Law and Policy* 271.

Manne, H. G., 'Mergers and the Market for Corporate Control' (1965) *J. Pol. Econ.* 110.

March, J., and Olsen, J., 'The New Institutionalism: Organisational Factors in Political Life' (1984) 78 *Am. Pol. Sci. Rev.* 734.

Markovits, R. S., 'Duncan's Do Nots: Cost-Benefit Analysis and the Determination of Legal Entitlements' (1984) 36 *Stanford LR* 1169.

Mashaw, J., *Bureaucratic Justice* (New Haven, 1983).

—— 'Explaining Administrative Process: Normative, Positive and Critical Stories of Legal Development' (1990) 6 *J. Law Econ. Org.* 267.

Matthews, R., 'The Economics of Institutions and the Services of Growth' (1986) 96 *Economic Journal* 903.

Matthews, S., 'Comparing Auctions for Risk Averse Buyers: A Buyer's Point of View' (1987) *Econometrica* 633.

Mayer, C., 'The Regulation of Financial Services: Lessons from the UK for 1992', in M. Bishop, J. Kay, and C. Mayer (eds.), *The Regulatory Challenge* (Oxford, 1995).

—— and Vickers, J., 'Profit Sharing: An Economic Appraisal' (1996) 17 *Fiscal Studies* 1.

MAYNTZ, R., 'The Conditions of Effective Public Policy: A New Challenge for Policy Analysis' (1983) 11 *Policy and Politics* 123.

MAZUR, A., 'Bias in Risk-Benefit Analysis' (1985) 7 *Technology in Society* 25.

MESSINGER, S., and BITTNER, E., *Criminology Yearbook* (London, 1979).

MEYER, J., and ROWAN, B., 'Institutionalised Organisations: Formal Structure as Myth and Ceremony' (1977) *Am. J. Sociol.* 340.

MILGROM, P., and WEBER, R., 'A Theory of Auctions and Competitive Bidding' (1982) 50 *Econometrica* 1089.

MINDA, G., 'Towards a More "Just" Economics of Justice: A Review Essay' (1989) 10 *Cardozo LR* 1855.

MITCHELL, R. C., and CARSON, R. T., *Using Surveys to Value Public Goods: The Contingent Valuation Method* (Washington, 1989).

MITNICK, B., *The Political Economy of Regulation* (New York, 1980).

MOE, T., 'Political Institutions: The Neglected Side of the Story' (1990) 6 *J. Law Econ. Org.* 213.

—— 'An Assessment of the Positive Theory of Congressional Dominance' (1987) 12 *Legislative Stud. Q.* 475.

—— 'Interests, Institutions and Positive Theory: The Politics of the NLRB' (1987) 2 *Studies in American Political Development* 236.

MORAN, M., *The Politics of the Financial Services Revolution* (London, 1991).

—— and WOOD, B., *States, Regulation and the Medical Profession* (Buckingham, 1993).

MORRISON, A. B., 'OMB Interference with Agency Rule-Making: The Wrong Way to Write a Regulation' (1986) 99 *Harv. LR* 1059.

MOWBRAY, A., 'Newspaper Ombudsmen: The British Experience' (1991) *Media Law and Practice* 91.

National Audit Office, *Report by the Comptroller and Auditor General: The Work of the Directors General of Telecommunications, Gas Supply, Water Services and Electricity Supply* (HC 645 Session 1995–6) (London, July 1996).

—— *Report by the Comptroller and Auditor General: Sales of the Government's Residual Shareholdings* (HC265, 1996/97) (London, 1997).

National Consumer Council (NCC), *Regulating the Public Utilities* (London, 1997).

—— *Paying the Price* (London, 1993).

—— *Self-Regulation* (London, 1986).

National Economic Development Office, *A Study of UK Nationalised Industries* (London, 1976).

NEWMAN, O., *The Challenge of Corporatism* (London, 1980).

New Zealand Commerce Commission, *Telecommunications Industry Inquiry Report* (Wellington, 1992).

NIELSEN, R., and SZYSZCZAK, E., *The Social Dimension of the European Community* (2nd edn., Copenhagen, 1993).

NISKANEN, W. A., *Bureaucracy and Representative Government* (Chicago, 1971).

NOBLE, C., *Liberalism at Work* (Philadelphia, 1986).

NOLL, R. (ed.), *Regulatory Policy and the Social Sciences* (Berkeley, Calif., 1985).

NORTH, D. C., 'Government and the Cost of Exchange in History' (1984) 44 *J. of Econ. History* 255.

OFFER, *The Transmission Price Control Review of the National Grid Company: Proposals* (London, Oct. 1996).

Office of Fair Trading (OFT), *Voluntary Codes of Practice* (London, 1996).
—— *Raising Standards of Consumer Care: Progressing Beyond Codes of Practice* (London, 1998).
OFGAS, *Value Plus: British Gas Trading's Pricing to Direct Debit Customers in the South West of England: A Decision Document* (London, Nov. 1997).
—— *1997 Price Control Review: British Gas Transportation and Storage: The Director-General's Final Proposals* (London, Aug. 1996).
OFTEL, *Consultation Procedures and Transparency* (London, 1995).
—— *Effective Competition Review* (London, Feb. 1998).
—— *Effective Competition: Framework for Action* (London, 1995).
—— *Meeting Customer Needs in Telecoms: The Role of Consumer Representatives* (London, 1996).
—— *Network Charges from 1997: Statement* (London, July 1997).
—— *Pricing of Telecommunications Services from 1997: Statement* (London, June 1996).
—— *Second Submission to the Culture, Media and Sport Select Committee: Beyond the Telephone, the Television and the PC: Regulation of the Electronic Communications Industry* (London, Mar. 1998).
OFWAT, *The Proposed Framework and Approach to the 1997 Period Review* (London, June 1997).
OGUS, A., *Regulation: Legal Form and Economic Theory* (Oxford, 1994).
—— 'Regulatory Law: Some Lessons from the Past' (1992) 12 *Legal Studies* 1.
—— 'Rethinking Self-Regulation' (1995) 15 *OJLS* 97.
OLSON, E. D., 'The Quiet Shift of Power: OMB Supervision of Environmental Protection Agency Rulemaking under Executive Order 12291' (1984) 4 *Va. J. Nat. Resources* 31.
OLSON, M., *The Logic of Collective Action* (Cambridge, Mass., 1965).
ORR, *New Service Opportunities for Passengers: A Consultation Document on the Development of the Competitive Framework of Passenger Rail Services* (London, Oct. 1997).
—— *New Service Opportunities for Rail Passengers: Statement* (London, Mar. 1998).
—— *The Periodic Review of Railtrack's Access Charges: A Proposed Framework and Key Issues: A Consultation Document* (London, Dec. 1997).
OSTROM, E., 'An Agenda for the Study of Institutions' (1986) 48 *Public Choice*.
OTWAY, H., 'Public Wisdom, Expert Fallibility: Towards a Contextual Theory of Risk', in S. Krimsky and D. Golding (eds.), *Social Theories of Risk* (Westport, Conn., 1992).
—— and WYNNE, B., 'Risk Communication: Paradigm and Paradox' (1989) 9 *Risk Analysis* 141.
PAGE, A., 'Self-Regulation: The Constitutional Dimension' (1986) 49 *MLR* 141.
—— and FERGUSON, R., *Investor Protection* (London, 1992).
PEARCE, F., and TOMBS, S., 'Ideology, Hegemony and Empiricism' (1990) 30 *BJ Crim.* 424.
PELKMANS, J., 'The New Approach to Technical Harmonisation and Standardisation' (1986–7) 25 *J. Common Market Studies* 249.
PELTZMAN, S., 'The Economic Theory of Regulation after a Decade of Regulation' (1989) *Brookings Papers Macroeconomics* 1.
—— 'The Effects of Automobile Regulation' (1975) 83 *J. Pol. Econ.* 677.

PELTZMAN, S., 'Towards a More General Theory of Regulation' (1976) 19 *J. Law and Econ.*

PERCIVAL, R. V., 'Checks without Balance: Executive Office Oversight of the Environment Protection Agency' (1991) 54 *Law and Cont. Prob.* 127.

PETERS, G. P., 'Bureaucratic Politics and the Institutions of the European Community', in A. M. Sbragia (ed.), *Europolitics: Institutions and Policy Making in the New European Community* (Washington, DC, 1992).

PILDES, R. H., and SUNSTEIN, C. R., 'Reinventing the Regulatory State' (1995) 62 *Univ. of Chicago LR* 1.

PLOUGH, A., and KRIMSKY, S., 'The Emergence of Risk Communication Studies: Social and Political Context' (1987) 12 *Science, Technology and Human Values* 4.

POSNER, R., 'Natural Monopoly and Regulation' (1969) 21 *Stanford LR* 548.

—— 'The Appropriate Scope of Regulation in the Cable Television Industry' (1972) 3 *Bell J. of Econ.* 98.

—— 'Theories of Economic Regulation' (1974) 5 *Bell J. of Econ.* 335.

—— *Economic Analysis of Law* (3rd edn., Boston, 1986).

—— 'Utilitarianism, Economics and Legal Theory' (1979) 8 *J. Legal Stud.* 103.

—— 'Wealth Maximisation Revisited' (1985) 2 *Notre Dame J. of Law, Ethics and Pub. Policy* 85.

POWELL, W., and DI MAGGIO, P. (eds.), *The New Institutionalism in Organizational Analysis* (Chicago, 1991).

PRIEST, G., 'The Current Insurance Crisis in Modern Tort Law' (1987) 96 *Yale LJ* 521.

PROSSER, T., *Law and the Regulators* (Oxford, 1997).

—— *Nationalised Industries and Public Control* (Oxford, 1986).

—— 'Appealing to the MMC: Or Elsewhere?' (1996) 7 *Utilities LR* 2.

—— and GRAHAM, C., 'Privatising Nationalised Industries: Constitutional Issues and New Legal Techniques' (1987) 50 *MLR* 16.

PURDY, M., and CULLUM, P., 'Utility Regulation: A Consumer Perspective' (1997) 8 *Utilities LR* 138.

PUTTERMAN, L., *The Economic Nature of the Firm* (Cambridge, 1986).

QUIRK, P., *Industry Influence in Federal Regulatory Agencies* (Princeton, 1981).

—— 'In Defence of the Politics of Ideas' (1988) 50 *Journal of Politics* 31.

Rail Regulator, *Competition for Railway Passenger Services* (London, 1994).

RAMIREZ, F. O. (ed.), *Rethinking the Nineteenth Century* (New York, 1988).

RAMSAY, I., 'The Office of Fair Trading: Policing the Consumer Market Place', in R. Baldwin and C. McCrudden, *Regulation and Public Law* (London, 1987).

—— *Consumer Protection* (London, 1989).

RAYNER, S., 'Culture Theory and Risk Analysis', in S. Krimsky and D. Golding (eds.), *Social Theories of Risk* (Westport, Conn., 1992).

REDFORD, E. S., *Administration of National Economic Control* (London, 1952).

REES, R., and VICKERS, J., 'RPI–X Price-Cap Regulation', in M. Bishop, J. Kay and C. Mayer (eds.), *The Regulatory Challenge* (Oxford, 1995).

REID, P., 'Regulating Airlines: Why the Arms-Length Approach has Failed', in T. Harrison and J. Gretton (eds.), *Transport UK* (London, 1985).

RENN, O., 'Concepts of Risk: A Classification', in S. Krimsky and D. Golding (eds.), *Social Theories of Risk* (Westport, Conn., 1992).

RICHARDSON, G., and GENN, H. (eds.), *Administrative Law and Government Action* (Oxford, 1994).

—— OGUS, A., and BURROWS, P., *Policing Pollution* (Oxford, 1988).

RIKER, W. H., 'Implications from the Disequilibrium of Majority Rule for the Study of Institutions' (1980) 74 *Am. Pol. Sci. Rev.* 432.

ROBINSON, C., 'Introducing Competition into Water', in M. E. Beesley (ed.), *Regulating Utilities* (London, 1997).

ROMANO, R., 'Law as Product: Some Pieces of the Incorporation Puzzle' (1985) 1 *J. Law Econ. Org.* 225.

—— 'Competition for Corporate Charters and the Lessons of Takeover Statutes' (1993) 61 *Fordham LR* 843.

ROSE-ACKERMAN, S., 'Efficient Charges: A Critique' (1973) 6 *Can. J. Econ.* 572.

ROVIZZI, L., and THOMPSON, D., 'The Regulation of Product Quality in Public Utilities', in M. Bishop, J. Kay, and C. Mayer (eds.), *The Regulatory Challenge* (Oxford, 1995).

ROWLAND, D., 'Enforcement of Health and Safety at Work, with Special Reference to the UK', in C. Harding and B. Swart (eds.), *Enforcing European Community Rules* (Aldershot, 1996).

Royal Society, *Risk: Analysis, Perception, Management* (London, 1992).

SAGOFF, M., 'At the Shrine of our Lady of Fatima or Why Political Questions are not all Economic' (1981) 23 *Arizona LR* 1283.

SAPPINGTON, D., and WEISMAN, D., *Designing Incentive Regulation for the Telecommunications Industry* (Cambridge, 1996).

SAWKINS, J. W., *Water and Sewage in Scotland: A Response*, Univ. of Aberdeen Discussion Papers (1993).

SAYER, S., 'The Impact of the European Union on UK Utility Regulation', in M. E. Beesley (ed.), *Regulating Utilities* (London, 1996).

SCHARPF, F. W., 'Political Institutions, Decision Styles and Policy Choices', in R. M. Czada and A. Windhoff-Heritier (eds.), *Political Choice: Institutions Rules and the Limits of Rationality* (Frankfurt, 1991).

SCHOLTZ, J. T., 'Co-operative Regulatory Enforcement and the Politics of Administrative Effectiveness' (1991) 85 *Am. Pol. Sci. Rev.* 118.

SCHWARZ, J., et al., *The 1992 Challenge at National Level* (1990).

SCHWARZ, M., and THOMPSON, M., *Divided We Stand: Redefining Politics, Technology and Social Choice* (Hemel Hempstead, 1990).

SCHWARZE, J., *European Administrative Law* (London, 1992).

SCOTT, C., *Competition and Co-ordination: Their Role in the Future of European Community Utilities Regulation* (London, 1995).

SCOTT, C., 'The Juridification of Regulatory Relations in the UK Utilities Sector', in J. Black, P. Muchlinksi, and P. Walker (eds.), *Commercial Regulation and Judicial Review* (Oxford, 1998).

—— 'Privatisation, Control and Accountability', in S. Picciotto, J. McCahery, and C. Scott, *Corporate Control and Accountability* (Oxford, 1993).

—— HALL, C., and HOOD, C., 'Regulatory Space and Regulatory Reform', in P. Vass (ed.), *CRI Regulatory Review 1997* (London, 1997).

SCOTT, W., 'The Adolescence of Institutional Theory' (1987) 32 *Admin. Sci. Qly.* 493.

Secretary of State for Transport, *Guidance to the Franchising Director* (London, 1994).

SELF, P., *Political Theories of Modern Government* (London, 1985).

—— *Administrative Theories and Politics* (2nd edn., London, 1978).

—— *Econocrats and the Policy Process: The Politics and Philosophy of Cost Benefit Analysis* (Basingstoke, 1975).

—— *Government by the Market?* (Basingstoke, 1993).

SEVENSTER, H. G., 'Criminal Law and EEC Law' (1992) *CMLR* 29.

SHAKED, A., and SUTTON, J., 'The Self-Regulating Profession' (1981) 47 *Rev. Econ. Stud.* 217.

SHARKEY, W. W., *The Theory of Natural Monopoly* (Cambridge, 1982).

SHAVELL, S., 'The Optimal Structure of Law Enforcement' (1993) *J. Law and Econ.* 255.

SHEARING, C. D., and STENNING, P. D. (eds.), *Private Policing* (Beverly Hills, Calif., 1986).

SHEPSLE, K. A., and WEINGAST, B., 'Structure-Induced Equilibria and Legislature Choice' (1981) 37 *Public Choice* 503.

SHLEIFER, A., 'A Theory of Yardstick Competition' *Rand J. of Econ.* 16 (1985) 319–27.

SHORT, J. F., 'The Social Fabric at Risk: Towards the Social Transformation of Risk Analysis' (1984) 49 *Am. Soc. Rev.* 711.

SHOVER, N., *Constructing a Regulatory Bureaucracy* (Albany, NY, 1982).

SHRADER-FRECHETTE, K. S., *Risk and Rationality* (Berkeley, Calif., 1991).

SIEBERT, H., and KOOP, M., 'Institutional Competition versus Centralisation: *Quo Vadis* Europe' (1993) 9 *Oxford Rev. of Econ. Policy* 15.

SIEDENTOPF, H., and ZILLER, J. (eds.), *Making European Policies Work* (London, 1988).

SLOVIC, P., FISCHHOFF, B., and LICHTENSTEIN, S., 'Perceived Risks, Psychological Factors and Social Implications' (1981) 376 *Proceedings of the Royal Society of London* 17.

—— —— —— 'Rating the Risks' (1979) *Environment* 4.

SMITH, R., 'The Feasibility of an Injury Tax Approach to Occupational Safety' (1974) 38 *Law and Cont. Prob.* 730.

SNYDER, F., 'The Effectiveness of European Community Law' (1993) 56 *MLR* 19.

SPENCE, M., 'Monopoly Quality and Regulation' 16 (1975) *Bell J. of Econ.* 417–29.

SPRENT, P., *Taking Risks* (London, 1988).

STEINMO, S., THALEN, K., and LONGSTRETH, F. (eds.), *Structuring Politics: Historical Institutionalism in Comparative Politics* (Cambridge, 1992).

STEWART, R. B., 'Crisis in Tort Law? The Institutional Perspective' (1987) 54 *Univ. of Chicago LR* 184.

—— 'Regulation in a Liberal State: The Role of Non-commodity Values' (1983) 92 *Yale LJ* 1537.

—— 'The Reformation of American Administrative Law' (1975) 88 *Harv. LR* 1667.

STIGLER, G., 'The Theory of Economic Regulation' (1971) 2 *Bell J. of Econ.* 3.

—— 'The Optimum Enforcement of Laws' (1970) 78 *J. Pol. Econ.* 526.

STOKES, M., 'Company Law and Legal Theory', in W. Twining (ed.), *Common Law and Legal Theory* (Oxford, 1986).

STONE, C., 'The Place of Enterprise Liability in the Control of Corporate Conduct' (1980) 90 *Yale LJ* 1.

—— 'Controlling Corporate Misconduct' (1977) *Public Interest* 55.

STREEK, W., and SCHMITTER, P. C., *Private Interest Government: Beyond Market and State* (London, 1985).

SUN, J. M., and PELKMANS, J., 'Regulatory Competition in the Single Market' (1995) 33 *J. Common Market Studies* 67.

SUNSTEIN, C., 'Paradoxes of the Regulatory State' (1990) 57 *Univ. of Chicago LR* 407.

—— *After the Rights Revolution* (Cambridge, Mass., 1990).

—— 'Cost Benefit Analysis and the Separation of Powers' (1981) 23 *Arizona LR* 1267.

SUTHERLAND, P., et al., *The Internal Market after 1992: Meeting the Challenge*, Report to the EEC Commission by the High Level Group on the Operation of the Internal Market (Brussels, 1992).

SWANN, D., *The Retreat of the State: Deregulation and Privatisation in the UK and US* (Brighton, 1988).

—— 'The Regulatory Scene', in K. Button and D. Swann (eds.), *The Age of Regulatory Reform* (Oxford, 1989).

SWART, B., 'From Rome to Maastricht and Beyond: The Problem of Enforcing Community Law', in C. Harding and B. Swart (eds.), *Enforcing European Community Rules* (Aldershot, 1996).

SZYSZCZAK, E., 'European Community Law: New Remedies, New Directions' (1992) 55 *MLR* 690.

—— 'L'Espace social européen: Reality, Dreams or Nightmare? (1991) *GYIL* 284.

TAIT, E., and LEVIDOV, L., 'Proactive and Reactive Approaches to Risk Regulation' (1992) *Futures* 219.

TELSER, L. G., 'On the Regulation of Industry: A Note' (1969) *J. Pol. Econ.* 937.

TEUBNER, G. (ed.), *Dilemmas of Law in the Welfare State* (Berlin, 1985).

—— *After Legal Instrumentalism? Strategic Models of Post-Regulatory Law*, EUI Working Paper No. 100 (Florence, 1984).

—— *Autopoietic Law: A New Approach to Law and Society* (Berlin, 1988).

—— (ed.), *Juridification of Social Spheres* (Berlin, 1987).

—— *Law as an Autopoietic System* (Oxford, 1993).

—— 'Juridification—Concepts, Aspects, Solutions', in G. Teubner (ed.), *Juridification of Social Spheres* (Berlin, 1987).

—— and FEBBRAJO, A. (eds.), *State, Law and Economy as Autopoietic Systems: Regulation and Autonomy in New Perspective* (Milan, 1992).

THOMAS, G., et al. (eds.), *Institutional Structure* (London, 1987).

THOMAS, G. M., *Revivalism and Cultural Change* (Chicago, 1989).

THOMPSON, M., ELLIS, R., and WILDAVSKY, A., *Cultural Theory* (Boulder, Colo., 1990).

TIEBOUT, C., 'A Pure Theory of Local Expenditures' (1956) 64 *J. Pol. Econ.* 416.

TINDALE, S., 'Procrastination and the Global Gamble', in J. Franklin (ed.), *The Politics of Risk Society* (Cambridge, 1998).

TOTH, A. G., 'A Legal Analysis of Subsidiarity', in D. O'Keefe and P. M. Twomey (eds.), *Legal Issues of the Maastricht Treaty* (London, 1994).

—— 'The Principle of Subsidiarity in the Maastricht Treaty' (1992) 29 *CMLR* 1079.

TRACHTMAN, J. P., 'International Regulatory Competition, Externalisation and Jurisdiction' (1993) 34 *Harv. J. of Int. Law* 49.

TREBILCOCK, M., 'The Social Insurance–Deterrence Dilemma of Modern North American Tort Law: A Canadian Perspective on the Liability Insurance Crisis?' (1987) 24 *San Diego LR* 929.

TURNER, B. A., *Man-Made Disasters* (London, 1978).

TURVEY, R., 'The Sliding Scale: Price and Dividend Regulation in the Nineteenth Century Gas Industry' (London, 1996).

VAN DYKE, B., 'Emissions Trading to Reduce Acid Deposition' (1992) 100 *Yale LJ* 2707.

VASS, P., 'The Methodology for Resetting X', in P. Vass (ed.), *CRI Regulatory Review 1997* (London, 1997).

—— 'Profit Sharing and Incentive Regulation', in P. Vass (ed.), *CRI Regulatory Review 1996* (London, 1996).

VAUGHAN, C. L., *Franchising* (Lexington, Mass., 1989).

VELJANOVSKI, C. G., 'Wealth Maximisation, Law and Ethics: On the Limits of Economic Efficiency' (1981) 1 *Int. Rev. Law and Econ.* 5.

—— *The Future of Industry Regulation in the UK* (London, 1993).

—— 'Regulatory Enforcement: An Economic Study of the British Factory Inspectorate' (1983) 5 *Law & Policy Quarterly* 75.

—— and BEBCHUCK, L. A., 'The Pursuit of a Bigger Pie: Can Everyone Expect a Bigger Slice?' (1980) 8 *Hofstra LR* 671.

VERWILGHEN, M., *Equality of Law between Men and Women in the European Community* (Dordrecht, 1986).

VICKERS, J., 'Concepts of Competition' (1995) 47 *Oxford Economic Papers* 1–23.

—— 'The Economics of Predatory Prices' (1985) 6 *Fiscal Studies* 24.

—— and YARROW, G., *Privatisation and Natural Monopolies* (London, 1985).

VIEHOFF, I., 'Evaluating RPI–X', Topics 17 (London, 1995).

VISCUSI, W. K., 'The Impact of Occupational Safety and Health Regulation' (1979) 10 *Bell J. of Econ.* 117.

VLEK, C. J. H., and STOLLEN, P. J. M., 'Rational and Personal Aspects of Risk' (1980) 45 *Acta Psychologica* 273.

VOGEL, D., *National Styles of Regulation: Environmental Policy in Great Britain and the United States* (Ithaca, NY, 1986).

WADDAMS-PRICE, C., 'Undue Discrimination and Cross-Subsidies: Price Structures in UK Utilities' (1997) 8 *Utilities LR* 191–200.

—— 'Competition and Regulation in the UK Gas Industry' (1993) 13 *Ox. Rev. of Econ. Policy* 47.

WALLACE, H., and WALLACE, W. (eds.), *Policy-Making in the European Union* (3rd edn., Oxford, 1996).

WATERSON, M., *Regulation of the Firm and Natural Monopoly* (Oxford, 1988).

WATERSTONE, M. (ed.), *Risk and Society: The Interaction of Science, Technology and Public Policy* (Dordrecht, 1991).

WEATHERILL, S., *Cases and Materials on EC Law* (London, 1992).

—— 'Implementation as a Constitutional Issue', in T. Daintith (ed.), *Implementing EC Law in the United Kingdom* (Chichester, 1995).

WEINGAST, B., and MARSHALL, W., 'The Industrial Organisation of Congress' (1988) 96 *J. Pol. Econ.* 132.

WEINRIB, E. J., 'Utilitarianism, Economics and Legal Theory' (1980) 30 *U. Toronto LJ* 307.

WEISBERG, H. (ed.), *Political Science: The Science of Politics* (New York, 1986).

WEISS, L. W., and KLASS, M. W. (eds.), *Regulatory Reform: What Actually Happened* (Boston, 1986).

WELLENS, K. C., and BORCHARDT, G. M., 'Soft Law in European Community Law' (1989) 14 *ELR* 267.

WELLS, C., *Corporations and Criminal Responsibility* (Oxford, 1993).

WHISH, R., *Competition Law* (3rd edn., London, 1993).

White Paper, *Financial Services in the United Kingdom: A New Framework for Investor Protection*, Cmnd. 9432 (London, 1985).

—— *Privatising Electricity* (London, 1988).

WILDAVSKY, A., *Trial without Error: Anticipation versus Resilience as Strategies for Risk Reduction* (Sydney, 1985).

—— *Searching for Safety* (New Brunswick, NJ, 1988).

WILKE, M., and WALLACE, H., 'Subsidiarity: Approaches to Power-Sharing in the European Community', RIIA Discussion Paper No. 27 (London, 1990).

WILLIAMS, S., 'Sovereignty and Accountability in the European Community' (1990) 61 *Pol. Q.* 299.

WILLIAMSON, O., *The Economic Institutions of Capitalism* (New York, 1985).

—— 'Franchise Bidding for National Monopolies: In General and with Respect to CATV' (1976) 7 *Bell J. of Econ.* 73.

WILLSON, F. M. G., 'Ministries and Boards: Some Aspects of Administrative Development since 1832' (1955) *Pub. Admin.* 43.

WILSON, G., 'Social Regulation and Explanations of Regulatory Failure' (1984) 32 *Pol. Stud.* 203.

—— *Interest Groups* (Oxford, 1990).

WILSON, J. Q., *The Politics of Regulation* (New York, 1980).

WINTER, R., 'State Law, Shareholder Protection and the Theory of the Corporation' (1997) 6 *J. Legal Stud.* 251.

WOODS, L., 'Quasi-Public Bodies: The European Dimension' (1996) 6 *Utilities LR* 220.

WOOLCOCK, S., *Competition among Rules in the Single European Market* (London, 1994).

—— 'Competition among Rules in the Single European Market', in J. McCahery et al. (eds.), *International Regulatory Competition and Coordination* (Oxford, 1996).

WOOLF, LORD, 'Public Law–Private Law: Why the Divide?' [1986] *PL* 220.

WOOLMAR, C., *The Great British Railway Disaster* (London, 1996).

WYNNE, B., 'Institutional Mythologies and Dual Societies in the Management of Risk', in C. Kunnreuther and E. Lay (eds.), *The Risk Analysis Controversy* (1983).

YALOW, R. S., 'Radioactivity in the Service of Humanity' (1985) 60 *Thought* 517.

YARROW, G., 'Regulation and Competition in the Electricity Supply Industry', in J. Kay, C. Mayer, and D. Thompson (eds.), *Privatisation and Regulation* (Oxford, 1986).

ZUPAN, M. A., 'Cable Franchise Renewals: Do Incumbent Firms Behave Opportunistically?' (1989) 20 *Rand J. of Econ.* 473.

—— 'Non-price Concessions and the Effect of Franchise Bidding Schemes on Cable Company Costs' (1989) 21 *Applied Economics* 305.

Index